Beyond Boundaries

oundaries

Rereading John Steinbeck

Edited by
SUSAN SHILLINGLAW and KEVIN HEARLE

The University of Alabama Press
Tuscaloosa and London

Typeface is Palatino

∞

The paper on which this book is printed meets the minimum requirements
of American National Standard for Information Science–Permanence of
Paper for Printed Library Materials, ANSI Z39.48–1984.

Excerpts from the following works are used by permission of Viking
Penguin, a division of Penguin Putnam, Inc.:
    From *The Grapes of Wrath* by John Steinbeck, copyright © 1939, renewed
© 1967 by John Steinbeck. From *Steinbeck: A Life in Letters*, edited by Elaine
A. Steinbeck and Robert Wallsten, copyright © 1952 by John Steinbeck,
© 1969 by The Estate of John Steinbeck, © 1975 by Elaine A. Steinbeck and
Robert Wallsten. From *The Log from the Sea of Cortez* by John Steinbeck, copy-
right © 1941 by John Steinbeck and Edward F. Ricketts, renewed © 1969 by
John Steinbeck and Edward F. Ricketts Jr. From *Cannery Row* by John Stein-
beck, copyright © 1945 by John Steinbeck, renewed © 1973 by Elaine Stein-
beck, John Steinbeck IV, and Thom Steinbeck. From *Burning Bright* by John
Steinbeck, copyright © 1950 by John Steinbeck, renewed © 1978 by Elaine
Steinbeck, John Steinbeck IV, and Thom Steinbeck. From *East of Eden* by
John Steinbeck, copyright © 1952 by John Steinbeck, renewed © 1980 by
Elaine Steinbeck, John Steinbeck IV, and Thom Steinbeck. From *The Short
Reign of Pippin IV* by John Steinbeck, copyright © 1957 by John Steinbeck, re-
newed © 1985 by Elaine Steinbeck, John Steinbeck IV, and Thom Steinbeck.

Library of Congress Cataloging-in-Publication Data

Beyond boundaries : rereading John Steinbeck / edited by
Susan Shillinglaw and Kevin Hearle.
    p.   cm.
Includes bibliographical references and index.
    ISBN 0-8173-1151-3 (cloth : alk. paper)
    1. Steinbeck, John, 1902–1968—Criticism and interpretation.   I. Shill-
inglaw, Susan. II. Hearle, Kevin, 1958–
    PS3537.T3234 Z619 2002
    813'.52—dc21

                    2002000360

British Library Cataloguing-in-Publication Data available

Contents

III. Rereading Steinbeck's Women

IV. Steinbeck's Science and Ethics

Acknowledgments

In March 1997, the Fourth International Steinbeck Conference, "Beyond Boundaries: Steinbeck and the World," was held at San Jose State University and in Monterey, California. The title of the symposium was taken literally: it was sponsored by both the John Steinbeck Society of Japan and the Center for Steinbeck Studies at San Jose State University. It was held in two appropriate locations—San Jose, near Los Gatos, where Steinbeck completed *Of Mice and Men* and composed *The Grapes of Wrath;* and Monterey, where, of course, Steinbeck spent his apprentice years from 1930–1936. This crossing of boundaries—be they international, logistical or theoretical—was and is the central concern of the conference and of this text.

Many people and institutions helped smooth the crossing of boundaries. Thanks to President Kiyoshi Nakayama and members of the Steinbeck Society of Japan who donated operating funds. Dean John Crane of San Jose State University generously gave funding for a keynote speaker. SJSU's School of Engineering, with the blessing of Robert Trammell, provided space, tactical assistance, and cleaning. Both the Fairmont Hotel and the Monterey Plaza Hotel generously lowered rates. And Julie Packard approved a modest conference rental of the new wing of the Monterey Bay Aquarium, where the magical final banquet was held. Appropriately, participants dined in front of one of the largest tanks in the world—the glass built and installed by Japanese technicians and engineers.

The Steinbeck Center's archivist, Jennifer Smith, offered unflagging service. She was helped by Barbara Tom and Bettina Hotelling, both of whom volunteered countless hours. Craig Kochersberger designed the publicity flyers as well as the program. Steve Webster, Senior Marine Biologist at the Monterey Bay Aquarium, helped organize events in Monterey—an invaluable mainstay of support. Kalissa Moore, as always, gave her heart and her food to participants in Monterey. The City of Monterey opened Ed Ricketts's lab to the public. Hopkins Marine Station opened its doors for tours, assisted by Joe Wible, Head Librarian, who prepared an exhibit on Ricketts's work for the event. Art Ring organized and led a splendid tour of Steinbeck's Stanford University—with the help of Maggie Kimball, Archivist of Stanford University.

Preparation of this manuscript was made possible by a sabbatical leave granted in the spring of 2001 to Susan Shillinglaw, and she is grateful to San José State University for this opportunity to complete several Steinbeck projects. The Steinbeck Center's assistant, Katie Rodger, was, as always, an invaluable resource: she double checked quotations and sources with the help of Stephanie Fielzer, student assistant. My warm thanks to both.

And thanks to all the participants who put up with logistical shifts, who fully appreciated both busy Silicon Valley and lovely Monterey Bay, and who wrote splendid papers and participated eagerly in discussions, tours, and events.

Abbreviations

AA = *America and Americans*
BB = *Burning Bright*
COG = *Cup of Gold*
CR = *Cannery Row*
EOE = *East of Eden*
FV = *The Forgotten Village*
IDB = *In Dubious Battle*
JN = *Journal of a Novel: The* East of Eden *Letters*
LSC = *The Log from the Sea of Cortez*
LV = *The Long Valley*
OMM = *Of Mice and Men*
PH = *The Pastures of Heaven*
SLL = *Steinbeck: A Life in Letters*
SOC = *Sea of Cortez: A Leisurely Journal of Travel and Research*
SQ = *Steinbeck Quarterly*
ST = *Sweet Thursday*
TAKA = *The Acts of King Arthur*
TF = *Tortilla Flat*
TGOW = *The Grapes of Wrath*
TGU = *To a God Unknown*
THG = *The Harvest Gypsies*
TMID = *The Moon Is Down*
TP = *The Pearl*
TWB = *The Wayward Bus*
TWC = *Travels with Charley in Search of America*
WD = *Working Days: The Journals of the Grapes of Wrath*
WOD = *Winter of Our Discontent*

Introduction

Rereading John Steinbeck

Susan Shillinglaw and Kevin Hearle

John Steinbeck, one of only seven American novelists awarded the Nobel Prize, has long been acknowledged as one of America's preeminent writers and has long attracted a substantial readership. So much is clear. *Of Mice and Men* and *The Pearl* are read by nearly all American high school students. *The Grapes of Wrath* has sold over 150,000 American editions a year for the past decade —and steadily for over sixty years; indeed, nearly all of Steinbeck's books have remained in print. Translated into most languages, his novels are read enthusiastically outside the United States. From 1939 (the year Lewis Milestone's *Of Mice and Men* was released) to 1955 (the year Elia Kazan's *East of Eden* premiered) more good films were made from Steinbeck's novels than from those of his contemporaries. Scores of artists and writers have been influenced by his social and ecological visions —Woody Guthrie, Bruce Springsteen, T. C. Boyle, and Russell Banks among others. As a writer who, beginning in the 1930s, gave voice to the ordinary man and woman, he came to be the conscience of America. With empathy and clarity he witnessed and recorded much of the political and social upheaval of the twentieth century: the Depression, World War II, the Cold War, Vietnam. And always he wrote a marvelously lucid, accessible prose. So much is clear.

But he has also been boxed in critically, his place in the much-debated literary "canon" unsettled, uncertain. Is he a "mere realist"? A regionalist? A California writer who abandoned his native land—and his own material—when he moved permanently to New York in the late 1940s? A writer to be read in high school and thus not sufficiently complex for a University curriculum? A writer who did his best work in the 1930s and then drifted into baggier, less probing novels? Such categories and opinions have frequently been imposed, like a Procrustean bed, on John Steinbeck's work. The purpose of this volume, as the title suggests, is to consider his prose in other contexts, to view it with other critical lenses. Readable and broadly appealing, his work is also highly complex and experimental. His avid reading of history and his lifelong attention to science make him a far more profound writer than many readers have acknowledged. He was a modernist outside the traditional boundaries of modernism, his prose shaped by myth; his sentences honed, like Hemingway's, to the essential; his visionary characters as thoroughly deflated as Fitzgerald's. He wrote again and again about the process of creativity itself, as a fine-tuned reading of *East of Eden* or *Cannery Row* makes readily apparent. John Steinbeck is a far more ambitious writer, his scope far broader, and his "layered" books (a description he coined) far more complex than many readers have acknowledged. These essays take this popular, accessible writer beyond the established critical boundaries, beyond well-worn thematic terrain, beyond the theoretically commonplace. And beyond America's shores.

Steinbeck himself was long suspicious of critical categories. As early as 1932, when he was sent the galleys for *To a God Unknown*, he confides in his notebook that "The critics will scream shame at me" (*LVN*). Since his previous two novels, *Cup of Gold* (1929) and *The Pastures of Heaven* (1932) had received hardly any notice at all, and that mostly positive, his remark seems odd, overly sensitive. But the anticipation of negative criticism —undoubtedly self-protective—also indicates the degree to which Steinbeck felt that his work would not be fully appreciated or understood. Each book was, for him, an experiment, a point he makes clear in a little essay he wrote in 1950, "Critics, Critics Burning Bright," after his highly unorthodox play, *Burning Bright*, received decidedly unfriendly reviews:

> Since by the process of writing a book I have outgrown that book, and since I like to write, I have not written two books alike. Where would be the interest in that? The result has been (and I

can prove it with old reviews) that every book has been attacked by a large section of the critical family. I can also prove by old notices that the preceding book is compared favorably over the current one and the one before over the preceding one ... having made up their minds what the next book would be like, the critics experienced anger when it was different. (21)

Steinbeck repeatedly and forcefully declared his independence from expectations: "A good writer always works at the impossible," he observes in the notebook he wrote for *East of Eden* (*JN* 4). Indeed, with his reputation established in the late 1930s, he enjoyed for the next thirty years the freedom to write, for the most part, whatever he pleased. In the year following publication of *The Grapes of Wrath*, for example, he severed his ties to the novelistic tradition, declaring that "I've worked the novel—I know it as far as I can take it. I never did think much of it—a clumsy vehicle at best" (*SLL* 193). To discover "the form of the new" he turned to widely different pursuits: "two theses for John Cage to set to percussion music: Phalanx and the Death of the Species" (*WD* 106); an allegorical play about Cannery Row, "God in the Pipes"—"In form ... almost like a ballet" (*WD* 116); a film script that became *The Forgotten Village* (1941), and a work of scientific inquiry, *Sea of Cortez* (1941). His "rebirth" is an explosion of creativity, of trying out new forms and approaches. During the war years that followed, he wrote with similar virtuosity, completing a non-fictional work about bomber crews, a film treatment called *Lifeboat*, a novella, *The Moon Is Down* (1942), a series of war dispatches for the *New York Herald Tribune* and perhaps the first ecological novel ever published, *Cannery Row*. These few years from 1939 to 1945 give ample evidence of Steinbeck's range. He refused to be pigeonholed as a realist, a writer of fiction, a committed social critic, a regional writer. This fierce independence is one of his most salient features as a writer.

The first section of this text embraces Steinbeck's independence of thought and approach, the essays considering the author's versatility. From a consideration of sentimentality in *The Grapes of Wrath* to studies of his influence on Bruce Springsteen and Native American writers, these essays note his willingness to experiment with style, structure, and content; his eagerness to embrace new disciplines and perspectives as ecologist, journalist, playwright and scriptwriter; and his considerable impact on writers, artists and readers. Perhaps what unites these essays is an insistence on Steinbeck's appeal to a wide audience. His novels are, as John Seelye, among others, asserts, a good read. His plots engage. His characters are accessible. He wrestles with issues that resonate with a diverse readership. Indeed, although none of these essays discusses Steinbeck's experiments with the play-novelette, it is perhaps that form that best conveys the versatility in Steinbeck that each of these essays explores. In 1936, finished with *Of Mice and Men,* he wrote a short piece explaining the experimental form he'd created, the play-novelette, in which he notes that the novel reaches a literate audience, and a play a broader audience. Combining both forms, a play-novelette would reach the widest possible audience. Furthermore, "not only might the novel benefit by the discipline, the terseness of the drama, but the drama itself might achieve increased openness, freedom and versatility" ("The novel might benefit" 51). Like Walt Whitman, Steinbeck reached broadly across America with his new form of expression, and the steady endurance of *Of Mice and Men* as text, play, and film gives testimony to the powerful versatility of form. The ghost of George Milton, who shoots his friend Lennie out of love and need, throws shadows over the twentieth century as fully as does "The Ghost of Tom Joad," who calls Springsteen, and others, to political and social engagement.

The second section considers Steinbeck as "world citizen," a stature he has certainly attained. This most American of writers is, in fact, a quintessential Westerner in his restless curiosity about new terrain. From the time he left his hometown of Salinas in 1919, he craved new experiences —at one point leaving a note for his college roommate at Stanford that he was bound for China, a trip that never materialized. But when he finally had the funds to travel in the mid-1930s, he started traveling widely and writing about the places he saw. In 1935 he and his wife Carol went to Mexico, a country he visited and wrote about with some frequency because, he notes, "there's an illogic there I need." Two years later he and Carol sailed to Scandinavia and

Russia. He went overseas as a war correspondent in 1943, covered post-war Russia in 1947, and, with his third wife, Elaine, wrote various magazine pieces about his travels to Spain, Paris and Italy throughout the 1950s. In 1963 he, Elaine, and Edward Albee toured Russia and Poland on a trip sponsored by the State Department. In 1967, he covered the Vietnam War for the Long Island paper, *Newsday*, in a highly controversial series called "Letters to Alicia." Steinbeck was at home in the world at large. Shortly before his marriage to Elaine in 1949, he writes, "You said that this [the Pacific Grove cottage] was my home but I have thought about it deeply. I think I have no 'place' home. Home is people and where you work well. I have homes everywhere and many I have not even seen yet. That is perhaps why I am restless. I haven't seen all of my homes" (*SLL* 382).

But Steinbeck's internationalism cuts more deeply, as these essays suggest. His novels and plays, most set in America, have won an international audience that has sometimes been more passionate about his writing than have been his American readers. When *The Moon Is Down* was published in 1942, for example, the American public, polarized by war, was tepid in its response to this fictional treatment of totalitarianism. Two influential critics, Clifton Fadiman and James Thurber, attacked the writer's patriotism and alleged that Steinbeck—"soft on Nazis" because he portrayed them as people, not automatons—had a naïve grasp of world politics. In France, England, and Norway, however, readers embraced the writer's parable about Nazi forces invading a country much like Norway. Foreign readers felt that this American writer, far from the European front, had captured, in the midst of war, their suffering and their unflagging spirit. Steinbeck's empathy knew no cultural boundaries. He understood ordinary people and relished small scenes of human drama: "I do not know what the people of France are thinking," he writes in his first article for *Collier's* magazine in 1952, "but I do know to a certain extent what the farmers, winegrowers, teachers and kids of the little village of Poligny are thinking and talking about. This seems important to me. People like these are the soul and guts of France" (26). And, one certainly might add, working people are the soul and guts of his fictional world. He sought urgently to "understand" and to help readers see clearly as well. "In every bit of honest writing in the world," he observes in 1938, "there is a base theme. Try to understand men, if you understand each other you will be kind to each other" (*LVN*). Throughout a long career that was his aim.

Steinbeck's signature fictional relationship is, undoubtedly, male friendship—George and Lennie, Casy and Tom Joad, Mack and the boys, Lee and Adam Trask to name only a few. But the role of what might be called a feminine sensibility is far more compelling in his fiction than a brief overview of his work might suggest. *The Grapes of Wrath* concludes, after all, not with Casy mentoring Tom but with Ma's final lesson to Rose of Sharon, delivered wordlessly. If Tom learns political engagement, Rose of Sharon appreciates the value of human connection, humility, and generosity of spirit. Men "figuring" gets the migrants only so far. Essays in the third section of this text look at Steinbeck's consideration of gender, and do so in ways which illuminate the extent to which feminist literary criticism and Steinbeck criticism have both become more subtle and more theoretically sophisticated over the last few decades. In her introduction to the anthology *The New Feminist Criticism*, Elaine Showalter notes that "In its earliest years, feminist criticism concentrated on exposing the misogyny of literary practice" (5). Steinbeck, with his platoons of happy prostitutes and his ranks of powerful but seemingly stereotypical maternal presences, received his share of comeuppance from early feminist readings. But as society began to explore the broad notion of what it means to be "feminine," and as feminist critics began to question the ways in which society and literary works construct gender roles, it became clear that Steinbeck's female characters were far from incidental, and that Steinbeck's relationship as an author to the gendering of his culture is far more complex than anyone had previously imagined.

Finally, the fourth section considers Steinbeck's lifelong interest in science. In his 1959 book *The Two Cultures and the Scientific Revolution*, physicist-turned-novelist C. P. Snow decried the growing cultural divide between science and literature. Snow noted that specialization within and among academic disciplines had created a situation in which the finest minds in science and the arts were no longer able to inspire each other across their "gulf of mutual incomprehension." The science section of this volume brings together a series of essays analyzing some of the many ways in which Steinbeck's works bridge that gulf. John Steinbeck and his best friend Ed Ricketts were a pair of Renaissance men. Together they wrote *Sea of Cortez*, which continues to be revered by marine biologists around the world. Mythology guru Joseph Campbell once admitted that in the months he'd spent with Steinbeck and Ricketts they'd taught him more about comparative mythology than he'd taught them. Clearly, John Steinbeck is the great pre-Thomas Pynchon exception, among twentieth-century American novelists, to Snow's pronouncement about our divided civilization. As these essays illustrate, Steinbeck's characters are thinking animals, and although they may behave in accordance with their sentimental beliefs, Steinbeck's books do not.

The science section of this volume includes one essay by a scientist, a number of essays by literary critics on the influence of the scientific method and contemporary science on Steinbeck's writing, and even one essay suggesting that Steinbeck became a less scientifically minded writer after Ricketts's death. The essays do not, however, universally support C. P. Snow's notion that we are becoming a civilization of two cultures: one scientific and another artistic and humanistic. One of the important trends of the last quarter century has been the increasing humanistic and historical contextualization of science. With such classic works as Thomas Kuhn's *The Structure of Scientific Revolutions*, the history of science has established itself as an important academic discipline with much to reveal about both the timeliness and the socially constructed nature of scientific truths. A number of the essays in this volume, in fact, suggest what Steinbeck and Ricketts acknowledge so frequently in *Sea of Cortez*, that far from offering timeless pronouncements of truth, everything they write is of contingent value: "its subject everything we could see and think and even imagine; its limits—our own without reservation" (1). These essays analyze Steinbeck's science in historical and social context to reveal not only how much Steinbeck broke through the boundaries between science and literature but also just how much in his scientific thinking he was a man of his time.

Reviewing a little-known book that Steinbeck published in 1948, *A Russian Journal*, William McFee wrote that Steinbeck possessed "an observant eye, a deadpan humor, and a command of the English language unsurpassed by any American of our time" (qtd. in McElrath xx). *Beyond Boundaries: Rereading John Steinbeck* nudges readers toward that kind of full appreciation of John Steinbeck's work.

I
Beyond Boundaries

1

Come Back to the Boxcar, Leslie Honey: Or, Don't Cry For Me, Madonna, Just Pass the Milk

Steinbeck and Sentimentality

John Seelye

Seelye answers Leslie Fiedler's attack on Steinbeck as a sentimental writer by comparing Steinbeck to sentimentalists—especially comparing Harriet Beecher Stowe's Uncle Tom's Cabin *to* The Grapes of Wrath. *Steinbeck uses sentimentality as an aspect of his characters and readers but then has chance, a quintessentially un-Christian and anti-sentimental force, crush it.*

I want to start by rendering a précis of a famous work of fiction: it is about the breakup of families, chiefly caused by the vagaries of staple-crop agriculture; it is about a man of humble origins and Christly virtues, a lay minister for a time, who emerges during the course of the novel as a scapegoat for the people he represents and who is killed by the forces of exploitative, capitalistic agribusiness, figured as intolerant, bigoted, and ignorant wielders of absolute authority; it focuses on family and on the values promoted by domestic virtues by means of scenes with women who are central to the plot, who prove far stronger than the men with whom they are associated; it stresses the importance of motherhood, figured as a positive force working to maintain the coherence of family even as the domestic unit is torn asunder by centrifugal social forces which have disempowered male authority. This work of fiction is founded on carefully gathered facts; it transcends the particular, however, and is epical in scope, for the action ranges widely along the length of a longitudinal geopolitical axis of the United States; it is a movement through space permitting a documentary series of vignettes demonstrating the social ills caused by an economic system indifferent to the integrity of the family, to the suffering of the dispossessed, to the basic needs of humanity. The action from time to time builds to violence, in which a courageous few do battle with the many who draw their strength from a code of laws that are based on the sacredness of private property essential to the Constitution.

It is a work of sentimental fiction, which attempts to enlist our sympathies, to draw from us tears of grief for the tragic lot of families torn asunder by economic forces, to move us to better the lot of our fellow human beings. It ends with the conversion of a son of one of the farming families to radicalism, virtually swearing on the grave of his Christ-like friend that he will join the growing ranks of those aroused to anger and action by the tragic inequities permitted in American society. We as readers are reached out to by his conversion, which is intended to move us to do likewise, to enlist us in the same struggle. We weep tears of anger but they are not idle tears. Thousands of our fellow readers weep also, a torrent of water that will sweep away the iniquities to which we have been vicarious witnesses, that will turn the wheels of the millstones of God, grinding a wrathful vintage from the perpetrators of injustice. A great war is coming, just beyond the closing pages of this book, a war that will lift the intolerable burden of suffering and poverty from the families and open the doors of opportunity wide to them.

The novel is, of course, *Uncle Tom's Cabin*, by Harriet Beecher Stowe. James Baldwin has called *Uncle Tom's Cabin* "Everybody's Protest Novel," in an essay that I for many years, not having read it, thought was about *The Grapes of Wrath*, by John Steinbeck, a novel which bears a certain resemblance to *Uncle Tom's Cabin* (149). These points of similarity are worth consideration, if only because Leslie Fiedler, who in *Love and Death in the American Novel* pronounced Stowe's book "the greatest of all novels of sentimental protest" (264) of the nineteenth century, has denounced *The Grapes of Wrath* as "maudlin, sentimental, and overblown" ("Looking Back" 55).

Now Fiedler is an icon, whose courage to make outrageous statements provides a model inspiring us not to walk the line but dance along the edge. It was courageous in 1960 to praise *Uncle Tom's Cabin*, and positively foolhardy in 1989 to stomp on

The Grapes of Wrath in the presence of a host of Steinbeckians: From this pressing came no sweet communion wine, but, as I have been informed, tears shed in maudlin and overblown grief at having to witness the public dismantling of a beloved object. But that has been Fiedler's mode ever since he shocked the literary establishment by proposing that the love between Huck and Jim was the kind that passeth the laws of Mississippi. Fiedler is a kind of lumberjack, whose critical dynamite loosens up academic log jams and gets the wood moving again, rafting it downstream toward the pulp mills that roll out the paper on which, according to Fiedler, our greatest masterpieces are written. And regarding his attack on Steinbeck's sentimentality, I am as always grateful to Fiedler because he has provided the fulcrum for the lever I am about to set in motion. To my mind, Steinbeck's book is assuredly the greatest sentimental novel of protest of the twentieth century.

Moreover, like *Uncle Tom's Cabin* in the 1960s, which owed its advent in the curriculum to the increased attention being paid to African Americans during the struggle for Civil Rights, *The Grapes of Wrath* is greatly relevant to the present, a time when the problems of migrant workers are once again being brought forward. And as for the homeless, well they are always with us, but never in such numbers I think as now. To borrow President Clinton's imaginative and highly evocative metaphor, if there is a bridge to the twenty-first century, a broken-down automobile with a family living in it is stuck half-way across, from which vantage point you may see a group of foreign nationals wading over to the farther side.

Before we join them, pending the universal loss of tenure, let us for a time consider the meaning of the word "sentimental," that being the problematic half of the whole, for surely all of us can agree what a protest novel is. And it is at the start important to point out some differences between Stowe's novel and Steinbeck's, which like the similarities are helpful in defining what the sentimental was to writers of far different cultural origins and historical generations.

First off, let me say that Steinbeck probably never read Stowe's novel, which during the 1920s and 1930s was thought of, when it was thought of at all, as a literary curiosity of the nineteenth century, which survived largely through the Tom shows that were a regular part of traveling carnivals. Steinbeck surely knew *about* Uncle Tom. Everybody knew about Uncle Tom, especially James Baldwin, for whose generation Stowe's hero was generally confused with Booker T. Washington as black men who danced Jim Crow to the white man's tune. We now know differently, having over the past thirty years developed a much more intimate and informed acquaintance with Stowe's novel, and realize that Uncle Tom is a latter-day Christ, who in refusing to take up the whip and flog his fellow slaves at the behest of Simon Legree guarantees his own crucifixion. It is an act not of cowardice but great courage, an act moreover that strikes at the very heart of the system of which Tom and his fellow slaves are victims, which corrupts whites as well as blacks because of the effects of absolute power. It is an extreme version of the civil disobedience about which Thoreau was writing at the time, and for which he logged a famous night in the Concord jail. It is, that is to say, an intensely political act, that reaches for its impetus beyond the laws of men to that higher law to which Thoreau himself had reference.

But where Thoreau thought of the higher law in general, perhaps even deistic terms, as that body of self-evident truths to which Jefferson made reference in the Declaration of Independence, Uncle Tom (and Harriet Beecher Stowe) were thinking about gospel truths. Tom draws his strength from the Bible, from the example of Christ. As Neitzsche observed, Christianity was the religion of women and slaves; it was (and is) the religion of the oppressed, that holds out the consolation of heaven to those who suffer without hope of relief here on earth. Women and slaves were equals in Rome in the time of the Caesars as persons without power; it was a situation that had not much changed by 1850 in America. Harriet Beecher Stowe responded in a characteristic evangelical manner, by holding out to women and slaves the promise of power implicit in the Gospels; indeed, she gave that power to the women and the slaves in her novel, as an example to her readers of what could be done through the liberating agency of faith—in opposition to the oppressiveness of man-made and unjust laws. That power is essential to the force of sentimentality in fiction.

Suffering in sentimental fiction, according to Jane Tompkins, may cause tears, but they are tears of identification and sympathy. Women, in effect, by prayerfully suffering abuse from drunken husbands and dying pious deaths from tuberculosis and other lingering diseases, gain terrific power by imitating Christ in his passion, who died from the effects of entrenched Orthodoxy and the Roman empire. But we need to add a third factor here; in Stowe's novel suffering in imitation of Christ is not empowerment per se, but is used to give impetus to the abolition movement. Along with her emphasis on the family, a strategy to gain the interest of her middle-class readers, Stowe's use of Tom as a black Christ, however heart-felt, was an effective device that appealed to that class of Americans who had political power. Hers once again is a protest novel, the strategy of which is to move her readers to take action; a call from the author herself comes at the very end of the book, when she instructs her readers to do that which makes them feel good. Obviously doing nothing was not what Stowe had in mind.

It perhaps helps here to remember that for Jane Tompkins the pluperfect sentimental novel is *The Wide, Wide World* by Susan Warner, the end of which brings the heroine to an absolute sense of her own unworth, a humility born of Christian doctrine that promises the ultimate reward: a heaven on earth identified with marriage to a minister. There is no reference in Warner's book to the social and economic inequities of her day, even though she and her sister were victims of the very unstable commercial situation that was typical of speculative capitalism in mid-nineteenth century America. For Christians like Warner, then and now, the evils of this world are simply irrelevant to the larger design, which is preparing oneself for the next and far, far better world to which they will be going, having done those far, far better things for others to which Charles Dickens, the ultimate sentimentalist of the day, made frequent reference. Dickens for his part was well aware of the inequities of this world, which are displayed in full in his fiction, but though he showed Stowe and Warner how sentimentality could be used to good effect in arousing sympathy for the underprivileged and dispossessed, Dickens did not write novels of protest. Thus, in *Oliver Twist,* having exposed the horrors of workhouse life, he proposed no alternative solution to poverty. Instead, he put considerable emphasis on personal benevolence, that is, the happy hearthside condition which his long-suffering orphan boy finally attains, not because of any government program, but through the agency of his regained birthright, an action that is providentially determined.

On the other side of the Civil War we have the instance of Bret Harte, who was, to borrow the title of his popular poem, "Dickens in Camp." Mark Twain sneered at Bret Harte's "saintly whores and sanctimonious sons-of-bitches," but Harte, like Stowe, owed a great debt to Dickens, from whom he abstracted the idea of his golden-hearted gamblers and open-handed gold miners. Harte went Dickens one better, for he had no social agenda at all; indeed, the world he wrote about had already disappeared by the time he began writing about it. He was merely playing with an idea that was given warrant by a situation, namely the essentially male makeup of California mining-camp life. But in eliciting his readers' often tearful sympathy for these rough-surfaced but tender-hearted and sensitive West-Coast guys, Harte was providing an almost linear demonstration of what is much more complex in both Dickens and Stowe, namely the exponential diagram implicit in "The Luck of Roaring Camp," in which the presence of a child brings out the mother in all of the men resident in the place, rendering "Roaring Camp" ambiguous in implication, at least to modern ears. For what are we talking about here but cross-dressing? But the effect of this transformation is to bring out as it were the mothers in all of us as well, so that we brim over with human sympathy and then weep at the ending when a sudden flood wipes out the camp and leaves the little Luck dead in the arms of one of the rough miners, who died in trying to save him. There is a certain element of mischief in Harte's fiction, and the flood that destroys the camp and child is the kind of water that turns the works in sentimental fiction. For the kid misnamed Luck is a male version of Little Nell and Little Eva, not used by Harte to move us to promote social reforms but assuredly to move us to tears.

What, you may be wondering, has all this got to do with John Steinbeck? Well, what Bret Harte demonstrates to a fault is the function of sentimental literature that is essential to protest fiction, which is to redeem what have been considered marginal persons by bringing them into the domestic center. It is a movement invariably associated, in Dickens, Stowe, Warner, and Harte, among many others, with women and children, whose mere presence can act to reveal the essential feminine in us all. By contrast, yet in complete synchronization with Harte, let me cut to the scene in which the remnants of the Joad family, along with other dispossessed emigrants, take refuge from rising flood waters in a boxcar on a railroad embankment. The men have struggled to preserve their vehicles from the flood by erecting a flimsy levee, a mud wall that is subsequently torn apart by a fallen tree in an episode that is diagrammatically illustrative of Steinbeck's naturalistic view of causality. During this same episode Rose of Sharon gives birth to a stillborn baby, a tiny corpse that her uncle sets adrift on the flood that rises above the cars and trucks so essential to their survival. We may doubt that Steinbeck was making a conscious allusion to the ending of Harte's most famous story, but the connections, as with parallel elements in *Uncle Tom's Cabin*, are useful here.

Because what the rising flood and the dead baby arouse in us are not tears of sympathetic grief, but a concomitant despair; we abandon hope not only for the Joads and their companions in adversity but for the humankind of which they are the lowest common denominator. The baby, ordered by Uncle John to "go down" like Moses and instruct America, can hardly set his people free. But then there occurs that final and famous moment in which Rose of Sharon gives her breast to a starving man, a gesture encouraged by her mother and which elevates these two women to a salvational and central position in the terminal tableau. It is a situation that would seem to recommend itself to us as a prototypical instance of the sentimental, yet though it draws upon our feelings, it does not I think move us to tears. It may end the novel on a note of affirmation, but not that rising organ chord associated with the operatics of soap. Fiedler admits to admiring this final moment, which attains the "mythopoeic" power, the "archetypal resonance," he finds in texts like *Gone With the Wind*, *Tarzan of the Apes*, and *The Adventures of Sherlock Holmes* ("Looking Back" 60). He even allows that it redeems all the rest of the book, with its cosmeticized sharecroppers, noble truck-drivers, and golden-hearted waitresses (Harte's miners, gamblers, and whores updated). He tells us that "Steinbeck himself has confessed . . . that [this] strange conclusion to a revolutionary and intendedly hopeful fable forced itself on him unbidden, which is to say, emerged out of his deep unconscious" ("Looking Back" 63). In contrast to the rest of the book, with its simplistic account of a complex economic and political situation, the ending is highly ambiguous, and ends with the word "mysterious." For Fiedler the transforming, even redeeming moment *has* to emerge from an archetypal resonance. Notably, the terminal passion of Uncle Tom famously came to Harriet Beecher Stowe in a dream vision, also.

Fiedler reminds us that the Hollywood version of the novel ends with the Joads attaining the felicity of a government camp, a clean, well-lighted place with the added bliss of flush-toilets, a heaven on earth conceived by a middle-class sensibility and an equivalent to that Dickensian center of domesticity which the characters in all sentimental fiction, including Bret Harte's, struggle to attain. But Steinbeck relegates the camp episode to an interlude, a periodicity that puts the government program into perspective, as a palliative perhaps but not a solution. Instead, he carried the remnants of the Joad family to that desperate hour on the railroad embankment and the final scene in the barn. This conclusion may, as Fiedler insists, have been generated in Steinbeck's unconscious, but it was also a carefully contrived artifact, which the author defended to Pascal Covici in a famous letter. There were those editorial readers who felt that the nameless vagrant to whom Rose of Sharon offered her breast should have been more tightly woven into the story, that the moment of hope should not have been a casual encounter but should have had some kind of foreplay by way of extenuating circumstances. But Steinbeck would have none of that. "The giving of the breast has no more sentiment than the giving of a piece of bread," he wrote. "If there is a symbol, it is a survival symbol, not a love symbol, it must be an accident, it must be a stranger, and it must be quick. To build this stranger into the structure of the book would be to warp the whole meaning of the book" (*SLL* 178).

Steinbeck seems to have wanted the moment to have the same

accidental force as the toppling of the cottonwood tree by the flood and its subsequent destruction of the feeble levee erected by the desperate men, who are forced to stand by as helpless witnesses to the event. Moreover, it is this emphasis on chance as a definitive force that provides a link between *The Grapes of Wrath* and Steinbeck's other novels about migrant workers: Like the disappearance of Jim Nolan's sister, in *In Dubious Battle*, the falling tree "was one of those things that happen." Like the murder by Lennie of Curley's wife in his second novel about migrant workers, originally entitled "Something That Happened," the encounter between Rose of Sharon and the starving man was a moment without causality, as casual as casual sex, "an accident, with a stranger, and quick." Most important, it was explicitly not, as Steinbeck emphasized, a sentimental gesture, which it might well have been had the man been tightly woven into the preceding events of the novel. Despite the familial grouping, centered by women, it was a classical moment, that, as Fiedler demonstrates, drew on a long iconographic tradition, Christian surely in implication, but not sentimental.

That is why Fiedler is drawn to it, as he tells us, such allusiveness being an archetypal resonance. But Fiedler is drawn to the conclusion of *The Grapes of Wrath* for other reasons, also: our leading connoisseur of kink, for whom all American fiction worth discussing has a sexual subtext, usually pathological, Fiedler was chiefly interested in *Uncle Tom's Cabin* because of the "rape" of Uncle Tom and the subliminal seductiveness of Little Eva. His *Love and Death in the American Novel* traces those aspects of our fiction that contain the gothic continuity, and there are no gothic bones showing in *The Grapes of Wrath*. Moreover, when Steinbeck deals with sexuality, it is seldom in a subliminal package but out in the open air, under a bush perhaps with Jim Casy but in plain view.

Fiedler, however, does manage to find an Oedipal message in *The Grapes of Wrath*, identified with the disempowerment of Pa Joad and the "loving" bond between Tom and his mother. These Freudian elements are agents of archetype that provide Fiedler welcome relief from the depressing soup kitchen of sentiment that is for him the novel as a whole, and they lead up to that final scene, in which Rose of Sharon as a perverse Madonna nurses an impotent father figure, "a total reversal of conventional generational roles" ("Looking Back" 62). But Fiedler's sexual "archetypes" can also be read as essential to the sentimental idea: if Pa is disempowered by his loss of patriarchal authority, which derives from an honest day's work, so Ma gains terrific strength, validating the maternal center of the sentimental mode; Tom's deep regard for his mother works to a similar end, for the action of the novel is clearly intended to move Ma Joad toward the center of power. It is a movement that, as in *Uncle Tom's Cabin,* identifies that center with the domestic idea, which likewise warrants the final scene in the book, even while that scene turns against its sentimental potential. Once again, the sentimental impulse is essential to novels of social protest.

But then Fiedler has never been much interested in either sentimentality or social protest, for having grown up in the age of hard-boiled realism and agitprop, he is immune to both. It was Fiedler, we should remember, who defended the execution of Rosenbergs, the Mom and Pop of the Communist Party who, third in line to Major André and Sacco and Vanzetti, were the dubious beneficiaries of liberally shed tears. Fiedler's was a position which in the 1950s took real guts. He is tough, the Mike Hammer of literary critics, and having punched out Steinbeck's generous truckers and butt-kicked "the improbably soft hearted waitress," he blows away what he calls the "pastoralism" of Steinbeck's novel, the Joads' fanciful dream of finding a little farm somewhere in California that will sustain their agrarian ideal ("Looking Back" 57).

But the Joads do not find that farm, a failure consistent with Steinbeck's intention, and in keeping with his decision to override the sentimental potential of his novel with his carefully chosen conclusion. *The Grapes of Wrath* may posit a pastoral ideal, but in terms of plot it is an epic, an action that moves not toward the domestic resolution of the *Odyssey,* nor the Promised Land of *Exodus* and the *Aenied,* but toward what in naturalistic terms must be called a tragedy. In sum, Steinbeck's greatest novel most certainly has sentimental elements, which work in the traditional, nineteenth-century way, engaging our sympathies with the characters. But in denying the Joads their dream, turning the plot away from a positive, hopeful resolution, Steinbeck turns the sentimental mode back on itself, a movement of which the dead baby, the flood, and the final scene with the starving, anonymous man are signifiers.

In an earlier moment in the novel, not discussed by Fiedler, the Joad family prepares to leave their Oklahoma farm. Departure from the home place has epical overtones but is an essentially sentimental event, as Uncle Tom's forced exile demonstrates, because it raises the domestic ante to an intolerable level of deprivation. Ma Joad is shown going through and discarding the memorabilia of her youth, as the melody from "Red River Valley" fills the air—in the movie, not the novel, not always easy to keep apart. Now we may harden our hearts like Fiedler, and ask how many Okie farm wives kept boxes of nostalgic keepsakes hidden away like a secret memory, but the function of this scene is not to provide us a realistic inventory of Okie farm-wife memorabilia. It is to arouse the sympathy of the reader/viewer for Ma Joad, and through her for all of the women who were displaced by the godawful Dust Bowl depression and forced to join the westward-moving army of the kinds of people we now call the Homeless.

Much as Harriet Beecher Stowe reached out to touch the hearts of her middle-class, white women readers by asking them if they had ever lost a child—not to slavery, of course, but to death—so Steinbeck is playing the same tune, albeit in a minor key, which in a protest novel in the United States must be gauged to harmonize with the values of the great American middle class, always the instrument of change then and now in this country. And most women of the great American middle class have a box in a closet somewhere filled with precious trinkets saved from their youth and understand what it means to have to discard a faded and shriveled rose of long ago, a momento not of death but of a past life hidden away, a sustaining secret memory of love.

It is moments like this, perhaps unconsciously conflated with the movie, that warrant Leslie Fiedler's charge of sentimentality, and there are other episodes, like the deaths of the Joad grandparents, that also correspond to tropes of the nineteenth-century model. For like Harriet Beecher Stowe, Steinbeck wanted to move his readers, and he could only do so by engaging them with the predicament of the Joads, which meant moving that family not only to California but into the familial center occupied by the great American middle class. At the same time, as his letter to Covici indicates, Steinbeck introduced elements that consciously worked against sentimental possibilities: significantly, having removed a few valuable trinkets, presumably to sell them, Ma Joad consigns her ephemeral treasures to the fire. It is a burning away of the past that like the deaths of that Anchisean pair, Granma and Granpa Joad, is an allusion to one of the several classical epics whose framework undergirds the family's heroic passage westward.

Although always drawn towards romantic models, like the Arthurian matter, Steinbeck is one of our great neoclassical writers, for whom form is a highly traditional even mandatory inheritance. The same may be said for his use of biblical patterns, whether the Exodus migration or the passion of Christ, which play such sustaining roles in *The Grapes of Wrath,* as they do in *Uncle Tom's Cabin* as well, albeit to much different ends. To put it briefly, Stowe's epic is Judaic-Christian in its implications, but for Steinbeck it is the classical version that holds, a Homeric, Virgilian, Mosaic errand underwritten by no providential guarantees but entirely dictated by the vagaries of chance, witnessed by the drought and the flood with which the action is framed. And of all the classical models, it is perhaps the *Iliad* that *The Grapes of Wrath* most closely resembles, being essentially a battle epic with no happy, empire-founding, promised-land-regaining conclusion.

Not only does the notion that life is dictated by casual happenstance connect Steinbeck's three labor-intensive novels, but chance is the factor that rules in all of his fictions, the accidentalness of events that disrupt the plans of men. And chance as the determining force of the universe is a notion foreign to the impulse that moves sentimental fiction. It is an ideology bordering on nihilism that operates, as in *Moby-Dick,* against the very basis of the sentimental tradition, which is so fruitfully rooted in the Christian idea of universal redemption. Once again, from Dickens's romances to Stowe's, causality in sentimental fiction derives from the gospel promise; it gives meaning to suffering and takes its form from the idea of salvation; God rules this world through the gracious intervention of Jesus Christ. Even the little Luck in Bret Harte's tearful parable suggests the redemptive role of Christ-child, for in the Christian plan the fall of a sparrow is part of a great and benign plan, providentially determined. The tears of sadness we are called upon to weep will yield to tears of gladness.

Thus, an emphasis on mere causality, on accident as the determinant factor of life, would seem to be downright hostile to the sentimental impulse. After all, we can identify this idea with realistic and naturalistic fiction, with the great continuity that connects Stephen Crane, Edith Wharton, and Theodore Dreiser with Hemingway, Glasgow, and Faulkner, among many others. It is a tradition which likewise operates outside the frame of social literature, the tradition of Dos Passos, Richard Wright, and Jack Conroy, which is shaped to illustrate a generally Marxist argument. For Marxism is keyed to a faith in immutable laws akin to those sustaining Judaic Christianity, not to the idea of the universe as an accident. It is perhaps not necessary to point out with Fiedler that *The Grapes of Wrath*, despite its points of similarity with texts like *Manhattan Transfer* and *U.S.A.*, is no more Marxist in its ideology than conventionally Christian. True, Tom Joad is not only given a messianic profile but is last seen shouldering a radical errand, which last, like Steinbeck's attack on what he defined as the "Fascist" elements of American agrarian capitalism, inspired ferocious reactions on the part of his contemporaries who assumed he was himself a Socialist when in fact his novel was in sync with Roosevelt's attempts to rescue the United States from Revolution.

In short, Steinbeck is a gravely misunderstood writer, as Leslie Fiedler's dismissal surely demonstrates. But that in some ways is his own fault, for much as Steinbeck, though a realist, often uses symbolic frameworks derived from archetypal sources, structures essentially romantic in implication, so as a realist he is anomalous in his use of sentimentality. But let us remember that Harriet Beecher Stowe was herself an early proto-realist, who turned from writing melodramatic protest novels to stories that are thought of as the foundation of the local color movement. Moreover, later, bona fide realists like Mark Twain, despite his contempt for Bret Harte and female purveyors of flapdoodle, could evoke the sentimental spirit as well. The reverse imprint of *Uncle Tom's Cabin* is *The Adventures of Huckleberry Finn:* The raft is an intensely domestic place. And Louisa May Alcott, who began her career writing penny dreadfuls, in *Little Women* provided a necessary corrective to *The Wide, Wide World*, not for its sentimentality but for its unbearable Christian burden. For American writers like Stowe, Alcott, Twain, and Steinbeck, the sentimental mode has its uses but was not an invariable necessity. Use it, as the saying goes, don't abuse it. Consider, then, some of the uses to which Steinbeck put sentimentality—and how he did not abuse it and why.

Let's start with *The Red Pony*, which veers toward the sentimental in its final, added chapter, when the grandfather recalls the pioneer past in which he took part only to be dismissed by the boy's father, thereby setting up a bond of sympathy between the boy and the old man and between the readers and both old man and boy. But in the original version of the book—which includes only the first three stories—there is no such opportunity, although there are plenty of situations that could have been worked for tears, like the death of the pony in the title. Deaths of horses are sentimental occasions, surely, or *Black Beauty*, published by the Humane Societies of Great Britain and America, was written in vain. *Black Beauty* is another sentimental novel written to forward reform, and when first published was subtitled *The Uncle Tom's Cabin of the Horse*, which makes the connection complete. Cut to *Bambi*, and the death of the deer mother, which makes the union of the fawn and his father, the great stag, possible; cut to *Love Story*, in which the death of Jenny makes the reunion of Oliver and his father possible. These are all sentimental fictions, and you may pick those which use tears to work reforms and those for which tears, as in Tennyson's poem that provides the title of the sentimental novel that serves as a target for aesthetic darts in *The Rise of Silas Lapham*, are merely idle, being for the sake of a good cry only. These are lacrimose lubricosities as it were, a kind of pornography of tears, intended to move us—but only to move us.

It serves a useful purpose here, I think, to mention also *The Yearling*, Marjorie Kinnan Rawlings's clone of *The Red Pony*, which plucks at your heartstrings to no purpose that I have been able to detect, or *My Friend Flicka*, a hybrid horsey out of *The Red Pony* and *The Yearling*, but with no perceivable connection to the ultimate horse's tale, *Black Beauty*. We are in these fictions set in Bret Harte country, which is to say we are back in California, the artistic capital of which is Hollywood, the place where Lassie always comes home. And it was of course Hollywood that added "Red River Valley" to Ma Joad's moment with her treasured past, whereas the song Steinbeck had chiefly in mind as he wrote his novel was "The Battle Hymn of the Republic," which keys both the epical and the gospel elements of the novel and provides another useful link to *Uncle Tom's Cabin*.

Let us now turn to Steinbeck's other novels about dispossessed field workers, specifically to *Of Mice and Men*, which took its title from a beloved poem by Robert Burns, the Robert Frost of his own day and as often misconstrued. It is about a plowman who has turned up by accident a mouse's nest, and who, holding the quivering victim in his hand, philosophizes about the vicissitudes to which all living creatures are heir, and over which they have no control. Now there is a sadness that permeates much of Burns's poetry, he who wrote what might have served as the epithet for much sentimental literature, that "Man's inhumanity to man/Makes countless thousands mourn!" ("Man Was Made to Mourn" 56–57). And the image of the "wee, sleekit, cow'rin', tim'rous beastie" in "To a Mouse" with the "panic" in its "breastie" like Bambi is certainly susceptible to a sentimental reading (2). The plowman, holding the mouse, begs its pardon for having destroyed its home, for in asserting "Man's dominion," he has broken "Nature's social union" (7–8). But a companion poem is Burn's "To a Mountain Daisy," which contains the following stanza, starkly unsentimental and yet in keeping with the concluding line from "To a Mouse" that Steinbeck took as his title:

Ev'n thou who mourn'st the Daisy's fate,
That fate is thine—no distant date;
Stern Ruin's ploughshare drives elate
Full on thy bloom,
Till crush'd beneath the furrow's weight,
Shall be thy doom. (49–54)

Of Mice and Men, like the poem from which it takes its title, does seem susceptible to a sentimental reading. Fiedler's dismissive essay ignores Steinbeck's still highly popular novel, which enjoys sales of over 300,000 paperback copies a year, preferring for obvious reasons to attack *The Grapes of Wrath*, which sells only 150,000 copies a year. His preference gives heft to his notion that Steinbeck, like Dos Passos and James Farrell, is no longer read, as mythopoetic an idea as any conjured up by Edgar Rice Burroughs. But for our purposes, *Of Mice and Men* is particularly useful, not only because it is still widely read, but because, although it deals with the lives of migrant workers, it does not have a social agenda of any detectable kind. Indeed, from a modern, feminist perspective, it is probably Steinbeck's most politically incorrect work of fiction, errors of attitude that turn on the role played by the woman known only as Curley's wife, whose actions disrupt and finally destroy the vision of a male-centered paradise, the Edenic parable beneath the pastoral weave.

In Lennie and George we have a pair recalling the two men in Bret Harte's "Tennessee's Partner," in which male bonding is taken to a sentimental extreme. As in "The Luck of Roaring Camp," moreover, domesticity in this novel is identified with the male hegemony, for the Joad family's dream of owning a little farm is shared not only by Lennie and George but by the other migrant workers they are cast among, a green, pastoral hope we are called upon to share likewise, but which finally proves futile.

Likewise, Lennie's proclivity for taking up little furry creatures in his hand seems to be a sardonic reference to the sentimental plowman in Burns's poem, given what happens to them as a result. And when he holds and then crushes Curley's wife, we must I think regard him as a heedless and callous natural force, arbitrary and casual in its effects. Lennie's attraction to little furry things is sentimentality itself but what he does to them destroys the sentimental impulse along with the little furry thing. And when George administers an anaesthetic of sorts to Lennie, by pointing to the distant green prospect of their long deferred domestic paradise before shooting him, we have a perfect diagram of Steinbeck's use of the sentimental mode, which is to hold it out to us in a promising form and then, like Lennie with a wee mousie, crush it.

Steinbeck's is not, however, a cynical gesture. It is in keeping with his non-teleological view of the world, which is essentially unfriendly to linear and progressive literary forms, the kinds of discourse that sustain an argument or a thesis or a solution, whether it be Christian or Marxist doctrine. The sentimental mode, like the pastoral and epic with which it is often conjoined in protest novels, is one of the most linear of forms, pointing always to some happy and regenerative—even transfiguring— conclusion, and when used for the purpose of protest literature it holds out a socially determined solution to a social problem.

Once again, there is no solution posited for the problems overwhelming the Joads and their fellow migrant workers, only expedient palliatives. That momentary relief experienced by the family in the government camp was derived from actual experience, as we know, but Steinbeck in his letters and articles also made it clear that the fascistic vigilante bands organized by local authorities in California were furiously antagonistic to those camps, fearing that they would provide the workers the opportunity to organize themselves into an effective force for change. In the novel, the migrants are able to forestall the attempts to invade their camp, but in truth the real strength, as in *In Dubious Battle*, was in the hands of local authorities who kept the vigilantes on a purposefully loose leash. And as for the vow that Tom Joad takes on the grave of Jim Casy, with its vague promise of a syndicalist agitation, we know from *In Dubious Battle* also how skeptical Steinbeck was about the activities of labor organizers, for whom the actual welfare of workers is secondary to furthering the Socialist cause in which the organizers serve.

In Dubious Battle, the critical first in Steinbeck's labor-intensive trilogy, would seem to be the one of the three that is without any bid for sentimental sympathy. It is also intensely male-centered, with only marginal roles for women, although the young mother, Lisa, with her ambitious husband, is clearly a prefatory sketch for that American Madonna, Rose of Sharon. Indeed, throughout the book we find points of contingency with *The Grapes of Wrath*, starting with Jim Nolan, the protagonist, who shares certain qualities with Tom Joad, but who, as his family name suggests—borrowed from that of the protagonist in Edward Everett Hale's "Man Without a Country"—is a permanent exile in the world, without family connections. As the central figure, a young man who is undergoing an education in radicalism, Jim should attract reader sympathy, and his sudden death in a vigilante ambush is certainly shocking. But in the end he serves merely as the occasion for yet another appeal by his mentor, the labor agitator, Mac, for the workers' attention and solidarity, forwarding a strike already defined as doomed.

With Mac slipping into his familiar rhetoric as he stands over Jim's bleeding corpse, Steinbeck obviously is blocking any bid for empathy with his cause, for where Mac is obviously appealing to the sentimentality of the fruit pickers, Steinbeck, by calling our attention to that ploy, puts massive distance between the reader and the message. The ending is not only unsentimental but also grimly realistic, holding out little hope for casual laborers in those factories in the field, the orchards of California. It is in this novel, once again, that the idea that things just happen is first made explicit. And though Steinbeck expresses the phalanx idea through the reflections of young Dr. Burton, we see no sign that the men Mac attempts to organize can muster anything but sporadic efforts to join in a common effort to better their lives. Mac's career seems a little better than an extended exercise in futility, from which he protects himself with a thick callus of rationalization, the repeated mantra that even a failed strike will serve a useful purpose. Likewise, the cost to the men he purports to help is written off as a kind of expense account, necessary to effect a greater good, resulting in another kind of protective callus, on the heart not the head. His is a higher realism, which Steinbeck's carefully flattened prose intensifies.

Yet at a critical point Burton observes that "Sometimes I think you realists are the most sentimental people in the world" (209), and a few pages later he tells Mac that he is "the craziest mess of cruelty and hausfrau sentimentality, of clear vision and rose-colored glasses I ever saw" (212). Increasingly it is Jim Nolan who sees "the big picture," the Marxist vision, and who by the time he dies has become a thorough socialist zealot, while Mac again and again gives way to a human impulse, a warmth perhaps attributable to his Irish blood but which I think is essential to the meaning of the book, and hence to Steinbeck's use of sentimentality in *The Grapes of Wrath* as well. As Warren French suggests, it is in Mac's mouth that Steinbeck places the words that will in terms of sentiments be repeated by Tom Joad, when he promises his mother that he will become an omnipresent force among the migrant families, being "there" wherever a few are gathered together, in effect becoming a secular Christ (14).

There is a depth of humanity in this connection that is I think essential to Steinbeck's often perverse use of sentimentality, his *lacrimosus interruptus*. If Tom Joad does play that role so central to sentimental fiction, the human semblance of Jesus Christ, it is not, however, the suffering Christ, the passive victim of established authority who in rendering unto Caesar what was Caesar's included his corporal identity, with the expectation that his spirit would rule in heaven, to which destination and triumph he recommended the meek and lowly of the world. That was the role, once again, of Uncle Tom, not Tom Joad. Let us return in that connection to the theme song of *The Grapes of Wrath*, "The Battle Hymn of the Republic," which is about quite a different Christ from the one found in sentimental literature, whose robes fit so easily on the suffering protagonists engendered by writers like Stowe and Susan Warner.

The Christ of Julia Ward Howe is the militant Savior, not warranted by the Gospels but produced by the uneasy union of Christianity and the old Pagan religion it displaced, with its furious berserker gods for whom violence and vengeance were a way of life. Howe's is the Puritan Christ, as well, that compound of the Old and New Testaments, the Gideon-like wielder of the sword of divine judgement. We should always keep in mind that deep within "The Battle Hymn of the Republic" there dwells not the moldering body but the undying spirit of Captain John Brown, whose solution to the problems dramatized in *Uncle Tom's Cabin* was quite different from Harriet Beecher Stowe's— not colonization but insurrection.

The Grapes of Wrath is, like *Uncle Tom's Cabin*, a very emotional book, but the emotion is one of anger. Steinbeck's letters from California during the period of the novel's gestation seethe with fury over the plight of the migrants, starving and drowned out by social and natural forces, victims of laws both man-made and natural over which they have no control. His anger was chiefly aimed at the vigilante groups who persecuted the Okies, and we know that the novel was first drafted as an attack on those groups, a version that lingers in detectable fragments in the book that finally emerged from Steinbeck's fury. And it is anger I think that he hoped to inspire in his readers, moving them to tears not of sad resignation but outrage over the fate suffered by the Joads as they strive to attain what was and is still a middle-class ideal, a decent job that could permit a degree of self-respect. Leslie Fiedler snorts the epithet "middle-brow" ("Looking Back" 61) but that was precisely the point, nor were Steinbeck's efforts to ennoble the Joads any different from the end sought by photographers like Dorothea Lange, whose sympathetic portraits of noble Okies and Arkies are patent exercises in primitivism that somehow escape Fiedler's censorious eye.

Moreover, Steinbeck saw in the anger of farm workers in California the seeds of a war, a populist uprising, much as John Brown saw in Nat Turner's and other slave rebellions hopeful signs that a general insurrection was possible in the South. Surely we take Tom Joad's promise to his mother as a threat to established order, as an errand that will carry Jim Casy's populist gospel to the circling watchfires of the migrant workers' camps. This is not to say that Steinbeck hoped by means of his novel to stir up revolution in California. Though he may have borrowed technique from *U.S.A.*, he hardly shared Dos Passos's Marxist ideology. It is to say that *The Grapes of Wrath* is a text that, like Luther's, is pinned as a warning to the gates of Heaven that something had better be done or else. Why otherwise the insistence on reprinting "The Battle Hymn of the Republic" on the endpapers entire, the hints to Pascal Covici that the song contained the essential message of his book?

That is, if he hoped to arouse outrage and anger in his readers, he also seemed to have sought to strike terror into the hearts of the authorities in California, and he appears to have been successful in this last regard, given the reaction of many Californians to his book. But like John Brown's raid, Steinbeck's literary terrorism was counterproductive in the long run, for if his only solution to the problem of the migrant workers was essentially the palliative already in place, those government camps that the fruit growers feared and hated as staging grounds for the revolution Steinbeck hoped to evade, then the record shows that his novel did not serve as an effective vehicle for change, and may even have worked against his purposes. On another plane, Steinbeck may have hoped that his rhetoric would override the essential circumstances of life, but things do just happen, and the greatest irony framing *The Grapes of Wrath,* as Fiedler points out, is the fact that a war did indeed end the plight of the Okies, not a revolution but the anti-Fascist conflict that America finally entered in 1941.

That is, the Okies and Arkies who seemed in 1939 at the point of taking up arms against their troubles escaped them by finding employment in armament factories. But Fiedler does not acknowledge that those jobs enabled many of the former migrants to realize their pastoral dream, buying the farms seized from resident Japanese, who were interned by those same paranoid fascist authorities who were aroused to panicked action by an invasion of swarms of alien migrants seeking a small piece of California landscape for themselves. And as the Okies and Arkies moved toward the middle-class center where Steinbeck had sought to place them, so the dispossessed Nisei were removed to camps far from the American gaze, most of them deported finally to the land of their ancestors as the Okies and Arkies became solid, even reactionary citizens of California.

In denying Steinbeck's novel the power of archetype, Fiedler overlooks the transforming role of the popular cinema, to which Margaret Mitchell's novel also owes its mythic force. By means of that mystic liminal grove known as Hollywood, Tom Joad as Henry Fonda became Mr. Roberts, and died a hero's death in the War, fighting fascism but not suffering martyrdom in the cause of the IWW. By such means he became "there" in a way hardly foreseen by John Steinbeck, suffering a death which, like those of Uncle Tom and Jim Casy, inspired the conversion of yet another, younger man to the cause of rebellion against arbitrary power (I speak of Ensign Pulver, soon enough grown old and grumpy). And in a former identity Tom Joad as Henry Fonda had been Jesse James's younger brother Frank, in the Hollywood version a populist hero whose career of robbing trains was revenge against the railroad company for the murder of his mother, who in the movie was played by Jane Darwell, who is Ma Joad in the movie version of *The Grapes of Wrath*. Tom/ Henry's daughter, also Jane, in her time espoused radical causes also, but then went on to marry a man who owned stuff like cattle ranches and baseball teams, including a television network that occasionally shows the Hollywood version of *The Grapes of Wrath*. None of this, once again, was the work of John Steinbeck, who, as we know, hated Hollywood as an alien presence that corrupted literature, but it is, I think, a marvelous irony that the movie is populated by actors who appear like members of some radical repertoire company in any number of films of the Thirties. For many of these movies celebrate, often by sentimental means, the common people who sustain the American economy or who, when betrayed by it, begin to think revolutionary thoughts and engage in revolutionary activities, which is ever the lesson of Captain John Brown, never mind Baby Face Floyd.

In conclusion, John Steinbeck's use of sentimentality is intrinsically and idiosyncratically his own, at once revealing the warm and passionate heart of a man who was moved to anger and outrage by the suffering of his fellow human beings but who in creating the kind of fiction that would call attention to that suffering stopped well short of calling for revolution or even holding out hope for positive social change. His belief in the accidentalness of life, a fatality without a supernatural agency behind it, was an ideological frame that blocked the championship of purposeful action. Steinbeck was, if you will, a Prometheus in chains of his own fashioning, whose rage was a signal of his powerful identification with the suffering of humanity, an anger exacerbated not, as Fiedler would have it, by guilt, but by a frustrating realization that bad things happen to good people, and cannot be set right by a specific political action.

Yet through all his fiction we find a terrific energy at work, the sort of force that across the highway drives the old tortoise, seeds borne between his drought-hard skin and carapace; that drives the Joads to California, that keeps them going against all adversity; that drives zealots like Mac to pick themselves up and hurl their bodies again and again against an apparently indifferent wall of inert mankind, that doubtful battle to which the epithet from Milton has reference. It is a characteristic that bonds Steinbeck's works to those of William Faulkner, in which endurance leads to prevalence, and no one has ever accused Faulkner of sentimentality in the negative sense, or "A Rose for Emily" was written in vain. So if you must ask to whom and for what purpose Rose of Sharon offers her breast, then I say she offers it to thee.

2

The Ghost of Tom Joad

Steinbeck's Legacy in the Songs of Bruce Springsteen

Gavin Cologne-Brookes

Like Steinbeck, Bruce Springsteen is a writer with a social conscience. And like Steinbeck's Tom Joad, Springsteen's down-and-out characters evolve from being self-reflective and self-absorbed to being socially conscious. Tom Joad's legacy is readily apparent in Springsteen's album The Ghost of Tom Joad.

Just as Elia Kazan's film of *East of Eden* inspired "Adam Raised a Cain" on *Darkness on the Edge of Town* (1978), so Bruce Springsteen cites John Ford's movie of *The Grapes of Wrath* rather than John Steinbeck's novel as the main influence on *The Ghost of Tom Joad* (1995). While Ford once claimed to have "never read the book" (Bluestone 169), Springsteen has clearly been influenced by Steinbeck's actual writing. In fact, he would read from the novel at the top of shows during his Joad tour (Sandford 382). But the adaptability of Steinbeck's vision to other genres remains extraordinary. It's hard to imagine a musician citing, say, a Hemingway or Faulkner novel or even a film adaptation as a primary influence, and not just because such movies have never been classics. Something about Steinbeck's vision crosses boundaries and transcends the mere text. *The Grapes of Wrath* has now traversed three genres. Like the characters themselves, it has meandered from the Oklahoma of noveldom through the arid New Mexican landscape of the movie to Springsteen's California-orientated folk songs of failed dreams in the Promised Land. This essay is specifically about Steinbeck's influence on Springsteen, but to assess this legacy properly is also to appreciate the ways in which genre-hopping illuminates both the meaning and social function of art.

The works of Steinbeck and Springsteen comment on and contribute to our understanding of social forces and injustices, and arguably help foster changes in the way individuals and communities respond. Whether art *really* makes a difference is, of course, a vexed question. In Steinbeck's novel, Al suggests to Uncle John that their struggle to find a better life is about as achievable as "huntin' skunks under water" (435). The phrase echoes Gustave Flaubert's that books are like pyramids: "There's some long-pondered plan" followed by "blocks of stone . . . placed one on top of the other, and it's back-breaking, sweaty, time-consuming work. And all to no purpose!" (Barnes 35–36). Both comments imply that art, as a form of questing human endeavor, must have its own reason for being because there's little hope that it will contribute to a better, fairer world. But the fact is that, perhaps partly because of its adaptability to other genres, *The Grapes of Wrath* has had, as works of art go, an unparalleled influence on America's awareness of its own social inequities.

To note that Steinbeck's migrant odyssey is peculiarly adaptable to other genres is nothing new. Bluestone explored this adaptability in his invaluable study of the novel and movie in *Books into Film* in the late 1950s. But Springsteen's album adds a new dimension to our sense of Steinbeck's legacy. Moreover, *The Ghost of Tom Joad* is not an isolated response on Springsteen's part to Steinbeck's moral vision. It is just the most obvious example of a profound, ongoing legacy that evidently began for Springsteen in the late 1970s when he was encouraged by producer Jon Landau and then-girlfriend Lynn Goldsmith "to get more 'arty'" (Sandford 143). Continuing through the 1980s and 1990s into the twenty-first century, it has deepened into a fundamental attitude toward the role of the artist-observer that is wholly evident in such *éngagé* songs as "Murder Incorporated," "Streets of Philadelphia," and "American Skin (41 Shots)." Springsteen's songs are no mere passive echoes of a vision filtered through the sentimental tendencies of Hollywood. His specific reference to Steinbeck in *The Ghost of Tom Joad* headlines a *Grapes of Wrath* influence characterized by an increasing tendency to reassert a political radicalism that exists more obviously in the novel than in the film. Brought to the novel via the movie, Springsteen responds both to the style(s) and the content of Steinbeck's novel in ways that restore much of the flavor of the original.

The Ghost of Tom Joad as a title indicates that, like Steinbeck, Springsteen is trying to create art that functions as social commentary. It suggests that the mature Springsteen lays claim to a shared view of artistic endeavor that is closely linked with the historical moment, emphasizing characters in relationships to one another and to their environment, and arguing for collective responsibility rather than individual isolation. For some, like the Hungarian Marxist critic, Georg Lukàcs, this is the course that art of long-term significance tends to follow. Seeing it as a question of realism versus modernism, he berates the latter for seeing people as by nature solitary, asocial, and unable to enter into relationships with others. In modernism, he argues, history is made "private" and all ties are broken "between historical events and private destinies" (*Contemporary Realism* 20). To seek escape is a modernist "yearning for harmony" that leads to "withdrawal before the contradictory problems thrown up by life. . . . By seeking inner harmony men cut themselves off from society's struggles" (*Writer and Critic* 89). For Lukàcs, in significant art the events of characters' lives are integrally connected to history. "The individual event," he argues, is seen to exist "in organic-historical connection with that infinite chain of individual events which in themselves are similarly accidental and in and through whose totality historical necessity always asserts itself" (*Historical Novel* 375).

The Grapes of Wrath is just such an example of artistic engagement. No mainstream modernist, Steinbeck built his novel on public, contextualized incidents in which individual actions affect the lives of families and communities. Even Steinbeck's American landscape is characterized by an attention to detail that fixes it within what Lukàcs might call its "organic-social connection." "One could easily read *The Grapes of Wrath* and drive along Route 66 today with a full sense of recognition," writes Jay Parini. "Chapter 15, for instance, opens with a vivid evocation of the roadside stands (whose names have, of course, changed)," and "Steinbeck's eye for details like these" helps make it such "a stunning book" (Parini 238). Significantly, this attention to detail is just as notable in Springsteen's *The Ghost of Tom Joad*. Take, for instance, the song "Youngstown." Where a younger Springsteen invariably contented himself with generic references to highways, back streets, cars, rivers and factories, here he documents a specific iron works founded in northeast Ohio in 1803 by James and Dan Heaton. He notes its role as a maker of Union cannon balls in the nineteenth century and tanks and bombs in the twentieth, and he carefully situates one blast furnace worker's story within a cultural, geographical and historical context. By the end of the song he has taken his listeners on a journey from the Monongahela Valley and the Mesabi Iron range to the Appalachian coal mines, and from the Civil War through World War II to Korea and Vietnam. At the same time he has given voice to an American worker as deliberately as that definitive American cultural witness, Studs Terkel. The legacy of Steinbeck's work in Springsteen's songs is therefore a matter of both theme and style. In the whole concept of the songs from sentiments to performance, Springsteen not only seeks, and finds, the ghost of Tom Joad, but through his career has become that ghost.

First and foremost there is the thematic legacy, in particular the relationship between the individual and the community. The songs mark Springsteen's maturation away from an individual desire to escape, to an awareness not only of his immediate environment—something evident in previous albums— but also that his story is part of American history and culture. Early in his career, Springsteen's travel motif is predominantly about individual dreams of escape, exemplified by such songs as "Born to Run" and "Thunder Road." The hero sees his hometown as a restrictive place full of losers from which he will pull out to find personal success elsewhere. From this Springsteen moves, via the family ties and reluctant separations evident in such *River* songs as "Independence Day," to something quite different. His theme in *The Ghost of Tom Joad* is *enforced* migration and individual *responsibility* as part of a wider group. While, between songs like "Johnny 99" and "Reason to Believe" on the Guthrie-inspired *Nebraska* (1982), hints of communal responsibility still vie with lonely personal ambition, at no point in that album does individual escape seem much of an option. By the time of songs like "Souls of the Departed" on the aptly-titled *Human Touch* (1992), and through much of *The Ghost of Tom Joad*, the emphasis is even less on individual escape. Rather, characters try to make connections between one another, the narratives of their lives and the forces around them.[1] In "Galveston Bay," for instance, a Vietnam veteran spares a Vietnamese immigrant who has killed two Texan Klan members in self-defense. As Jim Cullen puts it, the resolution of the song's racial conflict offers us "the ultimate definition of brotherhood: love that transcends boundaries" (Cullen 138).[2] Similarly "Sinaloa Cowboys" and "The Line" are songs which raise questions—again far from the early Springsteen—about how issues to do with friendship and responsibility relate to family and community issues.

Warren French's analysis of the change in Tom Joad describes much the same kind of change as is evident in the Springsteen heroes as the singer's career has evolved. It is, writes French of Joad, from a "selfish, violent individual concerned only with the survival of his touchy clan into a visionary operating selflessly in the background as an inspiring influence to his whole community" (*Fiction Revisited* 76). Springsteen, like Joad, has moved from merely celebrating the rebel figure, the early Joad, to being just that "inspiring influence." Again, like Joad, he has ultimately absented himself from his original community in the process—at least to the extent of owning a Beverly Hills mansion and becoming "a part-time Californian" (Cullen 191). But that "a fella ain't no good alone" (570) is as relevant to Springsteen's album as it is to Steinbeck's novel. Individuals—and the art that portrays them—mature when they grow out of youthful self-centeredness and see themselves as part of a larger context. The change between Springsteen's youthful and mature visions is put in relief on his 1989 video anthology. Introducing a 1987 live version of "Born to Run"—with all that stuff about towns full of losers the individual has to escape in order to "win"—he is recorded reminding the audience, however dubiously, that "nobody wins unless everybody wins." But still, "this is the beginning," writes Steinbeck, "—from 'I' to 'we'" (206). American myths of individualism strike at the heart of notions of community, and this is evident in both *The Grapes of Wrath* and *The*

Ghost of Tom Joad. Those Springsteen fans who prefer the romantic rebel to the emphasis on community may, as Sandford suggests, feel that "he never quite recovered from watching *The
Grapes of Wrath* on TV" (Sandford 147). But as Springsteen himself said in 1988, while introducing the acoustic version of "Born
to Run" recorded on the same anthology, "I realized that after
I'd put all those people in all those cars I was going to have to
figure out some place for them to go." "Individual freedom," he
came to acknowledge, "when it's not connected to some sort
of community or friends or the world outside ends up feeling
pretty meaningless."

Indeed, the way Springsteen's statements have changed through
his career corroborates the evidence of the songs. In a 1974 interview with Michael Watts, appropriately entitled "Lone Star,"
he admitted, "the main thing I've always been worried about is
me. . . . I had to write about me all the time," he said, "because
in a way you're trying to find out what that 'me' is." His links
with Tom Joad, then, are more profound than the fact that, in
Watts's words, he used to wear a hat "pulled down low over one
ear in the true style of the Depression era" so that he and his
crew resembled "young Okies" (Watts 55, 52). In a 1992 interview with David Hepworth, Springsteen again suggests a personal dimension to the journey from "I" to "we" evident in his
lyrics. His comments also perhaps explain why he would put
geographical distance between himself and his native region.
"I'd lived in New Jersey for a very long time and I'd kind of
written about a lot of things that had a lot to do—very tight into
my *past*, my *past*, my *past* always," he said, "different ghosts
you're chasing." Having taken this as far as he could, he was
now writing instead about "people trying to connect to each
other and that happens everywhere." Connection, as he says
about "With Every Wish" on *Human Touch*, means "dealing with
a life with consequences." "What does it mean to be a husband?" asks Springsteen rhetorically. "What does it mean to be
a father? What does it mean to be a friend to somebody? When
you finally get a good look at the world as it is, how do you not
give in to cynicism, not give in to despair?" His answer is that
you recognize—and this is Springsteen consciously or otherwise quoting the First epistle General of Paul—"a world of love

and a world of fear," and that the two go hand in hand. "Perfect love casts out fear," wrote Paul. But of course it doesn't, it just makes fear more palatable.

Such is the thematic aspect of Steinbeck's legacy in the songs of Springsteen. In Lukàcs's terms, Steinbeck and Springsteen both reject escapism, whether into aesthetic experimentation or private neuroses, in favor of living with, confronting and depicting life's struggles in wider contexts. Out of the world of love and the world of fear comes the world of responsibility. Springsteen's talk of "a world of love and a world of fear" is a confession of life's complex contradictions. Beginning with his own early wrath, he has come to see this class anger in context. This is not to say that he has become a Marxist songwriter. Ironically, he is as enmeshed in the capitalist system as one can imagine, and rich because of it. But the contradictions in his songs and story are by and large to do with the contradictory aspects of American ideals of equality and individualism.

While subject matter is a major source of Steinbeck's influence on Springsteen, it cannot be separated from style and approach. It is here that Springsteen actually reinforces something of the political dimension of *The Grapes of Wrath* arguably muted by the movie adaptation. In his analysis of the book into the film, Bluestone concludes that screenwriter Nunnally Johnson's streamlining of Steinbeck's oscillation between two differing styles—his juxtaposition of documentary naturalism with the Joad narrative—tends to retain the insistence on "family cohesion," "affinity for the land" and "human dignity" (Bluestone 158–59). "The leisurely pace of the novel," he writes, "gives way to a tightly knit sequence of events." But Bluestone notes that this approach also serves to mute and generalize the novel's political radicalism. This is partly because, as one would expect, Steinbeck's seventeen general commentaries find no place in the movie, yet are precisely where we find "the angry interludes, the explicit indictments" that contribute so much to the novel's moral tone (Bluestone 162–63). If part of the withdrawal from political implications exists in the novel itself—for instance with Rose of Sharon's final act of offering her breast milk to a starving man—Bluestone demonstrates how the film invariably uses the novel's "evasive answers" in preference to its "specific accusations" (Bluestone 159–60). "Thus the book, which is an exhortation to action, becomes a film which offers reassurance that no action is required" (Bluestone 167). A novel that is "remembered for its moral anger" becomes a film "remembered for its beauty" (Bluestone 168–69). In certain ways, then, by concentrating on the novel's narrative strengths, the film loses something of the novel's moral strength. It "improves" on the novel as narrative art but only by dropping a vital element of Steinbeck's overall approach.

Given the classic status of the movie version—and the fact that Springsteen chose to cite the film rather than the novel— it is certainly tempting to view Steinbeck's lasting impact in terms of subject matter over style. Some commentators have done this. "There is, finally, something crude about Steinbeck's book," Parini concedes. Rather than a stylist, suggests Parini, "Steinbeck is, foremost, a storyteller" (Parini 275). Harold Bloom, too, intimates that content rather than style accounts for its lasting impact. While there are "no canonical standards worthy of human respect that could exclude *The Grapes of Wrath* from a serious reader's esteem," he writes, it is hard to say "whether a human strength" is in itself "an aesthetic value, in a literary narrative" (*Steinbeck* 5). Steinbeck's style in *The Grapes of Wrath* is fairly rough and ready. His extensive research and a dry-run like "L'Affaire Lettuceberg" notwithstanding, the eventual novel was finally written at speed, the 200,000 words completed in six months, and produced "in the sequence of its publication with minimal revision" (French 193). And perhaps there's some truth in the view that the lasting legacy of much of Steinbeck's work has to do with qualities adaptable to other genres: the understanding of human motivation, the human story.

But if so, this is not the whole truth. For a start, Steinbeck is hardly in danger of being known about rather than read. A random glance at the booking ticket for *The Grapes of Wrath* in my local small-town library revealed that it has been taken out nearly once a month for the past five years. As with Tolstoy in *War and Peace* (which Parini notes might equally be described as in some ways "crude") his actual literary approach, involving both narrative and exposition, can have no equivalent when transferred to the streamlining demands of the screen. More-over, while the songwriter's art has its own demands and limita-tions, Steinbeck's legacy in Springsteen's songs certainly goes deeper than the influence of mere subject matter. If "Adam Raised a Cain" provides an early example of Springsteen on his way to being (in the words of *Tom Joad* reviewers) "a musical Steinbeck" (Schoenberg A7) or a "Steinbeck in leather" (Dawidoff) by the time of *Tom Joad,* the legacy had become less superficial than such phrases imply.[3] Quite aside from the similarities between Tom Joad's maturing vision in the novel and Springsteen's through his career, Steinbeck's legacy is also evident in Springsteen's changing approaches, including his choice of musical style, and the juxtaposition of narrative and explicit commentary.

For instance, it's not coincidental that *Tom Joad* is a folk rather than rock album. The translation of Steinbeck's images from novel into song lyric sees Springsteen returning to the origins of storytelling as folk art. Steinbeck's vision is recycled, refined, and updated, but it also reappears in an album that pays hom-age—in its acoustic intimacy as well as subject matter—to the kind of folk songs alluded to in *The Grapes of Wrath.* Songs like "Youngstown," about alienated labor, or "The New Timer," about an itinerant worker and railrider through Texas, New Mexico, California and back, echo the titles of songs documented in the novel, such as "Ten-Cent Cotton and Forty-Cent Meat" or "I'm Leaving Texas." Meanwhile, Springsteen's sometimes lulling, sometimes eerie rhythms call to mind Steinbeck's ubiquitous campsite guitarist. "And perhaps a man brought out his guitar to the front of his tent," writes Steinbeck. "And he sat on a box to play, and everyone in the camp moved slowly in toward him, drawn toward him," listening to "the deep chords beating, beat-ing, while the melody runs on the strings like little footsteps."

And now the group was welded to one thing, one unit, so that in the dark the eyes of the people were inward, and their minds played in other times, and their sadness was like rest, like sleep. He sang the "McAlester Blues" and then, to make up for it to the older people, he sang "Jesus Calls Me to His Side." The children drowsed with the music and went into their tents to sleep, and the singing came into their dreams. (272)

This, surely, is the effect Springsteen seeks with *The Ghost of Tom Joad*. It marks a return to music as intimacy—as if around a campfire with only the Joads and Wainwrights to hear—in contrast to his electrified anthems that filled arenas in the 1970s and 1980s. This is also why *The Ghost of Tom Joad* is so markedly warmer and more companionable, for all its dark subject matter, than the album it superficially resembles. The generally bleaker, harder songs of *Nebraska* would not exactly draw in and weld our imagined group of migrants, let alone lull their children to sleep.

Of course, a gulf yawns between Springsteen's position as a rock star, recording songs in a Los Angeles studio for mass consumption, and Woody Guthrie or, say, Joe Hill, who was not just a recorder but a participant, shot in the jailyard in Salt Lake City in 1915.[4] Perhaps there must always be something artificial—something even of postmodernist pastiche—about Springsteen seeking to re-create the fireside intimacy of folk tradition. On the other hand, Springsteen's motivation, and consequent appeal, seem to stem from a genuine commitment to those of his class (especially those who suffered as soldiers in Vietnam or still do as workers in America) that has subsequently branched outward. Seeing the fates of his friends and family in context, he has logically extended this to examine the plights of other beleaguered groups, climbing, in this case, into "the hearts and minds," as Mikal Gilmore puts it, "of a handful of undocumented immigrants" to California (Gilmore 434).

Springsteen, moreover, has learned much from the novel's oscillating use of both "cinematic" narrative and the verbal commentator's (as opposed to the film director's) scope for direct exposition. In a television documentary on Steinbeck, David Thomas recorded Gore Vidal's views on Steinbeck's general legacy. Again the emphasis is on subject matter rather than approach. "He looked at people nobody had ever looked at before and not many people have looked at since," said Vidal, "so I think, as a spirit of a country and of an age, and of his time, he was an honorable recorder." Such sentiments equally apply to Springsteen. That said, Vidal's phrase "honorable recorder" sounds slightly patronizing because it elides the fact that Steinbeck's novel does not simply record the plight of a people but gives it poetic voice through the Joad narrative and indicts the status quo through the alternating expository commentaries. Springsteen does much the same. "Got a lot of sinful idears—but they seem kinda sensible" is a line from *The Grapes of Wrath* (27) that could, as easily, be Springsteen's. But it's not just that Steinspeak and Springspeak grow out of an American vernacular first celebrated in *Huckleberry Finn*. Neither figure is merely "an honorable recorder."

Bluestone's analysis is again useful here. Whereas "the angry interludes, the explicit indictments, the authorial commentary" would have seemed "obtrusive" in the film, they find their "proper filmic equivalents" through direct action, and Steinbeck's narrative style is otherwise highly cinematic (Bluestone 162–63). "Except for the freewheeling omniscience of the interchapters," writes Bluestone, "the novel's prose relies wholly on dialogue and physical action to reveal character. Steinbeck's style is not marked by meditation, it resembles, in this respect, the classic form of the scenario" (Bluestone 163). Such a style "can also serve as precise directions for the actor," with a great many scenes that can "be turned into images of physical reality. Critics who seem surprised at the ease with which Steinbeck's work moves from one medium to another may find their explanation here" (Bluestone 164).

But while Nunnally Johnson's script and Ford's film may be hampered by the demands of the cinema, Springsteen as a songwriter and performer is free of the pressures imposed by the Hollywood system. In various ways, he is able to restore the expository side of Steinbeck's approach, and so the political bite. On the one hand, the songs on *Tom Joad* are full of precisely the same kind of cinematic narrative that Bluestone notes in Steinbeck's style. On the other hand Tom Joad, elevated in the film version to accommodate Henry Fonda and Hollywood's star-vehicle tendency, is again relegated to the role of "ghost" rather than hero as he reprises his oath to the book's strongest character, Ma Joad. In the album he is only one figure on a crowded canvas. Springsteen roams widely across America in a sequence of scenarios that add up to an essayistic indictment of the exploitation of ordinary workers and migrants from the blast furnaces of northeastern Ohio to the plight of Mexican wetbacks.

Also restored is the reference, excised from the film, to police brutality in that speech. If, as Bluestone argues, "the production crew effected alterations which mute the villainy of cops and tradesmen" and "cloud over the novel's political radicalism," Springsteen offers little of the comfort, respite or sentimentalism that arguably colors the movie (Bluestone 167–8). And if there still remains a degree of romanticism in Springsteen's depiction of Joad, romanticism can hardly be a charge leveled at "Balboa Park," about a border drug-runner who dies after a balloon of cocaine bursts in his stomach. Nor has it any place in those especially pointed songs of the 1990s, "Murder Incorporated" and "Streets of Philadelphia," or a song first performed in June 2000, "American Skin (41 Shots)." The latter, to the public dismay of Patrick Lynch, President of the New York City Patrolman's Benevolent Association, does nothing to flinch from detailing the facts of the forty-one shots fired into unarmed Guinean immigrant Amadou Diallo, when police mistook his wallet for a gun. In detailing some of the brutal incidents and aspects of contemporary American life, Springsteen has clearly revealed himself now as an artist whose understanding of Steinbeck's artistic vision goes beyond the mere, incidental influence of a single movie.[5]

Such then is Steinbeck's legacy in the songs of Bruce Springsteen. Both in content and approach, Springsteen's songs reveal some profound debts to Steinbeck's vision, and help to ensure that it continues to impact on American culture, and beyond. But perhaps the most significant debt has to do with a vision of the individual's communal responsibility, and therefore of art's social function. Ultimately Springsteen's return to folk music links with his finding a focus beyond his immediate self and environment: namely the relationship between a variety of individuals and groups and their historical contexts. Springsteen is continuing the tradition of hunting skunks under water. His mature pursuit of connection and community in place of the solipsistic escapism of youth echoes Tom Joad's journey of discovery. It's not a winnable journey except in terms of individuals growing into such recognition within their own lives, but it does shape the art itself. And the kind of art we choose to value, since our choice reflects our outlook, might matter more than we imagine in terms of the kinds of societies we shape. It may be that Steinbeck's legacy is especially important as part of a *collective* legacy. If, as members of a given society, we accept the consensus from Nietzsche and Freud to Wittgenstein and Kuhn that our sense of reality is always some kind of construct, it follows that our view of the function of art may in itself help *create* its function. The individual and collective choice between two kinds of art may, in turn, relate to the individual and collective choice between two kinds of futures. The ghost of Tom Joad may be a specter we, like Springsteen, should heed.

3

Changing Perceptions of Homelessness

John Steinbeck, Carey McWilliams, and California during the 1930s

Christina Sheehan Gold

In "Changing Perceptions of the Homeless," Christina Sheehan Gold examines the ways that homeless advocates sought to reinvent the public image of California's homeless in the 1930s in order to advocate for social welfare and assistance. Gold argues that in their seminal works, The Grapes of Wrath *and* Factories in the Fields, *John Steinbeck and Carey McWilliams effectively adopted the strategies developed by the homeless advocates to create greater empathy for the homeless. Employing an historical approach, the article relies heavily on newspaper and magazine articles and government agency reports.*

Introduction

In November 1939 eighteen cars full of people from the San Francisco Bay Area journeyed to California's San Joaquin Valley where they joined a similar contingent from Southern California. Newspaper advertisements boasted that participants in this quasi-tourist caravan would see the squalor and the poverty of California's agricultural migrants, visit squatters' settlements and government camps, and speak directly with homeless agricultural migrants. Carey McWilliams, Chief of the California Division of Immigration and Housing, organized the trip, calling it a "See For Yourself" caravan as a challenge to those who disputed the accuracy of the depictions of migrant life in John Steinbeck's controversial novel, *The Grapes of Wrath*. At the end of their tour, the caravaners reported that Steinbeck was accurate and that government assistance to the migrants was necessary ("See For Yourself"; Bay Area Committee). Five months later, Eleanor Roosevelt embarked on a similar, well-publicized trip through California. She was accompanied by the popular actors Melvyn Douglas and Helen Gahagan, drawing further attention to the event. The First Lady and her small Hollywood entourage toured from Bakersfield to Visalia visiting the homeless. In public speeches the First Lady described the deplorable migrant conditions, reaffirmed Steinbeck's accuracy, and adamantly advocated for federal assistance to the homeless ("First Lady and Film Stars"; "First Lady is New Ally"; "Mrs. FDR").[1]

These tours of homeless camps exemplify the broad fascination with California's migratory agricultural workers during the late 1930s. Popularly known as Okies, the growing numbers of migrants leaving the Southwest bound for California heightened American anxiety about the homeless.[2] Californians and Americans across the nation hotly debated what to do about the impoverished homeless migrants who flowed over California's border and up and down its highways. Some Californians felt threatened by the migrants and forcefully argued for their right to protect themselves and their communities from the perceived danger. Others were appalled at the human suffering caused by the economic depression and advocated greater compassion and social welfare.[3]

California's interest in the depression-era migrants has received excellent study by a handful of contemporary historians. James Gregory's important book, *American Exodus: The Dust Bowl Migration and Okie Culture in California,* explains the public misunderstanding of the conservative subculture of Southwestern migrants. Charles Shindo, in *Dust Bowl Migrants in the American Imagination,* extends Gregory's work in a careful analysis of the ways that artists and reformers misrepresented the migrants in order to advance their own political and economic agendas. Both authors examine the migrants in their specific historical context of the Dust Bowl and California in the 1930s. By contrast, this paper casts the migrants as part of a long history of transient homelessness in America. Very old beliefs about homelessness, inherited from the British, informed Californians' perception and treatment of homeless migrants from the Southwest. Placing the migrants in the broad context of American homelessness helps explain Californians' reaction to them and illuminates a shift in American conceptions of the homeless.

Homeless advocates in California during the 1930s combated traditional perceptions of the homeless as dangerous outsiders and thrust into the public consciousness a new view of California's homeless migrants as hardworking pioneers and farmers who cherished traditional American values. Homeless advocates attempted to re-educate the public about homelessness in order to argue for social welfare. John Steinbeck's fictional account of the migrants, *The Grapes of Wrath* (1939), and Carey McWilliams's factual account, *Factories in the Field* (1939), adopted the methods established by homeless advocates. These important books threw the advocates' agenda full force into the public consciousness, propelled a shift in perceptions of the homeless, and enhanced public support for related social welfare.[4]

Fear and Persecution: The Inheritance From England

Historians often trace American anxiety about the homeless far back to England between the fourteenth and seventeenth centuries when social and political changes created a growing homeless transient population.[5] The devastating plague, the enclosure movement, a population boom, and a surge in unemployed soldiers created an unprecedented number of transients. The British blamed homeless transients for contributing to the economic and social turmoil that threatened the stability of feudal life, and they responded to the rise of transiency with measures that criminalized and stigmatized the homeless. Vagrancy laws criminalized the condition of being homeless, and the Poor Laws (1601) made the homeless an economic burden to communities by requiring local governments to provide for their relief. Believing that homeless transients would drain town coffers and rob or attack local residents, towns "warned away" the homeless with threats and violence. The 1662 Law of Settlement and Removal empowered city officials to legally remove impoverished newcomers and to forcibly return them to their place of birth or previous residence. Legal action and social bias became, and remained, closely linked in the effort to exclude and persecute homeless transients in England.

The United States inherited, perpetuated, and even enhanced the British fear of homeless transients and the laws that punished them.[6] These inherited attitudes and laws played a central role in shaping the ways that depression-era Californians responded to agricultural migrants from the Dust Bowl. In California during the early 1930s, as in England during the seventeenth century, local governments were responsible for social welfare. Residency laws ruled that aid could be granted only to the resident poor, not to the homeless outsider. In 1933, California amended the Indigent Law of 1901 to require a three year waiting period for residency, raising it from one year. Counties and towns throughout the state used legal and illegal methods of warning away homeless outsiders in order to protect their relief budgets. Residents and police officers bullied migrants out of their counties with threats and violence. In 1935, the California State Relief Administration systematically excluded interstate transients from their purview, proclaiming that every effort should be made to return them to their place of legal residence (California State Relief Administration 26–30). Vagrancy laws were also widely used to punish and remove the homeless. As in England, these Californian laws reflected and intensified a growing fear of homeless migrants, who came to symbolize the chaos caused by the severe economic depression.

Fear: California During the Great Depression

The fear of homeless outsiders coalesced around the simple belief that migrants would victimize local residents because they had no investment in the community. A 1937 article in the socialist press acknowledged the growing interest in the migrants and its fearful tone:

> In addition to the statistical documentation, popular pamphlets and human interpretations of the plight of the footloose Americans have begun to pour from the press. Most of this literature indicates that the rootless or homeless, neglected family, in a community but not a part of it, is a breeding ground for crime, disease, ignorance or desperate radicalism. (Weybright)

Californians perceived the homeless migrants as unknown outsiders with a propensity towards radical politics, contagious disease, welfare dependency, and immoral behavior.

Californians worried that the migrants were fertile soil for communist and socialist agitators. Waves of agricultural strikes fueled the belief that migrants were radicals, and public commentary revealed a fear that migrants might destroy a season's crops by striking during the harvest. Accusations of migrant political radicalism were often aimed at government camps where communism supposedly festered. In a *Yuba City Herald* article titled "Migrant Camp is Red Hot Bed," Representative J. Z. Anderson asserted that the camps were "breeding grounds for agitators." An editorial in the *Bakersfield Californian* worried about the political outlook of migrant voters who "brought to California with them a moral and political philosophy alien to California. . . . Unless we educate these migrants and their children in the constructive way of thinking which characterizes our economic and social outlook, our free institutions are doomed."

Along with radical politics, residents accused the migrants of spreading disease and parasites. Migrant children, residents worried, would infect local children through contact at school. In Bakersfield, irate parents threatened vigilante action when migrant children spread epidemics of flu, skin diseases, and chicken pox through the classrooms (Frank Taylor 235). Responding to public outcry, County Health Departments throughout the state destroyed migrants' squatter settlements, which were seen as incubators of disease. The health hazards presented by squatters' settlements were highlighted in a publicity campaign by the Kern County Health Department, which issued warnings in the local press, radio, community meetings, and libraries (Kern County Health Department 3).

Many residents also believed that lazy migrants came to California to freeload off relief payments. The conservative Crescent City newspaper, the *American,* explained that "as long as our relief aid is the most generous in the nation, our relief rolls will remain the longest. . . . California has watched the destitute from other states surge across the borders at the rate of about ten thousand a month" (Baxter).[7] Thomas W. McManus, Secretary of the Kern County Citizens' Committee, argued that "the ever increasing horde of migrants is brought to this state because of the urgings of relatives already here. New arrivals' first relief checks are cashed at the telegraph office, where the folks at home are notified that California is a 'land of plentiful relief' " ("Pro-America Group"). One proposed solution to halting the incoming migration, then, was to stop providing relief to homeless migrants. Santa Clara County posted signs along its highways warning migrants that the county would not provide charity. The Los Angeles County Board of Supervisors sent a resolution to all the state governors warning that Los Angeles would provide no further aid to transients, and then the Sheriff's Office burned down a squatters' camp to emphasize the point.

In addition to being welfare dependents, migrants were perceived as immoral, ignorant, and even subhuman people, whose values and lifestyles were antithetical to those of their settled neighbors. *Country Gentleman* magazine offered a long list of the shocking habits of the migrants:

> 40 per cent . . . are shiftless trash who live like hogs, no matter how much is done for them. . . . Several years ago Doctor Stone [a Health Officer] found a family camped on top of a manure pile; they explained that it was warmer there. . . . Health officials in some communities report that incest is fairly common among the degenerate fringe. Going into one migrant home, a doctor found that one of the grown daughters was soon to have a baby. . . . he asked who was the father-to-be. Reluctantly the girl admitted the sire was her own father, and it then developed that the father had already had a baby by another daughter. . . . [N]umskull fathers and mothers spend their dole for cars, movies and liquor instead of proper food. (Hibbs)

And the list continued. Residents fretted over the impact of these unruly migrants on their children and local institutions.

The fear of homeless migrants was dramatically revealed by use of modern forms of "warning away." In a move known as the Bum Blockade, in 1936 the Los Angeles Police Department (LAPD) extended its jurisdiction to the entire state border, including the very northern side 805 miles away, and forcibly blocked the entrance of migrants into the state. The LAPD also searched incoming trains for indigents then forcibly placed them on outbound trains ("L.A. Police Chief"). In San Luis Obispo County residents warned migrants away at gunpoint. Even more dramatic were calls for the sterilization of homeless migrants. One Californian proposed "the adoption of a county ordinance . . . to legalize the sterilization of those relief clients who continue to have children while accepting public aid" ("Sterilizing Parents"). A County Health officer similarly posited that "the only solution to this problem is sterilization" (Pomeroy). These calls for the sterilization of migrants were extremist and rare, but demonstrate the intense hostility and fear felt by some and the extreme measures suggested to control the influx of homeless migrants.

Romanticization: A Competing Vision

A romantic vision of the homeless competed with the fear in both England and the United States. In a study of homeless transients, historian Henry Miller explains the dichotomy between the two perceptions:

> Society has been torn in the way it sees the unsettled or the wanderer; its ambivalence is painfully obvious. On the one hand, the vagrant is viewed as an enemy, a disrupter, a menace to established order, a parasite—he or she is someone to be shunned, stigmatized, or even killed. The vagrant of sixteenth-century England could be branded, imprisoned, or put to death. But the vagrant is also celebrated; he or she is sometimes perceived as the embodiment of all that is good in mankind. The holy wanderer who forsakes material comfort in the pursuit of spiritual fulfillment is beatified and canonized, like Saint Francis Assisi. And the vagrant is romanticized as a vagabonding, unfettered, free spirit. (Miller xiii)

Charlie Chaplin's tramp is a familiar example of the romanticization of homelessness in the United States. According to Chaplin, the tramp was "a gentleman, a poet, a dreamer, a lonely fellow, always hopeful of romance and adventure" (Chaplin 144). In *City Lights* (1931) and *Modern Times* (1936), the tramp was undefeated by his poverty, and probably happier and more fulfilled in it. During the depression, a plethora of social scientific studies confronted Americans with the harsh realities of homelessness and, aside from a few tenacious strands, the romanticization of homelessness faded into memory.

American Heroes: Recreating
the Image of Homelessness

The following quotation from a Works Progress Administration
pamphlet embodies the spirit of homeless advocates' efforts to
combat the fear of the homeless and to reinvent the image of
homeless migrants as traditional Americans.

> The fact that [migrant] poverty is a problem should not lead
> us into hasty condemnation of their moral character. The poor
> people coughing along the highways in their rusty cars are not
> shiftless bums trying to make life hard for thrifty, self-respecting
> citizens who know enough to stay home. Most of them, when you
> come to look closely at them, are just the opposite. They are the
> individualistic Americans who have the courage and vitality to
> go get it. They are the ones who are not liked but still have hope.
> It is not their fault that hope is slim, but it is to their credit that
> a slim hope is enough to keep them on their way. In our natural
> annoyance when some of them faint on our doorstep, let us not
> forget that the initiative and courage that we are preaching, they
> are practicing. They are Americans in the old tradition, doing
> their best to fend for themselves. If sometimes they are over
> whelmed by circumstances, it is not for lack of the pioneer spirit.
> In judging them, let us not hastily turn against the traditional
> standards of American history. (Coyle 18–19)

Homeless advocates, including social workers, government officials, artists, and local residents, struggled to redefine the public
conception of homeless transients in order to increase empathy
for the homeless and public support for social welfare. This new
perception of the homeless blended romantic imagery with an
emphasis on the structural causes of homelessness. The advocates' work involved an informal agenda, including five major
tactics that challenged fearful attitudes.

First, nostalgic descriptions created by advocates likened the
migrants to the courageous pioneers that settled the West. Ad-

vocates cast California's migrants as a new breed of pioneers that confronted even greater hardship than their predecessors and faced it with equal courage and tenacity. Newspaper articles and government reports compared the migrants' over-laden jalopies on Interstate 66 to covered wagons. Titled "Rolling Stones Gather No Sympathy: From Covered Wagon to Jalopy," an article in *Migrant and Farm Labor* described the migrants as "pioneers without a frontier" and "rural pilgrims." The author explained that "American progress has in large part been made possible by the mobile nature of our population," but rather than being rewarded for their efforts, the depression-era migrants were "penalized for their spunk" by losing relief eligibility and encountering hostile communities. The author advocated for relief, arguing that federal policy had "encouraged and aided the settling of the West," and the pioneering migrants in the 1930s deserved no less (Weybright). A *San Francisco Chronicle* article similarly admired the migrants' pioneer heritage:

> These people are of good pioneer stock—their grandparents followed such men as Daniel Boone through the Cumberland Gap and settled Kentucky, Tennessee, and later further West. Theirs is a history of generations of the soil, of decades of heart-breaking toil in their improvement and cultivation of their impoverished land. (qtd. in Coyle 4)

By associating the migrants with a familiar and admired American archetype, advocates combated perceptions of the homeless as dangerous outsiders.

Second, advocates cast the migrants as another favorite character from American history—Jeffersonian small farmers. They lamented a lost agrarian myth in romantic depictions of migrants as noble small farmers displaced from their land by cruel economic and natural forces. One author sentimentally proclaimed that the migrant "has the craving for land so deep he can taste it. . . . This hunger for land is the bright red thread of those people's lives, a bedrock affirmation" (Jaffe).[8] The idea that previously self-sufficient, hard working yeoman farmers had become landless, penniless vagabonds garnered immense sympathy for the migrants.

Third, advocates appealed to xenophobia and racism, frequently using the term "pure American stock" to contrast the Dust Bowl migrants with the workers from Japan, China, the Philippines, and Mexico, who had harvested California's crops in the previous decades. One homeless advocate explained that "the people who are coming in here from the Dust Bowl are not very different from the blood that settled the state. . . . If we can't take this problem with the realization that these aren't alien people who are migrating into California—they are good American stock, they aren't aliens—we won't solve the problem" (Bakersfield Conference).

Fourth, homeless advocates strenuously argued that migrants were not lazy welfare dependents, but hard workers who were victims of misfortune beyond their control. Appealing to fairness and the Protestant work ethic, advocates explained that public assistance was justified because the migrants worked hard and lived simple honest lives, yet they were impoverished nevertheless. In a radio broadcast, John Henderson of the Farm Security Administration was asked if migrants came to California to receive relief. "Emphatically no," Henderson replied. "We have records of thousands of these people which prove conclusively that almost all of them came to seek employment. A high percentage had never been on relief and are distinctly not relief-conscious" (Henderson).

Fifth, and finally, advocates strenuously maintained that migrants were not political radicals or social misfits that endangered local communities. Migrants, advocates said, fulfilled an essential economic function, and they held deeply conservative political and social beliefs. A *New York Times* article proclaimed:

> The probability of the Okies and Arkies enlisting under the hammer and sickle is minute. Most observers agree that they are political conservatives. They think and talk, not of marching on Sacramento or Washington, but of getting a little piece of ground. . . .
> [T]heir political beliefs are as orthodox as though each of them already owned that dream farm. (Darton)

Any tendency towards unionism or radicalism was born from their impoverished condition and would disappear once they were reestablished in financial security. Advocates also emphasized that the migrants sought out traditional communities and struggled to keep their families intact. Migrants, like all Americans, deserved to raise their families in a decent home with modest budgets.

By the late 1930s, homeless advocates were actively involved in recreating the public understanding of homeless migrants in order to allay entrenched fears and to build a climate sympathetic to public assistance and reform. It was in this historical context that McWilliams and Steinbeck published their seminal works.

John Steinbeck and Carey McWilliams

The public discussion of California's migrants heightened considerably, reaching national levels in 1939 with the publication of *The Grapes of Wrath* and *Factories in the Field*. These books complemented one another nicely, with McWilliams providing an objective, quantified analysis and Steinbeck providing a subjective, fictional account. Steinbeck tugged at the heartstrings, while McWilliams logically explained the problem.

John Steinbeck clearly adopted the homeless advocates' agenda. His understanding of the migrants was shaped in large part by his work and friendship with Tom Collins, a manager of a government camp for migrants. Collins, a homeless advocate, toured Steinbeck through the San Jaoquin Valley, imparting his understanding of the migrants in a way that paralleled the advocates' agenda. Prior to writing his epic novel, Steinbeck read through Collins' weekly camp reports to supply material for his story and characters. In those reports, Collins described the migrants as hard workers: "We greatly admire these men's determination to keep off the relief rolls. They leave camp as early as six o'clock in the morning and roam the whole country-side in search of employment" ("Report . . . April 4, 1936"). Collins referred repeatedly to the migrants' strong religious devotion, which was "their joy in times of distress" ("Report . . . February 22, 1936"). Collins' migrants were patriotic white Americans who yearned for the opportunity to once again farm their own land.

Before writing *The Grapes of Wrath*, Steinbeck authored a series of articles for the *San Francisco News* that mimicked the advocates' formulaic approach to studies of the migrants. In this 1936 series, "The Harvest Gypsies" (later published as a collection titled *Their Blood Is Strong*), Steinbeck described the migrants as "small farmers who have lost their farms" (22) and "good American stock" (43) who were "descendants of men who crossed into the middle west, who won their lands by fighting, who cultivated the prairies" (22). Exploitation by farmers pushed the migrants to "flares of disorganized revolt" (36–37), but when treated properly in government camps the migrants were good citizens: "They have shown in these camps an ability to produce and to cooperate. They are passionately determined to make their living on the land. One of them said, 'If it's work you got to do, mister, we'll do it. Our folks never did take charity and this family ain't takin' it now'" (43).[9] Conversations with Collins and research for "The Harvest Gypsies" provided Steinbeck with the foundation for *The Grapes of Wrath*.

The Grapes of Wrath portrayed Okie migrants as part of a long tradition of pioneering into the state. Steinbeck did not romanticize the tradition, however, and described the pioneering migrants as "a horde of tattered feverish Americans" who were "hardened, intent, and dangerous" (315–18). The earliest pioneering was born of a desperation that led the men to ruthlessly wrest the land away from its occupants. Even though Steinbeck criticized pioneering, the Joads, nevertheless, were part of this American tradition.

Furthering the advocates' agenda was Steinbeck's depiction of the Joads as Jeffersonian small farmers who were pitifully detached from their land and homes. The migrants, as opposed to California's commercial growers, were "true" farmers who shared a spiritual and physical attachment to the land. A Dust Bowl tenant farmer in the novel explained:

> If a man owns a little property, that property is him, it's part of him, and it's like him. If he owns property only so he can walk on it and handle it and be sad when it isn't doing well, and feel fine when the rain falls on it, that property is him, and some way

he's bigger because he owns it. Even if he isn't successful he's big
with his property. (50)

The displaced migrants had lived on the land for generations:
"We measured it and broke it up. We were born on it, and we
got killed on it, died on it. Even if it's no good, it's still ours.
That's what makes it ours—being born on it, working it, dying
on it" (45). The novel bemoaned the loss of this connectedness
with the land as banks, agribusinesses, and tractors dominated
agriculture in the state.[10]

The Grapes of Wrath alluded to issues of race, social welfare,
and family values in ways that also mirrored the advocates'
agenda. Although the novel did not use the term "pure American stock," or slander the minority workers, it repeatedly emphasized the migrants' American heritage. Steinbeck's fictional
migrants described their ancestry: "We ain't foreign. Seven generations back Americans, and beyond that Irish, Scotch, English, German. One of our folks in the Revolution, an' they was
lots of our folks in the Civil War—both sides. Americans" (317–
18). In addition, the Joads were by no means lazy welfare recipi-
ents who drained local budgets. The Joads' strong work ethic
compelled them to leave the comfort of the government camp
and return to their degrading, underpaid employment. In fact,
the farmers benefited financially from the exploitation of their
labor. The strength of family and community pervaded Steinbeck's book as Ma Joad struggled desperately to keep her family
intact.

Finally, like the advocates, Steinbeck illustrated that migrant
radicalism was born of poverty and social injustice. This radicalism would fester as a threat to the settled community unless
the problem were repaired. Tom Joad described his emerging
political philosophy: "I been thinkin' a hell of a lot, thinkin'
about our people livin' like pigs, an' the good rich lan' layin'
fallow, or maybe one fella with a million acres, while a hunderd
thousan' good farmers is starvin'. An' I been wonderin' [what
would happen] if all our folks got together an' yelled" (571). The
government camps provided a welcome amelioration of conditions, but Tom explained that they were not enough:

> I been thinkin' how it was in that gov'ment camp, how our folks
> took care a theirselves, an' if they was a fight they fixed it their-
> self; an' they wasn't no cops wagglin' their guns, but they was
> better order than them cops ever give. I been a-wonderin' why we
> can't do that all over. Throw out the cops that ain't our people.
> All work together for our own thing—all farm our own lan'. (571)

The novel warned that the suffering caused by an unjust system
would push the migrants to rebel against that system in order
to achieve their traditional dream—to farm their own land.

Steinbeck gave sympathetic faces to an anonymous and fright-
ening population, helping advocates combat the fear of migrants
as dangerous outsiders. The Joad family personalized the homeless for readers who became intimately acquainted with the fictional migrant family's plight. The Joads and their situation became synonymous with the larger migrant condition. A public
debate addressed the question, "What can America do for the
Joads?" ("Congress"). This was essentially the same question as
"What can America do for the migrants?" In speaking of the migrants, one journalist explained, "I know a great many of the
Joads in California; know them, like them and respect them"
("Speakers"). Advocates successfully co-opted the ground swell
of pity created by Steinbeck for the Joads in order to argue for
government assistance for the real homeless migrants.

Advocates used the detailed and sympathetic descriptions
of migratory life in the novel to support their pleas for enhanced public welfare. In the debate over federal camps, advocates pointed to Steinbeck's depiction of a government camp as
a virtual oasis in a desert of poverty and deprivation. An article
in the *Public Welfare News* described the gradual acceptance of
federal camps and the key role of Steinbeck's novel:

> Gradually the program [government camps] has received com-
> munity acceptance. . . . Economists, sociologists, and labor groups
> have seen the program meet problems for which there were not
> other solutions. And finally, John Steinbeck has produced his
> masterpiece, "The Grapes of Wrath," which has made the nation
> aware both of the problem and of the successful if not entirely
> satisfactory way in which the Administration's program has at

least ameliorated the living conditions of thousands of terribly underprivileged farm labor families. ("Housing")

The *San Francisco News* attributed legislative gains made on behalf of the migrants to Steinbeck's novel. "The magnitude of the program to date, and the prospect of further increase, can be largely credited to John Steinbeck's epic, 'The Grapes of Wrath'" ("Grapes of Wrath Yield Golden Wine").

In order for advocates to most effectively use *The Grapes of Wrath,* an essential question needed to be answered—did it accurately describe migrant conditions? Conservatives strenuously argued that the Joads were a complete fabrication, bearing no resemblance to real life. Carey McWilliams's book, *Factories in the Field,* gave advocates the proof they needed to counter these claims. Public commentary supporting *The Grapes of Wrath* repeatedly quoted facts and statistics drawn from *Factories in the Field.* Given Steinbeck's firm refusal to enter the public discourse about his novel, McWilliams became a primary spokesperson defending the accuracy of *The Grapes of Wrath.*[11] This made sense not only because of the contemporaneous publication of McWilliams's book, but also because of McWilliams's position as the Chief of the Division of Immigration and Housing (DIH), which inspected migrant living conditions. In newspaper articles, public speeches, and radio broadcasts, McWilliams vehemently defended Steinbeck's novel against accusations of inaccuracy, propaganda, and vulgarity. Philip Bancroft, the Director of Public Relations for the Associated Farmers, charged that *The Grapes of Wrath* was "straight revolutionary propaganda." In response, McWilliams argued that his DIH inspectors found many Hoovervilles as miserable as the one Steinbeck described and that he had seen the handbills advertising work in California that had been distributed out of state to attract migrants ("McWilliams, Bancroft Debate").[12] In the *New Republic,* McWilliams acknowledged that factual evidence from his own work helped convince the public that *The Grapes of Wrath* was accurate (McWilliams, "What's Being Done" 178).

Factories in the Field told the history of migrant workers, described the rise of large scale farming in California, and explained how agribusinesses abused the workers and squashed small farming. Although less widely read than *The Grapes of Wrath*, it was frequently quoted and referenced in discussions of migrants and adhered to essential aspects of the homeless advocates' agenda. McWilliams avoided using the romantic imagery of migrants as pioneers and yeoman farmers, instead focusing on more tangible issues, like race, unionization, public health, and potential solutions. McWilliams bitterly indicted the large farmers and championed self-sufficient small farmers. He, like Steinbeck, did not disparage the minority pickers, but noted with alarm that white migrants were being treated as if they were racial minorities (305–6). Because California's agricultural migrants were "native-born Americans, white, largely Protestant, and of Anglo-Saxon lineage," farmers could no longer exploit them: "These despised 'Okies' and 'Texicans' were not another minority alien group (although they were treated as such) but American citizens familiar with the usages of democracy" (306). McWilliams warned that radicalism would emerge from the exploitative agricultural system:

> Today some 200,000 migratory workers, trapped in the State, eke out a miserable existence, intimidated by their employers, homeless, starving, destitute. Today they are restless but quiet; tomorrow they may be rebellious. Before these workers can achieve a solution of the problems facing them, they will have to work a revolution in California landownership and in the methods of agricultural operations which now prevail. (10)

Californians could diminish political radicalism and union activity by simply improving migrant conditions. Pointing to government camps, McWilliams demonstrated that the migrants were orderly, clean, well-behaved, and responsible participants in their communities (300–303). Migrants were clearly not dangerous outsiders and moral degenerates.

McWilliams and Steinbeck garnered intense hostility from conservatives. Congressional Representative Lyle Boren charged that *The Grapes of Wrath* "exposes nothing but the total depravity, vulgarity, and degraded mentality of the author" (Boren 140). The Associated Farmers called Steinbeck an "arch enemy, defamer and slanderer" (McWilliams, "Californa" 103)[13] McWilliams was labeled "Agricultural Pest Number 1," and a farmer accused him of publishing propaganda rather than facts, saying that "there are other propagandists besides Messrs. Hitler, Stalin and Mussolini. And some of them live and publish their works right in America" (Ralph Taylor). Aside from angering conservatives, *The Grapes of Wrath* and *Factories in the Field*, guided by the advocates' agenda, drew a massive amount of interest to California's migrants, who could no longer simply be dismissed as criminals and welfare dependents.

Migrants as Entertainment

The broad interest in California's migrants became the focus of social gatherings of both advocates and opponents. A "Grapes of Wrath Party," held in honor of Carey McWilliams, included musical numbers by prominent performers and the proceeds supported a Christmas party for migrant children in Visalia. Social events like luncheons and teas included informative lectures by experts who had lived and worked with the migrants. Women at the First Baptist Church in Brawley "were entertained . . . at the home of Mrs. Jess Hutchison at which time Mrs. T. Mead, missionary from the local Migratory Labor Camp, spoke on 'The Missionary Work Among Migratory People'" ("Missionary"). The California Division of the American Association of University Women devoted its monthly meeting to a comprehensive, slide-illustrated review of the migrant condition ("Migratory"). Republican women at a Pro-America luncheon heard a speech by the Executive Secretary of the Associated Farmers, and they shared their anger at Steinbeck's and McWilliams' books and their frustration with the incoming migrants ("Pro-America;" "Migrant 'Smear' Novels"). The broad array of social gatherings illustrates the depth to which concern about the migrant issue had permeated Californian society.

Hollywood actors also expressed an interest in the migrants. By nature of their popularity, film stars drew attention to the migrant cause, and they spoke about the migrants in the terms created by homeless advocates. Actress and politician Helen Gahagan toured the state, publicly speaking about the migrants, emotionally pleading their case, and sharply criticizing government inaction. At a luncheon at the San Francisco Center, Gahagan drew upon racial comparisons saying that the migrants were "not Chinese, not Mexicans, but our own people." Her voice broke as she spoke of the impoverished little blonde children ("A Plea"; "Stage Star"). In January 1940, Hollywood celebrities were invited to the opening of a migrant labor camp, including Gahagan and her husband, Melvyn Douglas, Henry Fonda, Jane Darwell, John Carradine, and Phil Dunne ("Film Stars").

Hollywood moved into center stage of the migrant issue with the filmic version of *The Grapes of Wrath*. The film's sympathetic depiction of the migrant condition gave audiences not just the words to understand the migrants, but the images and sounds as well. These migrants, audiences saw, were respectable, hardworking, white Americans who had been displaced from their cherished land. Tom Collins continued shaping the public depiction of the homeless by serving as the technical adviser in the filming. Newspaper articles described the film as the most powerful educational tool yet to teach Americans about the migrants. The *San Francisco Chronicle* reported that the migrants' problems "may be brought to a satisfactory solution shortly through the vast educational powers of the motion picture. . . . What the book started the movie will carry on, only to many more millions than any novel possibly can reach" (Hefferan).

Conclusion

The massive amount of public attention and media focus on the migrants revealed the emergence of a new perception of the homeless that aligned with the advocates' agenda and broke away from the fear and disdain that had historically dominated Americans' feelings about the homeless. The *San Francisco Chronicle* pondered the change in attitudes:

> How has it happened that men may now meet and discuss this acute phase of the unemployment problem which makes itself felt in so many States, in so many ways? May meet and discuss causes and plan and urge remedies which must inevitably affect powerful vested interests? May do this without being publicly la-

beled, as happened so often a few years ago, "reds and agitators?" (Eggleston)

The State Chamber of Commerce asserted that it was "very much heartened by the discovery of what seems to be a new attitude of most people toward the transient labor problem." Harrison Robinson of the Chamber of Commerce said, "It's quite surprising. You no longer encounter a blank face or an impatient reaction when you mention this great problem to the average person" ("New Attitude"). Commentary generally maintained that *The Grapes of Wrath* (the novel and the film) and *Factories in the Field* brought nationwide attention to migrants and resulted in a more empathetic understanding of the migrants' plight and in sincere efforts to improve their condition ("Congress"; "Truth"; "Opinion"). In other words, Steinbeck and McWilliams helped the homeless advocates succeed in their efforts as many Americans began to perceive the homeless in a new way.

By the summer of 1940, California's migrants were a standard topic of conversation throughout the nation, but the excited interest over the homeless migrants quickly dissipated as Americans shifted their focus from the depression at home to the emerging war abroad. Migrants from the Southwest found salaried, settled jobs in the recovering wartime economy. Mexicans once again predominated as agricultural migrants, and the problem lost its urgency in Anglo-Saxon eyes. Even though homeless migrants lost the public gaze, the words and the images had been firmly ingrained in the public consciousness. Fear and distaste for the homeless continued, and probably dominated, but *The Grapes of Wrath* and *Factories in the Field* had showcased a tradition of homeless advocacy and empathy that would remain firmly entrenched in the American consciousness.

4

Steinbeck's "Self-characters" as 1930s Underdogs

Warren G. French

French argues that Steinbeck's self-characters were similar to the author psychologically rather than being in any way strictly autobiographical. His underdogs in Tortilla Flat, Of Mice and Men, *and* In Dubious Battle—*Danny, George, and Jim Nolan respectively—reflect Steinbeck's own vision of communal harmony and his own attendant sense of frustration at the failure to realize that vision. In the figure of Tom Joad in* The Grapes of Wrath, *this underdog changes significantly from a figure of failure to one who inspires hope in the struggling masses.*

John Steinbeck's agent, Elizabeth Otis, greeted a letter from the author, dated 26 April 1957, as "one of the most impressive letters that you or anyone else has ever written" (qtd. in Benson 811). Steinbeck considered this letter important enough to send a duplicate copy to his friend and advisor, Chase Horton, who was assisting him with his research on Sir Thomas Malory in connection with Steinbeck's long-planned modernization of Malory's *Morte d'Arthur*. In this letter, he explains his concept of a "spokesman" in a work of fiction, who can be called a "self-character," a central figure with whom the novelist, perhaps unconsciously, identifies and into whom "he puts not only what he thinks he is, but what he hopes to be. You will find one in every one of my books and in the novels of everyone I can remember" (*TAKA* 303–5). Since Steinbeck's main purpose in this letter was to identify Malory's Sir Lancelot as the author's "self-character," he mentions no specific examples from his own writings, but adds: "I suppose my own symbol character has my dream wish of wisdom and acceptance." He thus expresses the importance of recognizing that his "self-characters" do not necessarily share his experiences as thinly disguised self-portraits like Thomas Wolfe's Eugene Gant and Jack Kerouac's Jean Dulouz. In the same letter he mentions Ernest Hemingway as a novelist whose "self-characters" were "most simple and near the surface."

Despite the importance of these "self-characters" to understanding the "dream wish" underlying Steinbeck's fiction, little effort has been made to identify them. The importance, however, of understanding Steinbeck's sense of personal involvement in his fiction has been dramatically disclosed in another pair of self-searching letters to his editor/publisher, Pascal Covici, and his agent, Elizabeth Otis, written in 1938 and published, apparently with his consent, in 1946 in a revised edition of Covici's anthology *The Portable Steinbeck*. Explaining his reasons for destroying the manuscript of an eagerly awaited novel tentatively titled "L'Affaire Lettuceberg," Steinbeck lamented the consequences that his impulsive action might have for Covici's nearly bankrupt firm; he justified his action by explaining, "My whole work drive has been aimed at making people understand each other and then I deliberately write this book, the aim of which is to cause hatred through partial understanding" (qtd. in Benson 376). He found the manuscript unsuitable for publication because he saw himself as a writer with a mission—if not always a pleasant one for readers—to try to open closed eyes and closed minds to a better understanding of the conflicting forces at war in human nature. As he put this conception in a letter to his friend George Albee in 1935, when he was writing *In Dubious Battle*, "man hates something in himself. He has been able to defeat every natural obstacle but himself" (*SLL* 98). Steinbeck's aim, in short, was to connect with his readers through broader understanding of self.

That wish to connect is, perhaps, most clearly evident in three novels that solidified Steinbeck's reputation: *Tortilla Flat* (1935), *In Dubious Battle* (1936), and *Of Mice and Men* (1937). Each is an identifiable stage in the development of Steinbeck's "self-characters" that has been largely overlooked by critics because attention has focused on the dramatic events of the individual novels rather than inter-relationships between and among these three powerful stories produced in such rapid succession. *Tortilla Flat* is usually admired for its quaint local color but often dismissed as an escapist idyll of the devil-may-care paisanos' irresponsible lives and deaths. *In Dubious Battle* has been praised as America's greatest fictional depiction of a workers' strike and its potentially disastrous consequences, while *Of Mice and Men* is lauded as a timeless evocation of the poignant tragedy of nature's misfits. But all have also been criticized for not proposing solutions for the tragic problems that they dramatize, despite Steinbeck's frequent protests that he is writing *novels* not tracts. When I was asked to write the introduction to *In Dubious Battle* for the much-needed Penguin Twentieth Century Classics collected edition of Steinbeck's work, I began to reconsider it in conjunction with its predecessor and successor.

Looking at *Tortilla Flat* as something more than a tragicomic chronicle of a mock Arthurian roundtable on the edge of a sleepy California city, I perceived the novel as rather the downbeat story of Danny trapped between the contending forces of freedom in the wild woods behind his house and subservience to authority in the town. From the time that he is released from jail, where he has been incarcerated for antisocial behavior, inherits two houses, and assumes a respectable position in the community until the night he makes an unsuccessful attempt to return to life in the woods and struggles with an unidentified "Enemy" (who is the only one worthy of him), Danny is caught between the twin urges for peaceful prosperity and unregulated freedom. The mysterious foe on the night of that wild party is the pressure from the "civilized" community that was beginning to weigh heavily on Steinbeck himself. Danny is a creature of the wild whom society does not need to destroy because he destroys himself by seeking to change his nature. The novel is his eulogy.

Looked at from the perspective that *Tortilla Flat* provides, *In Dubious Battle* can be perceived as Jim Nolan's eulogy. Often, however, the novel has been read as dated social history, a book that both chronicles an apple-pickers' strike against heavy odds and highlights an unresolved debate between a labor organizer (Mac) and the humanitarian Doc Burton, who provides essential medical aid to the strikers, about the difference between men acting on their own and melding together in an organized and directed group. The prominence of this debate over Steinbeck's "phalanx" or group man theories led the prolific Yale critic Harold Bloom to claim, in 1987, that at its half-century mark, the novel is "now quite certainly a period piece, . . . of more interest to social historians than to literary critics" (1).

The difficulty about this judgment is that it turns the novel into not just a tract, but a pointless one, since the dispute between the theorists is never resolved and their contribution to the immediate action is never examined as part of the closure—the narrative ends abruptly with Jim Nolan's grotesque death after assuming a leadership role for which he was not ready. The movement of the narrative is relentlessly focused upon Jim from the moment when, like Danny in *Tortilla Flat*, he is released from jail, where he had been confined on trumped-up charges; to when he decides to join Mac's Party, which is organizing the local strike; to his death a few days later in that Party's service. His eulogy is a timeless account of impetuous youthful ambition and noble intentions gone amok in an exploitative world.

Of Mice and Men ends also with the death of a principal character and may also be viewed as a eulogy for another victim whose fate is inevitable. The final emphasis in this novel, however, is not on the inescapable demise of the physically powerful Lennie, who does not have the mental ability to control his great strength, but on George, a physically less powerful but more thoughtful and visionary individual in control of his actions but unable to protect Lennie, around whom he has built a dream world from an unpleasantly real world that Lennie cannot understand or control. When George must finally kill Lennie himself quickly to protect him from a torturously cruel death at the hands of an enraged lynch mob, he must also destroy his own dream. His is a kind of living death, since he has been forced to destroy what had made his life worthwhile.

All three of these relatively short novels move toward inexorable conclusions that are parallel variations on the tragic failure of schemes that "gang aft agley," in the words of Scottish poet Robert Burns (from whom Steinbeck takes the title *Of Mice and Men*). Social outcasts all, they are on their way to inevitable dooms, though none of the "plans" around which the novels are built could be considered among the "best laid." All three portray the outcome of aspirations that exceed one's potential. The trio can be most cogently categorized as *Bildungsroman* ("education novels") that end disastrously with the deaths of dreams as a result of impulsive behavior that robbed key characters of constraints that organized society demanded.

In *John Steinbeck's Fiction Revisited*, I summed up the argument for treating these three interrelated narratives as a trilogy of "underdogs," those at the bottom of society and disappearing even below there: "although there is no evidence that Steinbeck had any conscious intention of shaping these three . . . into a kind of ironic trilogy about men's fate, viewed jointly as a phase in his development, they provide a vision of three principal forces responsible for the 'going under' of one who is not able in the words of Sir Henry Morgan in Steinbeck's first published novel, *Cup of Gold*, to 'split' before 'civilization'" (72). The term "underdogs" here both borrows from and connects the novels with the English translation of the Mexican novelist Manuel Azuela's harrowing novel about his country's dispossessed, *Los de Abajo* (literally "Those from Below")—although I have found no evidence that Steinbeck was familiar with the novel.

But what does the steadily downbeat viewpoint of this trilogy have to do with Danny, Jim and George as Steinbeck's "self-characters" or alter egos? The author was neither an untamable creature of the vanishing woods, nor an aspiring labor leader, nor an itinerant field hand with an unworkable dream. Yet despite his cultured, middle-class difference from his creations, he shared with the trio dreams of what they hoped to become, as he supposed his "symbol characters" would. All three dream of a moderate, comfortable lifestyle that they could share with others who need help. At the time each story unfolds—during the post World War I boom in *Tortilla Flat* and during the Depression —Danny, Jim and George dream of establishing communities that will provide them opportunities for leadership benefiting others; but they have no sound, practical ideas of how to improve their situations in communities that threaten their dreams. By implication Steinbeck reflects a general discontentment with the communities he knew well; but he also projects a vision of a better society in the familiar communities of Monterey and San Jose.

He was very reticent during the 1930s to discuss details of his own life in interviews, which he usually shunned. He was more concerned that outsiders would snoop into his personal problems or criticize his dreams than that they would recognize his characters' problems and share in his search to improve the community. If they could identify with the frustrations of Danny, Jim and George as Steinbeck dramatized them, others might be moved to share his self-searching dissatisfactions with society that could lead to a desire to do something. Even so, one wonders how Steinbeck could continue to identify his dreams with those of his socially marginal characters once his work began to attract profitable attention. Steinbeck's sympathetic relationship to Danny, Jim and George must be viewed in relation to his own insecure situation at the time he was writing the novels and not the time of their subsequent publication, as his situation changed rapidly and materially with the publicity surrounding each.

The three books appeared in rapid succession from 1935 to 1937. By the time he began "Something That Happened," as *Of Mice and Men* was originally titled, he was still plagued by the same doubts and fears with which he was endowing his characters. Although he was not particularly pleased to receive four thousand dollars for the film rights to *Tortilla Flat,* he took the money for government bonds "for the lean years that he was sure were ahead" (Benson 323). Even after he moved into his new home in Los Gatos in July 1936, he mused in his ledger that "for the moment now the financial burdens have been removed. But it is not permanent. I was not meant for success" (qtd. in Benson 330). Only after the success of *Of Mice and Men* as both a novel and a play did Steinbeck feel that his fortunes had turned around, and even then, as Benson observes, he continued to be haunted by the conviction that his success was only a temporary fluke (331)—as the journals kept while he wrote *The Grapes of Wrath* testify. Steinbeck could not easily overcome the underdog syndrome that made him a success.

In short, to recognize the significance of Danny, Jim and

George as Steinbeck's "self-characters" is to see why these novels are not "dated" social protest tracts. As Steinbeck explained in the letter to aspiring fellow novelist George Albee in January 1935, "I'm not interested in ranting about justice and oppression, mere outcroppings which indicate the condition. But man hates something in himself. He has been able to defeat every natural obstacle but himself he cannot win over unless he kills every individual" (*SLL* 98). The importance of these three novels lies in Steinbeck's deep psychic relationship with his characters.

His writing about underdogs did not end with this trilogy and its doomed characters any more then did the conditions which inspired them. His next novel focuses even more powerfully and memorably on the lonely figure of a besieged social outcast.

When we first meet Tom Joad in the second chapter of *The Grapes of Wrath*, he has been recently released from jail—like Danny and Jim Nolan. But Tom has not served time for drunken rowdiness like Danny or for ill-timed curiosity like Jim; he was convicted for murder, albeit in self-defense, and he has been released early for good behavior. Yet still he is a killer, and as the novel nears its end, he will kill again in momentarily maddened retaliation for the killing of his mentor and friend Jim Casy, a former preacher turned labor organizer.

The Grapes of Wrath, however, does not end as another tragedy of the bold fighter against overwhelming odds, although both Tom and Jim Casy are certainly underdogs. There is a striking difference between this epic and its three predecessors, all narrowly focused narratives. This novel does not rush readers through a downward movement toward defeat, but interrupts the account of the tribulations of the Joad family with panoramic reflections on past and present situations affecting their lives. And this novel ends with the central character momentarily triumphant and optimistic about his own future role and improvement of his people's situation. Here Steinbeck employs a technique that Charles Dickens used a century earlier in *Hard Times* (which would certainly also be an apt, though less stirring title for Steinbeck's own novel) by leaving the future disposition of his characters in the hands of his readers. The readers' response was a chorus of international praise, though some social activists found the ending too romantic while many fellow Californians condemned it and made threats even against the author's life.

How did this change come about, from the pessimistic conclusions of the "underdogs" trilogy to the inspiring feeling that troubled situations can be improved? Such questions are not easily answered, unless the writer explains his intentions publicly, as Steinbeck was not inclined to do, and the answer on this occasion is even more complicated because of missing evidence.

Between *Of Mice and Men*, in which the last words are those of the sadistic fascist Carlson, who looks at the psychopathic Curley and asks, "Now what the hell ya suppose is eat'in them two guys"—referring to Slim leading away the inconsolable George—and the controversial tableau at the end of the *The Grapes of Wrath*, in which Rose of Sharon Joad offers her breast milk to an old man, there is a missing link in the development of Steinbeck's attitudes as projected through his "self-characters." Perhaps "L'Affaire Lettuceberg," a searing attack on his home town of Salinas, included an important "self-character" who would have been very different from his earlier oppressed "underdogs." A possible clue to the nature of this character might be found in "The Time the Wolves Ate the Vice Principal," a short story which appeared after World War II in the first issue of *47, The Magazine of the Year*. In this gruesome tale, an overworked public servant from the Salinas High School is coming home exhausted late one night when a pack of hungry wolves falls upon him, as the town sleeps serenely on—another blameless individual like Jim Nolan and George Milton doomed by an unfeeling community and another offshoot of the defeatist vision that shaped the underdog novels.

It can be argued, however, that whatever Steinbeck's reasons for providing this unflattering picture of his home town to a new magazine attempting (unsuccessfully) to establish itself, after completing "L'Affaire Lettuceberg," he had undergone, if only temporarily, the same kind of spiritual change that he portrays through Casy and especially Tom Joad. Both the author and the self-character experience a painful ordeal that ultimately ends not destroying them, but enabling them to achieve a vision that transcends self-indulgent action. I use the term "self-indulgent" here because in devising "L'Affaire Lettuceberg," Steinbeck had, from his own account to his agent and editor, succumbed to a personal pique of the kind that made the Joads put the "fambly fust" without pondering whether hope for survival might depend upon collective action.

While Steinbeck had many times experienced defeat and despair trying to establish himself as a writer, he had not had to face the devastating despair experienced by the Joads and other homeless migrants. Since in *The Grapes of Wrath* he also speaks—even lectures—threateningly in his own voice for the first time in his fiction, he seems distanced from the main action, a troubled observer who feels intense sympathy for his agonized characters but in no way identified with them. He's not writing from his own experience except as a sympathetic observer.

In creating the central spokesman, however, he needed to create a character capable of experiencing the same kind of inspirational change that he had when he realized that he must destroy "L'Affaire Lettuceberg." As a result of Casy's vision, although Casy has insisted he is no longer a preacher, Tom realizes that he must fight for all his people, the underdogs, not just his family; but he realizes also that he must avoid Casy's untimely fate if he is to succeed in his mission. In Tom's climactic conversation with Ma Joad, he explains Steinbeck's enlightened realization that violence is no longer the most effective method of working for his people. Just as Steinbeck refused to join many others seeking a better society by battling at the barricades and chose rather to share his message with a wider audience through his writing, so Tom realizes that he must become an inspiring voice speaking out of the darkness, serving his people unperceived, unrecognized: "I'll be all aroun' in the dark," he tells Ma. "I'll be ever'where—wherever you look" (572). In this much admired passage, Steinbeck has Tom Joad explain what Steinbeck hoped to achieve through writing *The Grapes of Wrath*. He had done an about face, writing here with a new inspiration and hopefulness replacing the angry despair of the earlier underdog novels. He was taking a great risk and staking his own and his backers' futures on a new vision.

Remarkably, the relationship between the author and the "self-character" in this novel is most unusual. When Tom Joad describes himself as "a voice in the dark," he depicts precisely the author's own long-sought role that he achieved through his novel. He has created a "self-character," who indeed shares his "dream wish of wisdom and acceptance." *The Grapes of Wrath* provides one of those rare, illuminating occasions when a dream comes true. Steinbeck did not extend his trilogy of the underdogs into a tetralogy. The underdog here has become a top dog.

It was risky indeed to contemplate such an outcome for an untested work upon which so much depended for author and publisher; but Steinbeck's faith in his vision during the demanding months of intense writing conveyed the message that he wished: "I hope to God it's good," were the last words he wrote in the journal he kept while writing the novel. Unlike many such high hopes, this one was fulfilled. He had become what he had hoped to be.

Afterglow

Although Steinbeck's cycle of underdog fiction was predominantly tragic in concept and cautionary in tone—even *The Grapes of Wrath* ends equivocally with a voice crying out in the wilderness and a hopeful gesture rather than any promising solution for the migrants' problems—it has generally been overlooked that the cycle did not end until Steinbeck ventured into the new medium of film with one of the most undeservedly obscure of his creative works, *The Forgotten Village*. This short film ends not with a voice coming out of the dark but rather with the proud cry of a young Mexican, shouting as he marches straight toward Mexico City determined to become a doctor who will bring new hope and health to his often oppressed people. "I am Juan Diego," the boy cries.

A young Mexican boy may seem a strange "self-character" for Steinbeck, but I feel that if Steinbeck had been a young Mexican boy, he would have been capable of such a defiant gesture. Juan

Diego is as much the author's "self-character" as is Jody Tiflin in his memorable *The Red Pony* stories. By telling Juan Diego's story, he ended a decade of uncertainties as he sought to realize his artistic and humanitarian ambitions on the highest possible, positive note.

5

Propaganda and Persuasion in John Steinbeck's *The Moon Is Down*

Rodney P. Rice

According to Rice, The Moon Is Down *has been respectfully examined in its historical and sociological contexts, and all too often dismissed as poor literature. As propaganda, however, the novel is highly effective in its rhetorical structures and propaganda techniques.*

At various points in his career, especially during World War II, John Steinbeck produced some exceptionally effective propaganda. One of his most successful efforts describes what happens when a small, unnamed coastal town, which looks suspiciously like a Norwegian fishing village, is overrun by an unnamed force that strongly resembles an invading Nazi column. Created in 1941 and published in 1942, *The Moon Is Down* was written as "a kind of celebration of the durability of democracy" that resulted from Steinbeck's voluntary service in a variety of governmental agencies ("My Short Novels" 39), the foremost of which was the Office of Coordinator of Information (COI), a precursor of the CIA (Benson 486–89; Coers 6–12). An eager participant in the war effort, Steinbeck offered his services as early as 1940, when he wrote a letter to President Roosevelt warning him concerning an imminent "crisis in the Western hemisphere," which Steinbeck believed could only be met with an "immediate, controlled, considered, and directed method and policy" (*SLL* 206). While working for the COI, Steinbeck began associating with escapees from occupied nations and concluded that these "silent figures" needed advice, encouragement and supplies to carry on the struggle. Years later Steinbeck described the experience in "Reflections on a Lunar Eclipse," when he said he was attempting to provide a so-called "blueprint" to set forth what "might be expected and what could be done" about the Axis invasion (qtd. in Benson 487–88). Although Steinbeck referred euphemistically to *The Moon Is Down* as a "blueprint," to the extent that it represented a carefully designed plan to manipulate, shape, and direct the attitudes and actions of groups suffering from the Nazi invasion, the novel more properly qualifies as propaganda.

In the book *Literature and Propaganda*, A. E. Foulkes claims that there are two general modes of inquiry associated with the study of propaganda. While the first concerns itself with sociocultural and historical conditions under which propaganda is produced, the second focuses on formal aspects of propaganda, that is, how propaganda functions as a system and what distinguishes it from other forms of communication (8). But because many of the historical and sociocultural conditions associated with the production of *The Moon Is Down* have been well documented, this study will focus on propaganda as rhetoric.[1]

Even though many other studies recognize elements of propaganda in Steinbeck's rhetoric, most prefer examining the novel as literature.[2] In the main, critics agree that the work is not one of Steinbeck's best artistic efforts.[3] In contrast to that critical tradition, however, this essay examines how Steinbeck used special propaganda methods in *The Moon Is Down* for the deliberate propagation of democratic principles in order to champion threatened values and encourage resistance to totalitarianism. To that end, some definitions and a critical framework are in order. In particular, it is important to differentiate some relevant aspects of conventional persuasion from those of propaganda. A good working definition of propaganda is provided by contemporary rhetoricians Garth Jowett and Victoria O'Donnell, who define propaganda as the "deliberate and systematic attempt to shape perceptions, manipulate cognitions, and direct behavior to achieve a response that furthers the desired intent of the propagandist" (16). As well, I shall employ the research of Leonard Doob, whose seminal *Propaganda: Its Psychology and Technique* helps clarify the terms of the discussion and provides the framework for analysis of elements of propaganda relevant to this particular communication situation.

Although both propaganda and persuasion are forms of communication that include classical rhetorical elements such as a speaker or writer, an audience, a text or message, and a purpose, the fundamental difference is that persuasion often can be neutral. Generally, persuasion attempts to promote what Jowett and O'Donnell call "interactive dependency," a reciprocal situation in which writer or speaker and audience are dependent upon one another to fulfill mutual needs. Therefore, persuasion is "transactional" and focuses more deliberately on complex and continuing voluntary interactions between writers and speakers and their audiences (24–25). By contrast, propaganda is more concerned with manipulating behavior and managing public opinion to exert what Terence Qualter calls "control" (15). As a result, rather than emphasizing voluntary transactions, propaganda works to promote the objectives of a writer or speaker in a way that may or may not be in the best interests of the target audience. Generally, the most common way propagandists promote objectives is by using *suggestion,* which Doob defines as the systematic

> manipulation of stimulus-situations in such a way that, through
> the consequent arousal of pre-existing, related attitudes there oc-
> curs within the mental field a new integration which would not
> have occurred under different stimulus-situations. (54)

For Doob, "stimulus-situations" are special circumstances or conditions that influence people or produce a cognitive and affective response because the agent or action that caused the response somehow becomes isolated from the competing background of objects, ideas, and persons. Furthermore, Doob states that successful use of suggestion is based on manipulation of four central principles: (1) The principle of perception; (2) The perceptual principle of simplification; (3) The perceptual principle of auxiliary attitudes; and (4) The perceptual principle of repetition (98). Not surprisingly, all four are present in *The Moon Is Down.*

According to Doob, the *principle of perception* is one in which the propagandist makes the "stimulus-situation stand out from the competing ground" (98). Conceptually, the idea is akin to the Gestalt principle of "figure-ground segregation," the notion that one of the ways the mind configures experience and organizes perceptions into holistic patterns is by perceiving objects or "figures" as they stand out from their background (Koffka 177–210; Rock 65–66). When applied to propaganda situations, the assumption Doob makes is that audiences, even those in isolated situations, are constantly bombarded by several stimuli which may be said to present a ground against which the propagandist must make the stimulus situation stand out as a significant "figure" (95). In other words, to be successful, the propagandist must find a way to make his message emerge from the noise of competing information.

In operational terms, Steinbeck achieves figure-ground segregation by relying heavily on what Kenneth Burke has described as the "basic" figure of speech, *synecdoche*, the substitution of parts for wholes or wholes for parts (25–26). What makes it especially effective in this case, however, is that Steinbeck uses the technique thoughtfully and intelligently. Thus, rather than relying on more facile propaganda methods that employ hyperbole and highly charged emotional tactics in order to lend line and definition to the subject, Steinbeck adopts a more sophisticated approach that eschews stereotypes and expands the range of interpretive possibilities. In doing so, he eliminates one of the most popular propaganda cliches of the time. Gone, for instance, are the ubiquitous monocle-bedecked, goose-stepping Nazis frequently found in Hollywood films and popular media of the day. Instead, Steinbeck substitutes characters with motives and desires that correspond to more complex benign and malign parts and wholes associated with the circumstances of the story. For example, though Colonel Lanser is hardly an admirable figure, he is not purely evil. Rather, he has been dehumanized and victimized by war, and as such stands for the many—civilian and soldier alike—who have also fallen prey to the "great gray dream" in which "real things become unreal and a fog creeps over the mind" (23). As if to highlight the universal essence of this dehumanization, Steinbeck refuses to mention actual, particular historical figures like Hitler, political groups like the Nazis, or probable locations like Norway. Instead, he employs euphemistic terms like "the Leader" or "the invader" or "the town" to outline a broader image and evoke appropriate positive and negative audience reactions. Even the scapegoat figure, the infamous Norwegian fascist, Vidkun Quisling, escapes direct identification. As a substitute, Steinbeck uses Mr. Corell, whom he originally named "Curseling" in an early manuscript of the book (Coers 41).

In addition to synecdoche, Steinbeck also structures the plot in theatrical fashion so as to produce a concentrated communication of theme that emphasizes particular actions and subsequently grounds them against the backdrop of the ever-growing resistance of the townspeople. Originally intended as drama, Steinbeck actually classified *The Moon Is Down* as a "play-novelette," a term he invented to justify a dramatic structure that orders events in a novel in similar fashion to those in a play. As early as 1938, for example, Steinbeck spoke about *Of Mice and Men* as a failure in the genre, but suggested that simplifying narrative and theme, and then ordering a novel as if it were a play produces a pure dramatic structure that intensifies novelistic values (Levant 130). In *The Moon Is Down*, the method does not produce powerful art, but it does succeed in giving vivid outline to the invasion scenario. In so doing, the play-novelette manifests another of Doob's precepts, the *perceptual principle of simplification.*

As Doob defines it, the propagandist uses this perceptual principle to "simplify his stimulus-situation to bring it within the range of perception" (98). Essentially, the idea is to present intricate and subtle materials in such a way that even laymen believe they understand them. Here, Steinbeck uses a terse story structure that closely resembles an easily identifiable rhetorical pattern, in this case the five stages—exposition, complication, climax, falling action, and resolution—of the classical plot pyramid. Chapters 1 and 2 focus on the townspeople and the invaders, respectively, in order to introduce information relative to characters, the situation, and the conflicts between the conquered and the conquerors. Next, Chapters 3 and 4 provide complication by amplifying opposing positions and intensifying conflicts. The climax occurs in Chapter 5, and it is given emphasis by the portrayal of the eroding morale of the conquerors, the "spiritual siege" (60) or crisis that results from the stark realization that blind will and force alone cannot subjugate a free people. This is underscored in an epiphanic moment when one of the invaders, Lieutenant Tonder, utters in a state of near hysteria, "Conquest after conquest, deeper and deeper into molasses. . . . Maybe the Leader is crazy. Flies conquer the flypaper. Flies capture two hundred miles of new flypaper!" (68). Subsequently, in Chapters 6 and 7 the falling action shifts focus from the eroding morale of the conquerors to the increasing morale of the conquered. Finally, in Chapter 8, Steinbeck resolves the story by having Orden, captive yet undaunted, utter a closing speech that invokes the spirit of Socrates as the quintessential symbol of the quest for truth and freedom.

Steinbeck reinforces the concentrated communication of theme through simplification of character. Actually, the figures who people *The Moon Is Down* look more like allegorical types than fully rounded characters. And, although most of the characters —townspeople and invaders alike—are somewhat wooden, they effectively serve the propagandist's aims in that they suggest a rudimentary range of human dispositions that is easily apprehended. In Chapter 2, for instance, the qualities of the invaders are carefully catalogued and presented. In quick succession, we are given the "man of figures," Major Hunter (20); the "family man," Captain Bentick (20); the cold, ambitious careerist, Captain Loft; a pair of romantic idealists, Lieutenants Tonder and Prackle; and their seasoned, unquestioningly obedient leader, Colonel Lanser. Together, these men constitute Steinbeck's symbolic embodiment of the malign elements of the novel; these are the "Herd men" (111), those who are trapped by reductive, idealistic and artificial forms of perception that vitiate experience, those who Steinbeck also suggests are "not expected to question or to think, but only to carry out orders" (23). On the opposite side are the townspeople, whom Steinbeck clearly identifies as the "Free men" (111), or those who approach experience openly and holistically, and not in accord with unflinching ideology. Foremost among this group are Mayor Orden, "the leader of men," and Doctor Winter, the simple historian and physician, both of whom calmly refuse to compromise with their symbolic opposite, Colonel Lanser. Caught in the middle is George Corell, the traitor, who is trapped in a moral wasteland because he is useless to the invaders and detested by the townspeople, and who therefore cannot be part of either group. To broaden the social spectrum, Steinbeck also adds a cast of minor characters that includes Alexander Morden, the heroic alderman who dies for his country; his avenging wife, Molly, who kills for the cause of justice; and Joseph and Annie, the servants who struggle to a new sense of patriotic awareness.

Although the strategy invoked the ire of some American critics like James Thurber and Clifton Fadiman, who favored a more direct, hard-hitting approach and claimed Steinbeck's "fairy-tale" was too soft on the fascists (Coers 13–17), on the whole the technique worked well for European audiences. In Norway, for instance, *The Moon Is Down* became known as the epic of the Norwegian underground (Coers 53). For one Norwegian reviewer, the book stood apart from other propaganda efforts because it divined universal feelings, "there were our problems, our hopes, our sorrows about [Germany's] victory" (Coers 51). According to Danish underground leader Jorgen Jacobsen, because *The Moon Is Down* helped galvanize increased resistance, he felt it was "more important to Denmark during the war than to any other country" (Coers 76). In France, Jacques DebuBridel called the book a "masterpiece of understanding" (Coers 110). And in Holland, one Dutch translator stated that the book succeeded so well because "Steinbeck gave the mind of the people to such a small space" (Coers 98).

By eschewing propaganda stereotypes, and using an easily accessible plot structure and simplified characters, Steinbeck was able to manipulate form and organization so as to sharply outline the rhetorical focus of his invasion scenario. Significantly, the above testimonies also suggest that *The Moon Is Down* successfully created "resonance" with the audience, a concept associated with Doob's third precept, the *principle of auxiliary attitudes* (98). As Doob describes it, this principle is tantamount to "baiting" the audience with an attractive object, symbol, or idea that induces them to perceive that which the propagandist wishes (96). In this case, the bait is the appeal to freedom, unity, and solidarity—manifestations of democratic strength—all of which Steinbeck believed could not be subverted by force. Simplistic as this idea may seem, he nonetheless personifies it with Mayor Orden. Early on, for example, Steinbeck states that, "grown people, when they saw the word 'mayor,' printed or written, saw Mayor Orden in their minds. He and his office were one" (7). Essentially, Orden embodies public opinion and executes public will. As such, he *is* the town. He may fall, but the spirit and will of the people cannot be broken permanently. "The Mayor is an idea conceived by free men," Orden asserts, "It will escape arrest" (112).[4]

Ultimately, then, the lines of conflict—herd man versus free man—are sharply etched and the figure-ground boundaries are unmistakable. Moreover, the propagandist's message in *The Moon Is Down* is an encouraging one for the resistance. Orden's last words are, "The debt shall be paid" (112), an optimistic indication that herd-cum-teleological man is doomed to defeat. However, to reinforce the message and ensure it resounds clearly with the audience requires *repetition*, Doob's fourth principle, one that assumes that the more often an idea is presented, the more likely it is to be perceived as the propagandist intended it (98). For plangency, Steinbeck employs repeated motifs, including images, words, objects, phrases, and actions. The "flies conquer the flypaper," for example, is first mentioned in Chapter 5 (68), and then repeated in Chapter 8 (111), as if to punctuate Orden's recitation of Socrates to Colonel Lanser. Also, there are recurring references to the townspeople as "good," "nice," and "peaceful" (25, 29, 35), and to the invaders as "time-minded" and "orderly" (3, 11, 15), references that by the end become ironic, as indicated when Doctor Winter says, "A time-minded people . . . and the time is nearly up" (105). As well, there are ironic descriptions like this one given by Doctor Winter:

> Your Excellency, our friend, George Corell, prepared this town for the invasion. Our benefactor, George Corell, sent our soldiers into the hills. Our dinner guest, George Corell, has made a list of every firearm in the town. Our friend, George Corell! (13)

Here the rhetorical device is *anaphora*, the technique of repeating the same word at the beginning of successive clauses or sentences, a method Steinbeck also uses at the start of Chapter 4 through several references to falling and piling snow. In the above example, however, the repeated phrases, "friend," "benefactor," "dinner guest," and again, "friend," underscore the fact that Corell is none of these things, but in reality is a betrayer.

Elsewhere, Steinbeck uses other rhetorical devices such as *chiasmus* and *conduplicatio* to achieve balance and repeat significant words and images. In Chapter 5, the eroding morale of the conquerors is nicely captured in the following:

> And the men thought always of home. The men of the battalion came to detest the place they had conquered, and they were curt with the people and the people were curt with them, and gradually a little fear began to grow in the conquerors, a fear that it would never be over, that they could never relax or go home, a fear that one day they would crack and be hunted through the mountains like rabbits, for the conquered never relaxed their hatred. (58)

In this instance the word "curt" is nicely balanced to signify the nexus of the relationship between conqueror and conquered. In addition, the threefold repetition of the word "fear" in the dependent clauses of the second sentence underscores the growing emotional crisis experienced by the invaders.

In the final analysis, the repetition of ideas, the terse style, compact structure, and stiff characterization produce mediocre art, but good propaganda. Certainly, when judged solely on artistic merit, *The Moon Is Down* pales when compared to Steinbeck's great works like *The Grapes of Wrath, In Dubious Battle,* or *Of Mice and Men.* Nonetheless, as propaganda, the book represents an ideological triumph for the human spirit. In the dim and gloomy early days of World War II, Steinbeck offered a commodity for which he was a consistent champion—freedom and hope and resolve, especially for the underdog. In fact, as a testament to the novel's enduring appeal, between 1945 and 1989, no fewer than 76 editions appeared in 28 countries around the globe

(Coers 137). Moreover, the Norwegians felt so strongly about Steinbeck's contribution to the resistance that they awarded him the King Haakon medal in 1946 (*SLL* 767–68). Ultimately, then, in terms of what it was intended to do—encourage democratic principles, boost morale, and reassert basic Western values—the book succeeds masterfully.

6
Steinbeck's Influence upon Native American Writers

Paul and Charlotte Hadella

Although Steinbeck's works include few Native American characters, he nonetheless has exerted a profound impact on contemporary Native American writers. Steinbeck's empathy for marginalized characters and his commitment to social issues are key concerns for these writers; but perhaps the theme of loneliness most compellingly echoes in works such as Thomas King's Medicine River, *Louis Owens's* Wolfsong, *and James Welch's* Winter in the Blood *and* The Death of Jim Loney.

Louis Owens, author of two books and numerous articles on the work of John Steinbeck, is not writing about Steinbeck these days. He is writing fiction whose main characters are mixed-blood white and Native American, reflective of his own Choctaw, Cherokee, and Irish descent. Yet his transformation from Steinbeck critic to Native American novelist is less of a departure than it might seem. In fact, other contemporary Native American writers besides Owens have been influenced by Steinbeck. Making that Steinbeck connection visible is the purpose of this paper.

Owens was born in 1948, before a discernible body of fiction that could be called "Native American" even existed. When he was a young man, there was nothing like a Native American literary movement, as there is today, nothing like an active roster of Indian writers whose work he could read and admire. Before 1968, when Scott Momaday won a Pulitzer Prize for his novel, *House Made of Dawn*, only eight novels by Native Americans had ever been published, and most would have been out of print and unknown to all but a few scholars. In the absence of Native

American literary mentors, it was Steinbeck who spoke persuasively to Owens, and to others of his generation. The Blackfoot poet and novelist, James Welch, who was born in 1940 and began publishing in the mid-seventies, has, he says, "been very influenced by" John Steinbeck: "And a lot of the influence has just kind of sunk in without my having known it" (Coltelli 198). Thomas King, born three years after Welch, is another native writer who owes a considerable degree of debt to Steinbeck.

Before exploring Steinbeck's mark upon Native American fiction, however, we must briefly consider Steinbeck's treatment of Native Americans in his own work. Louis Owens, in his book on *The Grapes of Wrath,* surveys Steinbeck's work and finds just one time when the figure of the Indian is not presented as "an abstraction," either a romantic symbol of "profound, unconscious impulses, a link to the mystical," or else "a mirror reflecting back at America its own fantasies and its own guilt" (*Trouble* 60, 64). The one exception to this rule is Jule, the half-Cherokee mixed-blood in *The Grapes of Wrath* who is appointed Gatekeeper for the dance at the Weedpatch labor camp. " 'Wisht I was a full-blood,' " muses Jule at one point. " 'I'd have my lan' on the reservation. Them full-bloods got it pretty nice, some of 'em' " (464). "Here, for an instant in Steinbeck's work," observes Owens, "a present-day American Indian is made to share in the real difficulties of American life. The Indian, for a brief moment, steps out of the world of shadow and into the mundane light of reality" (62–63). Yet Steinbeck's accomplishment is diminished, in Owens's view, by the fact that Steinbeck here demonstrates his ignorance of U.S. policy in regards to how land is allotted to tribal peoples. He also seems unaware that the Cherokee reservation "had long since ceased to exist" (63).

Thus, Steinbeck appealed to Native American writers despite failing to do his research, and despite the fact that he never created a believable, fully rounded Native American character. If Native Americans, then, did not see themselves in any of Steinbeck's Indians, what did they see in Steinbeck's work that spoke to them? Was it a vision of America that matched their own? Indeed, with Steinbeck's sympathy for the dispossessed, and his devotion to social and economic themes, one feels a strong kinship between Steinbeck and Native American writers. Like

Steinbeck, most contemporary Native American writers are concerned primarily with life away from the cities; they depict individuals struggling against powerful forces within society that would deprive them of self-definition; and they issue a clear repudiation of the American Dream, which adds a decidedly political edge to their fiction. No doubt Steinbeck's socio-economic liberalism influenced Owens, Thomas King, and James Welch. However, there is a more universal theme in Steinbeck's fiction that dominates certain novels by these three writers: it is the theme of loneliness.

For example, Thomas King's first and best known novel, *Medicine River*, recalls crucial elements of *Cannery Row*, a book that Ed Ricketts called "an essay in loneliness." Several months ago, we contacted Thomas King, who grew up in California, to ask him about Steinbeck, in particular the strong *Cannery Row*–like feel to *Medicine River*. "I've read Steinbeck, of course," he replied, "but most of the inspiration for *Medicine River* came from the ten years I spent among the Blackfoot people in Lethbridge, Alberta, Canada. Particularly the time I spent playing basketball for the native Friendship Centre." Although King's own life experiences provided him with the subject of his novel, they do not explain the book's narrative structure, which depends upon the comic tension that arises between two dichotomous characters, Will and Harlen. For that, King reproduces, however unconsciously, the relationship in *Cannery Row* between Doc and Mack. "I see your point," King admitted to us. "*Cannery Row* and *Medicine River* do share some similarities." Indeed, they do.

In the vein of *Cannery Row*, the episodes involving Will, the loner, and Harlen Bigbear, the extrovert, are often juxtaposed with tales featuring other residents of Medicine River, tales which fracture the surface levity of the book. The community of Cannery Row has seen its share of depression victims and suicides, just as Medicine River is home to people whose lives have been shattered by domestic violence and alcohol addiction.

But it is in the way that King understands the tension between Will and Harlen that *Medicine River* comes even closer to mirroring *Cannery Row*. Will, a photographer, spends much of his time studying people from behind his camera but remaining detached from them. In this way, his job, like Doc's, perfectly complements his asocial personality. The other major part of his job involves spending many hours alone in his darkroom, developing the images he has captured on film. Similarly, Doc gathers specimens from tide pools, then brings them back to his lab for quiet and methodical study.

Furthermore, Harlen is a dead ringer for Mack. Apparently unemployed, Harlen nevertheless stays constantly busy by keeping up on all of the latest tribal gossip, attending every wedding and funeral, coaching the men's basketball team (the equivalent of Mack's "boys"), and overseeing the next money-making project for the tribe. The hardest job he has undertaken is to try to bring Will into the fold, into the tribe, by involving him in community activities, such as basketball, as well as in social events on the reservation adjacent to the town of Medicine River. Harlen can no more stand seeing Will alone than can Mack stand to see Doc by himself in his laboratory. Just as Mack decides that Doc is "a lonely and set-apart man" (96), and attempts to do something about it by throwing him parties, Harlen sets his mind upon liberating Will from loneliness, even going as far as to play matchmaker for the shy bachelor. Never mind that Will's favorite way to relax is by watching football by himself. Harlen has his own ideas about how Will should be spending his time.

How well does Harlen succeed in converting Will to tribal thinking? At the beginning of the novel, Will visits Medicine River to attend his mother's funeral. Harlen achieves his initial victory when he persuades Will to establish a photography business there. We learn through a series of flashbacks that Will, a mixed-blood, grew up in the big city, Toronto, where he has continued to live as an adult disconnected from any sense of community. We learn, too, that he had been in a serious relationship with a white woman. We discover, in other words, that Will has lived to this point without identifying with being Indian. In a crucial scene near the end of the novel, Will is persuaded to step from behind his camera and to take a place in the group portrait he is shooting at a family reunion on the reservation. It seems, then, that Harlen has finally won: he has weaned Will of his city ways and brought him into the tribe. The last chapter, however, finds Will home alone, and fairly content, on Christmas day. Has Will become more group-oriented, more "Indian," since moving to Medicine River? Yes. But the ending of the novel also indicates that he will continue to placate that side of him—the self-reliant "white" side of him, if you will—that desires distance and freedom from the group. There can be a balance, King is saying.

In *Cannery Row* Doc, too, must choose between solitude and fellowship, but never within the context of his own racial identity. This quest for identity, which, as Louis Owens contends, is the master theme of all contemporary Native American fiction, is what sets *Medicine River* apart from *Cannery Row*. We must emphasize this point since it seems that we have been subordinating King's novel to Steinbeck's, implying that *Medicine River* can be read simply as a duplicate of the earlier model. Like *Cannery Row*, *Medicine River* does offer an "essay on loneliness." But King goes his separate way when he extends the theme of loneliness to address questions of race and identity.

Moving from *Medicine River* to a consideration of Louis Owens's fiction, we propose that the Steinbeck stamp can be found all over Owens's first novel, *Wolfsong* (1991), a book that combines Steinbeck's economic themes with his keen sensitivity to human loneliness. It is the former that are most noticeable at first. *Wolfsong* has been called an environmental novel, a label that it rightly deserves given Owens's regard for the rain forests of the American Northwest and his plea to save the wilderness from those industrial interests—namely, mining and logging—that would plunder it. It is also, then, a novel of social protest, one that, like *The Grapes of Wrath*, registers its opposition to corporate greed. In the Cascade Range of northwest Washington, Tom Joseph, a young Skagitt Indian who has gone to California to attend college, returns home for his uncle's funeral and finds himself caught up in the old man's fight to stop a copper company from creating an open-pit mine in a wilderness area. Tom's uncle has died of a heart attack while firing potshots at the bulldozers that have come to dig roads to the mine; these machines, like the tractors in the Oklahoma section of *The Grapes of Wrath*, symbolize blind, brute force.

The comparison between *Wolfsong* and *The Grapes of Wrath*

should not be pressed too far, since a great difference in scope, structure, and style does exist between them—for one thing, Owens's fidelity to Native American values, which hold the land to be sacred, adds a dimension to *Wolfsong* that, of course, is not developed fully in Steinbeck's novel. Though the Okies express close connection to the land, working the land is viewed in economic rather than in spiritual terms. Moreover, the entire aspect of the epic journey, so crucial in *The Grapes of Wrath,* has no correlation in Owens's book. Nevertheless, it is reasonable to assume that a critic-turned-novelist who has devoted so much of his intellectual energy to writing about Steinbeck—including an entire book on *The Grapes of Wrath* itself—has dropped bits and pieces of that great novel, consciously or not, into his own fiction. Consider: the protagonist's name, "Tom Joseph," perhaps was intended to evoke the famous hero of the Nez Perce tribe, Chief Joseph; but does it not sound like "Tom Joad"? Also, should we ignore the attention to setting and landscape in *Wolfsong,* reminiscent of the emphasis Steinbeck gives to them in *The Grapes of Wrath*? Owens's precise evocation of the rugged, rain-drenched terrain in and around the Stehemish River valley, complements, by way of contrast, Steinbeck's memorable description of the flat, drought-stricken land in *The Grapes of Wrath.* In the Cascades region of Washington, Owens has found the direct opposite of the Dust Bowl of Oklahoma, two very different places that nevertheless share a similar history of environmental catastrophe due to economic exploitation.

Furthermore, Tom Joseph is destined to become, like his near-namesake in Steinbeck's book, a fighter in a seemingly hopeless battle. His homecoming at the beginning of *Wolfsong,* though from college rather than prison, sets up a similar situation to that in *The Grapes of Wrath,* when Tom Joad returns home to find his family and community in crisis at a time of economic change and uncertainty. Both Toms even hitch rides in trucks on their way to reaching home. More important than such incidental parallels, however, is the fact that both men, over the course of these novels, will become committed to a cause that transcends self, and thereby rejects the more typically American rule of "me first." This ideal of commitment has been passed to Tom Joseph from his uncle, to Tom Joad from Jim Casy.

Like Jim Casy, Jim Joseph, the uncle in *Wolfsong*, is a martyr for his cause; and like their mentors, both Tom Joad and Tom Joseph evolve into bigger-than-life characters, determined to transcend the powers of earthly evil and merge with the forces of goodness for which they do battle. In subverting selfhood for the greater cause, both Toms choose loneliness over family and community ties. When Tom says farewell to Ma Joad in *The Grapes of Wrath*, he announces, "I'll be all aroun' in the dark. I'll be ever'where—wherever you look. Wherever they's a fight so hungry people can eat, I'll be there. Wherever they's a cop beatin' up a guy, I'll be there. . . . I'll be in the way guys yell when they're mad an'—I'll be in the way kids laugh when they're hungry an' they know supper's ready. An' when our folks eat the stuff they raise an' live in the houses they build—why, I'll be there" (572). Just as Tom Joad becomes one with "the folks" whose cause he represents, Tom Joseph becomes one with the wilderness at the end of *Wolfsong*. After sabotaging the mine site that promised to destroy his sacred tribal land, Tom Joseph escapes his pursuers and flees north toward the Canadian border. Wounded and half-starved, he regains strength as "he listened to the rising howl of the wolf" and lives into his dream of following the wolf's song. Reminiscent of Pepe in "Flight," Tom Joseph loses pack and rifle, stripping himself of civilization, so to speak, as he climbs the last glacier between himself and freedom. We leave him running "with long, smooth strides down the mountain, the moon hurling his shadow northward before him listening to the rising howl of the wolf that went on and on until the night seemed ready to burst" (249). In this wolf-like state, Owens's Tom merges with the wilderness for which he is willing to sacrifice his life. A lone fugitive from the law, he has broken all ties with home and loved ones.

Louis Owens, in his critical book, *John Steinbeck's Re-Vision of America*, uncovers themes in *The Grapes of Wrath* that play an important role in his own novel. The first is man's failed responsibility to steward the land, the blame for which the common people must share along with the rich. "Regardless of his professed admiration for the 'Okies,'" writes Owens," not for a moment does Steinbeck exempt the sharecroppers from their portion of blame for the ruined and impotent earth" (132). Like

Steinbeck, Owens shows that the poor have bought into the belief, dear to the rich corporations, that the land is an exploitable commodity. Indeed, with Tom Joseph's family living in poverty, they, like the rest of the community, welcome the copper mine for the jobs it will bring. If Tom is a hero, then, he is certainly a lonely one, for his spiritual bond with the land has alienated him from his family, his girlfriend, and his neighbors. He acts alone, against the wishes of all of these people, to block its exploitation. Thus, what Owens calls "the all-important lesson" of *The Grapes of Wrath* goes largely unheeded in *Wolfsong*. Whereas several of the Joads do learn "that spiritual and even physical survival depend upon commitment to a larger whole, to 'the one inseparable unit man plus his environment'" (133), no one in *Wolfsong* but Tom and his deceased Uncle Jim embrace this ideal.

The last author whose work we would like to discuss in connection to that of John Steinbeck is James Welch, a major figure in the field of contemporary native American literature. With the novels *Winter in the Blood* and *The Death of Jim Loney*, published in the 1970s, Welch became part of the so-called "Native American Renaissance," the blossoming of the native writing in this country that established the reputations of Scott Momaday and Leslie Marmon Silko as well. Welch has continued to publish important books since the 1970s, most recently a revisionist account of the Battle of Little Bighorn called *Killing Custer*.

With Welch's professed debt to Steinbeck in mind, it is impossible to read *The Death of Jim Loney*, Welch's second novel, and not think of *Of Mice and Men*, though there is little in the circumstances of the novel that actually recall Steinbeck's small masterpiece. True, at one point Loney, the depressed, mixed-blood protagonist, and his white girlfriend, Rhea, daydream about building a cabin, just as George and Lennie sustain each other with an Edenic vision of living off "the fatta the land." "Let's build a cabin," Rhea tells Loney. "We can cut down these little old trees. We'll build a log cabin and you can hunt. Just like your ancestors. You can dress me up in furs" (14). In *Of Mice and Men*, two factors combine to ensure that George and Lennie will never see the day when they are living in harmony with the land on their own piece of property. The first is the grim economic reality that, as transient workers, George and Lennie will never earn the capital needed to finance their dream. Steinbeck expects the reader to realize the unfairness of an economic system that denies equal opportunity to all. The second factor is Lennie himself. His uncontrollable attraction to soft, furry things, and his brute strength, which can erupt into violence if he is provoked, have gotten himself and George into trouble before. From the opening scene in the sycamore grove, where further misfortunes for the two men are foreshadowed, the reader realizes that the same will undoubtedly happen again.

In *The Death of Jim Loney*, Welch avoids Steinbeck's economic message and concentrates solely on flaws in character as the reason for Jim Loney's demise. After all, Loney and Rhea could afford a modest "dream home" in the woods: she is a school teacher and he, though currently unemployed because it is winter, has had no trouble finding seasonal ranch work. But if Welch does not feel Steinbeck's need to critique capitalism, he does share his pessimism. Indeed, the feeling of doom is pervasive in Welch's novel, as Loney alienates himself, one by one, from those people who try to reach out to him: Rhea, his sister, and an old high school buddy. In fact, he winds up shooting and killing the latter in a bizarre hunting incident. Critic Philip Fisher contends that a distinguishing feature of the naturalistic novel is the "plot of decline" (169). Both *The Death of Jim Loney* and *Of Mice and Men* are, in this respect, works of naturalism. The reader, well understanding that the characters have never stood a chance, can only watch without hope as the plot works its way to its inevitable, tragic outcome.

But if economic conditions are not responsible for Loney's decline into depression, insanity, and ultimately, self-annihilation, then what is? The answer would have to be "too much winter." Throughout the novel, Welch uses the Montana winter as a metaphor for the deep-freeze that has overtaken Loney, whose inertia is as solid as it is inexplicable. Alone at last, after the hunting episode, Loney leads the police on a chase that will result in his fatal shooting. Ironically, orchestrating his own death, the event forecast in the novel's title, becomes the only empowering act of Loney's life.

Nothing can explain the flaw in Loney's character, his craving for self-destruction. He simply *is* that way, just as Lennie *is* mentally deficient. A bottle of whiskey, the container that holds the one thing that can warm and comfort Loney, appeals to him on the same sensual level as soft, furry things appeal to Lennie. Left on his own, Lennie would have gotten himself killed long ago. Through George's guidance, Lennie has managed to survive —but for how much longer? The companionship that the men have forged, renewed periodically by George's recitation of their dream, saves both men from the condition that Jim Loney cannot escape: loneliness. As Louis Owens states, "The dream of George and Lennie represents a desire to defy the curse of Cain and fallen man—to break the pattern of wandering and loneliness imposed on the outcasts and to return to the perfect garden. George and Lennie achieve all of this dream that is possible in the real world: they are their brother's keeper" (*Re-vision* 102). In *The Death of Jim Loney*, Welch shows us a man who has lost this will to connect with his fellow man and woman, and to be spared from the torment of loneliness. He steadily sheds every last bond of companionship, a process that can lead only to death. Technically, Loney dies of bullet wounds, but the real cause of his death is loneliness—a loneliness that totally overpowers him and that he seems, on some level, to desire. By giving his character a name that sounds so much like "lonely," Welch underscores the grim, deterministic point that this man was cursed from the moment he was born, and that there is nothing anyone could do about it. That his name sounds like "Lennie" is perhaps no coincidence either. Both Lennie and Loney are victims of forces beyond their control, though Lennie, through George, has at least given and received love. Not even with Rhea could Loney feel love, which, in the end, makes Welch's novel an even bleaker book than Steinbeck's.

Born in the 1940s Thomas King, Louis Owens, and James Welch belong to a generation that came of age when Steinbeck received the Nobel Prize. Does this mean that Steinbeck claims no hold upon the imagination of younger native writers? Proof that Steinbeck is indeed still relevant surfaces in the writing of Sherman Alexie, born in 1966. Currently recognized as the standard-bearer for a new generation of Native American writers, Alexie is prominent enough to speak at a BBS roundtable on race with President Clinton. Alexie dedicates one of his books, *The Lone Ranger and Tonto Fistfight in Heaven,* to the native quartet of "Leslie" [Silko], "Adrian" [Louis], "Joy" [Harjo], "Simon" [Ortiz], for the young native writer of today finds no shortage of literary heroes of his own race to praise and emulate. Nevertheless, Steinbeck has apparently made an impression. In a recent volume of poetry, *The Summer of Black Widows,* Alexie places the name of "John Steinbeck" near the top of the list of authors, living and dead, whom he respects. Alexie calls these list poems "Totem Sonnets," after totem poles of the Northwest, the massive wood carvings constructed to honor a tribe's most powerful animal guides and ancestors. Steinbeck's high place on this totem pole speaks for itself.

Another of Alexie's "Totem Sonnets" lists the names of fictional characters. We are generalizing here, but kinship in the existential predicament of the twentieth century seems to be the bond that unites all of these characters. Characters from Native American fiction reside upon this totem pole, such as Tayo from Silko's novel *Ceremony* and Cecelia Capture from Janet Campbell Hale's novel *The Jailing of Cecelia Capture.* Also, we find Flannery O'Connor's The Misfit here and Toni Morrison's Sula. Given that Alexie's latest novel *Indian Killer* features an extremely introverted and troubled character, John Smith, who drifts numbly through life without really knowing who he is, we aren't surprised to find Welch's Jim Loney on Alexie's totem pole, clearly the prototype in Native American fiction for John Smith. Victims all, the characters on this totem pole have been cursed by such modern maladies as loneliness, alienation, deracination, and despair. At the very top of the totem pole is the name of "Lennie." With his simple list of names, Alexie confirms the connection between himself, the native writers that we have addressed in this paper, and John Steinbeck. Uniting all races, it is profound loneliness, ironically, that could bring all people to a greater appreciation of their shared humanity.

II
Steinbeck as World Citizen

7

Cannery Row and the Japanese Mentality

Hiroshi Kaname

Teikan (resignation/acceptance) is a core Japanese belief and accords well with Steinbeck's non-teleological thinking in general. Kaname offers Cannery Row *as perhaps the finest example of this principle in action in Steinbeck's work.*

Cannery Row attracts the Japanese because it shares a key aspect of the traditional Japanese worldview, *teikan* (resignation). *Teikan* means being well contented, accepting everything as it is—including death, loneliness, or poverty. Although *teikan* may appear to be a negative way of thinking, the idea is positive, though very complicated. The Japanese make desperate efforts to achieve their aims. Once they find something impossible to achieve, however, they promptly relinquish the attempt. In Japan, there is a saying: "You should know when and how to quit." A related expression, "Cherry blossoms bloom out suddenly and are gone soon," leads to *bushido,* the feudal Japanese code of chivalry. The *bushi,* or *samurai,* do not adhere to life. They do not adhere to anything. *Bushido* thus reinforces the traditional Japanese acceptance of, and praise for, *hakanasa* (transience). Together, these concepts are central to a way of thinking that is deeply concerned with the idea that we should accept death, loneliness, or tragedy for what it is.

The idea of acceptance is also found in *Cannery Row.* At the heart of *Cannery Row* is a philosophy most clearly articulated in *The Log from the Sea of Cortez* when Steinbeck discusses "non-teleological" thinking: the phenomenon should be understood as "what actually 'is,'" not as "what should be, or could be, or might be" (112). *Cannery Row* refuses to depend on the law of causality and accepts one deviation after another, an approach that critic Peter Lisca identifies as the book's lack of structure (*Wide World* 207). Indeed, the book consists of fragmented affairs and episodically depicts not a few events which have no close relationship with each other. But the novel also arranges episodes to create a story. Steinbeck approves of "continuity in discontinuity." For example, Chapter 23 reflects a refusal to place absolute trust in the law of causality:

> Sam Malloy had a number of fights with his wife. . . . The nice bouncer at the Bear Flag threw out a drunk . . . and broke his back . . . a group of high-minded ladies in the town demanded that dens of vice must close to protect young American manhood. . . . Dora was closed a full two weeks. . . . Doc had to get a loan at the bank to pay for the glass that was broken at the party. Elmer Rechati went to sleep on the Southern Pacific track and lost both legs. A sudden and completely unexpected storm tore a purse-seiner and three lampara boats loose from their moorings and tossed them broken and sad on Del Monte beach. (136–37)

What is important is that "there is no explaining a series of misfortunes like that" (*CR* 137). Throughout the novel events occur in many places, although their causal relation is not clear. The only clear fact is that misfortunes happened. Events mentioned in Chapter 23 may or may not have some definite causal relation. The important thing is to understand them as they are.

Chapter 11 is similarly based on "is" thinking, for example, in Steinbeck's attitude to prostitution. He understands and accepts prostitutes. Doc is kind and understanding to Dora and her girls: "Take the girls at Dora's. All of them had at one time or another gone over to the laboratory for advice or medicine or simply for unprofessional company" (157).

This acceptance is reminiscent of Walt Whitman and democracy. In the first edition of *Leaves of Grass*, Whitman acknowledges Ralph Waldo Emerson's inspiration; it was Emerson who first said that America is a poem. Whitman says, "I have wish'd to put the complete Union of the States in my songs without any preference or partiality whatever" (572). Similarly, Steinbeck says, "Cannery Row in Monterey in California is a poem" (5). The intention of the truly national poet, Whitman, is to depict how various things American are accepted and united; he finds "unity in multiplicity" which is the principle of democracy.

"Unity in multiplicity" is related to the idea of "continuity in discontinuity" in *Cannery Row*. Throughout the novel, scenes of disorder and scenes of stasis are proof of multiplicity. For example, in one scene that highlights disorder,

> [t]he lights blazed in the laboratory. The front door hung sideways by one hinge. The floor was littered with broken glass. Phonograph records, some broken, some only nicked, were strewn about. The plates with pieces of steak ends and coagulating grease were on the floor, on top of the bookcases, under the bed. Whiskey glasses lay sadly on their sides. Someone trying to climb the bookcases had pulled out a whole section of books and spilled them in broken-backed confusion on the floor. (119)

An equally compelling scene emphasizes quietude:

> Early morning is a time of magic in Cannery Row. In the gray time after the light has come and before the sun has risen, the Row seems to hang suspended out of time in a silvery light. The street lights go out, and the weeds are a brilliant green. The corrugated iron of the canneries glows with the pearly lucence of platinum or old pewter. No automobiles are running then. The street is silent of progress and business. And the rush and drag of the waves can be heard as they splash in among the piles of the canneries. It is a time of great peace, a deserted time, a little era of rest. (81)

Both the principle of disorder and that of serenity must be given equal significance. Indeed, for Steinbeck democracy means accepting various things as they are, an idea that he returns to in his final text, *America and Americans*:

> Our land is of every kind geologically and climatically, and our people are of every kind also—of every race, of every ethnic category—and yet our land is one nation, and our people are

Americans. Mottoes have a way of being compounded of wishes and dreams. The motto of the United States, *"E Pluribus Unum,"* is a fact. (13)

The form of *Cannery Row* is thus deeply related to "non-teleo-logical" thinking. Seemingly unrelated interchapters in fact support Steinbeck's philosophy. "No critic has discovered the reason for those little inner chapters in *Cannery Row*," Steinbeck wrote to his editor, Pascal Covici (qtd. in Lisca *Wide World* 208). Steinbeck deeply regretted critics' failure to understand the interchapters. But later critics have recognized the significance of the non-teleological interchapters. As Susan Shillinglaw says, *"Cannery Row* is Steinbeck's purest non-judgmental, 'non-teleological' text" (ix). Steinbeck's intention in *Cannery Row* is to make it an artistic manifestation of "non-teleological" thinking.

This idea of "unity in multiplicity" also helps explain the author's complex intentions. Steinbeck made a rather offhand comment about the novel in "My Short Novels":

> I saw a piece of war as a correspondent, and following that wrote *Cannery Row.* This was a kind of nostalgic thing, written for a group of soldiers who had said to me, "Write something funny that isn't about the war. Write something for us to read—we're sick of war." (39)

But in fact, his deep intention was more complicated. *Cannery Row* is not just funny and humorous. As John H. Timmerman says, "Steinbeck's vision darkens considerably in *Cannery Row*" (156). Still another motivation may be related to Ed Ricketts, for *Cannery Row* is dedicated to Ed Ricketts, who influenced Steinbeck enormously, and Steinbeck's biological thought is similar to Ricketts's. Furthermore, the prologue of *Cannery Row* notes the complexity of design in the novel:

> How can the poem and the stink and the grating noise—the quality of light, the tone, the habit and the dream—be set down alive? When you collect marine animals there are certain flat worms so delicate that they are almost impossible to capture whole, for they break and tatter under the touch. You must let them ooze and crawl of their own will onto a knife blade and

then lift them gently into your bottle of sea water. And perhaps that might be the way to write this book—to open the page and to let the stories crawl in by themselves. (6–7)

In fact, the sentiment that Steinbeck expresses in "My Short Novels," Timmerman's observation about the novel's darkness, Steinbeck's friendship with Ed Ricketts, as well as the book's structural complexity are all true, for *Cannery Row* includes all these aspects. *Cannery Row* has depth and surface. L. J. Marks says:

It is probable, moreover, that *Cannery Row* will retain its popularity on the basis of its surface humor and bawdiness, . . . But this observation only reaffirms that Steinbeck's method is intentionally comic; it in no way impairs the fact that his comedy is, at its heart, serious. (92)

Though we should not miss the novel's cheerful and humorous tone, the essence of *Cannery Row* is the author's tragic view, his awareness of the mortality as well as the solitude of human beings.

The central plot of *Cannery Row,* if the book can be said to have one, is Mack's plan to throw a party and console Doc. He fails in the first plan, but succeeds with the second. It's a simple plot. But the reason that Mack thinks of giving a party is that he becomes aware of Doc's solitude, and he hopes to save him from being lonely, detached and depressed. Charles Metzger says: "Doc is isolated in part by his work. . . . He is isolated also by his unusual intelligence" (24). Frankie is isolated because he is a backward boy. Even Mack feels isolated. He confesses to Doc: "Ever'thing I done turned sour. . . . I don't do nothin' but clown no more. Try to make the boys laugh" (124). Doc, whose model is Ricketts himself, is a "non-teleological" thinker, and accepts both his own solitude and others' isolated feelings as they are. L. J. Marks calls Doc "the complete Steinbeckian hero. . . . His philosophical point of view is, of course, non-teleological, which leaves him free to be what he is and to accept others as they are" (97).

Loneliness is an important theme in many Steinbeck novels. For example, in *Of Mice and Men* George deplores his loneliness, saying, "Guys like us, that work on ranches, are the loneliest guys in the world" (15). And Candy in *Of Mice and Men* is similar to the old Chinese man in *Cannery Row* in that they are both very lonely. In *The Grapes of Wrath*, Uncle John is lonely.

Death is also ever present in *Cannery Row*, the gloom probably derived from Steinbeck's war experiences. There are four suicides depicted: Horace Abbeville (Chapter 1), William (Chapter 3), a beautiful girl (Chapter 18), and Joey's father (Chapter 26). Steinbeck does not ask why these four characters kill themselves. They simply are not survivors.

Fate ordains that human beings cannot escape loneliness and death. Human beings are born alone and die alone. In Chapter 31, for example, the gopher cannot find a mate, however hard he tries. Even if he can escape, loneliness or death awaits him. There are traps put out every night. The gopher shares this fate with the human beings of *Cannery Row*. Steinbeck insists on the acceptance required by "non-teleological" thinking.

In Japan, one of the traditional ways of accepting life as it is is to live a non-materialistic life in an honest and honorable way. This manner of living is Taoist in origin, which is espoused in *Manyoushuu*, one of the oldest and greatest collections of Japanese poems. It is why the *samurai* demean themselves with dignity in poverty, and it is one reason why Steinbeck with his "non-teleological" approach is so loved by the Japanese in general.

For the Japanese, true artistry is realized only when the writer is released from commercialism and materialism. Release from the world purifies and enhances art. Steinbeck, like Thoreau, seems to transcend worldliness. He wants not to be bound by the world. And Steinbeck as an artist may find out his dream in the way of living of Mack and the boys, who live as they want to. They are not negative about their non-materialistic way of living. Rather, they are proud to be non-materialistic and socially isolated from commercialized society. They want to live as naturally as possible. They accept things as they are.

In short, *Cannery Row* is read with favor by the Japanese because, as we have seen, it shares a central idea with the traditional worldview of the Japanese: *teikan*, accepting what actually is. In this sense, the spiritual world of *Cannery Row* is similar to that of the Japanese.

8

"Consonant Symphonies"
John Steinbeck in the Indus Valley

P. Balaswamy

Indian readers appreciate Steinbeck's work more than they do that of other American authors because they understand his philosophical stance and approve his support for the underdog. Balaswamy particularly argues for the essential monism of To a God Unknown *and of Steinbeck's non-teleological thinking in* Sea of Cortez *and elsewhere.*

Of the twentieth century novels included in an American fiction study list at an Indian University, the students enjoyed John Steinbeck's *Of Mice and Men* better than all other novels prescribed—the list included *The Great Gatsby, The Sound and the Fury, Invisible Man,* and *Catch 22.* The greatness of these modern American classics, in terms of artistic excellence and formal complexities, was certainly recognized and appreciated by this set of students, but the human appeal of *Of Mice and Men* and the elementary conflict portrayed therein seemed to touch a core in their hearts, making their responses rather spontaneous. It is illustrative of the fascination Steinbeck holds for Indian readers, vouchsafed by the considerable following this American writer enjoys in the academic circles, particularly in Indian Universities. Steinbeck's appeal has crossed all boundaries—national, religious, cultural and social—and has solidly reached readers in India and other nations. It is not "Dissonant Symphonies" that Steinbeck has orchestrated in his works, but what we may term as "Consonant Symphonies"—tunes and tones that create harmonious relationships among peoples and nations of the world. This paper analyzes the internationalism of Steinbeck and his appeal across the Western boundaries.

Perhaps the "pleasure of discovery" is the first factor in Steinbeck's appeal to Indian readers. They are pleasantly surprised when they find not merely echoes of, but overt references to, Indian thought. The philosophical base of Steinbeck's noteworthy works, *The Grapes of Wrath, Cannery Row,* and *To a God Unknown* has many strands similar to the Indian philosophical systems and the Indian view of life. Commenting on "the sources of Steinbeck's thought," Jackson J. Benson states that "we have been led into a good deal of speculation after the fact." Admitting that our author's reading of philosophy has not been deciphered yet, Benson cautions that "working backward from fiction to underlying philosophy from a specific source can be dangerous work: the critic is going to see in the background those sources he may be familiar with, not necessarily those which may have shaped the thoughts of the writer" (233). While not disagreeing with the logic of this biographical estimate, and clarifying that one does not search for "evidence" in Steinbeck's reading list, one may resort to the age-old practice of intense textual analysis as the basis for his conclusions. Two Steinbeck texts may be examined in the light of such a theoretical stance.

To a God Unknown, considered by many readers as a tale of westering, or as an account of a farming community's failure to face the ravages of a drought, is more than that: it is a parable, a complex and carefully constructed allegory. Steinbeck wrote in a ledger:

> This story has grown since I started it. From a novel about people, it has become a novel about the world . . . Joseph is a giant shouldering his way among the ages, pushing the stars aside to make a passage to God. . . . The story is a parable. . . . The story of a race, growth and death. Each figure is a population and the stones, the trees, the muscled mountains are the world—but not the world apart from man—the world and man—*the one inseparable unit man plus his environment* [emphasis added]. (Valjean 122–23)

Even though the mythical vehicle of *To a God Unknown* is a composite of Christian, Hindu and the Grail legends, in the typical syncretic method adopted by Steinbeck in some of his other fiction (such as *Cup of Gold, In Dubious Battle* and *The Grapes of Wrath)*[1] the title and the main burden of the theme of this early novel by an ambitious, young, idealistic writer have been drawn from an ancient Hindu text, the *Rig Veda,* and Steinbeck has provided as the epigraph a hymn from this classic Sanskrit text.

The changes made in the title during the revisions of the novel, from "To the Unknown God" to "To an Unknown God" and finally to *To a God Unknown* were necessitated, according to Steinbeck, by the shifts in thematic emphasis as well as the meaning of the novel (*SLL* 56, 67). The self-sacrifice made by Joseph Wayne to this Unknown God based on his belief that the universe and he are inseparable may be "unknown" to western readers, but Indian scholars recognize the *Advaidic* or non-dualistic root of that concept. The epigraph to the novel is a clear indicator that Steinbeck must have had more than a passing acquaintance with Vedic texts of ancient India.

Further, Steinbeck himself has provided categorical information about the source of the title for his third work in a letter to a friend:

> The title will be *To a God Unknown.* The transposition in words is necessary to a change in meaning. *The unknown in this case meaning "unexplored." This is taken from the Vedic hymns.* I want no confusion with the unknown God of St. Paul [emphasis added]. (*SLL* 67)

For his novel, Steinbeck has drawn from the Hindu sources not only the title, but the main symbol of a monolithic rock,[2] a legend[3] (Thomas 67), a form of worship, and the name *Rama*[4] for one of the main characters. Endorsement comes from an early Steinbeck scholar: "This epigraph, together with the name of the characters (Rama, wife of Thomas) and the novel's title, indicates one area of the novel's reference, the monistic and pantheistic philosophy based on the ancient sacred literature of Hinduism" (Lisca 37–38). One Indian critic has already pointed out that "the sacred rock" which plays a crucial role in the spiritual progress as well as in Joseph's final sacrifice "represents the Hindu God, Lord Shiva" (Sathyanarayana 97).

Joseph's discovery of this "sacred rock," described by him as "ancient and holy" (*TAGU* 32) is accidental, in true Indian tradition. According to Indian legends, the chosen man has a dream about the holy place or is led to it by a strange coincidence. A close reading of Steinbeck's descriptions of the "holy place" reveals surprising similarities between the grove (30) and a Hindu wall-less temple containing Lord Shiva's form *Lingam*[5] as its main deity:

> They had come to an open glade, nearly circular, and as flat as a pool. The dark trees grew about it, straight as pillars, and jealously close together. In the center of the clearing stood a rock as big as a house, mysterious and huge. It seemed to be shaped, cunningly and wisely, and yet there was no shape in the memory to match it. (31)

Among the numerous explications of the *Lingam*, its enigmatic quality is often stressed: it is acclaimed as the "shapeless shape" —*rupa arupa*, in Sanskrit. The Judeo-Christian memory has indeed no shape to match it (Maxwell 42, passim). A mode of worship in the Shiva temples is the pouring of the sacred water, milk, honey, and other substances considered holy, in an act known as *abhisheham* in Sanskrit. Joseph performs this rite during the drought episode by pouring bucketsful of water over the rock (167). His is an act of appeasement to his personal god at a time of crisis, in true Indian fashion. This monolithic rock or *Lingam*, in a metonymic function, represents the Supreme Being. Indians believe that since this Universe is the creation of *Brahman*, the Cosmic Being, every object in this world is a manifestation of that Supreme Soul, and hence a rock, wood, atom or any other being or object could be considered the minimal aspect or realization of God.

The most important principle is that the underlying theme of *To a God Unknown* is derived from the *Advaitic* concept of non-dualism or monism expressed in the *Upanishads* and popularized by Emerson in America. The Vedantic concept may be summarized thus: the ultimate reality is one undifferentiated homogeneous consciousness called Brahman; the universe is a creative expression of this Brahman under the influence of *maya*; the existence of individual souls and their apparent separation from Brahman is due to this *maya*; once the barriers constituting the illusory differences are removed the souls merge with Brahman (Sharma 202).

Joseph reaches the state of non-dualism on the rock, the *Lingam*, the "shapeless shape." This rich symbol shows in material form the merger of all dualities in the Universe, the negative and the positive, the neutrons and the protons, the male and the female, the *Atman* [the individual soul] and the *Brahman* [The Supreme Being] (Sharma 1–10).

If some American readers and critics find that *To a God Unknown*, one of Steinbeck's earliest works, is not mature enough, nor a great artistic success, and is even "corny," a more weighty illustration can be offered in *The Grapes of Wrath*, where Casy declares: "There was the hills, an' there was me, an' we wasn't separate no more. We was one thing. An' that one thing was holy" (110). Tom expresses this abstract concept of Casy's in his own native idiom: "Says one time he went out in the wilderness to find his own soul, an' he foun' he didn' have no soul that was his'n. Says he foun' he jus' got a little piece of a great big soul. Says a wilderness ain't no good, 'cause his little piece of a soul wasn't no good 'less it was with the rest, an' was whole" (570).

The non-dualistic philosophy envisages that every atom of the living and non-living things originates from and ultimately merges with the Universal Being, and therefore deserves due respect and veneration. (This concept is more inclusive than the medieval theory of the Great Chain of Being. The Eastern concept embraces even non-living things as possible receptacles and manifestation of the Supreme Being.) Accordingly, the Joads, the turtle, the ant, the wild oat's seeds (as portrayed in Chapter 3 of *The Grapes of Wrath*) are all parts of the Universal Soul.

Steinbeck makes an overt statement of this concept in *The Log from the Sea of Cortez:*

it seems apparent that species are only commas in a sentence, that each species is at once the point and the base of a pyramid, that all life is relational to the point where an Einsteinian relativity seems to emerge. And then not only the meaning but the feeling about species grows misty. One merges into another, groups melt into ecological groups until the time when what we know as life meets and enters what we think of as non-life: barnacle and rock, rock and earth, earth and tree, tree and rain and air. And the units nestle into the whole and are inseparable from it. (178)

In an earlier passage from *The Log from the Sea of Cortez* (where also he talks about Emerson and his concept of Over Soul), Steinbeck has made a categorical declaration about his adherence to the Indian concept of non-dualistic being:

> The whole is necessarily everything, the whole world of fact and fancy, body and psyche, physical fact and spiritual truth, individual and collective, life and death, macrocosm and microcosm (the greatest quanta here, the greatest synapse between the two), conscious and unconscious, subject and object. The whole picture is portrayed by *is*, the deepest word of deep ultimate reality, not shallow or partial as reasons are, but deeper and participating, possibly encompassing the Oriental concept of *being*. (125)

Even though this concept has been analyzed from an ecological/ environmental angle, and quite plausible and acceptable theoretical positions have been taken by scientists and literary scholars in the recent book, *Steinbeck and the Environment: Interdisciplinary Approaches*, there is a mystical tone present in many passages of *The Log from the Sea of Cortez*, which justifies the "holistic vision" and the philosophical slant this paper has ascribed to Steinbeck's views on man and his world. Chapter 14 of *The Log from the Sea of Cortez* is so full of speculative philosophy—with sprinklings of words such as "being," "living into," "all-truth," "infinite whole"—that one cannot but conclude on the positive influence of Oriental thought on Steinbeck's writing.

Steinbeck's statements in *The Log from the Sea of Cortez* endear him to the Indian reader, the kinship having been established at the intellectual and philosophical level. Steinbeck attributes in an open manner the link between his non-teleological philosophy and the Oriental concept of oneness of all living things. In an oft-quoted passage, Steinbeck declares:

> Non-teleological ideas derive through "is" thinking, associated with natural selection as Darwin seems to have understood it. They imply depth, fundamentalism, and clarity—seeing beyond traditional or personal projections. They consider events as out-growths and expressions rather than as results; conscious accep-tance as a desideratum, and certainly as an important prerequi-site. Non-teleological thinking concerns itself primarily not with what should be, or could be, but rather with what actually "is".
> . . . (112)

This word, "is," synonym for "being," had been earlier consid-ered by Steinbeck as "the deepest word of deep ultimate reality," taking him to higher realms of Indian philosophy.

A corollary to the non-dualistic philosophy is the concept of *maya*, part of a doctrine of Reality as non-dual. This concept at-tempts to explain the experience of multiplicity by assigning to it some kind of ontological status. What is perceived by one can be illusory and the truth of the matter can be the opposite of it. Steinbeck's light-hearted version of the concept of *maya* is *Can-nery Row*, which shows "whores, pimps, gamblers, and sons of bitches" through one peephole. Through another peephole, the same persons are revealed as "Saints and angels and martyrs and holy men" (*CR* 1).

Steinbeck's angle of vision of the wastrels of Cannery Row is quite uncannily reminiscent of the vibrant and iconoclastic per-ception of a modern saint of India, Swamy Vivekananda. In one of his speeches made in the West, Vivekananda declared, send-ing shock waves through the minds of his cultured audience:

> The woman in the street, or the thief in the jail, is the Christ that is being sacrificed that you may be a good man. Such is the law of balance . . . All the thieves and the murderers, all the unjust, the weakest, the wickedest, the devils, they are all my Christ! That is my doctrine . . . I have to sneer at the woman walking in the street, because society wants it. She, my saviour, she whose street-walking is the cause of the chastity of other women! Think

of that! . . . Whom shall I blame? Whom shall I praise? Both sides
of the shield must be seen. (Tapasyananda 184–85)

It is amazing that Steinbeck could see "both sides of the shield"
in such an unpanicky manner, the whole point missed by the
Western detractors of Steinbeck; they blame it on the author's
sentimentality, whereas this Indian reader can see it for what it
exactly is—Steinbeck's affinity with the Indian thought!

Steinbeck's appeal crosses national boundaries in another significant way. The Steinbeck protagonist is generally a deprived
individual who fights courageously for his needs as well as to
retain his integrity and dignity. This "underdog" condition/
status has always a particular appeal to the Indian sensibility
due to our more than 300 years' colonized status. The Joads, Jim,
Joseph Wayne, George and Lennie, the inhabitants of the Pastures of Heaven, Pepé, and a host of others are specimens of
mankind who have to struggle for their basic needs and peace
of mind, but often in vain. Through their fight against formidable
forces which too often overcome them, these men and women
come closer to the Indian reader's heart, followed by an empathetic process of identification.

A third factor that makes Steinbeck a favorite among the
Indian/Eastern readers is the absence of any despair in his fiction, perhaps with a couple of exceptions such as *In Dubious
Battle*. Even though Steinbeck dons the robe of a satirist, he cannot simply give up on humanity. Readers in the East have generally found the nihilistic, absurd vision of the great modernists
such as Hemingway, Kafka, Camus, Becket *et al* a bit unconvinc-
ing and life-denying. The arid, humorless and rather mechani-
cal Mersaults and Ks of the celebrated fictions of the world mas-
ters leave the Indian readers cold and uninspired.

The reasons for such a response are not far to seek. Westerners
have gone through a religious crisis during the late nineteenth
and early twentieth century, driving them to a faithless condition or to a belief in the Absurd vision of humanity. On the other
hand, Indians have not experienced any crisis of faith, anyway
not recognizable or with any sizable impact. So the existentialist
philosophy has only a limited appeal to the imagination of East-
erners. They find Steinbeck's affirmation of life and his celebra-

tion of human spirit quite meaningful and exhilarating. In *The Grapes of Wrath,* in spite of all his fierce denunciations and wry satire, Steinbeck is a mellowed, optimistic and kind sage and seer. So he declares:

> This you may say of man—when theories change and crash, when schools, philosophies, when narrow dark alleys of thought, national, religious, economic, grow and disintegrate, man reaches, stumbles forward, painfully, mistakenly, sometimes. Having stepped forward, he may slip back, but only half a step, never the full step back. This you may say and know it. (204–05)

Steinbeck's Nobel Prize acceptance speech that "a writer who does not passionately believe in the perfectibility of man has no dedication nor any membership in literature" strikes a perfect chord in the undespairing Indian/Eastern mind.

The feature of sentimentality, though condemned by almost all the Western critics as a negative aspect of Steinbeck (or any other writer), is considered more positively in the Indian perspective. Adopting a sentimental view is natural to a compassionate and comprehending person, whose worldview enables him/her an understanding beyond dry logic. A coldly objective western mind may abhor that art which has a maudlin element in it, but Indians delight in sentimentality. So they love the climactic scenes of *The Grapes of Wrath* and *Of Mice and Men,* the scenes in *Tortilla Flat, Cannery Row,* and *The Moon Is Down.* Man is, after all, a bundle of emotions, sweet and bitter, and a writer such as Steinbeck is loved since he portrays such basic emotions in a dramatic and convincing fashion.

Certain aspects of the contemporary urban Indian scene serve as a vital factor in Steinbeck's appeal to the modern man everywhere. The "dubious battles" being fought on the Indian streets today for religious, regional, casteistic, linguistic and economic causes have turned India into a strife-torn land. For that matter, most countries suffer from such strife. Steinbeck's analysis of the "dubious battle" in the Californian orchards and his implied suggestions through the portrayal of the bitterness generated on both sides have very valid hints for the embattled psyche of the modern man. A calm awareness of the issues involved, an objective attitude toward all persons, and a readiness to understand the 'other', opposite point of view, as suggested by Steinbeck, are quite relevant to any country of the world today.

A great writer transcends his age and his environment, and affects readers going beyond boundaries. That Steinbeck belongs to that class is a matter of quiet pride for Steinbeck scholars the world over.

9

Living In(tension)ally

Steinbeck's The Log from the Sea of Cortez as a Reflection of the Balance Advocated in Lao Tze's Tao Teh Ching

Michael J. Meyer

Although Steinbeck did not own a copy of Lao Tze's book, the text was available to him at Ed Ricketts's lab. The Log from the Sea of Cortez is evidence that Steinbeck was undoubtedly influenced by Taoism, and that, indeed, Taoist thinking and Lao Tze's thoughts extend widely into the Steinbeck canon.

When Peter Lisca's second book on Steinbeck, *John Steinbeck: Nature and Myth,* appeared in 1978, few were surprised when he pointed out the strong influence of Eastern philosophy, especially Lao Tze's *Tao Teh Ching,* on Steinbeck's *Cannery Row.* Noting that two well-known editions of the text by Witter Bynner (1944) and Lin Yutang (1942) had been published just previously to the novel, Lisca contended that Steinbeck was familiar with *The Way* and cited Steinbeck's words in *The Journal of a Novel* as evidence. There, Lisca reminds us, Steinbeck lists Lao Tze along with Plato, Christ and Buddha as "one of the great ones" (183). In addition, Lisca also uses textual evidence from *Cannery Row* and the letters and unpublished papers of Ed Ricketts to support his argument that many of the basic principles of the *Tao* are generally visible throughout Steinbeck's post-war novel and that specific passages of the text are reinterpreted and rephrased by Steinbeck as if designed for digestion by a more modern audience (116–23).[1]

In fact, many Steinbeck texts, notably *Tortilla Flat, The Wayward Bus* and *East of Eden,* contain a central story which retells a classic—reinterpreting the tales of King Arthur and the knights of the Round Table, the play *Everyman,* and the myth of Cain and Abel. Other Steinbeck titles further indicate the author's interest in revisiting texts. For example, *The Winter of Our Discontent* reiterates Shakespearean and Biblical themes, and *Of Mice and Men* and *The Grapes of Wrath* both contain echoes of events in Greek mythology. In each work Steinbeck modernizes the message to make it more accessible and relevant to twentieth century readers. Later in his career he spent a good deal of time rewriting Malory's *Morte D'Arthur* as *The Acts of King Arthur and His Noble Knights.* Thus, it is not far-fetched to believe that he also found an opportunity to rewrite or reinterpret some of the insights in Lao Tze's great masterwork, incorporating it not only into *Cannery Row,* but into much of his later fiction and non-fiction as well.

Although Steinbeck did not own Lao Tze's book, a copy of it was available to him in Ed Ricketts's library, as Robert DeMott has noted (67). Since this information was not available to Lisca in 1978, his assertions regarding the Taoist principles incorporated in *Cannery Row* seem all the more perceptive and convincing. This study will carry his observations further, extending them to *The Log From the Sea of Cortez,* Steinbeck's non-fictional account of his voyage to Mexico's Gulf of California in 1940, and arguing that Lao Tze's precepts as found in the *Tao* (also known as *The Way*) greatly influenced Steinbeck's thought, perhaps to a far greater extent than Lisca envisioned.[2]

Taoism's rejection of the desire for material goods, fame, power and even the holding of fixed or strong opinions (Lisca, *Nature and Myth* 118) may be the most important factor in Steinbeck's initial fascination with the religious tenets proffered in the text. Both Jackson J. Benson and Jay Parini have suggested that Steinbeck feared that wealth and success would cause artistic failure as a writer. Steinbeck's letters offer further evidence of the author's desire to enjoy the simple pleasures and to cultivate the inner life. For example, in an April 1939 letter to his friend Carlton Sheffield, he writes about going into seclusion: "I don't know how long I'll be away. A month or so anyway. It serves a valuable purpose too—gets me out from under the mess of this book" (qtd. in Benson 397).

Using Huston Smith's breakdown of essential Taoist beliefs in his *The World's Religions* (196–220), it is possible to trace even more closely the parallels between Steinbeck's philosophical expressions from *The Log from the Sea of Cortez* and those expressed by Lao Tze in the *Tao*. Of central importance are the abilities to prefer creative quietude to force and to understand that polar opposites have interrelationships as well as differences; other shared qualities are the desire to seek inner peace and the difficulty of putting the meaning of *The Way* into language, resorting to symbols instead; all can also be found in Steinbeck and Ricketts's *The Log from the Sea of Cortez*.

Smith lists creative quietude as the first essential of the *Tao*, and clearly Steinbeck explains in *The Log* what Lao Tze calls *wei wu wei*—doing not doing (*World's Religions* 204, 207–11). Followers of Taoism believe that things happen effortlessly without interference of the conscious will, as indicated in this quotation:

> Less and less do you need to force things
> Until finally you arrive at non-action.
> Where nothing is done, nothing is left undone.
> . . . .
> True mastery can be gained by letting things go their way.
> It can't be gained by interfering. (Lao Tze ch. 48)[3]

Some critics of Eastern philosophy have misinterpreted this Taoist principle as advocating passivity and non-action and dismissed it as diminishing human intellect. Smith, however, defines *wei wu wei* as allowing genuine creation, as releasing the subliminal self, as letting go and allowing the conscious mind to relax and stop standing in its own light (*World's Religions* 208).

In the *Tao*, Lao Tze similarly suggests that it is possible to find perfect harmony with the way things are. In order to foster such thoughts, however, the art of contemplation must be practiced and the most obvious solutions to dilemmas must be discarded. In the process, believers in the *Tao* will find there is supreme power in "the suppleness, simplicity and freedom that flows from us, or rather through us, when our private egos and conscious efforts yield to a power not their own" (Smith, *World's Religions* 208). Only then will they understand that the way to do is "to be." Like Junius Maltby of *The Pastures of Heaven*, Lao Tze invites readers to attain education through what others deem laziness or sloth. Like Casy in *The Grapes of Wrath,* Lao Tze encourages a contemplative time in the wilderness where individuals observe valid connections or relationships between opposites (like religious precepts and sexuality). Like Kino in *The Pearl,* Lao contends that men can only understand true wealth through poverty. Finally, The Master advocates, as does Steinbeck in *The Log From the Sea of Cortez,* that individuals inevitably discover new insights through contemplation and unintended probing. Steinbeck states in *The Log* that his journey on *The Western Flyer* was not only a practical voyage to obtain biological data and animal life which would sustain Ricketts's business, but it was later transformed into "[a] search for something that [seems] like truth to us; [a] search for understanding; . . . for that principle which keys us deeply into the pattern of all life; [a] search for the relations of things, one to another" (92).

Of all Steinbeck's works, *The Log* espouses a personal contemplative effort similar to that recorded in the *Tao.* For example, he seeks a "warm wholeness, wherein every sight and object and odor and experience seems to key into a gigantic whole" (101), a place where even "human sacrifice has the same effect of creating a wholeness of sense and emotion—the good and bad, beautiful, ugly, and cruel all welded into one thing" (101). As Richard Astro writes regarding Ed Ricketts's philosophical influence on Steinbeck, Ricketts hoped that his friend would reach a plateau where the ultimate and best writers discover "there is no right and wrong, all things are 'right,' including both right and wrong; and there are no clay feet, although the poet will know clearly about the things called 'clay feet.'" Eventually he will also "attain a 'creative synthesis,' an 'emergent viewpoint' as [he livesl into the whole and know[s] that 'it's right, it's alright,' the 'good,' the 'bad,' whatever is" (33).

In the Easter Sunday chapter of *The Log,* Steinbeck labels such attempts to find wholeness as non-teleological, mirroring the Taoist principle of just being, or *wu wei:*

> In their sometimes intolerant refusal to face facts as they are, teleological notions may substitute a fierce but ineffectual attempt to change conditions which are assumed to be undesirable, in place

of the understanding-acceptance which would pave the way for a more sensible attempt at any change which might still be indicated. (112)

Later in the same chapter, Steinbeck advocates non-teleology as a way for men to "break through" to larger understandings than at first seem possible or probable. Like Lao Tze, Steinbeck would have his readers accept what *is* rather than force or impose an unnatural order.

Non-teleology, as Steinbeck defines it in the fourteenth chapter of *The Log*, provides the opportunity to see beyond traditional and personal patterns. It concerns itself not with what should be but rather with what actually is. It does not attempt to ask why, nor does it presume an end pattern in which conditions are better than what they originally were (138). The precept of non-teleology concurs with Lao Tze's precepts in the *Tao* when he concedes that "all calculated systems, every attempt to arrange life in apple pie order is pointless and that man's general tendency is to approach life in the wrong modes, ones which will create acrimony rather than peace" (Smith, *World's Religions* 210). As Lao Tze says:

Look, and it can't be seen,
Listen, and it can't be heard,
Reach, and it can't be grasped,
. . . .
Approach it and there is no beginning
Follow it and there is no end (ch. 14)

Therefore, Steinbeck argues for non-teleological approaches primarily because all teleologies assume a common *post hoc ergo propter hoc* pattern. Rather than attempting to answer the already sufficiently difficult question of what or how, teleologies concentrate on the impossible why. In a manner reminiscent of a passage from the *Tao*, Steinbeck is in agreement with Lao Tze that there can be no definitive answer to that sensitive question: Why? Instead there can only be "pictures which become larger and more significant as one's horizon increases" (*LSC* 113). Compare Lao Tze:

You can't know it, but you can be it,
at ease with your own life.
Just realize where you come from:
this is the essence of wisdom. (ch. 14)

Yet despite the human realization that relative answers are the only ones that are truly available, Steinbeck points out in *The Log* that humans often defy the Taoist principles of wholeness by insisting on a definitive response; a common human tendency is to embrace deceiving absolutes and dismiss opportunities for wholeness. Such absolutes are, according to Steinbeck, "wishful thinking" although he concedes that "everyone continually searches for absolutisms" and "imagines continually that he finds them" (117). Since human desire for definitive answers involves a need to be in charge rather than to rely on non-active waiting, it is difficult for any individual to engage in what Smith labels "alert-waiting," sitting with a blank mind, arriving at pure consciousness and attaining peace and stillness and selflessness in an aura of emotional calm (*Religions of Man* 202).

Since contemplative seeking evaluates all possibilities, it holds that considering all truth is an attainable goal. As a result, the seekers and practitioners of non-teleology embrace not only traditional teleologies of their pasts but also acknowledge error as part of the whole picture of truth, since many times errors contain a part of truth, even if it is restricted. Steinbeck encourages readers of *The Log* to attempt to "live into" situations. Like Lao Tze, Steinbeck offers his readers an escape from the guilt and fear associated with assuming responsibility for actions. Nothing need be condoned or extenuated, says Steinbeck; it just *is* (121). Such Taoist acceptance of non-action will then provide "the crust to break through," moving beyond blame or cause to understand the union of two opposing viewpoints," a breakthrough which "very frequently sheds light over the larger picture, providing a key which may unlock levels not accessible to either of the teleological viewpoints" (123).

Such dialectical oppositions also suggest Smith's second element in his analysis of Taoist belief: the relativity of all values and the correlate of this principle, the identity of all contraries (*World's Religions* 214). The inherent dualism of the *Tao* must have fascinated Steinbeck who often mentions the appeal of paradoxes in his philosophical musings in *The Log from the Sea of Cortez*. Indeed, Taoism is generally associated with the traditional Asian symbolism of a circle containing two equal parts, yin and yang. Yin, pictured with the color black, stands for a passive approach while the white, yang, implies active pursuit of a goal. Jointly, they reflect life's basic oppositions: sun / moon, positive / negative, light / dark, summer / winter, male / female, dry / wet (*Religions of Man* 211). Yet though such principles remain in tension, they are not flatly opposed to one another; rather they complement and counter-balance one another. Each invades the other's hemisphere and establishes itself in the very center of its opposite's territory. In the end both are resolved in an all-embracing circle, symbol of the final unity suggested in the *Tao*. Constantly turning and interchanging places, the opposites are but phases of a revolving wheel. "Life does not move onward and upward toward a fixed pinnacle or pole," notes Smith. "It bends back on itself until the self to come, full circle, to the realization that all is one and all is well" (*World's Religions* 215).

Lao Tze expresses this view in several chapters of the *Tao*, notably in chapter 2, where he states:

When people see some things as beautiful,
Other things become ugly.
When people see some things as good,
Other things become bad.
Being and non-being create each other.
Difficult and easy support each other.
Long and short define each other.

High and low depend on each other.
Before and after follow each other.

Similarly, in chapter 28, the Master offers the following suggestions for true integrity.

Know the male
Yet keep to the female

. . . .

Know the white
Yet keep to the black:
Be a pattern for the world.

Chapter 26 also records Lao Tze's belief in the interaction of opposites by stating "The heavy is the root of light. The unmoved is the source of all movement."

A similar discussion of the premises of yin and yang can also be found in *The Log* where Steinbeck examines the existence of ethical paradoxes and moral ambiguity as a major dilemma that needs to be faced by all human beings. Reflecting on the contradictions he has observed on the collecting voyage, he states: "We have definitions of good qualities and bad; not changing things, but generally considered good and bad throughout the ages and throughout the species." He then continues by pointing out that "so-called and considered good qualities are invariable concomitants of failure, while the bad ones are the cornerstones of success" (80).

Steinbeck's assessment holds that all human beings perceive themselves in a simplistic way, torn between two alternatives. Not surprisingly then, his text, like Lao Tze's, suggests the difficulty individuals encounter in seeing the integrated whole while maintaining labels which suggest the existence of polar opposites. Steinbeck asks his readers to confront the inextricable interrelationships of opposites even if such relationships seem highly unlikely. Steinbeck wants to stress, as Lao Tze did:

If you wish to shrink something,
You must first allow it to expand.
If you wish to get rid of something,
You must first allow it to flourish.
If you wish to take something,
You must first allow it to be given. (ch. 36)

Throughout *The Log*, Steinbeck repeatedly affirms the interrelationship of opposites: "bad grows toward good;" he writes, "and down toward up, until our little mechanism hope . . . manages to warp our whole world. . . . [Hope] cushions the shock of experience, that one trait that balances the directionalism of another" (72). Elsewhere in *The Log*, Steinbeck remarks: "Any investigation . . . will run into the brick wall of the *impossibility* of perfection while at the same time insisting on the *validity* of perfection" (124). And in chapter 14, he speaks of combining "fact and fancy, body and psyche, physical fact and spiritual truth, individual and collective, life and death, macrocosm and microcosm, . . . conscious and unconscious, subject and object" (125). The whole (like Taoism's circle) is necessarily composed of everything "deeper and participating, possibly encompassing the Oriental concept of *being*" (125). From his close observation of the paradoxes he found in the waters off the Baja coast, he drew philosophical conclusions that coincided with those expressed in the *Tao*.

Finally, in chapter 16, Steinbeck reiterates his belief in the balance suggested by the circle symbol, asserting: "Everything is potentially everywhere. . . . These things are balanced. A man is potentially all things too, greedy and cruel, capable of great love or great hatred" (136). He goes on to compare man to "two animals, and yet the same thing—something the early Church would have been forced to call a mystery" (136). And he reflects that "only in laziness [meaning non-action] can one achieve a state of contemplation which is a balancing of values, a weighing of oneself against the world and the world against itself. A busy man cannot find time for such balancing" (151). Indeed, in Mack and the boys' "laziness" in *Cannery Row*, Steinbeck praises a "balanced" life in which individuals are not overwhelmed by work but take time to contemplate and appreciate the world around them.

In short, both Taoism and Steinbeck eschew simplistic dichotomies by realizing that no perspective can be considered absolute—even Steinbeck's own ideals as he moved from his 1930s focus on the behavior of men in groups to his focus on individual moral responsibility in his later work. Therefore, Steinbeck's comments in the 1930s about the necessity of men to form groups in order to attain any goal may be as true as his later remarks that nothing ever was accomplished by a group and that it is only through the single clear mind that any progress is made (*EOE* 132).[4] Consequently, this apparent contradiction cannot be read as some Steinbeck critics would contend—as evidence of the author's vacillation and his inability or unwillingness to defend a philosophy. Instead of a change of mind, it may more accurately be seen as evidence of his adherence to a major Taoist principle, the belief that yin and yang always intersect and are true at the same time.

Besides the significant concepts of *wei wu wei* and *yin and yang*, several other Taoist precepts evident in *The Log from the Sea of Cortez* and elsewhere in the Steinbeck canon solidify claims that the *Tao* and its philosophical base form an important core of Steinbeck's personal beliefs, beliefs that regularly appear in his writing.

The Master finds value in emptiness, comparing it to a bellows that is never exhausted and continues to pump out air without exertion. He urges followers to "coax your mind from wandering/ and keep to the original oneness/ . . . let your body become/ supple as a newborn child's" (ch. 10). Steinbeck similarly espouses avoiding stress and strain when he states: "We do not think a lazy man can commit murders, nor great thefts, nor lead a mob. He would be more likely to think about it and laugh. And a nation of lazy contemplative men would be incapable of fighting a war unless their very laziness were attacked. Wars are the activities of busy-ness" (151). Surely this passage advocates the development of the inner spirit of men and women finding contentment in mild rather than forceful movement.

Lao Tze's concept of flexibility also needs to be developed by a believer in *The Way*. For example, in chapter 76, Lao Tze states:

> Men are born soft and supple;
> dead, they are stiff and hard
> Plants are born tender and pliant;
> dead, they are brittle and dry.
> . . . .
> The hard and the stiff will be broken.
> The soft and supple will prevail.

A similar message is communicated in the Master's words in chapter 9, where he says:

Fill your bowl to the brim
and it will spill.
Keep sharpening your knife
and it will blunt.

That Steinbeck is a similar advocate of human flexibility can be shown by his comments in chapter 16 of *The Log*. Reacting with wonder to some of the unlikely observations and conclusions he has drawn from the voyage of *The Western Flyer*, he states: "the process of gathering knowledge does not lead to knowing. . . . An answer is invariably the parent of a great family of new questions. So we draw worlds and fit them like tracings against the world around us and crumple them when they do not fit and draw new ones" (137). Of course, a flexible attitude is required for such action.

Yet another tenet expressed in the *Tao* is the inability of the Master to express its truth in a formal language or to use words to define the Way: "when you have names and forms know that they are provisional" (ch. 32). When the Master tries to express his insights, he inevitably finds words and language inadequate for the task:

But words that point to the Tao
Seem monotonous and without flavor
When you look for it, there is nothing to see
When you listen for it, there is nothing to hear
When you use it, it is inexhaustible. (ch. 35)

That Steinbeck felt similarly about his ability to express his Taoist thought in words is evident on the last page of *The Log*, as he attempts to draw conclusions about his discoveries, to express the way in which the marine life he had observed provided lessons for his own life. He states: "There was some quality of music here, perhaps not to be communicated, but sounding clear and huge in our minds" (224). Yet the so-called "real-picture," Steinbeck is quick to point out, is primarily incommunicable because it is a product of pure thought.[5] Similarly, just as Lao Tze envisions the *Tao* as teaching without words (ch. 43; ch. 2), so Steinbeck speaks of trying to find symbols for the wordlessness in his *Journal of a Novel*. In addition, when Lao Tze claims that "Those who know don't talk. Those who talk don't know." (ch. 56), Steinbeck seems to recognize in *The Log* the risks he takes by attempting to transmit the insights he has gained and by trying to explain his radical new philosophy through a language which may impede rather than foster understanding. Steinbeck's task, like Lao Tze's, was to try to transcribe (albeit incompletely and imperfectly) by means of imagery the complexity of thoughts that defy the ability of language.

If language proves inadequate for expressing *The Way*, symbols are often more effective. The primary image used by Lao Tze to describe the tenets of the *Tao* is water. Water, in fact, serves as a metaphor by which Lao Tze can reach his reader's consciousness and help him to conceive what seems improbable when expressed in language. Water is also a powerful signifier for Steinbeck. As Smith points out, water in the *Tao* illustrates the power of *wei wu wei*, doing not doing. (*World's Religions* 209–10). Moving gently forward, seeking its own level, adapting to its surroundings, water to Lao Tze offers a perfect example of how man should act. In quietude, water possesses both yin and yang. It can become stagnant and prove a home for death and decay, or it can become very clear and lucid, allowing the observer to see deeply and observe what is at the bottom of things. Despite its apparent weaknesses, water is strong enough to support ships and ocean liners and, after an amount of time, it is capable of wearing away the hardest stone. Appropriately, it also possesses the quality of flexibility so desired by Lao Tze and Steinbeck as a human trait; its willingness to bend when confronted with opposition is in communion with its ability to be either a source of life or a source of death.

The Steinbeck canon, of course, is also rich in water imagery, as David Cassuto has demonstrated in his analysis of *The Grapes of Wrath*. One need only recall the river and the flood in *Grapes*, the drought and need for rain in *To a God Unknown*, the little pool where George meets Lennie in *Of Mice and Men*, the frog pond and the tidal pool in *Cannery Row* and *Sweet Thursday*, and Ethan's place (the ocean cave) in *The Winter of Our Discontent* to be aware of a recurring use of an image that offers both positive and negative (yin and yang) connotations. Water can be both harsh and mild, can imply laughter or tears, can cause joy or pain. As a symbol for the wordlessness, it helps Steinbeck express the inexpressible. As Lao Tze reminds us, "The great Tao flows everywhere" (ch. 34) "The supreme good is like water, / which nourishes all things without trying to. / It is content with the low places that people disdain. / This is like the Tao" (ch. 8). If, as Lao Tze asserts, "It [the Tao] flows through all things, / inside and outside, and returns / to the origins of all things" (ch. 25) then water is an appropriate way for each author to express the paradoxical qualities that typify both Taoist thought and Steinbeckian philosophy.

In fact, Steinbeck's connection to Eastern thought—particularly Taoism—may account for the author's popularity in Asia, especially in Japan, where Steinbeck scholarship has been fostered for over 30 years. Certainly, Asian scholars have recognized that in spite of the fact that Steinbeck's stories are about a western culture and contain western values, they also reflect the code of ethics and religious expression of Far Eastern thought, embracing duality and flexibility, seeing paradoxical items as related or as integral parts of attaining wholeness and complete integration of opposite ways of knowing. By understanding that Lao Tze's treatises exist in tandem with *The Log*, readers will no doubt discover why Steinbeck advocated living in(tension)ally in the balance advocated by the old master, a wise teacher whose text is, even today, the third most translated document in the world.

10

Recent Steinbeck Dramatic Adaptations in Japan

Hiromasa Takamura

Between 1994 and 1995, three dramatic adaptations of Steinbeck's novels Of Mice and Men, The Grapes of Wrath, *and* East of Eden *were produced in Japan. Prior to that, only* Of Mice and Men *had been seen on the Japanese stage, and that only three times in the years between 1939 and 1993. Takamura comments on each production in the 1990s and suggests reasons for the resurgence of interest in Steinbeck's work in Japan.*

John Steinbeck's books, particularly *The Grapes of Wrath,* are ubiquitous in Japan. Since translation of part of the novel in 1939, there have been at least eight different Japanese translations of *The Grapes of Wrath* as well as five of *Of Mice and Men,* while a sixth one came out in 2001. An ambitious project to translate and/or retranslate all of Steinbeck's books by leading Steinbeck scholars into contemporary Japanese was completed in 2001. In spite of the popularity of Steinbeck's novels in Japan, however, dramatic productions have been infrequent. The first performance of a Steinbeck play in Japan was *Of Mice and Men,* staged by an independent theater group in 1939. In the 54 years between 1939 and 1993 *Of Mice and Men* was staged only three times: In 1950, the first commercial stage production played in Tokyo, and in 1957 it was staged again in Tokyo. No other work of Steinbeck was performed at all. But in the 1990s a renewed interest in Steinbeck was apparent, reflected in part by three much-heralded dramatic adaptations.

Since the Meiji Restoration in 1868, Japan has been open to foreign plays, almost always through translation, ranging from those of Shakespeare to off-Broadway plays. Works by Henrik Ibsen, Eugene O'Neill, Tennessee Williams, and Arthur Miller have substantially influenced the development of the modern Japanese theater. While foreign theaters have little impact on the lineage of such traditional Japanese theaters as Noh, Bunraku, or Kabuki, the influences of foreign theaters cannot be ignored when discussing the development of many modern theaters in Japan which have produced both Japanese plays and Western ones in Japanese. Indeed, Japanese audiences have shown un-flagging interest in foreign plays and playwrights for over a century. In 1898, the Shimpa Geki (New School of Theater) started in Tokyo, and the actor Otojiro Kawakami and his wife, Sadayakko, went to the United States as the first Japanese actor and actress of straight plays to cross the Pacific Ocean. They went abroad three times and came back to Japan in 1901 to per-form adapted plays of Shakespeare. The Shingeki (the Japanese modern theater) began in 1907, and the history of the modern Japanese theater started then.

At present there are about 350 modern professional theater groups in Japan, including the Gekidan Shiki, the Haiyuza The-ater, and the Takarazuka Revue Company with its female-only cast, which performs at both the Takarazuka Grand Theater (2,527 seats) and the Tokyo Takarazuka Theater (2,000 seats, to be rebuilt in 2001). The Globe Tokyo (713 seats), a replica of the Globe Theatre in London, annually performs approximately 40 plays, including about four Shakespearean plays. Such large theater groups as the Haiyuza or the Mingei produce about ten plays a year and travel with their repertories around the coun-try. Each touring theater usually performs for two days in every city it visits. Some of these groups have their own theaters. The Shiki has five theaters of its own in Tokyo, Sapporo, Nagoya, Osaka, and Fukuoka. One of the Shiki's longest-running shows, *The Phantom of the Opera*, has been performed 2,160 times in ten years, and 2.34 million people have seen it. Modern theater in Japan reflects the country's rich cultural diversity.

In spite of the popularity of translated and imported plays, Japanese audiences had to wait nearly 40 years before they could see a production of a Steinbeck play other than *Of Mice and Men*. In 1994 and 1995, however, there were three significant productions of Steinbeck's plays—all in Japanese by Japanese performers. The staging of *The Grapes of Wrath* by the Mingei Theater in Tokyo in 1994 closely followed the highly acclaimed Steppenwolf Theater's adaptation of the novel. It was performed only in Tokyo for 19 days, and the house was nearly always packed. In the same year, Japanese audiences enjoyed *Of Mice and Men* presented by the Haiyuza Theater Group in Tokyo. And in 1995, a unique production of *East of Eden* was produced, the Takarazuka Revue Company's musical adaptation. The Company claimed that it was the world's first musical derived from the novel. For the past 80 years the Takarazuka Revue Company, with theaters in Takarazuka and Tokyo, has been a successful all-actress revue group performing musicals. The group is unique, and entrance requirements for the actresses are very tough. There are difficult examinations and auditions, but many young girls (only those from 15 to 18 years old are eligible) want to enter the Revue Company's training school to wear their Kimono uniforms, to live in the dormitory, and ultimately to perform in one of the productions the company makes each year.

I

One underlying reason for Steinbeck's recent popularity is the Japanese identification and sympathy with Steinbeck's pacific worldview, a holistic view of man and nature. Unlike Ernest Hemingway, for example, who, in the minds of many Japanese, cultivated a macho American image in both life and in his fiction, Steinbeck empathizes with the deprived, the suffering, and the weak. Hemingway eulogizes the winner—at least he praises the indestructible man even if he may be defeated. In the Japanese consciousness, Hemingway is the American embodiment of the samurai tradition of stoicism and excellence in swordsmanship, while Steinbeck has affinity with the farmers who have endured under the oppression of the samurai society. Just as Akira Kurosawa in his classic film, *The Seven Samurai* (1954), depicts the strength and endurance of the peasants who eventually win over the samurai, Steinbeck roots for the powerless and often celebrates their ultimate survival and triumph. As does Steinbeck, Kurosawa focuses more on the weak and vulnerable, and Japanese readers and theater-goers find his viewpoint more akin to their worldview than Hemingway's representation of manhood.

This inclination toward Steinbeck's humane worldview has been accelerated by the social change that Japan has experienced since the "bubble economy" burst in the late 1980s. The prolonged economic recession has caused some to doubt the theory of the survival of the fittest, and instead to look for ways for the less privileged to survive. The economic situation has forced the Japanese to look more critically at social justice. Japan may not need powerful macho role models, but it does need role models who can be more sympathetic toward the suffering people. The Japanese realize that economic prosperity, ephemeral as it was, was possible only with the sacrifice of the weak, such as foreign workers who came to Japan to work manual jobs. In the past the Japanese society had never seen such an influx of foreign manual laborers (630,000), legal or otherwise. This dramatic increase has caused serious social problems such as illegal employee/employer relationships, insufficient medical care for workers, and alleged association with organized crime. The Japanese, however, now realize that they are not only the victims of the economic downturn but also the victimizers of their fellow human beings. In such a climate, Steinbeck seems increasingly relevant.

II

Besides this social and economic undercurrent, there are three other reasons for the recent popularity of Steinbeck, sparking interest in Steinbeck on stage. The surge of interest in Steinbeck in Japan was triggered by the release of the latest film version of *Of Mice and Men* (1992), starring Gary Sinise and John Malkovich as well as by the 1989 dramatization of *The Grapes of Wrath* by the Steppenwolf Theater company, a work that commemorated the 50th year of the novel's publication

Japanese moviegoers loved Gary Sinise's film, *Of Mice and Men*, a faithful remake in color of Lewis Milestone's classic version. Sinise's film, as well as the classic version of *East of Eden* with James Dean—which is regularly shown on TV—and the first appearance in 50 years of the play version of *The Grapes of Wrath*, have all reminded the Japanese of the fact that Americans have not forgotten their proud heritage and the tradition of the American Dream. And they revived Japanese interest in Steinbeck, who looks at the other side of America and Americans with understanding.

Stimulated by the popularity and success of the film version of *Of Mice and Men* in Japan, the Haiyuza Theater Group produced its adaptation in 1994. It ran thirteen days in Tokyo, and was staged again in Osaka to meet the demand in the third largest city in Japan. In the same year, the Mingei Theater produced *The Grapes of Wrath*. Usually, successful commercial plays in Tokyo go on tours to such large cities as Yokohama, Osaka, and Nagoya. Possibly because of the need for a highly mechanized stage (as in the American production, heavy rain fell on the stage during the storm scene) and because of financial restrictions, however, *The Grapes of Wrath* did not travel to any other cities in spite of the expectation of fans living elsewhere. *East of Eden*, by the Takarazuka Revue Company, was received warmly not only by the devoted Takarazukan fans but also by regular theatergoers, and the performance was later marketed on video.

The fine acting was largely responsible for the popularity of *The Grapes of Wrath* production. Translated into fluent spoken Japanese by Hiroko Watanabe and Ikumi Tanno, the play starred Tomoko Naraoka, a seasoned actress, as Ma Joad. Any new adaptation of *The Grapes of Wrath* is inevitably compared to the classic Twentieth Century-Fox film made in 1940, starring Henry Fonda and Jane Darwell who, as Ma Joad, won the Academy Award for Best Supporting Actress. Naraoka acted the part of Ma Joad so energetically and convincingly that she must have reminded many in the audience of the courageous, die-hard mother of Bertolt Brecht's *Mutter Courage und Ihre Kinder* (1941). As Ma, she was also successful because she represented the plight of a great number of migrant manual workers from foreign countries currently working, legally or otherwise, in Japan, as well as many homeless Japanese in big cities. And she embodied the universal motherly strength and compassion essential to unite the disintegrating family, to defend and preserve the disappearing old values, and to comfort and inspire the underprivileged. These feelings resonate in Japan.

The only thing that the audience would have missed in the Japanese version but witnessed in the Steppenwolf production was the starving black man whom Rose of Sharon breastfed at the end, insuring the universal message which that casting conveyed. Rose of Sharon's symbolic gesture to the black actor broadened the universality of the novel's ending; the Japanese version achieved this same sense of universality, however, with its very perspective. The presence of the "Japanese Rose of Sharon," with her English name retained in a California locale, pushed the play's allegorical message toward broader universality. The internationality of the Japanese version paradoxically makes it a far more expressive and richer play because it more compellingly "emphasizes" race, color, nationality, and culture. The very fact of the Japanese cast compensates for the omission of the black actor in the last scene. This could be said of all three versions produced in Japan, or of any other foreign adaptations for that matter, and yet in the case of *The Grapes of Wrath*, particularly the final scene, the blend of cultures enforced Steinbeck's original universal message.

Another aspect of cultural difference conveyed by Tokyo's production of *The Grapes of Wrath* is the audience's awareness of historic relations among Korea, China, and Japan, a situation that parallels that described in *The Grapes of Wrath*. Some in the audience took the confrontation between the oppressors and oppressed as paradoxical precisely because the Asian performers were playing both victimizers and victims. This ironically and dramatically confused the audience as to whose side the performers were really on. This dramatic irony resulted in a unique but important interpretation. Professor Jin Young Choi, commenting on the original *The Grapes of Wrath*, made a similar point about the Koreans' response:

Korean farmers, likewise portrayed in Korean novels, . . . against their every wish, had to emigrate to Manchuria during the Japanese occupation of Korea. Certainly Manchuria was no California to the Korean Okies, but they thought they could build a new life there without oppression. The truth, however, was that they encountered, just as the Joads did, Chinese and indigenous land-owners who tried to and indeed succeeded in exacting a heavy price from the Korean immigrants. The Koreans were discriminated against, persecuted, and exploited. (23)

Here, Chinese and Japanese become the oppressors while Koreans the oppressed. Her explanation of the Korean reading of *The Grapes of Wrath* reminds the Japanese that they themselves were and are potential oppressors.

In short, *The Grapes of Wrath* production in Tokyo conveyed more clearly, perhaps, than the original version a compelling universal message. Although there will always be the conflict between the depriving (victimizers) and the deprived (victims), the latter will eventually have enough courage to take a stand against the former.

III

Of Mice and Men was staged in both Tokyo and Osaka by the Haiyuza Theater with the same staff and cast. Paradoxically, the "unrealistic" stage conventions made the play more compelling for Japanese audiences: Candy's "ancient" dog was offstage and the characters on the stage pretended that the unseen dog was a live one sitting just outside the open door; and Lennie's puppy, which he kills near the end of the play, was a doll. These imagined stage properties, however, did not hamper the audience's full imaginative involvement. On the contrary, because of the unrealistic use of the stage which many in the audience might think similar to that often found in Japanese theaters such as Noh, Bunraku puppet shows, and Kabuki, the audience took Steinbeck's play about the plight of migrant workers as an allegory of all people in the same situation, regardless of their race and nationality. The story conveyed a universal message more forcefully than just "Something that Happened," Steinbeck's original "non-teleological" title for the play.

Jiro Kawarazaki, the Japanese Lennie, was physically much smaller than those Lennies in the three films which many in the audience would have seen: Lon Chaney, Jr. (1939), Randy

Quaid (1982), and John Malkovich (1992), the latter of whom appeared on a pair of elevated shoes in the film as did heroes of the Greek tragedy. But Kawarazaki acted so powerfully that the audience was convinced that he was strong enough to "bust every bone in Curley's hand" and, eventually, break Curley's wife's neck. The Japanese Lennie represented the plight of the migrant workers in Japan (from Iran, the Philippines, or China, for instance), the deprived (the homeless), and the weak (the handicapped), and he reminded the Japanese audiences of the mechanism of Japan's prosperity (the second largest economically developed country in the world) and its fall after the "bubble economy" had burst.

Steinbeck plays have, in short, come to the right place at the right time to succeed—particularly the *East of Eden* production by the Takarazuka Revue Theater. What makes the Takarazuka Revue unique in the theater world is that, unlike Kabuki which is performed all by male players, the Takarazuka's musical players are all actresses. The colorful stage scenes and beautiful actresses of *East of Eden* gave the audience a feeling of a dream being enacted in a fantasy world. Below the surface of the dreamlike beauty, however, lay Steinbeck's persuasive moral message. The Takarazuka version epitomized Steinbeck's two major purposes in writing a novel—education and entertainment—as he says, " . . . but there is one purpose in writing that I can see, beyond simply doing it interestingly. It is the duty of the writer to lift up, to extend, to encourage" (qtd. in Hayashi, *JS on Writing* 33). As in most of his works, Steinbeck suggests here that humanity can better itself. Steinbeck's works, particularly the Takarazuka's *East of Eden*, fit in this pattern. Many in the audience who were first entertained by the enchanting music, the breathtakingly beautiful scenes, and the exciting dances, eventually embraced the musical as something more than a usual Takarazuka revue by the time the final curtain fell.

At first glance, the Takarazuka musical may seem to have replicated on stage Elia Kazan's 1955 film, sequence by sequence, scene by scene. However, there were many important differences and inventions that make the Takarazuka version unique, with one particularly noticeable difference involving two characters, one old and the other new—Lee and Moses. Omitted from Kazan's film, Lee, the central pillar of the Trask family in both the novel and in the 1981 television version, was back with a sense of humor. Moses and children representing Cain's descendants were invented and inserted before the first scene in the chorus to suggest to the audience the significant biblical background of the story (Tani 2). Despite the universal message of *East of Eden,* a boundary, be it cultural, religious, or traditional, certainly exists between the original and the translated version. The Japanese audience, mostly Buddhists and Shintoists, required an introduction to the biblical background of the story, and Masazumi Tani, director, playwright, and poet, thus interpolated the biblical Moses and his children for the benefit of his Japanese audience.

Lee voiced the philosophical aspect of *East of Eden* that was not fully conveyed in Kazan's film. The Takarazuka version, however, more than corrected this defect. Director Masazumi Tani made Hikari Amachi play a dual role, Lee and Moses, a meaningful double casting, indeed. In the very first scene, Moses appeared on the stage surrounded by children to whom he explained what had happened to Cain and Abel, and eventually to Cain's descendants. Amachi, having played Moses, appeared as Lee in the following scene, and the implication of her dual role was apparent as Lee finally helped both Adam Trask and Cal Trask experience an epiphany—to acknowledge true feelings and their genuine love for each other and for all fellow humans through that family-centered love.

The Japanese audience felt deeply sympathetic about the ironical and still most appropriate message that Steinbeck conveys to us through his *East of Eden,* since this musical was played in a city just a few miles away from Kobe, the city devastated by the 1995 Kobe earthquake which claimed the lives of more than six thousand people. Steinbeck's message that all people have to go on living in a fallen world full of tragedy, be it natural or human-made, and that we must have "the courage to be" was one that a Japanese audience in a city so close to Kobe could not help but appreciate. With the famous theme music of the film playing in the opening scene, many who suffered directly or indirectly from the Kobe earthquake took the production as Steinbeck's resounding acknowledgment and encouragement of humankind's gallantry and courage in the face of uncontrol-lable tragedy.

The staging of these three translated and adapted plays was successful not only because the originals were appealing to the readers, but also because the translated plays proved to be so outstanding. Elaine Steinbeck wrote in the pamphlet of the Ta-karazuka's *East of Eden*, "I am sure that my husband would love what has been done to bring it alive for you upon the stage" (52). But what has been done by the Takarazuka theater and the other two plays in Japan proved to be far more diversified than Stein-beck could have imagined. Each production demonstrates that Steinbeck's originals transcend the boundaries of time, place, culture, and race. The success of Steinbeck productions in Japan is mainly caused by three kinds of interactions: between foreign and Japanese cultures, between the depriving and the deprived, and between the past and present of Japanese social, political, and moral contexts. Today, foreign actors and actresses may well have greater opportunities than do their original English and American counterparts to become keenly aware of Steinbeck's original message. Cultural "boundaries" surely exist and can-not be crossed over easily without additional explanations (i.e., the Biblical background for the Japanese audience), but the very presence of a "boundary" can be the advantage if it reminds the audience of the interaction/collision of the opposing forces—a truly dramatic situation—as did the three Steinbeck adapta-tions in Japan.

11

Staging *Tortilla Flat*

Steinbeck in a Thai Context

Malithat Promathatavedi

John Steinbeck is enormously popular in Thailand because the plight of the homeless is so readily appreciated, because he so tellingly conveys human suffering, a pivotal Buddhist doctrine, and because his novels are so readily translated and, most recently, adapted for the stage. Promathatavedi explores the Thai elements in a recent stage version of Tortilla Flat: Waniphok Ramphueng, *or* The Vagabonds' Lament.

One factor that makes John Steinbeck a very popular author with Thai readers is that many of his themes are universal and some can be related to Thai culture and situations. Proof of Steinbeck's immense popularity is that almost all of his novels are available in translation in most bookstores in Bangkok and other big cities in Thailand.

The plight of the Joad family in *The Grapes of Wrath* can be readily understood by Thai readers since it is similar to that of the poor farmers of Esarn, the arid northeastern region of Thailand. Many of them have to leave their drought-stricken rice fields and farmlands to migrate to the metropolitan areas to find jobs and make a living. Once in the cities, they find themselves in unfamiliar and sometimes hostile surroundings where they are looked down upon and taken advantage of by the city people. Having little education and insufficient skills, they find few good jobs available to them. The only jobs most of them can find are as day-laborers at construction sites, taxi drivers, or hired household help. Some who are even less fortunate may end up as drug addicts, thieves, or prostitutes. The lives of these people have been poignantly portrayed in the works of prominent Thai writers, such as Kampoon Boontawee's *Luk Esarn* (which means *Son of Esarn*) and Pira Sudham's *People of Esarn*.

The greed reflected in *The Pearl* appears to be innate in human nature and, according to Buddhist belief, is one of the chief causes of suffering. *The Doctrine of the Four Noble Truths*, which is the main theme of the Lord Buddha's teaching, pivots on the facts of suffering: suffering, cause of suffering, cessation of suffering, and the path leading to the cessation of suffering. Desire, or craving, is considered to be the root cause of suffering. Thus, *Nirvana* (the total extinction of suffering), becomes the ideal goal of every true Buddhist.

Another reason for Steinbeck's popularity is his language which is simple yet poetic. There are no long words or complicated structures in his works that will cause difficulty for Thai readers. As Thais are said to be poetic by nature, and possess a tonal language, they are easily attuned to his rhythmic language. Thus, it is not surprising that many of Steinbeck's novels have been used as reading materials in Thai high schools and universities. Almost all of them have been translated into Thai for the benefit of those whose English reading ability may not be adequate. The reasons for Steinbeck being so widely translated seem to be that translators are fascinated with his work and the novels readily lend themselves to translation. Even though Steinbeck's novels are widely read in Thailand, however, only two of them, *The Grapes of Wrath* and *Tortilla Flat* have been adapted for the stage. In this paper the stage version of *Tortilla Flat* will be explored to show how it has been adapted to fit into the Thai and Buddhist context.

The structure of *Tortilla Flat* is based on Malory's *Morte D'Arthur*. Steinbeck acknowledged this in his preface. "For Danny's house was not unlike the Round Table, and Danny's friends were not unlike the knights of it" (3). Clear parallels are drawn between the adventures of Danny and his friends and the feats of King Arthur's knights, though some of the paisanos' adventures are more parody than parallel to the knights' heroic deeds. Danny himself is the Arthurian figure around whom all activities revolve. His death can be seen in the same light as King Arthur's demise. In the end, each of the paisanos goes his own way after the house, the bond that held them together, has burned down. This is reminiscent of the breaking up of the Round Table caused by the knights going their separate ways on their quest for the Holy Grail. The similarities, however, end here, for the paisanos of *Tortilla Flat* live a life of their own with a code of chivalry quite different from that of the medieval knights. It is the dynamism of their personal interrelationships that inspired Chonprakan Chanruang, a professor of dramatic arts at one of the leading universities in Bangkok, to give the paisanos life on the stage.

Chonprakan Chanruang is the producer and director of the New Heritage Drama Troupe, an experimental group emphasizing Thai heritage. It considers social changes occurring in Thai society to find the appropriate format for the plays. Its most important challenge is turning foreign elements into Thai ones. Rather than changing Thai heritage, the troupe tries to find a place for it in modern society and show that it is not in conflict with the modern world. Instead, it offers alternatives for society. Chonprakan relates why he decided to stage *Waniphok Ramphueng* or *The Vagabonds' Lament*, the Thai version of *Tortilla Flat*.

> *Tortilla Flat* is a full-fledged novel. As far as I know, it has never been made into a play. This is not surprising since novels and plays belong to different media. The logic in their presentation is also different. . . . Since my first encounter with Steinbeck, I have been following his works and have stumbled upon *Tortilla Flat*. I promptly made up my mind and declared that I would show it to Thai people. This story is very beautiful. The five or six dirty, ugly, lazy, jealous, drunken, rootless, futureless, vagrant, lustful people make attractive principal characters. I find that this story is written for everyone regardless of country or language. It is universal. What has been told in the novel, especially concerning desire or craving and real happiness, is really in the mind. This is too great to be left only as printed words in the book. More importantly, this is Buddhist in nature. The character like Boonting (Danny) who never thinks about the future and never knows where his next meal is coming from, knows only whenever hunger strikes he will take whatever comes his way by whichever manner convenient to him, including stealing.

Happy with his friends and wine, he unexpectedly inherits two houses! Isn't it beautiful? Think of it this way. Those of you who have a job, a house, a family, a fixed bank account, relatives, stability in life, suddenly wake up to find that everything is gone. It is the same thing. If we look into this a little deeper, the houses are material things that cause the vagabonds to have a desire. They are a symbol of disaster. The houses pose a problem since they have to be taken care of. Here is where the comparison comes in. The gain of the vagabonds is the loss of people like us in society. It is just the other way around. This is part of the charm of this story.

When I plan to turn this novel into a play, I have to think in terms of staging a play. I have to first find out what it is that Steinbeck has said in the novel that affects us the most, what it is that agrees best with our world view, and then make it the theme or the message of the play. I must emphasize here that it is I who give the message, not Steinbeck. This is very important, for I will never be able to fathom him out thoroughly. We are not one and the same person. The point that impresses me is that real happiness does not lie in material things but in the mind itself. This is the statement I would like to make in this play and this is the beginning point of adapting *Tortilla Flat* into a stage play. (17–18)

Having his theme, Chonprakan sought a central character to relay his message to the audience and chose Pungkee (Pilon). One theory of finding a central character in a play is to make this character the very opposite of the theme of the play. In the novel, Danny is the one who inherits two houses but is unhappy with his inheritance, with material things. Since Chonprakan's focus was that real happiness does not lie in material things, his principal character had to be happy with material things to create a contrast. Pungkee (Pilon) believes that the possession of material things brings pleasure and it is he who does everything in his power to obtain them.

The Vagabonds' Lament was staged as a musical. Many well known folk songs like "Beggars' Song," "Gong Song," "Lullaby," "Boat Song," and "Rowers' Song" were interspersed throughout the play, which opened with a chorus introducing the general background. Songs were accompanied by drums from the balcony and the staging was particularly effective and free. Similar to the Greek theater, with an orchestra providing major movements, this play employed three side stages as well, and a ladder to the theater's ceiling, representing a cliff-face over the sea. There was also an additional audience seating facing the main auditorium and balcony seats; additional performers were divided into groups and merged or separated according to the requirement of the acts.

The setting of the play, a small village called Lang-yu, is more or less similar to Tortilla Flat in that it is situated on a hill and does not have electricity. In the production the audience learns both that electricity is coming to the village of Lang-yu and that there is a scenic point on Kuan Hua Haek hill where many tourists fall to their deaths every year because the rocks are slippery—but the villagers' mishaps at the spot come from their own carelessness. For instance, the year before Uncle Maak, the undertaker, won a big prize in a lottery and built two houses. Celebrating his good fortune, he got drunk and fell down the hill and died. His two houses were inherited by Boonting (Danny).

Soon Boonting's friends, a group of vagabonds who are social outcasts, come to share the fortune with him. The only person who associates with them is Yeesoon (a combination of Sweets Ramirez and Senora Teresina Cortez), a beautiful woman with numerous husbands and a brood of children in tow. She hangs around with Boonting because she wants his houses.

In the novel, Danny, returning home from the army, finds that he has inherited two houses from his grandfather. In the play, Boonting is of doubtful parentage; his mother is a prostitute and his father might have been any male in Lang-yu. Even his name hints at his being unwanted, "Boon" meaning "merit" and "ting" meaning "abandoned." With his mother going off with her various male companions, he grows up to be a vagabond without kin, money, or love. Homeless, he only has his gang of wretched friends, Pungkee (Pilon), Pla Bu (Pablo), Tane (Jesus Maria Corcoran), Wanpen (Big Joe Portagee), and Mong Klae (The Pirate), who are all as dirty and hungry as he is, and they join him in his drinking sprees. His life is changed overnight by the inheritance of the houses and all his happiness departs, leaving only sadness and troubles.

Overall, the play follows the plot of the novel closely. The main difference lies in Chonprakan's treatment of the characters. Whereas each of the novel's main characters is a fully developed individual—a fact Steinbeck emphasizes—the play puts more emphasis on the characters' actions, which is suitable for the stage. Except for Boonting and Pungkee, the characters receive superficial treatment and the audience sees only what these characters do; they cannot reach deep into their minds and feelings. The intricately woven bond between Danny and his friends, which has been so subtly and beautifully built up by Steinbeck, is also missing in the play. In reading the novel, one can more clearly see the pride and dignity of the characters, however poor or illiterate they may be.

Another character in the play whose role deviates from the novel is Chin Kee, the ruthless and cunning Chinese shopkeeper who assumes the place of the Italian Torrelli. The original Chin Kee who owns the squid-cutting yard is never mentioned in the play. This change is natural and understandable since the Chinese property-owners form a familiar part of Thai society. They are the ones who hold economic sway, especially in rural villages. With his wife Jee Choi (Mrs. Torrelli), who is as greedy as himself, Chin Kee tries every way, no matter how dubious, to get hold of Boonting's houses. Towards the end of the play, the couple assumes the function of a Greek chorus narrating the story. Compared to them, Torrelli and his wife seem rather benign, especially Mrs. Torrelli, who lets herself be talked into giving the vagabonds a quart of wine in exchange for an old pair of pants, only to have them stolen from her.

The character of Ramphueng, a prospective borrower of the company that Boonting and his friends are going to set up, is based on Senora Teresina Cortez. Very poor, with numerous children, she pitiably feeds them daily by throwing scraps of food on the floor. In the novel it is the old grandmother who strews boiled beans on the kitchen floor for them to eat. Out of pity for the children, Boonting and his friends cook duck porridge for them. However, since the children are not accustomed to this kind of food, they die on the spot, whereas in the novel the children, whose staple food is tortillas and beans, are very much alive, hale and healthy. Having mortgaged her house to her debtors, Ramphueng hangs herself out of desperation. In the novel, however, Senora Cortez does not die but becomes pregnant, the child fathered by one of Danny's friends, although she does not know which one.

The comic scenes in the novel arise from situations rather than words. The play, additionally has an overtone of vulgarity in the characters, especially in their language and actions. Thai words readily lend themselves to punning and double meaning. The witty folk singers and poets can speedily make up verses, especially with sexual connotations, on an impromptu basis to entertain their audience. For example, Boonting proposes to name his baby "Dok Mai" (flower) with a nickname of "E Dok" if it is a girl. "E" is an old word commonly used by country folk to call a female, especially a girl, intimately without connoting impoliteness. On the other hand, "E Dok," the shortened form of "Dok Thong" (golden flower), is also a derogatory term for a promiscuous woman. It might be that the director is trying to give a stereotyped picture of unrefined, uneducated villagers that, in a way, provides a basis for the comic elements which constitute a part of Thai theater. Even in the most tragic movie or play, there is always a place for humor. For example, in a scene at Boonting's second house where he is living with Yeesoon, there are vehement and rather coarse exchanges between the vagabonds and Yeesoon's daughters, Elizabeth, Hideko and Moei Chin, whose names hint at the multiple and international paternity of the girls, providing comic relief for the Thai audience.

In the play, there are numerous adaptations so that some of the points in the novel do not appear so foreign to the Thai audience. Christian elements such as the mystic treasure hunt on St. Andrew's Eve and the Pirate's dogs seeing a Holy Vision give way to the more familiar local beliefs in spirits and superstitions. Early in the play the audience learns how the friends follow Mong Klae into the woods to see where he has hidden a hoard of money he has earned from selling forest products. In the stage version, the money is intended for buying offerings for a spirit presiding over a shrine on Kuan Hua Haek Hill as a token of gratitude for the spirit's part in helping to heal Mong Klae's bitch from diarrhea (to die of constipation later on). This is a shift from the Christian act of buying a gold candlestick for Saint Francis, an example of how a foreign element is adapted to a Thai setting.

When Boonting's friends inform him that his other house has burned down, each of them tries to blame the other for having caused the fire. Since no one wants to accept the blame, it is concluded that liquor was responsible for the fire. In Thailand, wine is associated with high class society and would be incongruous with rural life, where homemade liquor or moonshine would be more appropriate.

In the novel, Danny is lured into buying a vacuum cleaner even though there was no electricity on Tortilla Flat. The play substitutes an electric rice cooker for the vacuum cleaner, which is more suitable to the Thai audience, since rice is the staple diet in Thailand and a vacuum cleaner would be out of place in a thatch-roofed house, not to mention its price, which is far too expensive for a poor villager to afford.

The whole business of mortgaging the house and setting up a company is another deviation from the novel. It may have been introduced to show Pungkee's calculating nature and also to show that no matter how lazy or vagrant these vagabonds are they still have dreams like everyone else. In the novel, it is the cunning Torrelli who tricks the drunken Danny into selling the house to him for twenty-five dollars.

Pungkee begs the spirit of the shrine on the hill to show him the way out of trouble. Looking up, he sees Mong Klae's money bag hanging on the wall and takes it down, intending to use the money to redeem the house. When the bag is opened, its content is not money but rocks. After a thorough search, the coins fall from Wanpen's body; still, he denies having taken them. This scene follows the novel where Big Joe steals the coins from the Pirate, with a comic twist. When Wanpen argues that he has marked the coins by licking them, Mong Klae just says that he has marked his coins with excrement so that no one would dare take them from him. His words cause Wanpen to vomit. He is then badly beaten up.

Racking their brains trying to find some money to pay for the mortgage, the friends resolve to go out with the fishing boats to catch a certain kind of fish as expensive as gold that swims around the island only once a year. All of them join the trip, leaving Boonting behind. In the novel, there is no mention of a fishing trip. Perhaps it is added to the stage version so that the Boat Songs could be introduced.

The vagabonds come back empty-handed. Chin Kee gives them two days to move out of the house. A boat full of fish is seen coming into the harbor out of the blue. Pungkee says that his boat has run into a deserted boat filled with the precious fish. He offers to sell the boat together with the fish to Chin Kee in exchange for the contract. The cunning merchant tricks him into getting Boonting to redeem the house and tear the contract up himself. While waiting for Boonting, Pungkee orders Chin Kee to bring out all the expensive food his shop has to offer for he will entertain his friends. Chin Kee suggests that Pungkee hold a big feast for the whole village, something in the nature of a temple fair. The villagers must pay for the admission charge and buy tickets to play games. At Boonting's house the villagers arrive and join in the games. This scene provides a setting for a village fair, something that is rarely seen by the city audience, and something very different from the wild party at Danny's house. Chin Kee and Jee Choi arrive in their best attire and set up a small stall selling all kinds of goods. Then they use free porridge and a ferris wheel ride to lure the villagers into attending the village chief's funeral on the other side of the river. Thus, Boonting and his friends will never be able to raise enough money by midnight to redeem the house since the money from the sale of the boat and the fish has been spent on the preparation for the fair. This scene emphasizes the ruthless nature of the Chinese merchant, a stereotyped villain in many Thai novels and short stories about rural life.

Boonting asks Pungkee whether the house makes him happy and the latter says yes. Boonting then reveals that he has never been happy with the house. When he did not have any food to eat, he could steal and a house was not a necessity. Now that he owns one, it makes him uncomfortable and tired. He is, at the moment, happy since he is going back to his former state. Chasing everyone away, he desperately announces that he can no longer bear the burden of this world.

For dramatic effect, at this point in the plot the play was performed simultaneously on two stages, one with Mong Klae going after Boonting and the other with Pungkee arguing with Chin Kee. Boonting walks toward the cliff where he stands absorbing the beauty of the moon, the sky with glittering stars and the sparkling sea. He is seized with a severe headache and seems to be in pain and a terrible fright, but not quite as delirious as Danny. Saying that he is so tired and cannot take it any more, he jumps off the cliff.

On the other stage, Chin Kee and Jee Choi claim that since Boonting is now dead his house must belong to them. The villagers then collect some money to give to Jee Choi who tears the contract up and throws the pieces of paper in the vagabonds' faces. Everyone else makes an exit and the friends are left alone. Then a lamp is upset and the house catches fire. The others try to put the fire out, but Pungkee tells them not to bother; so the house burns down, symbolically putting an end to all the troubles. The play ends in a philosophical note with a lullaby summing up the theme of the story.

> Alas! Poor humans,
> Never really happy are,
> Clinging to everything,
> Running round o'er a fire.
> Desire and passion,
> They all grasp as their own,
> Not one does realize,
> Happy is not having.
> Have not, know not, be not.
> Not realizing thus, unhappy they'll be.
> Be aware of non-attachment,
> To be happy, one must own nothing. (30)

The major theme of *The Vagabonds' Lament* is very much the essence of Buddhist doctrine. The Buddha preached about *Anatta* (Non-Self) which is a path to escape from suffering. He proclaimed the *Three Characteristics*, or *Signs*, of being, namely, *Im-*

permanence, Instability, and *Non-Self.* His purpose was to help beings attain a state of non-attachment to all phenomena, for attachment is the cause of desire and aversion. If we do not hold on to anything, we will not suffer the loss of it. *Atta* (Ego, Self) makes us want to be or to have this or that. Since desire or craving is the root cause of suffering, if we can get rid of *Atta* and attain *Anatta,* then we can find happiness. "There is no other happiness than peace," according to the Lord Buddha, and the peace he meant is peace of mind. Even though the body may be in pain, if the mind is at peace, the pain cannot affect the mind. On the contrary, the body can also be relieved of the pain. Through the Buddhist *Three Steps of Practice, Sila* (Precepts), *Samathi* (Meditation), and *Panya* (Wisdom), we can train ourselves to attain inward peace.

At first Boonting believes that owning the houses (having material things) will make him happy. As the play advances, we see that this is not the case. His possessions only bring him troubles and unhappiness. Still, he cannot detach himself from them. Unable to find peace with himself, Boonting loses his mind and chooses to leave the world at last.

No matter how different *The Vagabonds' Lament* is from *Tortilla Flat,* it has grown out of the novel as a token of admiration for Steinbeck. In its own way, it has successfully relayed the universal message that the author wants to express to people of a different culture and geographical setting.

12

Novella into Play

Burning Bright

Kiyoshi Nakayama

Nakayama documents Steinbeck's revision process on Burning Bright *from typescript novella to published novella to play version, and argues that the play version is the best of the three works.*

John Steinbeck's third play-novelette or novella, *Burning Bright: A Play in Story Form*, was published by Viking Press on 20 October 1950, two days after the premiere of the play *Burning Bright* at the Broadhurst Theatre in New York. Steinbeck wrote the book in three weeks, January 9 through 31 January 1950 (*SLL* 401). Its initial working title was "Everyman," later changed to "In the Forests of the Night." This second title was retained even while the book was being printed, but was finally changed, as Pascal Covici's 26 July 1950 letter mentions, to "Burning Bright" (Fensch 135). On September 5, while writing the play version of the work, Steinbeck reported in a letter to Frank and Lynn Loesser, "I am going over the lines a last time before rehearsal this Labor Day weekend. And of course there will be other word changes during rehearsal" (Benson 662). As he noted in another letter to Pascal Covici, "little changes take place in the play right up to opening night" (*SLL* 404-05); he continued polishing it even during the try-outs in New Haven and in Boston. This kind of work was unusual to him, for he always thought of his finished work as "dead."

This essay traces how Steinbeck wrote the final play version, *Burning Bright: Play in Three Acts, Acting Edition*, by adapting it from the novella version, *Burning Bright: A Play in Story Form*, which he wrote first. I shall point out variants between the published texts of the novella and the play versions of the work in order to illustrate how Steinbeck made deletions, emendations, additions, and even drastic alterations. In addition, I shall compare the author's 104-page carbon typescript of the play version —with the corrections and additions he made under the title of "In the Forests of the Night"—with the published play version, *Burning Bright: Play in Three Acts, Acting Edition.*

I

As the subtitle of the book clearly shows, even the novella is more play than novel. It is divided into acts and scenes instead of chapters. The contents page announces three acts: "Act One: The Circus," "Act Two: The Farm," "Act Three, Scene I: The Sea," and "Act Three, Scene II: The Child." Four characters—Joe Saul, his wife Mordeen, Victor, and Friend Ed—are present or implied in the action throughout the play; but their professions change from act to act. As Steinbeck observed in an essay, "Critics, Critics Burning Bright," "In an attempt to indicate a universality of experience I placed the story in the hands of three professions which have long and continuing traditions, . . . " (43). Accordingly, in Act One they are all trapeze artists, except for Friend Ed, who is a clown. Then in Act Two, Joe Saul is a farmer, Victor a farm hand, and Friend Ed a neighbor; in Act Three, Scene I, Joe Saul is the captain of a freighter, Victor the mate, Friend Ed the captain of another boat; and finally in Act Three, Scene II, Joe Saul and Mordeen are in a hospital room, with a baby lying beside her.

Joe Saul is around fifty, and sterile because he had rheumatic fever as a boy. He does not know this and is eager to have a child with Mordeen, who has been married to him for three years. To please her husband, Mordeen chooses Victor to be the father of her child; she intends to bring up the child as Joe Saul's. But Victor is hard to get rid of. When he becomes too troublesome, and tries to force her to go away with him, she wants only to kill him. In a crucial scene, Friend Ed appears. When Mordeen had appealed to him earlier for advice, he had evaded the problem. Now he thinks he ought to take the responsibility he had evaded, and kills Victor. In the final scene, Joe Saul, having learned the truth, heroically overcomes his personal feelings, and accepts

Mordeen's son as his own, saying, "Mordeen, this is The Child. I love The Child. I love our child. Mordeen, *I love my son*" (play 52).

The 104-page typescript of "In the Forests of the Night" can presumably be regarded as the original play version: it is the text in which Steinbeck meticulously made various revisions for the play as well as being the basic version used for rehearsal in September 1950. The author's revisions are printed without change in the published *Acting Edition*. By comparing "In the Forests" with the *Acting Edition*, I have found approximately thirty major variants. Among them, however, are included a dozen stage directions which were deleted or added in "In the Forests," and which I presume are of less importance than the revisions of the characters' lines.

Small but important variants are revealed in a comparison of the published novella and "In the Forests." In the latter, Steinbeck wisely eschews using such hyphenated words as "wife-loss" and "friend-right" (4, 5), which are part of what he called a "universal language" (Benson 656), and which the critics have unanimously abhorred since the novella was published. In the novella, Friend Ed says, "Three years it is since Cathy died. You were strong in your wife-loss" (4), whereas he says in the play, "Why, I remember when your Cathy died. You were strong when you lost your wife" (6). In Friend Ed's speech in the play, the author also avoids giving the exact number of years, "three," since Joe Saul's first wife died. This indicates the emphasis on "timelessness" which he aims for in the play. In the same manner, Friend Ed simply says to Joe Saul in the play, "Do I have the right to ask a question?" (7) instead of using the expression, "the friend-right."

In addition, the play version drops the theme of facelessness, while the theme of universality is retained. Both are introduced near the beginning of the novella, where Joe Saul says, "I know it is a thing that can happen to anyone in any place and time—a farmer or a sailor, or a lineless, faceless Everyone!" (9). But in the play, "a farmer or a sailor, or a lineless, faceless Everyone" is deleted. It is also dropped in the final part of the play. Steinbeck must have realized that the theme was hard to understand, and thus ineffective in the play.

Other lines are significantly altered. In the novella Mordeen asks, "Am I a good woman to you?" (13), while in the play Joe

Saul asks, "Am I a good husband . . . a good lover to you?" (12). In response to the question, Mordeen immediately answers, "Oh, my dear . . . wonderful . . . gentle and fierce and . . . wonderful" (12). Her words, which clearly connote not only his love but his manner of love-making, are, in the published novella, told to Friend Ed later in the text, when he asks her, "Is he [Joe Saul] a good lover?" (27). In the play, this initial love scene between Mordeen and Joe Saul is extended somewhat longer than in the novella, the purpose of which would presumably be to ensure that their conjugal love impresses itself more strongly and profoundly on the audience.

A significant alteration in the plot takes place toward the end of Act I of the play. In the novella, Victor playfully tries to seduce Mordeen, saying, "Let's get the hell out of here. Your old man's drunk. We'll go to a show. We'll go to town and have dinner. Say, how would it be if I rent a car and we go for a ride?" (35). In the play, however, it is Mordeen who is determined to lure Victor when she hears him say, "I'm not running away. Get that, . . . I'm leaving on my own!" (21). There is no mention of Victor's leaving in the novella's Act One. Thus, hearing his abrupt decision, Mordeen in utter astonishment makes the firm decision to stop him: "Victor, don't go now. I want to talk to you. Maybe . . . maybe we could go into town and have dinner . . . where we could talk quietly" (21). That is why Victor asks her: "Dinner in town? . . . You mean without Joe Saul and his eternal friend? . . . Just you and me?" and then suggests, "And after dinner I could rent a car. We could go for a drive" (21–22). This new scene in the play does not imply that Victor is a villain at all, but reveals that Mordeen makes up her mind to use him like a horse at stud.

When the two disappear, in the second paragraph from the end of Act One of the novella, Joe Saul comes back and says, "Mordeen, . . . Mordeen, I'm drunk. I'm sorry but I'm drunk," and then, "Mordeen, . . . I hurt Friend Ed. Sent him away" (38), his last words in Act One. In the play, however, there is added a new scene between Joe Saul and Friend Ed, which completes Act I:

JOE SAUL: Stop following me! . . . I want you to get out. Now, get out!
FRIEND ED: Easy, Joe Saul, easy. Go to bed. Try to sleep.

JOE SAUL: I cannot sleep. I am dead. My blood is cut off. I have no son.

FRIEND ED: You are not alone. Perhaps on a farm somewhere there is a man who cries for a child to inherit his labor and his land. You are not alone.

JOE SAUL: . . . What do I care about that? I am dead. . . . I have no son. (22–23)

With these lines, Steinbeck tries to keep the plot line consistent between Act I and Act II. Friend Ed suggests that "somewhere there is a man who cries for a child"; and that man turns out to be Joe Saul himself in Act II, set in a "A farm kitchen." And Joe Saul's last lines alluding to his symbolical death or his dead seed convey his desperate situation more clearly than his last words in the novella.

Another major alteration between novella and play takes place toward the end of Act II of the play. In spite of Mordeen's plea for him to go away, Victor stays at the farm because Joe Saul persuades him to do so. In the novella, however, Victor leaves the farm in desperation without heeding Joe Saul's request. To Mordeen and Friend Ed, it would be easier and less troublesome if Victor left for good, but Joe Saul does not know the truth about Victor's fathering the child. By this time Victor has grown as a man, not merely as an ardent but rejected lover to Mordeen but as the biological father of the baby to be born. Even in the novella, where he goes away, he returns to Mordeen at the opening of Act Three and tries to take her with him by force. But when revising for the stage, Steinbeck undoubtedly found it to be more natural and more believable—and perhaps more dramatic —to have the villainous Victor stay on the farm. Whereas in the novella Joe Saul himself decides to go to the doctor for a check up in order to give his unborn child a "present" of a clean bill of health, in the play it is Victor himself who malevolently suggests that Joe Saul go to the doctor, knowing that Joe Saul will find out he is sterile: "Why don't you have the doctor go over you, head to toe? That would be a present. . . . Make sure. Hang your health certificate on the tree for his [the baby's] first Christmas present" (play 40–41). Joe Saul agrees with him, saying, "Why, that *would* be a present. Of course! Then I could say to this child, 'That's what your father gave you first of all . . .

strength and health and cleanliness'" (41). In the novella, these last are the same words Joe Saul uses to Friend Ed after Victor leaves the farm. In the play, Friend Ed opposes Joe Saul's idea, saying, "This is foolishness. What do you need a check-up for? You're perfectly healthy" (41). Victor suggests again, however, that Joe Saul go to the doctor, until at last Joe Saul makes up his mind to have a check-up, in spite of Friend Ed's sincere anxiety and opposition. Thus in the play Victor becomes a much more villainous character. Not all agreed, however, that the shift in motivation was an improvement: in his *New Yorker* review John Lardner contends that "In the book, Joe Saul thinks of the idea himself, which makes the scene more convincing" (qtd. in McElrath 359).

II

One of the most crucial scenes of the novella is Act Three, Scene I, when Victor is killed. This scene, as it is described in the unrevised galley-proof, reads:

> Slowly [Mordeen] followed [Victor]. She walked to the rail and looked over. And her voice came back. "Victor," she said. "See the water—how it is broken, how the lights are shattered in the water."
>
> "Hurry!" he said sharply.
>
> She moved along the rail toward him, and her voice drifted back. "Only see the black water." A bottomless sadness was in her tone. "See the black water under the pier."
>
> There was a silence and then a crunching blow and in a moment a soft splash.
>
> Mordeen crept back into the wardroom. She was bent over and crushed like an insect. Her teeth were fastened on her lip and there was a glaze of pain in her eyes. She moved painfully to the wall and then carefully she wiped the club on her coat, knobbed black head and short thick handle. She bent over it, moaning. And then she hung it back on the wall and moved it a little so that it covered its right place on the wood paneling. She turned then and looked around the room, and then a great convulsion shook her and beat her down, and another struck her to her knees. She

struggled and writhed on the floor and she screamed hoarsely in labor.

Although dropped at an early stage, Steinbeck's original idea was to have Mordeen kill Victor by herself just before she goes into labor. He presumably wrote this scene because it is not natural for her to rely on someone like Friend Ed who has previously declined to advise her and/or offer his assistance both in the novella (30) and in the play (19–20). But it is hardly credible that pregnant Mordeen could alone kill a "large and powerful" (novella 13) young man like Victor.

In an unpublished 16 May 1950 letter, therefore, Annie Laurie Williams asked Steinbeck to revise the scene for the play:

> By this time you probably have worked out the new scenes between Friend Ed and Victor. I can feel the rightness of having Friend Ed come back to protect Mordeen and have to face Victor in a fight. Mordeen has already said she would be forced to kill Victor. Then Victor has started his scene with Mordeen when Friend Ed appears.
>
> I think that he would tell Victor that he will be forced to strike him if he doesn't stop. Victor hits Friend Ed and there is a hard fight. The audience can't see the fight but they can hear it. Victor is knocked down by Friend Ed and hits his head and dies. Friend Ed pushes him into the water, or he falls into the water.

Although Steinbeck did not write it exactly the way that Williams suggested, both the published texts of the novella and the play have similar scenes in which Friend Ed declares his strong intention of taking responsibility. He heroically executes what Mordeen is about to do; he urges Victor to come to the deck of the boat and kills him offstage.

In the play, the scene is elaborately rewritten for production; it is altered and considerably longer than in the novella. While Victor is offstage to get her suitcase for the hospital, Mordeen goes to the locker to get a cloak. The stage direction notes, "*she goes to the desk R., looks a moment at the Oriental dagger on the wall over it, then draws it from its sheath. Meanwhile* Friend Ed *has come down into the room and sees her action. He comes behind her, grasps her wrist and takes the dagger from her. He tosses it on the deck, hold-ing her tight"* (45). On the other hand, in the novella, Mordeen "drew a short thick knife from its sheath and concealed it in the folds of her cloak. And as she did, she saw Friend Ed standing just inside the door, shaking his head slowly at her" (79). After killing Victor, Friend Ed "took the knife from her and replaced it in its sheath" (80). In the novella, Friend Ed had earlier de-clared that "Once I wouldn't help you. I wouldn't take the re-sponsibility. Now I will" (79). He says this in the presence of Victor when the young man comes back from the sleeping cabin. In the play, however, Friend Ed speaks the same lines to Mor-deen while Victor is offstage. Likewise, in the play, Victor has no idea of the other words exchanged between the two, either: Friend Ed declares, "Whether you want it or not . . . you have it," and Mordeen responds, "Stay clear of this! What I have started, I will finish" (46). Determined to separate Victor from Mordeen, Friend Ed invites him to come to his boat which is to sail at mid-night, saying in part, "Will you sail with me? I have a berth for you. . . . It would solve many things" (46). Young Victor stub-bornly declines the offer: "I am taking Mordeen and my child away. You and old Joe Saul can shout, can weep, and howl . . . but you cannot stop me" (46). Friend Ed changes his strategy. In-sinuatingly, he tells Victor to give Mordeen happiness, and adds, "there is one thing I can give her through you. . . . There is one knowledge only I have. I want to lay it in your hands for her. . . . It's a secret thing. I will give it to you to hold for her" (46–47). And at last, Victor tells Friend Ed to "come out on deck and tell me" (47).

In the novella, however, Friend Ed simply says to Victor, "Will you come on deck with me? I have a message for you. . . . it's a secret. Come!" (80). These are his only words to Victor in Act Three, and they sound too short and abrupt to tempt the young man to leave the cabin. The reader would naturally wonder why Victor, having heard what Friend Ed said to Mordeen, obediently/naively follows Friend Ed out on deck to be killed. In the play version, however, the sequence of this particular scene consists of thirty-four lines, whose effect is to persuade Victor to trust Friend Ed, who offers him "a secret thing." And yet there re-mains a question of credibility as to whether someone would kill a young man just because he is selfish and a nuisance.

III

Another four-page typescript, "Act Two, Scene Two," containing several additions by the author, becomes Act III, Scene 2 in the published texts. These appear to be the only authorial emendations extant for the final scene of the play. During the summer of 1950, Burgess Meredith recollects, Steinbeck was "struggling with the ending for quite some time" (Benson 661).

The first three paragraphs of Act Three, Scene II of the novella correspond to the stage directions of "In the Forests." Although Steinbeck initially used the first three paragraphs of the novella as stage directions, they are all dropped in the final version of the play. Thus, in contrast with the novella, Mordeen's face is *not* masked with gauze in the play, and Joe Saul's face is *not* covered with a surgical mask. He does *not* have to wear "cap and long white tunic" (90), either. The author dropped the novella's theme of "facelessness" from the play. He deleted lines given to Mordeen in "In the Forests" which are taken verbatim from the novella: "You are JOE SAUL? Faceless—only a voice and a white facelessness," and "Where is your face? What's happened to your face, Joe Saul?" Also deleted is Joe Saul's reply: "It's not important. . . . It is the race—the species that must go staggering on." Thus the image of facelessness, the theme of impersonality, which is prominent in the novella, is completely erased from the play.

At the beginning of Act III, Scene 2, Mordeen's first words are taken from the novella. Being semi-conscious, she says, "Dead . . . dead . . . the whole world is dead" (51), and then, instead of saying, "Victor dead" (91), as in the novella, she says in the play, "And burning. Everything burned and black. Nothing left" (51), which emphasizes the image of a waste land. Here the image of "burning bright" turns out to be that of the corrupted world burned to ashes by the flames of divine wrath. Mordeen's words, "Victor dead," which appear in the novella, are dropped, and instead, Mordeen's words to Friend Ed follow, as in the novella: "Friend Ed, I wanted—I wanted Joe Saul to have his child—I wanted—but everything is dead" (novella 91; play 51). She utters these words subconsciously, revealing how traumatically she suffered in mind and body in the last crucial scene with Victor. To Mordeen, Friend Ed is her only true friend/confidant. He has done for her most selflessly what her husband was unable to. For her to speak to him so truthfully is, virtually, to say more to him than to her husband.

Another noteworthy variant in the play is that Mordeen says, "Joe Saul is dead," instead of asking, "Is Joe Saul dead?" as she does in "In the Forests." Joe Saul replies, "Part of Joe Saul is dead. Part of him died in the darkness" (51). These lines do not appear in the novella, where Joe Saul says, "I'm here. I went away into an insanity, but now I'm back" (91); these words are deleted in the play. His new lines including the words "[p]art of him" and "dead," can be found among the deleted lines at the beginning of the scene just after Mordeen says, "Victor dead!" Joe Saul's first lines in "In the Forests" read, "No, Mordeen. Only a little part of *him* could die—Victor will never be dead— Here and alive always" (emphasis added). The reader should notice that this "part of him" means "part of Victor," whereas the above-quoted words by Joe Saul, "Part of him died in the darkness" (51), obviously mean "Part of Joe Saul." Here, in the play's last scene, the name of Victor is never mentioned. And yet, Steinbeck symbolically suggests here that Victor is even "part" of Joe Saul who has finally come to know and accept the whole thing. Responding to Mordeen's words, "Maybe he'll never know" (51), he declares, "I know, and I am content, content as I have never been" (51). What he has gotten is an intuitive perception that the whole includes part of him, Victor, and everybody. Therefore, at least, Victor's death becomes, not an actual, bloody incident, but a symbolic loss, so that no one is to blame for it.

Apart from these variants, the most important fact about Act III, Scene 2 in the play is that the number of words is surprisingly reduced: from the 930-word text of "In the Forests" to the 496 words in the *Acting Edition*. In *Of Mice and Men*, "when Steinbeck transferred the story into final dramatic form for the New York stage he took 85 percent of his lines bodily from the novel" (Moore 49); but in Act III, Scene 2 of *Burning Bright*, the author used only 53 percent of "In the Forests" in the process of polishing it into the play text.

In order to write the concluding scene of the play, Steinbeck revised "In the Forests," which was adapted from the novella. He tightened the structure and action to such an extent, especially after the climactic scene of Victor's death, that even a highly sophisticated audience was often unable to understand the themes of the play fully. The final scene was too compact, as William Hawkins notes in his review: "that whole development takes place in only the last few minutes of the play" (239).

Reviewers' criticisms aside, Steinbeck revised the play sufficiently to create a "morality play, completely timeless and placeless" (*SLL* 408). Martha H. Cox is right when she notes that "the reviewers usually also found elements in the production to praise —the powerfully moving last act, the acting, direction, sets, lighting, and Steinbeck's attempt to create serious and original drama. Reviewers were, in fact, often kinder to the play . . . than to the book, though comments about the two are so intermingled that they are difficult to distinguish" (47).

Terse and compact, the play is a more effective piece of writing than the novella, in part because Steinbeck first wrote the novella, adapted it for the stage, and then kept polishing it, while receiving a number of suggestions from the actors, the director, the producers, and even from his agent, Annie Laurie Williams. He deleted hyphenated words, added new scenes, and made several drastic alterations. Perhaps if the novella had been published a few months later, and not, as it was, only two days after the opening of the play, the stage production may have survived a few months longer. Critical pounding of the novella, *Burning Bright*, must have had a devastating influence upon the play's run—only thirteen performances.

I would like to thank the staff of the Rare Book and Manuscript Library of the Butler Library of Columbia University for their generous, capable assistance in my work on this and many other Steinbeck studies when I did research there in the cold, early spring of 1989.

Also I am truly indebted to Dr. Tetsumaro Hayashi for his invaluable advice and inspiration over the years, and to Roy S. Simmonds for his inspiring article, "Steinbeck's *The Pearl:* A Preliminary Textual Study" [*Steinbeck Quarterly* 22 (Winter-Spring 1989)].

13

Beyond France

Steinbeck's The Short Reign of Pippin IV

Christine Rucklin

Rucklin argues that Pippin *has been underestimated because it has been read as merely a satire of the IVth Republic of France, 1945–58.* Pippin, *she says, employs Steinbeck's sophisticated understanding of French history to explore historiography—especially the role of the individual within cycles of history.*

"Vielle France, accablée d'Histoire, meurtrie de guerres et de révolutions, allant et venant sans relâche de la grandeur au déclin, mais redressée, de siècle en siècle, par le génie du renouveau"
Charles De Gaulle, *Mémoires de guerre*, "La Salut"

The Short Reign of Pippin IV is one of three Steinbeck novels not set in North America (*Cup of Gold* and *The Moon Is Down* are the others). This may partly explain the unease of critics when dealing with this novella, the most critically neglected Steinbeck text. General studies by Warren French, Jackson Benson, Howard Levant and Peter Lisca, of course, include interesting analyses of the book. But it has been dismissed as bland and superficial by those who read it only as a satire of the short-lived and unstable governments of the IVth Republic which ruled France from 1945 to 1958. In his authorized biography, Jackson Benson notes that Steinbeck's "works in response to France (*Pippin*) and his research in England (*Arthur*) were not . . . very successful" (706). Moreover, there are few articles devoted to *Pippin*. And Steinbeck himself contributed to the novel's slight reputation; many of his letters of that period testify to the fun he experienced while he composed the text. On 20 March 1956, he wrote to Webster Street: "It's fun and I could not resist writing it" (*SLL* 524), and in another letter to Pascal Covici the same year, he declared: "that's the reason for this book. Because it's fun" (*SLL* 537).

It seems odd, however, that Steinbeck wanted to poke fun at France, since he had a particular liking for the country where, in 1954, he stayed quite a long time with his third wife, Elaine. In *Un Américain à New York et à Paris*, a series of 1954 articles for *Le Figaro* magazine, he made it clear that he felt at home in Paris and that he appreciated the monuments, the French heritage, and the French culture. This positive experience in France also comes to light in *Pippin*, and there are many elements in the novel which show the extent of his personal knowledge of the country. Indeed, Steinbeck's interest in France appears not only in personal experiences evident in the novel, but also in the text's historical sources. *Pippin* outlines a far broader idea of history and of man's fate than has been noted in most analyses which focus only on the book's satirical intent.

In *Steinbeck's Reading*, Robert DeMott mentions two histories of France in the writer's personal library: François Guizot's *The History of France*, translated by Robert Black, in 8 volumes, of which Steinbeck owned 5; and H. A. L. Fisher's, *A History of Europe* (1939) in 3 volumes. These two works may have been Steinbeck's primary sources for historical material in *Pippin*. Guizot's work gives a few clues about the Merovingians, but Fisher's book seems to have played a more important part in the writing of *Pippin*. Fisher's study stretches from the dawn of history up to the 19th century, whereas Guizot's 8 volumes stop at the French Revolution at the end of the 18th century.

Paradoxically, Steinbeck notes those kings who fell into oblivion and whose reigns did not leave any significant mark on history. His knowledge of the 8th Century Merovingians, for example, is true to history. The writer accurately indicates that "Pippin the Short, son of Charles Martel . . . died in A.D. 768" (27): this detail is significant only insofar as it is one of the few dates reported in Guizot's book. Steinbeck's acuteness lies not only in this detail but also in his general understanding of the Merovingians who, according to Guizot, "are hardly historical characters, and it is under the name of *rois fainéants* that the last

Merovingians find a place in history" (143). The historian adds that "except two or three names somewhat less significant . . . than the others, Merovingian kings only deserve being forgotten" (144). In *Pippin*, Steinbeck simply states, "Merovingians were not able to produce a prince of clear and direct descent" (35) and Pippin IV behaves as his ancestors did.

Guizot notes that "Pippin (the son of Charles Martel) was apt to carry out and implement what he perhaps would not have created and begun to do. Like his father, he proved temperate or even self-effacing, as he came into power . . . he sought, in whatever obscure retreat, a forgotten Merovingian, the son of the penultimate roi fainéant, Chilperic III, and made him king, under the name of Childeric III" (186). As far as the latter Childeric is concerned, Fisher must be left aside as a source, since the historian does not even mention the king's name. For Steinbeck, Childeric is the very king who chooses to have Pippin on the French throne, as he knows that the Merovingians were of an unpretentious descent. "We Merovingians do not want the crown" (43), the character says, adding: "I have the honor to propose that we unite under His Gracious Majesty Pippin of Héristal and Arnulf, of the line of Charlemagne" (45). For Steinbeck, Childeric is more than a reminder of the ancient king: he is also the speaker of former times, the very voice which revives the Salic (meaning Frankish) customs. He recalls what France was like centuries ago: "In the days of my ancestors . . . these matters of succession were handled in a nobler manner—with poison, poniard, or the quick and merciful hands of the strangler" (43). This echoes Guizot's assertion that "between the various . . . members of a common family, rivalries, enmities, hostile plots, acts of violence and atrocity, and struggles quickly became something common" (145).

Not only does Steinbeck remember Frankish customs, but he also recalls Salic laws which prevailed at that time: "Pippin II of Héristal, ignoring the Salic custom of partition, gave all his realm to his son Charles—later called the Hammer" (44). Fisher is in this regard much more explicit than Guizot, for he does not simply describe the chronological succession of the kings of France, but he also outlines a few of their laws. He observes, for instance, that "since females were excluded from the succession to a certain form of property under the law of the Salian Franks, they were incapable of sitting on the French throne" (316). This is exactly what Steinbeck brings up in the conversation between Pippin and the American Egg King: "The French kings have always observed the Salic Law, is that not so? And this law says that women cannot succeed. Isn't that true also?" (103-04).

If the title Steinbeck chose for his novel makes it clear that the writer meant to recall the image of the Merovingians, his familiarity with France was not limited to that period of history. Steinbeck additionally alludes to the French Revolution on several occasions. Indeed, Pippin has points in common with Louis XVI, whom he often thinks or reads about. The king's reading about his ancestors can, of course, refer to Steinbeck's own reading about the 18th century king. Fisher, whose account of the French Revolution is a compact one, reveals the disastrous side of Louis XV's reign, after which Louis XVI, crowned in 1774, appeared to be "entirely unfitted (for reforming the state)," and although he "had every private virtue, honesty, piety, amiability, good sense . . . he could not govern" (795). Like Louis XVI, Pippin has nothing else in mind but what an ordinary man has. He just wants his "little house, [his] wife, and [his] telescope— nothing more" (180). As soon as he knows he is the new king, he remains where he is and starts reading about his ancestors instead of devoting himself to his bounden duty. Furthermore, he thinks of Louis XVI, who was "a good man" whose "intentions and . . . impulses were good" (67), but who nevertheless "was a fool" (67). Fisher relates the execution of the king, a central event in the history of France. And Pippin, at the end of the novel, confesses he wants to be guillotined like his ancestor.

Beyond the comparison between the real and the fictional kings, Steinbeck seems in accord with Fisher's general idea of France during the Revolution. According to Fisher, what triggered the Revolution was that even though France was urbanized, it remained medieval in its agriculture. The same idea is developed in *Pippin*: "The peasant, counting his profits, found time to wonder how much he had lost to the wholesaler. The retail merchant could be heard to curse under his breath when the wholesaler turned his back" (130). This obsolete system is stressed because the writer depicts at the same time the American system of corporations, embodied in the Egg King, who gives Pippin advice on American farming.

The notion of Revolution as it appears in *Pippin* is not only a reminder of the downfall of Louis XVI, but also of the collapse, broadly speaking, of monarchy itself. This brings us to another king whose story is also relevant to *Pippin:* Louis Philippe. After the failure of monarchy, Steinbeck was aware that "The Royalists of France, or for that matter of any country where royalty has been eliminated as a governing principle, have never given up" (40). In this regard, Steinbeck also had in mind the attempts of Royalists to govern France after the revolutionary watershed. He probably considered the Revolution of 1830 and the Monarchy of July. Fisher appears to be the only source here, for Guizot's history stops at the French Revolution. Fisher first reported the original and somewhat eccentric personality of Louis Philippe, this "Bourgeois King with his large 'sentimental umbrella' and his obtrusive domestic virtues [who] was condemned by the common citizen as a bore" (905). He then adds that "the monarchy of Louis Philippe . . . ended in a Paris Revolution" (904). Steinbeck's description of the king is very close to Fisher's: "I ask you to remember Louis Philippe, the so-called Bourgeois King, who dared to walk the streets in ordinary clothing and moreover to carry an umbrella. He was banished from France by an outraged people" (159). Furthermore, there is a more general resemblance between the reign of Pippin and that of the Bourgeois King, whose basic flaw was to be the head of a government which was "neither true monarchy, nor true republic, nor true empire, but a hybrid, without the historical glamour of the legitimate crown, or the democratic appeal of the republic, or the military renown of the House of Bonaparte" (904). This aspect of early nineteenth century history seems to be in the background of Pippin's fictional reign, which is an uneasy attempt "to reactivate a monarchy" (57) during the angry republican 1950s.

Steinbeck's novel tackles deeper subjects than critics have considered: it reflects the writer's idea of history. Steinbeck conceived of history as a cyclic process, and if this aspect appears more clearly in his early fiction, it is far from being absent in *Pippin.* He expresses this theory at the beginning of the novel:

"The events of 19— in France should be studied not for their uniqueness but rather for their inevitability. The study of history, while it does not endow with prophecy, may indicate lines of probability" (31). This assertion that the 1950s are but the recurrence of former times, combined with the elements in the history of France cited above, demonstrate that for Steinbeck, history repeats itself. And certainly he emphasizes these periods for a reason. There is a link between the Merovingians and later kings who were unfit for governing: Louis XVI who was overwhelmed by the crowd in Paris and by a duty he was unable to carry out; Louis Philippe who was banished from the City; and the failed French governments of the IVth Republic. "Guizot endured for 241 years (from 482 to 716). During that period, 28 Merovingian kings reigned and this makes an average reigning time of 8 years and 5 months" (144). These were very short reigns at a time when kings ruled until their deaths. French governments of the 1950s were also short-lived: 24 governments ruled in 13 years; and people took increasingly less interest in what was going on in the French Parliament, where there was an outstanding supremacy of political parties. The instability of the country at that time made Edgar Faure, one of the leading figures of the IVth Republic, call it a "gouvernement à secousses" (shaking government).

History works by cycles, and the human mind seems to be well acquainted with this, for Steinbeck asserts in *Pippin* that "it is a part of the nature, even of the triumphant gallantry of an aristocracy, that it does not, it cannot, abandon the certainty of its return, bringing with it the golden days, the prosperous and courteous days" (40). Even Pippin's wife knows that a "king only repeats old mistakes" (111). So does Uncle Charlie who tells the King that "If suicide does not appeal to you . . . you may relax in the certainty that in the near future there will be attempts at assassination" (53), as he is aware that the king's fate is written in the lines of history. His fate is to measure up to his ancestors, and in particular to Louis XVI, who inspires Pippin. In addition, the cyclic vision of history is reinforced by the use of the image of the mirror. Steinbeck draws a parallel between the Elysée—the dwelling place of French presidents—whose Ballroom "is not only wainscoted with mirrors but also has mirrors on its ceiling" (33) and Versailles—the dwelling place of French kings—which "was a madhouse of scurrying noblemen . . . walking before mirrors in the robes of their station" (161).

Steinbeck not only insists on the certainty of recurring events, but he also questions the breaking of the cycle. When his wife asserts that "the Kings of France, with singularly few gifts, have done very well for themselves. There are some exceptions, of course," Pippin answers, "it is the exception I am thinking of" (66). It seems as if the very periods Steinbeck focuses on were but an exception to the cyclic course of history. Moreover, the writer questions this breaking of the cycle further at the end of the novel, when the protagonist in disguise converses with an old man who tells him that kings "run out. They disappeared, they're ex – ex . . . extinct. Seems like there wasn't room for them" (154). By stating this self-evident truth that there are not kings any more in France, Steinbeck shows that the long reign of monarchy is gone for good, and that it's a loss one can mourn, for it is a loss of the French heritage.

Steinbeck also gave *Pippin* a deeper dimension by dramatizing man's struggle against his own fate. That this struggle changes in the course of history also manifests itself in the novel. Pippin is an amateur astronomer preoccupied with the purchase of a new camera and with observing the sky. He is so engrossed in this activity that his real life appears somewhat unreal in comparison; Pippin, for instance, is one of the last people in the country to know that he is made king. Paradoxically, his urgent need of a new camera is caused by the appearance of a meteor which was "unpredicted" and which "had a sharp effect on the Héristal household" (17). The appearance of this phenomenon seems to be linked to the coming of the reign of Pippin, since the king says "it is unusual to find showers of meteors at this season. Who knows what is going on up there? Do not forget that it was I who first reported the Elysée Comet. I was commended by the Academy. It is whispered that in the not too distant future I may be elected" (22–23).

Fate seems to be written in the stars, and man, like Pippin, is unable to escape his own fate, whatever may be his knowledge of what will happen to him: "I did not ask to be king. I was picked like a berry from a bush and placed in a position where there are many precedents" (108). Becoming a king was in no way Pippin's "choice of profession" (86), and he is incapable of governing; he is scared of what might befall him. He also knows that it "is the tendency of human beings to distrust good fortune. . . . The one thing our species is helpless against is good fortune. It first puzzles, then frightens, then angers, and finally destroys us" (130). Though he did not choose his position—he thinks it is his fate to become a king—he thinks he can escape his doom by dint of a strong will and learning. The perusal of the lives of his ancestors is a means to help him transcend the likeness he sees between present and past events. And knowledge is the one thing he most relies on in this fight against his destiny. Reading about Louis XVI, Pippin declares: "To a certain extent I think I am like him. I am trying to see where he made his errors. I should hate to fall into the same trap" (67).

As much as he relies on knowledge of history and culture, he also swears by science. Howard Levant remarks that "Pippin is much like the early Doc, a scientist dedicated to seeking truth and to doing good" (276). Steinbeck does indeed compare his character's attitude towards fate with a scientist's. But the writer also compares Pippin to the guinea pig used by the scientist to highlight the idea of man's fight against his destiny: "During his long and slow peramble it is more than possible that his mind, like a rat in a laboratory maze, sought every possible avenue of escape, explored runways and aisles and holes, only to run against the wire netting of fact. Again and again he butted his mental nose against the screen at the end of a promising passage, and there was the fact. He was king and there was no escaping it" (55). Yet, science and learning prove useless against fate. Pippin's reign is a complete failure, and he is eventually deposed. Whatever may be man's knowledge of his fate, there is nothing strong enough to defeat it.

Beyond its satirical aspect, *Pippin* thus entertains a deeper reflection on history. By comparing the past events with those of the 1950s, Steinbeck asserts that history works by cycles. By depicting an individual's struggle against his own fate, Steinbeck additionally makes of man an infinitesimally small unit overwhelmed by the gigantic and undefeatable law and order of history. It is by crossing the geographical, chronological and satirical boundaries that the writer proved successful in endowing this novel, so long underrated, with a depth that cannot be a sign of decline. At a time when French people are rediscovering *Pippin*—the only translation of this book into French has been republished recently—critics may learn to reevaluate the novel, by considering it not as one of the writer's masterpieces, which it is not, but as a work deserving more attention than is has received in the past.

14

"The Capacity for Peace—The Culmination of All the Others"

The Internationalism of John Steinbeck and Narrational Technique

John Ditsky

Within the context of Steinbeck's consideration of the American experience, Ditsky argues for a growing internationalist character to Steinbeck's work, culminating in his Nobel Prize acceptance speech, which equates literature with the communication necessary for peace and understanding among peoples.

On accepting the Nobel Prize in Stockholm in 1962, John Steinbeck echoed the emphasis placed on humanistic values by his predecessor in receiving the Award, William Faulkner. Steinbeck's speech, like Faulkner's, was framed by the threat of nuclear catastrophe and war. Speaking of Alfred Nobel himself, a man whose career was associated with the unleashing of physical power, Steinbeck chose to interpret the prizes Nobel had instituted as "a control—a safety valve"—over raw power, and that he had found the control in "the human mind and the human spirit." The awards

> are offered for increased and continuing knowledge of man and of his world—for understanding and *communication*, which are the functions of literature. And they are offered for demonstrations of the capacity for peace—the culmination of all the others. (*Speech* 10)

On such an international occasion Steinbeck emphasizes not his Americanness, but stresses peace among people, and peoples, as an ultimate purpose in writing. Thus Steinbeck made his last statement on behalf of humanity in the aggregate as being the cause for which artists as individuals create their works. No such artist can be primarily at the service of any exclusively defined community, but rather the one that is universally human. The writer's concerns culminate in a striving for peace that, of its very nature, must be international in scope.

William Faulkner's remarks gained great currency, but John Steinbeck's comments in a similar vein went largely unnoticed. Were the minions of J. Edgar Hoover listening to the Nobel Prize Address, they might have discerned in Steinbeck's speech a final statement on humanity in the collective sense, that is, as what he would once have termed the "group-man." And yet it is the individual artist who, in the end, must lead the masses towards peace. A reading of selected passages from Steinbeck's writings leads one to the conclusion that the artist performs the function of broad understanding by treating borders as though they did not exist. It is this trampling of borders with impunity that is the hallmark of John Steinbeck's internationalism: the refusal to see national differences as constituting obstacles to a world view of humanity.

Such an internationalism might be traced, very likely, to Steinbeck's liberal, evolving personal philosophy, reflecting the influences of the thoughtful individuals who entered his life at its various stages. His very catholic reading taste broadened his perspectives. Furthermore, he was by nature a rebel against the smug mores of small-town respectability. In fact, throughout his career John Steinbeck seems to have been free of all or most of the insularities regarding the "foreign" or unfamiliar that afflicted many of the supposedly more cosmopolitan members of his generation of writers. What we expect from a survey of Steinbeck's fiction and non-fiction is a consistency of vision even beyond the scope of a Nobel Prize Address and its occasional and necessarily universal nature.

But such a consistency is hardly possible. At the earliest stages of his career, John Steinbeck was too busy establishing himself as a writer to be occupied with internationalist concerns, an aspect of his work that developed later on. Moreover, his preoccupation with "is" thinking and the group-man or "phalanx" theory during the 1930s was a philosophical stance that did not begin to break down until the writing of *The Moon Is Down*. The success of *Tortilla Flat* and the stylistic breakthroughs of the third of the "work" novels, *The Grapes of Wrath* (followed by *Cannery Row*), made a broader outlook possible, one not as much myth-based as history-based, but concerned with real problems of real and specific people. Of course, this approach had been adumbrated in such earlier works as *In Dubious Battle, Of Mice and Men,* and even the not-so-comical *Tortilla Flat;* but in *The Grapes of Wrath* we see a shift-in-progress towards the presentation of characters with a truly broader, Whitmanesque, world view. By 1939, Steinbeck was on his way to becoming a writer whose ultimate concerns were international, that is, universal and not merely American, or regional. This new stage in his development tallies with his emergence as a public figure and his stature as a companion to celebrities; this matter of stylistic innovation is also crucial to this discussion.

For examples of such a coincidence of changes of style and attitude, we can look to the later works. In Steinbeck's final novel, *The Winter of Our Discontent,* for example, Ethan Allen Hawley—in an often-quoted passage, but one that is also almost intrusive, coming how and where it does towards the novel's ending—digresses for some Independence Day musings on the year of the novel's creation:

> It must be that there are years unlike other years, as different in climate and direction and mood as one day can be from another day. This year of 1960 was a year of change, a year when secret fears come into the open, when discontent stops being dormant and changes gradually to anger. It wasn't only in me or in New Baytown. Presidential nominations would be coming up soon and in the air the discontent was changing to anger and with the excitement anger brings. And it wasn't only the nation; the whole world stirred with restlessness and uneasiness as discontent moved to anger and anger tried to find an outlet in action, any action so long as it was violent—Africa, Cuba, South America, Europe, Asia, the Near East, all restless as horses at the barrier. (248–49)

In fact 1960 was no such thing. The year was not characterized by the feverish and often violent activism that marked the rest of the decade, one that Steinbeck did not live to see the end of. The world, if not quiescent, was also not more agitated than usual: new nations were emerging in great part through peaceful dereliction of colonial-power responsibility. But this passage does represent the novelist's opening up of the book's concerns to those of the world at large. Steinbeck uses the key word "discontent" in this novel almost as often as he cites "anger." It is obviously meant to be a key quote, the point at which the novelist brings his concerns about personal ego to the fore, now that he has freed his text from third-person, objective narration. It represents the corrupted ego of Ethan Allen Hawley projecting itself upon his nation, as his son's plagiarized "I Love America" essay has done. Specifically, it brings to a boil the earlier conclusion to Part I of the book, when Ethan—having succeeded in getting the Taylor property willed to him—celebrates the Easter of his betrayal of his friend by singing Shakespeare's lines from the opening of *Richard III*, the source of the novel's title, and thus ironically waxing festive (*WOD* 157).

Shakespeare's lines are characteristic in identifying the festering of the state with the rot in its government; the irony subsists in Richard's frank confession that the season of hope, the eastering of the year, is an unreal one. Steinbeck, of course, loved both of Shakespeare's Richard plays; but in this instance, he would have been unavoidably mindful of the pretensions to national power of Richard Nixon. Purged of his "anger" by his experiences in the Second World War, Ethan will become briefly and dubiously "content" by utilizing Nixonian tricks. As he looks at his 1960 world, Ethan also sees it as his oyster—or his ulcer—by projecting his own obsessions upon it.

Steinbeck, fairly clearly speaking in Ethan's voice and thus putting himself on trial in his final novel, has sent the guiltiness of his own American ego out into the world. It embraces, in a kind of breast-beating, the anger and violence of the planet. It identifies the moral guilt of a nation with events beyond its borders—events taking place in other "violent" and "restless" nations. This is, it could be argued, a particularly harrowing kind of confession, and one that it would take a psychologist to muddle through. In the end, there is very little that Steinbeck/Hawley does not seem to have accused himself of in the name of a broader context, including lust and indirect murder.

In *Winter,* Steinbeck reaches out to a genuinely international world consciousness which has also become a sounding board for especially American issues. The artist is at one and the same time on one side of his characters, observing and presenting them, and yet also leaping past or through them to a sphere of specifically cited—arguably gratuitously—larger concerns.

Of course, one can trace the first glimmerings of Steinbeck's internationalism even in the universality and pan-nationalism of the fraternity of freebooters in *Cup of Gold,* or in the reduction of human nature to discernible and universal types in *To a God Unknown.* We sense there the influences that would be epitomized by such conversational intimates as Edward F. Ricketts and Joseph Campbell. But when the artist is conspicuously present as a voice as he is in the work after *The Grapes of Wrath,* however, we find a foreshadowing of the tenor of the later works. In the narrative part of *Sea of Cortez,* for instance, the writer's voice can be coolly objective about foreigners:

> We do not know whether Mexicans are happier than we; it is probable that they are exactly as happy. However, we do not know that the channels of their happiness or unhappiness are different from ours, just as their time sense is different. We can invade neither, but it is some gain simply to know that it is so. (83)

And again, speaking of Japanese fishermen:

> We liked the people on this boat very much. They were good men, but they were caught in a large destructive machine, good men doing a bad thing. With their many and large boats, with their industry and efficiency, but most of all with their intense energy, these Japanese will obviously soon clean out the shrimps of the region. . . . (206)

We see here the present artistic consciousness in the act of transmuting apparently disparate traits into a neutral matrix of a developing internationalism. Suddenly Steinbeck had discovered the liberation of entering his own writing without artistic pretense to the contrary.

This arguably intrusive presence of the artist—once he has been freed to come and go within Steinbeck's fiction—appears in even such relatively insignificant but interesting moments in *East of Eden* as the passage at the beginning of Chapter 42 where the narrator reflects, "A war comes always to someone else," and then goes on to discuss the opening days of the American involvement in World War I, when it was at first assumed that Americans were naturally the superiors of the Germans when it came to marksmanship, just as they had once mistakenly assumed that the raiding Mexicans under Pancho Villa were "lazy and stupid." Though the narrator goes on to note a second phase in this process, one in which home folk ran in panic to the opposite assumption that the Germans were going to invade and conquer (*EOE* 484–85), what is interesting in this minor passage is the fact that the narrating voice, neither exposing nor denying identification with America, refutes any claims of American superiority while refusing to concede superiority to anyone else. In other words, the free-floating narrational voice of *East of Eden* leaps past nationalism to embrace an equality with the other citizens of the world, a refusal of claims to inherent American invulnerability that embraces all humankind in its ability to do anything pro or con in its "capacity for peace."

We might remember the criticisms of *The Moon Is Down* for its failure to show in caricatured form the evils of Nazism, just as the author had earlier meant to show that such an invasion by fascistic powers could take place in America, its initial setting, in effect equating the Axis and Allies as far as human capacities were concerned. Systems differ, and so do modes of human organization; the basics of human capacity do not. Steinbeck rather daringly, therefore, simultaneously embraces internationalism without denying his specific American identity. As early as *The Pastures of Heaven,* the boy Takashi Kato deflects racism towards the Japanese by showing his excess of Americanness (even as the author lets Robbie Maltby plant the expectation of war with the Japanese someday) (86–87). Takashi's convert's willingness to be more enthusiastic than "born Americans" serves to diffuse his playmates' chauvinism.

The above instances are not deeply significant in novelistic context, yet they adumbrate more serious critical issues. For while the narrator himself is now free to interject commentary as he will, his positioning in the work makes it possible for other, supposedly "fictional" characters to assert themselves likewise. This is true not only of the familial presence of Samuel Hamilton but also of the faithful house servant Lee, whose Chineseness—and ostensible foreignness—only Sam, Cal, and Abra seem to penetrate—perhaps because they have adopted his internationalism, his holistic acceptance of a world both different and without boundaries. Lee's Oriental philosophical stance and his bizarre input of biblical scholarship is of true importance to the plot line. We need to pay attention this time to his outsider's observations about American society and his eventual conclusion that he is not excluded from what he has seen and described, and to recognize that his foreignness is but an aspect of his Americanness, with national distinctions falling down around him.

With respect to ostensible nationalism, then, John Steinbeck includes himself in his final document, *America and Americans.* In spite of his specific ethnic roots, the writer maintains, he is instantly taken to be an American. He muses, "Somewhere there is an American look. I don't know what it is, and foreigners cannot describe it; but it is there" (16). Then Steinbeck goes on to say that Orientals he has known in California also have this American look, and he speculates further to the effect that evolutionary changes have already made Americans of Oriental descent look different from their ancestors and their cousins in the old country (17). Steinbeck seems content to see Americans as bridges to the wider world, incorporating and processing as they do that whole world's physical and psychological traits and features.

Thus it is possible that some would find Steinbeck's assertions here at least partially contradictory in terms of the isolationism of the times, especially when so much is asked to rest upon them. In the later chapter "Americans and the World" (131–36), Steinbeck discusses American apartness, the fact that for decades few Americans traveled abroad, and only reluctantly involved themselves in foreign quarrels. But, he concludes, "I believe the time of American insularity is over" (133), and with it political and private isolationism; Americans who venture beyond the confines of their country find that the citizens of other nations are "just like us!" (132). If there are arguably Emer-

sonian or Whitmanian contradictions at work here, John Steinbeck embraces them all. Not surprisingly, the chapter quickly
moves to credit America's writers with elucidating and recording American disparities with other societies, the end result being that Americans in the early part of the second half of the
twentieth century can confidently claim cultural parity with
those societies, and on the basis of that claim assert the right to
Americanize the globe. Steinbeck must have read the opening
language of the United Nations Charter, and known that it echoed that of the American Constitution. Naturally foreigners
would view such an attitude with suspicion and alarm; it is one
small step from the celebratory quality of Whitman's "Passage
to India"—where a universe is invited into a union of peoples
that is a benign projection of the American achievement—to
an arrogant and patronizing attempt to dominate a new world
order.

Of course, nothing of the sort was present in Steinbeck's imagination, except as a perceived threat anchored in the same American homogeneity he seemed to have been praising in the deliberately narrowed ethnic representation in *The Grapes of Wrath*.
But one doesn't praise a country's writers in the name of hailing
their depictions of sameness and dullness. Long before *Travels
with Charley* comes to an abrupt and disappointed halt with a
precipitate rush for home, Steinbeck had begun to sense that
some aspects of American culture had become a kind of Vel-
veeta of the soul. Somewhere in North Dakota, the writer grum-
bled to Charley that American food, with little to enliven it but
ketchup and mustard, was much like local radio: " . . . the mental fare has been as generalized, as packaged, and as undistin-
guished as the food" (109). Characteristically, Steinbeck one page
later recalls a conversation with a Minnesotan about how we
need the Russians, or some enemy, to spice our radio food, so to
speak (110). But we have lost the Russians.

But Steinbeck's moods could swing, as regards internationalism, and the swings are more apparent in the later works for the
stylistic, narrational reasons mentioned above. In *Travels with
Charley*, he admits that his observations and his musings have
become a mental "barrel of worms." That leads him naturally
to recall the days of classifying collected marine animals, and

how "what I found was closely intermeshed with how I felt at the moment. External reality has a way of not being so external after all" (159). Steinbeck waxes almost Shakespearean next in saying that "This monster of a land, this mightiest of nations, this spawn of the future, turns out to be the macrocosm of microcosm me" (159). Foreigners might have shared his experiences and come up with as many different conclusions as they represented nations or groups, but he feels that Americans would agree with him, and that what that would show is that "we are alike in our Americanness." For all their sectional and other differences, Americans are "a nation, a new breed," and this homogeneity has been the work of an astonishingly brief period of historical time (159–60).

By now John Steinbeck had painted himself into something of an oxymoronic corner as regards the true significance of national identities—towards the end of *Travels with Charley* he makes a sturdy effort to extricate himself, attempting to resolve the apparent contradictions in his attitudes towards national identity. In doing so, he strains to be a Crèvecoeur of clarity. He begins a late chapter by asking himself a rhetorical question he imagines Europeans asking: "What are Americans like today?" Steinbeck has a ready answer for those foreigners who claim to dislike Americans generally and yet make exceptions for individuals. "Traveling about," he states, "I learned the difference between an American and the Americans." Admitting that "I had always considered this a kind of semantic deadfall," he accepts that challenge:

> Americans as I saw them and talked to them were indeed individuals, each one different from the others, but gradually I began to feel that Americans exist, that they really do have their generalized characteristics regardless of their states, their social and financial status, their education, their religious, and their political convictions. (185)

But if there is an American image "built of truth," what is it? Steinbeck was not sure, and pushes the matter aside with the admission, "It appeared to me increasingly paradoxical, and it has been my experience that when paradox crops up too often for comfort, it means that certain factors are missing in the equation" (186).

Thus Steinbeck has found the title for his final volume, and yet it hinges on the fact of paradox. If the distinction between the characters of individual Americans and the fuzzy image of a perceived national character seems patently a truism possibly not worth stating, can it say anything of value? Can it be expected to relate to the dual aspects of our title, internationalism and narrational technique? We might cite a fictional example of such ambivalence from the period over a dozen years before *Travels with Charley*. In *The Wayward Bus*, Steinbeck has already conjured this character in a more caricatured form as the hypocritical Mr. Pritchard. Surely it is Steinbeck the narrator who makes Pritchard into such an antitype of his own values. Steinbeck reads us Pritchard's thoughts:

> Now he was nervous. He was going on a vacation he didn't really want to take. He was going to Mexico which, in spite of the posters, he considered a country not only dirty but dangerously radical. They had expropriated the oil; in other words, stolen private property. And how was that different from Russia? Russia, to Mr. Pritchard, took the place of the medieval devil as the source of all cunning and evil and terror. (33)

In other words, Mexico and its oxymoronically named Institutional Revolutionary Party (PRI) have, by setting up the state oil monopoly Pemex, acted like Bolsheviks, creators of the Evil Empire. Pritchard is a prophetic vision of a man ready to embrace the forthcoming Senator from Wisconsin as his kind of man. Yearning for the good old days of Coolidge and Hoover, Pritchard is close to being a cartoon capitalist. He is certainly, in his xenophobia, no version of John Steinbeck, whose internationalism excluded exclusionism, and whose visits to both Mexico and the USSR were characterized by sympathy and warmth.

With regard to the Soviet Union, in his own *A Russian Journal* Steinbeck had concluded as one might have expected him to, but as many at that time would not have wished him to:

> We found, as we had suspected, that the Russian people are people, and, as with other people, that they are very nice. The ones we

met had a hatred of war, they wanted the same things all people want—good lives, increased comfort, security, and peace.

... We have no conclusions to draw, except that Russian people are like all other people in the world. Some bad ones there are surely, but by far the greatest number are very good. (212)

Here, "Russian" means the whole USSR, or as much of it as Steinbeck was allowed to visit—including non-Slavic Georgia, which had produced the local hero/monster Josef Stalin. This point would be trivial except that it opens even wider the spirit of Steinbeck's internationalism. His vision seems unsentimentalized, given the capacity of his materials to have been worked in either emotional direction; he is still the observant reporter, objective to the point of limiting himself to such a neutral qualifying adjective as "nice." In short, he refused to draw conclusions.

Steinbeck's humaneness is also an aspect of his having been trapped by the tendency to generalize about peoples. Once stuck with his own genial overall views of nationalities, for example, he could only open outwards; and inward-going nationalism, or chauvinism, was not for him. Here, in *Once There Was a War*, he chats about a naval operation about to begin, one that he says the men refer to as a "Thing":

Dozens of the little ships are going out. It is an Allied operation. There are Dutch boats, and Polish boats, and English. The Poles are great fighters. This is their kind of work. When the little ships attacked the *Scharnhorst*, slipping through the Channel, it is said that a Polish sailor was down on the prow of his torpedo boat, calmly firing at the great steel battleship with a rifle. The Dutch have a calm, cold courage, and the British pretend, as usual, it is some kind of a garden party they are going to. (67)

Of course anyone who knows anything about the heroic resistance of Poles and Polish Jews in the two Warsaw uprisings cannot question the fact of enormous and widespread Polish courage; and the stoicism of the Dutch and the British has been severally reported. The gentle entrapment of John Steinbeck here lies with his tendency to think the best of all peoples, or at least the best of the best—for he is not reluctant to point out exceptions. If he is not sentimental, then, he seems in the later works to have toned down any residual Americanism to the point of accepting foreigners as being, like Americans—or most of them—"nice." This will never satisfy those who wish for harsher judgments, but it is highly unlikely that John Steinbeck was put on earth in order to pass sentences at anyone's trial. And what to make of his tendency to make generalizations—positive or negative—about whole peoples?

In the preface to *The Forgotten Village* John Steinbeck observes that "It means very little to know that a million Chinese are starving unless you know one Chinese who is starving" (*FV* 5). This line can be taken as an objection to unfocused altruism or a vague goodheartedness, but it is probably much more accurate to see in it a statement to the effect that it is all well and good to make benign generalizations about Russians, Dutch, Poles, and—yes—Chinese, but it takes individual contact to recognize the stranger as someone much like oneself and to relate to him and his needs. We may remember here the famous fourth chapter of *Cannery Row,* in which the mysterious old Chinaman is introduced, the fellow who carries his wicker basket down to the Bay every evening and disappears under the piers, only to reappear again at dawn, his basket now "heavy and wet and dripping" and one shoe's sole flapping. "It had been happening for years but no one ever got used to him. Some people thought he was God and very old people thought he was Death and children thought he was a very funny old Chinaman, as children always think anything old and strange is funny." In other words, people at the three stages of life read their own prepossessions into the strange figure, though no one troubles to get to know him; and even the children "did not taunt him or shout at him as they should for he carried a little cloud of fear about with him" (24–25).

Notice here the narrator's word choice: the children do not taunt or shout at the Chinaman "as they should"; taunting and shouting at what is strange is what children do at their stage of life. There is an exception, however. A "brave and beautiful boy of ten named Andy from Salinas" visiting in town makes it a test of his courage to confront the Chinaman, marching along behind him while singing "in a shrill falsetto, 'Ching-

Chong Chinaman sitting on a rail—'Long came a white man an' chopped off his tail'" (25).

We all recall what happens next, when the Chinaman turns around and confronts the boy, lips moving:

> What happened then Andy was never able either to explain or to forget. For the eyes spread out until there was no Chinaman. And then it was one eye—one huge brown eye as big as a church door. Andy looked through the shiny transparent brown door and through it he saw a lonely countryside, flat for miles but ending against a row of fantastic mountains shaped like cows' and dogs' heads and tents and mushrooms. There was low coarse grass on the plain and here and there a little mound. And a small animal like a woodchuck sat on each mound. And the loneliness —the desolate cold aloneness of the landscape made Andy whimper because there wasn't anybody at all in the world and he was left. (25–26)

Andy closes his eyes and when he opens them, the vision is over; and he never tries to do the same thing again.

This passage is one of the strangest in all of Steinbeck's work, even more chilling, perhaps, than the events in "The Snake." Andy's taunting allows him a glimpse into the incredible loneliness of the Chinaman, so far from home and without known human contact. Andy suddenly knows one Chinese, and he will never chant his racist chant again. Another observation. We notice that for no apparent reason, Andy is said to be "from Salinas," and to be "brave and beautiful." As interesting as Andy's hometown's name is to the Steinbeck reader, the adjectives "brave and beautiful" are revealing, for in being positive they do not mock a boy who has done a boyish thing and learned a lesson from doing so. It does not seem much of a claim to suggest that Andy is an idealized version of a very young Steinbeck who may have, at such an age, learned a very useful lesson about people who are different—and yet not that different at all. That a Californian writer should have been able to rise above native, and nativist, prejudice, and in doing so set himself on a path towards giving us the key character of Lee in *East of Eden* is crucial to his ability to speak to us about the "capacity for peace."

The examples used in this paper are all from the works of John Steinbeck, rather than from secondary sources. Moreover, the intention of letting Steinbeck speak in his own voice—or that of his characters, which so often is the same thing—has expressed itself here by the deliberate inclusion of passages which may seem incidental to the works from which they have been taken. But it is in his less guarded moments that the writer characteristically reveals himself. The latter phase of John Steinbeck's career, during which he became increasingly political, public, and well-traveled, did more than simply coincide with his changing from a writer of ostensibly amoral fiction to one who projected himself into characters he identified with—like Joe Saul in *Burning Bright*, Cal Trask, Ethan Allen Hawley, Sir Lancelot, and possibly even Pippin IV. The era of his moral fiction is also the era when he developed an internationalist stance, one that makes the paean to peace and the duties of the writer in the Nobel Prize Address more than simply his rising to an occasion. If, as has been suggested, there is always an Ed Ricketts figure in John Steinbeck's works, it could readily be conceded that this is particularly true of the earlier works; for it might be said with equal legitimacy that in the later writings, there is always a John Steinbeck figure, or nearly so. This figure is characterized by moral concerns and not "is" thinking, and in spite of being severely aware of his own moral shortcomings he manages to deny the final necessity of a nihilistic, or perhaps even negative, direction to life.

Paralleling these guest appearances in his own fictions as *character*, of course, have been those in which he becomes the often-subjective narrator; and here the fiction tallies with the journalistic work of the last decades of Steinbeck's life: *A Russian Journal, Once There Was a War, America and Americans*, and of course *Travels with Charley*, though it could be argued that this last title, along with some of the others and with *Journal of a Novel*, can be viewed as partial fictions as well. At any rate, the line is a blurred one, and the blurring results from the split in voices already referred to extensively. Steinbeck had become that kind of good teacher who performs and yet has a part of him watching his own performance. This split voice can be called *conscience*, in this case the artistic one; and it tallies with the process by which Steinbeck learned to project his own self and its concerns against sometimes contradictory national ones. Thus, America and one American were locked in combat. Over the rim of its foxhole, Steinbeck was able to observe a larger world that his American concerns might apply to. If this was not the distance from the tide pool to the stars any longer, it was certainly that from the community microcosm to the global village. Thus style, or voice, and global moral concerns are ultimately related. In this melding resides John Steinbeck's internationalism.

Last summer, a bus overtook a truck on a European highway. On the back of the truck was a corporate name that sounded a keynote for this paper. The truck was owned by "Steinbeck Global Logistics." Exactly the point. This "found poem" on the side of a truck encapsulated a basic change in Steinbeck's voice and style. In leaving behind his own village, Steinbeck also left behind his old style and his old perceptions. Whatever Californians may think of his move east, it did accompany changes that projected his thinking well beyond New York, so much further that his concerns came to encompass the planet.

III
Rereading Steinbeck's Women

15

Beyond the Boundaries of Sexism

The Archetypal Feminine versus Anima Women in Steinbeck's Novels

Lorelei Cederstrom

While critics have objected to Steinbeck's one-dimensional view of women as either sexual object or "maternal figure, who is nearly sexless," Cederstrom sees Steinbeck's women as far more complex and, indeed, integral to his non-teleological approach that "emphasizes the feminine values of wholeness, relatedness, and the interdependence of ecological groups."

Steinbeck has been criticized for the one-dimensional quality and limited range of his female characters. Claude-Edmonde Magny, Robert Morsberger and Joseph Fontenrose, for example, refer to two primary types: the Virgin Whore, who is the "mythical prototype of Steinbeck's woman as sexual object" and the "maternal figure, who is nearly sexless" (Fontenrose 129). While these character types are often present, these categories fail to assess the depth of Steinbeck's presentation of the archetypal feminine and the philosophical premises which underlie his work. In spite of the sexism ingrained in American culture and the masculine scientific approach to the natural world and life-processes that surrounded him, as early as 1933, Steinbeck wrote of the earth as "our mother" which gives life and takes it. While the American powers of commerce focused on the conquest of nature, Steinbeck described the dire results of sucking all the fish out of the Sea of Cortez with large vacuum hoses, and raping the fields of Oklahoma and California with iron machines. In the face of the masculinist view of nature as an object to be studied and analyzed, its mysteries penetrated by the probing objective mind of the scientist with his cause-and-effect theories, Steinbeck developed a non-teleological approach, which emphasizes the feminine values of wholeness, relatedness, and the interdependence of ecological groups. Although the male characters in Steinbeck's novels frequently respond to the natural world or the female characters in negative ways, these reactions reflect the general devaluation of the feminine in Western culture and do not represent sexism on the author's part. A closer look at nature and landscape as well as the female characters in several novels indicates that Steinbeck was celebrating the feminine and advocating the necessity of feminine values for a balanced life. The novels discussed here are taken from various stages in Steinbeck's career, each representing a different approach to the feminine in his overall emphasis on the restoration of gender balance. These representative samples include: first, his most obviously archetypal novel, *To a God Unknown,* in which Steinbeck sets out the parameters of his attitude toward nature, the feminine, and the feminine in nature; secondly, two novels which continue his discussion of male/female relationships and attitudes toward nature in a comedic vein, namely *Cannery Row,* which introduces the saga of Doc, and *Sweet Thursday,* in which the saga continues with Suzy and Doc; and finally, *East of Eden,* the novel with the most difficult and controversial female character, namely, Cathy Trask. In spite of the diversity in technique and approach, these novels nonetheless reveal Steinbeck's consistent appreciation of the archetypal feminine.

Steinbeck's holistic conception of life and deep appreciation for the value of the feminine is articulated clearly in his first and most overtly archetypal novel, *To a God Unknown* (1933). In his depiction of the female landscape of the Nuestra Señora valley and the men who live there, Steinbeck establishes a paradigm for the ideal balance between masculine and feminine, the human world and the world of nature. Joseph Wayne escapes from the patriarchal Christian culture of the East to make his home in the Valley of Our Lady, a place that the Indians of the region associate with more ancient deities than Christ. In his depiction of Wayne, a man who lives close to the earth which he approaches as a living being, Steinbeck has invoked two primordial archetypes: that of the earth as the Great Cosmic Mother[1] and her companion, the "Green Man,"[2] who ensures her health and fertility. The Great Cosmic Mother is the archetype of the living earth demanding reverence and respect for her power over life and death. The Green Man is her consort and protector, manifested in mythical characters like the Green Knight, the Fisher King and various fertility gods who sacrifice themselves and their lives to her protection. By invoking these archetypes, Steinbeck brings back to life the earth consciousness of the matriarchal age and valorizes the long-degraded feminine principle in our lives. Wayne, like the Green Man of mythology, builds his life in relationship to the earth as a primordial feminine spirit and rediscovers ancient rituals of the tree, the rock and the stream upon which the fertility of his land depends. From the moment of his arrival in the Valley of Our Lady, Wayne is attuned to the feminine spirit of the land; he sees immediately that even the forests of the valley of Nuestra Señora have a "curious femaleness" about them "as obscure and promising as the symbols of an ancient religion" (5). This female landscape overwhelms him, and he becomes spiritually reborn from the moment of his first contact: "Joseph felt that he had been dull and now suddenly was sensitized; had been asleep and was awakened" (5). To counteract the overpowering female landscape which he feels "might possess him" (5), he draws upon an image of "the calm, peace and eternal rightness of his father" as a balance. His perception that "his father and this new land were one" (5), even though it brings with it the understanding that his father must have died in his absence to be present so powerfully in the spirit, enables Joseph to inhabit the land. He further unites his own masculine spirit with the great goddess by making love to the earth, drawn to her by a "pain of desire" (8) so powerful that "she had been his wife" (8). Wayne's self-appointed destiny, like those of the Fisher King and other Green Men of mythology, is to love the earth as a living being, dedicating himself to bringing about and sustaining her fertility.

As Steinbeck develops the relationship between Wayne and the land, he utilizes another important symbol related to the Green Man of mythology, the tree. The union of masculine and feminine elements that sustain Joseph's life on the ranch is symbolized by a large oak tree; he believes that his father's spirit lives in the tree, which is sustained through its connection to mother earth. The tree, particularly the oak, also played a primary role in the rituals of the Green Man associated with the renewal of fertility in pre-historic Europe. In his book, *The Green Man,* which surveys the European archetype, William Anderson writes of the symbolic value attached to trees in various mythologies: "There would seem to be few cultures in which the Sacred Tree does not figure: as an image of the cosmos, as a dwelling place of gods or spirits, as a medium of prophecy and knowledge, and as an agent of metamorphoses" (23). The large oak under which Joseph builds his house is all of these and more. He believes his father "is that tree" (19) and turns to it for sustenance and wisdom. At the same time, Joseph recognizes that the entire landscape is haunted by spirits, which he perceives as primordial images, archetypal forces more real than the tangible world. Joseph confides this to Juanito: "'Since I have come, since the first day, I have known that this land is full of ghosts.' He paused uncertainly. 'No, that isn't right. Ghosts are weak shadows of reality. What lives here is more real than we are. We are like ghosts of its reality'" (19). Juanito clarifies this theory of the living archetypes around them by telling Joseph the basic belief of his own matriarchal culture: "My mother said how the earth is our mother, and how everything that lives has life from the mother and goes back into the mother" (19). The life Joseph Wayne hopes to establish on his ranch, like the tree, depends upon the living earth to sustain it.

The most important function of the Green Man in mythology is to ensure the fertility of the earth. Supported by the powerful union of masculine and feminine in tree and land, Joseph takes on himself the fecundating spirit of the Green Man:

> All things about him, the soil, the cattle and the people were fertile, and Joseph was the source, the root of their fertility, his was the motivating lust. He willed that all things about him must grow, grow quickly, conceive and multiply. The hopeless sin was barrenness. . . . It was the heritage of a race which for a million years had sucked at the breasts of the soil and co-habited with the earth. (24)

Because of this lust for fertility, Joseph decides to take a wife. His choice, Elizabeth, is neither the Virgin Whore nor the sexless mother, but rather a woman who has grown up with masculine values and, at first, understands neither the value of the feminine nor her place in the world. Elizabeth's initial confusion is described through an inversion of stereotypical masculine and feminine perspectives in her relationship with Joseph. She embodies the masculine Logos and tries to find classical models for her ideas, while Joseph, like the feminine Eros, communicates through the intensity of his feelings. A need for balance brings Joseph, with his intuitive, feeling connections to mother earth, to Elizabeth, the schoolteacher, who, Athena-like, has been raised with a patriarchal respect for the life of the mind. Elizabeth is particularly fond of Homer, and when she tries to share this with Joseph she discovers that he recalls only the part of *The Odyssey* which warns about the dangerous feminine, the story where "a man went to an island and got changed into a pig" (35). Yearning at first for an intellectual understanding of the passion of her suitor, Elizabeth tries to cast Joseph in a classical heroic mode. As he continues to try to teach her about instinctual impartial passion, she yearns to turn him into the Centaur Chiron, tutor of the heroes, complaining: "If only he had the body of a horse, I might love him more" (48). Although Elizabeth wants to be free enough to express her sexual yearnings openly—standing alone at her window, she longs for Joseph's brother among a group of young men on the prowl below—she is unable to do so until she marries Joseph.

Throughout the relationship between Joseph and Elizabeth, Steinbeck indicates his understanding that masculine and feminine qualities exist in male and female alike, regardless of gender, and emphasizes through their union the necessity for a balance between the two. The wedding of Joseph and Elizabeth speeds their transformation; it is described as an hierogamous union of masculine and feminine. Both of them chafe against the Catholic rituals of wedlock with which society would sanctify their union. Joseph, in particular, feels a "falseness," a "doddering devil worship" (49) in the rituals that surround their marriage, finding in the church bells a truer representation of the masculine and feminine elements of their joining. Steinbeck uses images from the mythic *hierosgamos,* the mating of earth and sky, to describe the bells: "It is the sun sticks, striking the bell of the sky in the morning; and the hollow beating of rain on the earth's full belly" (50). The hierogamous nature of their union is also emphasized in the wedding journey toward Joseph's homestead, as a multitude of cosmic symbols combine to indicate that they have crossed the threshold from the profane separateness of their individual selves to enter into a sacred union. Without words, Joseph conveys to Elizabeth his sense of their union: "Yesterday we were married and it was no marriage. This is our marriage—through the pass—entering the passage like sperm and egg that have become a single unit of pregnancy. I have a moment in my heart, different in shape, in texture, in duration from any other moment. . . . this is all marriage that has ever been, contained in our moment" (54). Elizabeth had been afraid of this marriage, but, like Eve leaving Paradise behind, she enters her new life with Joseph willing to accept that "the bitterness of being a woman may be an ecstasy" (55). Their sacred union gives each of them a moment of cosmic consciousness as well, in which "all things are one, and all a part of them" (63).

The lives of Joseph and Elizabeth on the homestead are full of rituals which emphasize their special connection to the land and its spirits. Elizabeth and her mysterious sister-in-law share women's mysteries associated with the domestic sphere, while Joseph continues his communion with his father's spirit in the tree. The central rituals, however, revolve around a large moss-covered rock that rests beside a tree in the center of a grove. Joseph and Elizabeth both feel a special connection to this rock which is described as the "heart" of the land, an archetypal *axis mundi* and its waters as coming "out of the center of the world" (74). Mircea Eliade, in *Cosmos and History,* has described the significance of such earth centers in fertility rituals and sacrifices like those which center around the rock here. In spite of their connection to the archetypal spirits of their land, both Elizabeth and Joseph are sacrificed to the needs of the great goddess, the living earth, at the rock. Elizabeth is killed as she climbs the rock to "tame it" (132), erring in her need for control against the feminine principle which had sustained her, and Joseph gives his own life blood to keep the moss rock heart alive when the stream that nourishes it dries up. Joseph's sacrifice is his final gift to the earth, a symbolic recognition that all life comes from earth and returns to her: "I am the land," he avows, "and I am the rain. The grass will grow out of me in a little while" (184). Like the Green Man, he lives and dies through his connection to the feminine earth. Joseph's act may be extreme in contemporary terms, but in terms of the mythos by which he lives, it is a fitting end. Barbara Walker's studies of the various rituals ensuring the fertility of the land by means of sacrifice to the archetypal feminine indicate that archaic societies frequently practiced blood sacrifices like Joseph's. She writes:

> Human or animal sacrifice victims were almost always male. . . . The savior-hero gave his lifeblood to Mother Earth as a fertility charm, to help replace the world's supply of life-giving blood produced by women. One of the oldest theories of the origin of life was as the Bible puts it, "the blood is the life" (Deut. 12:23). As women were thought to create their own inner fountains, so men's earliest idea of taking part in the creative process was to contribute their own blood. (47)

Thus, although both Elizabeth and Joseph have died, Steinbeck makes it clear that the archetypal principles they represent will return with the fertility of the land.

Characters in Steinbeck's later works are plotted across a landscape less infused with mythical allusions than the story of Joseph and Elizabeth in *To a God Unknown*. Rather, Steinbeck's later characters move across the wasteland yearning for cosmic connections as they sort through the disharmonious fragments of their lives. Steinbeck continues to emphasize the importance of achieving a balance between masculine and feminine, however, and points out through the use of various symbols and disturbed man/woman relationships how central that balance is. Several works focus on the relationship between men imbued with various Judeo-Christian masculine biases and women who represent more primitive and powerful female forces. Often the men, equally victimized by the devaluation of the feminine in our culture, see the women in terms of simple projections of good and evil. Certain characters, like Suzy in *Sweet Thursday* and Cathy in *East of Eden,* bring about disruptive and dangerous situations, as the simplistic anima projections of the men confront the reality of feminine complexity and power.

The necessity for the balance between the elemental masculine and feminine established in *To a God Unknown* is emphasized in another mode as Steinbeck explores Doc's empty life in the mock-Arthurian epic, *Cannery Row.* The epic involves the restoration of the feminine to a world ignorant of its value, which culminates in Doc's relationship with Suzy in *Sweet Thursday.* Doc's lack of fulfillment mirrors life on the sterile wasteland of mythology that sent the knight out on his quest for the grail. A modern man in search of his soul, Doc seeks a cure for his loneliness and lack of connection to the world through his scientific studies and alcohol. In spite of the warm regard for Doc as protector and benefactor by the male characters, the novel emphasizes in various ways the limitations in Doc's approach to life. Steinbeck immediately establishes the world of *Cannery Row* as one in which female nature is dominated by masculine science, and the domestic world of the female is studiously avoided by Doc and his friends. Mack and the "boys," who live from day to day by their wits, pray not to our mother the earth, but to "Our Father which art in nature" (18) for their gifts of survival.

Doc's life is particularly one-sided, out of tune with the feminine nature which Joseph Wayne worships. His work in the lab reflects the scientific, masculine consciousness run amok. He is a twentieth-century man, making his living at the expense of nature. He plunders the tide pools, breeding beds of the great mother of life, for creatures to dissect and "sells the lovely animals of the sea" (27) to be probed at research institutions all over the country. There is no reverence for life in the "little unborn humans, some whole and others sliced thin and on slides" (27) that decorate his shelves. Unlike Joseph Wayne, who dies saying "I am the rain" (*TGU* 184), Doc "has one great fear—that of getting his head wet, so that summer or winter he ordinarily wears a rain hat" (29). He lives in ignorance of the feminine in his personal life as well. The lab is his home; he cannot even bother to prepare healthful food for himself, and he abates his loneliness talking to the prostitutes across the street. All of Doc's friends recognize his loneliness, but do not correctly diagnose his illness. Although they know he needs a woman in his life, the boys of Cannery Row do not understand, any more than Doc himself understands, how much he needs to be reconnected to the feminine in nature as well as life. Hence, the parties they throw, including the long-awaited party that concludes *Cannery Row*, result in destruction and a deeper loneliness for Doc. The final image in *Cannery Row* of Doc standing alone in his lab speaking to his rats symbolizes his need for a connection with the feminine, and a realignment with the feminine elements in the cosmos. He recites a poem called "Black Marigolds" to his lab animals and specimens, suggesting the cosmic harmonies denied him. It movingly expresses his yearnings for a "forgotten time" when, "I have had full in my eyes from off my girl/ The whitest pouring of eternal light" (185).

The continuation of Doc's story in *Sweet Thursday* begins with Steinbeck's description of the universal alienation from the feminine from which Doc also suffers. The whole world supports the masculine war machine which now has a justification for tearing every last resource from mother earth: "The canneries themselves fought the war by getting the limit taken off fish and catching them all. It was done for patriotic reasons, but that didn't bring the fish back. . . . It was the same noble impulse that stripped the forests of the west and . . . pumped water out of California's earth faster than it can rain back in" (1). Doc's war experiences have only intensified his alienation from the feminine. Steinbeck symbolizes the depths of his imbalance in his cruel experiments on baby octopi. Indifferent to the many that die from the collecting, Doc forces the remaining to interact, projecting his own masculine rage onto the pinkening of the young octopi that precedes their death in the unnatural circumstances he has created. He plans to document the emotions of the octopi in their death throes and to write a scientific treatise to be called " 'Symptoms of Some Cephalopods Approximating Apoplexy' " (28).

It is easy to become confused about the orientation of Doc's experiments since he states that he is concerned with the nonteleological "how" (39) rather than the teleological "why."[3] Steinbeck makes evident the limitations of Doc's approach, however, for in spite of Doc's assertions to the contrary, his octopus study is fundamentally teleological; it isolates and manipulates one part of a complex system that Doc cannot begin to duplicate in his laboratory. Also, it is clear that Doc's interest in his study is dictated by his flight from the feminine. When Mack suggests that a wife might be the answer to his alienation and lack of focus, Doc says that the experiment will give him the "direction" he needs, protesting: "Don't let anybody give me a wife though —don't let them give me a wife" (28). His yearnings for a true relatedness to the feminine irrupt in spite of himself, however, and create endless diversions and interruptions in his experiments.

From the moment of her introduction into the men's world of Cannery Row, Suzy is the ultimate disruption. Although she is the prototype of the "Virgin Whore," a "lady" though a prostitute, she is more, for she brings the transformative aspect of the archetypal feminine into Doc's life. Her degradation is symbolic, as well, of the societal alienation from the feminine. Even when employed by the Bear Flag whorehouse and given a "tomato red" (38) dress, her smile is like that of "somebody's sister" (36), making men uncomfortable who would prefer to use her sexually in ignorance of the primal relationship they might share.

After his first glimpse of Suzy, Doc himself recognizes the basis of his problem. He sees that he has been looking for himself in the tide pools, "searching among the hydroids" for his soul, using the "secret priestly words of science to cover his own nothingness" (42). After this admission, one of the octopi confirms his self-evaluation by waving a tentacle at him, "gay and free and fluid—like the swinging thigh and knee and ankle" (42) of Suzy. Doc's failure to connect to the feminine is reinforced at his meeting with the Seer, who, like Joseph Wayne, is another Green Man. As Doc's foil, the Seer lives on nature's bounty without exploiting her. The Seer, who is so in tune with the archetypal feminine that he has "seen the mermaids playing on the shore," informs Doc that the reason for the failure of his quest to understand nature is that he has approached her "without love" (69).

The first time that Doc and Suzy meet, each recognizes an archetypal opposition and balance in the other, which is thinly disguised by their verbal sparring. Each speaks the truth when Doc tells Suzy that the life of a prostitute is "a poor substitute for love" (100), and Suzy retorts that Doc's whole life is a substitute for his lack of a woman. In spite of their immediate psychic connection, it takes the work of their friends to cut through their defenses and bring them together. Fauna, Suzy's madam, plays a central role as matchmaker. In spite of her occupation, she believes strongly in the value of a good marriage, and understands the mechanics of the Jungian anima, in which men are drawn to women who contain the projections of the inner feminine other they need to be whole. In her own words, Fauna describes this process to Suzy, pointing out that men need help in separating love from their projections:

> Well, when a guy picks out a dame for himself he's in love with something in himself that hasn't got nothing to do with the dame. She looks like his mother, or she's dark and he's scared of blondes, or maybe he's getting even with somebody, or maybe he ain't quite sure he's a man and has to prove it. Fella that studied stuff like that told me one time—a man don't fall for a dame. He falls for new roses, and he brings his own new roses. The best marriages are the ones pulled off by someone that's smart but not sucked in. (112)

As she instructs Suzy and orchestrates her relationship with Doc, Fauna symbolizes the archetypal Wise Old Woman, bringing masculine and feminine together through her instinctual knowledge. Fauna arranges Doc and Suzy's first date, which begins with a conventional meal in a restaurant and ends with an archetypal journey to the same beach where Doc had been instructed by the Seer. Their union takes place in this harmonious setting where Doc abandons his scientific intellect and communes with living nature, and Suzy leaves the reminders of her social degradation, her red shoes, behind.

Although Doc struggles continually to escape from his bond with Suzy, the inevitability of their relationship is recognized by everyone else. Doc's resistance is so extreme, however, that his friend, Hazel, eventually has to break Doc's right arm to bring Doc to acknowledge his need. When Doc accedes to ac-

cept Suzy's aid, there seems to be, at first, little change in his
approach to life, as he merely agrees to let her assist him on a
collecting trip. However, the final image in the novel makes it
clear that Suzy will bring Doc a different orientation toward his
life and his work, as he is now totally dependent upon coopera-
tion with the feminine. Suzy, in fact, controls the direction of
their journey physically as well as symbolically, for Doc's broken
arm prevents him from driving. Since Suzy has learned, on the
very morning of their trip, to drive a stick shift in a mock car
made of an apple box and a mop—two symbols that are more
readily associated with a domestic Eve rather than a scientific
Adam—it is unlikely that the couple will arrive at the tide-pool
in time for the collecting. Also, although Doc's car is packed
with his collecting tools, he still lacks the microscope that had
been inhibiting his scientific studies for some time. Instead, Doc
has been given a telescope by Mack and the boys whose confusion over the scientific terms has appropriately brought about a
significant shift in Doc's scientific focus. As Suzy drives Doc into
the setting sun, symbolic of the decline in Doc's Apollonian perspective, the gift makes perfect sense. With Suzy at the wheel,
as the masculine sun sets, Doc will be able to make perfect use
of the telescope, touted as "strong enough to bring the moon to
his lap" (259).

Many of the same elements that troubled Doc and Suzy's relationship are described in a more serious vein in *East of Eden*.
The lack of a positive relationship with the archetypal feminine
underlies and complicates the lives of all the male characters in
this novel, just as it does for Doc. For the most part, the feminine
is almost totally repressed, irrelevant to the structured roles and
relationships in the Christian lives of the settlers, but irrupting
dangerously as a result of that repression. Cathy is the negative and destructive face of the feminine in this novel, rejecting
both the moral universe of her father and husband and the roles
they expect her to play. Cathy is drawn as an elemental power
that cannot be fit into the role of the obedient daughter, good
woman, or dutiful wife, as the male characters demand, and
challenges all who would force her to submit to such limitations. In contrast, Abra acts as the positive and transformative
aspect of the feminine, restoring balance and bringing peace to

Adam and his son, Cal. She, too, however, must first rid herself of the projections of the male characters. In her relationship with Aron, in particular, she has been drawn into playing a limited role based on his needs and misperceptions about the feminine. Between Cathy and Abra, however, Steinbeck analyzes clearly the nature of the feminine and the way men will attempt to bind the feminine to suit their own desires.

Cathy has proven to be particularly enigmatic because the forces she represents cannot be integrated with the Judeo-Christian values that the male characters assert, and which seem, on the surface, to represent the views of the author. In each encounter, she brings the men in her life into a confrontation with the aspects of the feminine most antagonistic to the Biblical moral vision of the male characters. Steinbeck seems to have been aware of the difficulties with Cathy; for although he describes her as a monster (72) when he speaks of her in terms of the simple Christian values of the Salinas settlers, he qualifies that judgment on several occasions. Perhaps most telling is the assessment that in other times, both times in which the Judeo-Christian ethic and the scapegoating demanded by the sexual repressions of the age were most strong, Cathy would have been regarded as either "possessed by the devil" or "burned as a witch" (73). Like the possessed woman and the witch, or Curley's wife in *Of Mice and Men*, Cathy is the carrier of the anima projections of the men who encounter her, and because the projected qualities arise from the unconscious, Cathy is perceived as both divine and demonic.

Adam Trask is a complete victim of such projections. It is clear that whatever Adam sees in Cathy has little to do with Cathy herself. After describing Adam's rapture at seeing her for the first time, Steinbeck adds that "perhaps Adam did not see Cathy at all. . . . Burned in his mind was an image of beauty and tenderness, a sweet and holy girl . . . and that image was Cathy to her husband, and nothing Cathy did or said could warp Adam's Cathy" (133). Throughout their life together Adam remains totally oblivious to the real Cathy, seeing only what he wants to see in her silence and seeming acquiescence. He becomes the victim of his own inner feminine in his failure to acknowledge that the goodness he perceives in her is actually a part of himself. Thus, when Cathy leaves him, he is bereft of all the positive qualities he projected onto her.[4] Sam Hamilton tries to make Adam aware of the lack of reality in his perception of Cathy, telling Adam: "To you she was [beautiful] because you built her. I don't think you ever saw her—only your own creation" (262).

The most negative critical evaluations of Cathy are based upon Sam Hamilton's description to Adam of her ownership of the "most vicious and depraved" whorehouse in Salinas, a place that "takes the fresh and young and beautiful and so maims them that they can never be whole again" (306). It is important to remember that this description is intended as a medicinal corrective to the glorified image Adam has substituted for the reality of Cathy. Sam had tried earlier to awaken Adam, telling him to "find a new Cathy," one who could "kill the dream Cathy" (297). He knows that if Adam is to reclaim the positive qualities of his anima, he will have to be shocked into separating the real Cathy from his projection. After Adam's visit to Cathy at the whorehouse, where he believes he sees her as she is for the first time, his words reveal clearly that he has withdrawn his projection: "I'm free!" he exclaims, "She's out of me" (330).

In truth, however, Adam is not free. He has merely withdrawn one projection, his view of Cathy as angel, only to replace it with another, his neighbor's view of her as devil. As long as Cathy is seen in terms of these simplistic polarities, her power to constellate anima projections remains to trouble the next generation. As a result, Adam's relationship with his sons continues to be troubled by the lack of connection to the feminine that led him to Cathy in the first place, and his motherless boys seem destined to repeat his mistakes. Aron's life, in particular, is based upon illusions about his mother which have been projected onto Abra, whom he hopes to marry. When his brother Cal's jealousy destroys Aron's illusions and forces Adam and Cathy into a recognition of their failures, Abra's sympathetic understanding becomes the agent bringing about the restoration of the feminine necessary for their healing. Lee describes Abra to Cal as the embodiment of all the positive qualities of the archetypal feminine: "She's a good woman—a real woman" with

"the loveliness of woman, and the courage—and the strength—
and the wisdom. She knows things and accepts things" (575).
With the help of Abra's instinctive womanliness and wisdom,
Cal learns to forgive himself. She enables Cal to assimilate his
anima by teaching him about the mingling of good and evil that
resides in each person, and by giving him the unqualified love
he needs to be whole. She frees him from his guilt about his
brother by telling him that Aron was as much a victim of his
own projections as of anything Cal did to him. Not only had
Aron projected an idealized anima image onto the mother he
believed to be dead, but he had also created a story, a projected
image of his future and the way things must be, and he refused to accept any variation from the image. Abra tells Cal:
"He wanted the story and he wanted it to come out his way. . . .
He couldn't stand to know about his mother because that's not
how he wanted the story to go—and he wouldn't have any other
story. So he tore up the world" (577–78).

Once free of Adam's simplistic conception of good and evil,
and the various projected images of Cathy that have so clouded
their world, Abra and Cal are free to form a real relationship,
one based upon true knowledge and acceptance of each other
as a mingling of good and evil, strength and weakness, masculine and feminine. Their mating, like that of Joseph Wayne and
Elizabeth, is described in terms that suggest a union of archetypal masculine and feminine, as they come to each other at the
beginning of their relationship in a natural landscape, among
the azaleas on the Alisal (591–92). The novel concludes with a
powerful image of the restoration of the balance between masculine and feminine as Adam's blessing unites with Abra's love
to free Cal to be whole.

As these representative samples have shown, throughout his
career Steinbeck was concerned with affording the archetypal
feminine its proper value. As represented in landscape, the archetypal feminine becomes a force that must be reckoned with
and even sacrificed for, as Joseph Wayne's offering of his life's
blood at the rock makes clear. Although Steinbeck never returned
to such overtly mythical terms again, he repeatedly evoked the
tradition of the Green Man, presenting a clear ecological message throughout his career. This emphasis ranges from his pro-

test over the devastation of the fishing stock in Monterey Bay and the Sea of Cortez to the destruction of the farmlands of Oklahoma and includes his clear-eyed depiction of the human significance of the loss of living contact with the land suffered by the migrant workers in *The Grapes of Wrath* and *Of Mice and Men.* Steinbeck also dealt with the psychological ramifications of the devaluation of the feminine in human experience as shown through the sufferings of various male characters, like Doc and Adam Trask. The female characters in the novels, although often depicted as "anima" figures, sketched in sexist terms that reflect the male characters' projections onto the feminine, nonetheless force a new focus upon characters like Doc and Trask, who must learn to accept the female as a power and value equal to their own. Thus, the superficial and seemingly sexist characteristics of the women in Steinbeck's novels are much less at issue than the attitudes of the male characters toward them. Through the depth of his social and psychological vision, Steinbeck has become a Shaman, showing us the limitations of our current attitudes toward the feminine in both the natural world and in life. Above all, Steinbeck's novels reveal his deep respect for the balance between masculine and feminine upon which not only every man/woman relationship but also the health of the earth itself depends.

16

Of Mice and Men
Creating and Re-creating Curley's Wife

Mimi Reisel Gladstein

Gladstein traces the evolution of Curley's wife in the 1939, 1981, and 1992 film versions of Of Mice and Men.

Curley's wife, the lone woman in Steinbeck's poignant tale *Of Mice and Men*, has been a source of question and query almost from her conception. George S. Kaufman, the play's Broadway director was the first to suggest that more was needed for her dramatic realization. He encouraged Steinbeck to enlarge her part: "The girl, I think, should be drawn more fully: she is the motivating force of the whole thing and should loom larger" (*SLL* 136).

Steinbeck did just that for the play version, giving her a troubled background of battling parents and an alcoholic and lost father. Obviously, Claire Luce, who played the role on Broadway, still needed more and Steinbeck was moved, halfway into the play's run to provide a fuller exposition, explaining her predatory behavior as defensive. She is, he explains "a nice, kind girl and not a floozy" (*SLL* 154). We do not have a record of Luce's performance, so we cannot see for ourselves how she resolved the contradictions in this woman who was called a "tart" (28) and "jail-bait" (32) by the men in the play, but "not a floozy" by her creator.

In the ensuing half-century since "something happened" to Curley's wife, Steinbeck's poignant tale has continued to inspire interpretation in a variety of media. It has motivated four major film productions, two for the big screen, 1939 and 1992, and two television productions, one in 1968 and another in 1981, plus a stage-musical (1958) and an opera (1976). Luckily, there are readily available copies of three of the film productions and so we can study how different manifestations of Steinbeck's timeless fable have dealt with the apparent contradictions between the outer and inner being of the only woman in this male domain.

Judith Crist once commented that when Hollywood makes an historical movie, it tells us more about Hollywood at the time of the making of the film than it does about the time period the film portrays.[1] The same might be said about the portrayal of Curley's wife. A cursory exploration of the multiple possibilities that comparisons of the three film versions suggest to us are instructive, not only for what they demonstrate about this problematic character, but also about the times in which each text was produced. To illustrate, I have chosen three significant components of the characterization of Curley's wife as she is presented in the 1939, 1981, and 1992 film productions. They provide a beginning (how we are introduced to the character) (figure 1); a middle (some justification for her behavior) (figure 2); and, of course, her end or death (figure 3).[2]

The earliest film version followed shortly after the Broadway run. Lewis Milestone's 1939 cinema rendition starred Lon Chaney, Jr. and Burgess Meredith. Betty Field played the role of Curley's wife. The audience introduction to her is spotlighted by Candy's cue line: "Just wait'll you see Curley's wife."

And our first sight is a revealing one. Her sexuality is foregrounded; her legs are what we see first, encased in dark silk stockings. She is wearing high heels, lifting and lowering a puppy, precariously clasped between her ankles. The setting is in the barn, where she is lying on her back in the straw, blond hair tightly curled. This provocative introduction is softened emblematically by showing her in conjunction with a cute, fuzzy puppy, a connection that also foreshadows her demise. Milestone's semiotic choices, first silk stockings, then puppy, convey the ambiguity of this pivotal character. On the one hand, she is dressed in sexually provocative clothing, like a thirties screen vamp. On the other hand, her universality is highlighted by her delight in the cute puppy, an emotion the audience can share.

Figure 1. Curley's wife, 1939, 1981, 1992: The introduction to the character.

Her petting the puppy in the barn creates motivation for her final visit to the barn to get it before she leaves. (See figure 1.)

Robert Blake's nineteen eighties television version was produced some two generations later. However, except for the change from large screen to the small one and the addition of color, it does not often stray far from its predecessor.[3] In fact, it is consciously modeled on the 1939 production, even dedicated to Lewis Milestone. For many scenes, the same script was used. This complicates my thesis somewhat, because sometimes, rather than being a reflection of its times, it is an homage to its inspiration and therefore highly derivative. The Blake script replicates not only scenes added in the Milestone production, such as the farmhouse eating scene, but exact shots, such as the close-up of the pie, Mae's fingers breaking off a piece of crust. There is also a marked similarity between Betty Field's and Cassie Yates's initial scenes with the puppy, a scene that is not in the novel.

Blake retains the barn setting for our introduction to the character, but, perhaps in response to some consciousness raising about the sexual objectification of women, we see Mae's hands first, not her legs. On the other hand, the reason for this change could also be cultural. The sight of a woman's legs, in silk stockings, did not carry the same sexual impact in the eighties that it did in the thirties. The thirties is the decade when Claudette Colbert, in *It Happened One Night,* stops traffic by lifting her skirt to show her stockinged leg. By the nineteen eighties the sight of a woman's legs, either in or out of silk stockings, did not have the same erotic punch. Instead, her provocative character is communicated by the camera's focus on her cleavage in a tight-bodiced, low-cut cotton dress. Her blond hair is still tightly curled, but she is not on her back, at least at first. The suggestiveness of a woman on her back in the hay is another of the time-coded sexual signs of an era when even married couples could not be shown lying in bed together. Like her predecessor, she is playing with the puppies, appealing to the audience's sense that someone who loves dogs and children can't be all bad. (See figure 1.)

In both of these film versions, the contradictions inherent in this character are telegraphed in this opening scene, a scene not from Steinbeck's text, which changes the way Curley's wife is introduced to the audience. Rather than having her intrude into masculine space, the bunkhouse, as Steinbeck does, in the Milestone and Blake versions she is shown first alone in the barn. In these films, her loneliness, and its connection to her being the only woman in this male domain, is further underlined by another scene Milestone includes from the additional matter in the Eugene Solow screenplay. In both of these early productions, a scene just outside the barn follows this introductory scene. The camera pans from Mae, lying in the straw, to the open barn door which frames an interaction between Curley and his father. Curley is looking for his wife; the boss, his father, suggests that Curley needs to get his mind on his work and leave his wife alone. In the 1939 version, the boss speaks his understanding of her loneliness, noting that it would be better for her if she had some women to talk to. She is even named—Mae. Much has been made in the critical literature of the fact that Steinbeck never named this woman, identifying her only by her relationship to a man, as Curley's wife. Both Milestone and Blake remedy this situation. By giving her a name, she is humanized, achieving the same status as the men in the story. She becomes the subject of her own story with an identity other than the one given her by marriage to Curley.

By adding the scene in the barn Milestone can show the audience that Curley's wife is alone and innocently engaged in playing with a puppy. Therefore, her husband's suspicions are probably unfounded and the audience is moved to sympathy. The boss, Curley's father, also voices his disapproval of his son's obsession with his wife's activities. However, this sympathy is balanced by her looks, and emphasized by Candy's preparatory line, "Just wait'll you *see* Curley's wife." How she looks helps explain his disparaging attitude toward her and is accentuated by the voyeuristic camera focus on legs in the first film, cleavage in the second.

These additional introductory scenes are nowhere in the 1992 production. Gary Sinise's film owes its inspiration not to either previous film version, but to Sinise's early affection for Steinbeck's work. He played Tom Joad in the successful translation of *The Grapes of Wrath* from text to stage. Sinise and John Malkovich had performed Steinbeck's *Of Mice and Men* onstage in Chicago (1980) while part of the Steppenwolf Company. With Elaine Steinbeck's approval, Horton Foote wrote his own adaptation for the screen, a screenplay which is, in some ways, more and, in other ways, less faithful to Steinbeck's texts. Like Steinbeck, Foote does not name Curley's wife.

As in the play and novel, we first meet Curley's wife, as do Lennie and George, at the bunkhouse. In the novel, she plays her first scene in the doorway, using the doorframe to pose for the new men, leaning against it to arch her body forward. Foote's script brings her into the bunkhouse. However, there is a marked contradiction in the visual message of her costuming and actions. Unlike her prototype in the novel, she is not "tarted" up in the little red ostrich feather mules nor is her hair tightly curled into little sausages. Sherilynn Fenn, as Curley's wife, definitely shows the effects of a nineties production. Her sexuality is less dependent on costume and make-up, better conveyed by her manner than her looks. She bursts into the bunkhouse with a breathy little girl quality. To add to her youthful mannerisms, she is toying with her skirt, pulling it up and playing with the hem. (See figure 1.) Her breathy, girlish voice resonates with a quality reminiscent of Marilyn Monroe.[4] This change in the nature of allure plays into a contemporary infantilization of sexuality, epitomized by such things as pre-pubescent high-fashion models hawking tight jeans and/or Calvin Klein's perfume ads featuring awkward young boys and girls, photographed in their underwear.[5] Her girlish behavior and voice qualities are a counterpart of what Susan Bordo, in a recent article for the *Chronicle of Higher Education*, calls the "eroticization of children" (7). Myra Macdonald writes of the creation in the 1990s of the "little girl lost look," a reconstruction of feminine sexuality from that of power into a "waif-like innocence and insecurity" (112). Fenn's portrayal partakes of those characteristics. The concurrent qualities of innocence and sexuality are emphasized by the parting thrust of her breast and her form-fitting dress.

Once the audience is introduced to Curley's wife, made aware of her ambiguous nature, both predatory and needy, the script must furnish motivation for her behavior. Why is she so needy? In the novel, the reader first learns about the situation from the men's perspective. There are few early clues to provide understanding of the problems between her and Curley from her perspective. Curley's threatening behavior is explained by Candy to George and Lennie. After their initial unpleasant encounter, Candy notes that Curley is "worse lately" (27). Candy attributes this change to the fact that he "got married a couple of weeks ago . . . [and is] cockier'n ever since he got married" (27). He also calls attention to Curley's gloved left hand. Candy tells George that the glove is full of vaseline, which Curley says is to keep the hand soft for his new wife. George judges that as "a dirty thing to tell around" (28). However, it is not until three-fourths of the way through the novel that the reader gets the wife's viewpoint, her explanation of the problems in the marriage, what has created the situation that puts her in such need of company and consequently such jeopardy. Her words to Lennie, Candy, and Crooks tell of her frustration with being left at home while Curley goes off with the boys, "Think I like to stick in that house alla time?" (76). She speaks of Curley's one note conversations about how he is going to "lead with his left twict, and then bring in the ol'right cross" (76). But the men do not acknowledge her perspective. They view her as a danger and want her out of their living space.

When her dead body is discovered, Candy reproaches her for "messing" everything up. His final epitaph, over her dead body, is: "You Goddamn tramp . . . You lousy tart" (93). Is she to blame for her own demise, as Candy's eulogy suggests? Are we to believe Whit's diagnosis that "she can't keep away from guys"? (51). Or is it that she has "the eye" (28) as Candy explains? Curley is always looking for her, but then always leaving her alone, in a situation of such isolation that she is content, in her own words, to be talking to "a bunch of bindle stiffs" (77). Even on Saturday night. "Ever'body out doin' som'pin'. Ever'body! An what am I doin?" (76–77). In her final scene, she corroborates what we already know from Curley's behavior throughout the novel, "He ain't a nice fella" (86).

In the play and the novel, we can only speculate about what life with Curley is like. This is not true in all three films. Each provides scenes that counterbalance Candy's condemnation of her. The Milestone version takes us into the ranch house to provide justification for the woman's need for congenial company. In a scene created for the Milestone film we encounter Mae, the boss, and Curley at the dinner table. The camera focuses on a pie, as Curley and the boss cut off huge pieces, while Mae's fingers nip off a small piece of the crust. The men then drench their portions in cream. Noisily, they devour the pie and slurp coffee. There is no conversation; Mae is so overwhelmed by the eating noises, that she puts her hands over her ears. Obviously, we are meant to sympathize with "Mae's" disgust. The men are uncouth and animalistic. They "wolf" down huge pieces of pie, while she barely eats. Still, her looks convey another message, one not so sympathetic. She is bejeweled and made up, wearing a low-cut dress. (See figure 2.)

Blake's fidelity to Milestone goes far toward proving that imitation is the sincerest form of flattery. The dinner scenes are almost a carbon copy, the major difference being the addition of color. The camera eye first focuses on the pie; the men pack away pie and guzzle coffee. Once again, "Mae" is revolted by the gross and slurping dinner noises. If anything, either as a result of better sound equipment or by a conscious choice of the film

Figure 2. Curley's wife, 1939, 1981, 1992: The middle, or some justification for her behavior.

editor, the noises are louder. The men are even more unmannered, going at their food with an added two-handed boorishness, fork in one hand, coffee cups in the other. We are ready to join her, putting our hands over our ears. During this entire scene, the audience is put in the position of empathizing with Mae. After the meal, our sympathy is evoked again when Curley leaves her at home to go out with the boys, although she expresses her desire to go out. Since both the men's bad table manners and Curley's lack of consideration for her feelings are material that is not in the novel, the added text for the 1939 and 1981 film scripts provides opportunity for audience commiseration with Mae's plight. The scenes inside the ranch house make her more sympathetic, justifying her dubious quest for company, even to her detriment.

There is no analogous scene in Horton Foote's screenplay. True to the novel, we are kept outside of the ranch house. But if a 1992 conception doesn't turn our stomachs against Curley, his brutal nature is transmitted in another way. Annoying noise making, but of a more violent kind, is used to telegraph Curley's failures as a human being and husband. In an added scene that shows the men coming in from the fields, we encounter Curley pounding a punching bag. The scene is mid-way through the film and relevant in that it continues the motif of Curley's penchant for fighting, his violent nature. His wife's loneliness, even when they are together, is transmitted in their separation, the lack of interaction. She is sitting on the porch, some distance from him, uninvolved and eating something out of a white bowl. She speaks no lines. Her dress is pale and nondescript. It is not provocative in any way. (See figure 2.) Curley's father, the boss, is the one who expresses irritation at the noise, wanting a stop to the racket. The scene ends, punctuated with a last blow to the punching bag. Though brief, the scene is not in the play or either of the earlier film versions. It does not advance the plot in any way. It serves to establish Curley as a boxer and its purpose may be to sensitize the audience to his brutality and his wife's isolation, foreshadowing Curley's pummeling of Lennie. Curley's wife is in the scene, but not part of it.

Further indication of the impact of the time of production on how Curley's wife is portrayed in the 1992 film is Foote's importation of the contemporary issue of wife-abuse. This is accomplished in another of the few instances where Foote does tamper with Steinbeck's plot by adding a scene that clearly conveys an image of this woman as victim, more sinned against than sinner. First Foote omits her most unappealing scene from the novel, the one where Curley's wife goes into Crooks's room and throws cold water on the men's dream of owning a place of their own. Left out is her threat of lynching. Gone is her derogatory depiction of the men as "a nigger, a dum-dum and a lousy ol' sheep" (77).

Instead, Lennie and George come out of Crooks's room and encounter her in the yard, almost crying. Curley has gone to town after breaking all her records. Contemporary audiences, sensitive to wife-abuse, respond all too readily to her plaintive lament about her broken records. She had only four. Not only does Curley leave her alone, but also he destroys her means of entertaining herself. What else can she do but seek the company of others? And even those pitiful outcasts reject her. She runs crying from the yard. The addition of scenes like this and an earlier one where she and George have a quiet exchange in the barn, an exchange that is almost suggestive of a possible romantic connection, elicits our sympathy for her and softens the femme fatale nature of her character. An added heart-tugging touch is her naming of the records Curley broke. One is "Am I Blue?" A telling title.

How, then, if all three films add scenes to provoke our sympathy for Curley's wife, is the negative or dangerous side of her nature communicated? The ambiguous nature of the characterization is communicated in essentially time-coded ways, ways that play on recognized signals of the time of production. The semiotics of costume and make-up choices is particularly revealing.[6] In other words, the way the character is dressed is a sign or code by which we evaluate her in her specific cultural context.

The 1939 film's visual presentation of "Mae" falls clearly in the trampy category. When we first see her, she is in high-heeled sandal shoes and dark-toned hose. This speaks of her alienation from her setting. It is difficult to negotiate a barnyard in open-toed shoes and easily torn hosiery. In the farmhouse dinner scene, she is heavily made-up, with a big ring on her finger, wearing a low-cut dress, all signs of her attempts at appearing alluring. Her décolletage is emphasized when she pulls a movie flyer out of the bodice of her dress. In the visual codes of 1930s movie-making, nice women did not use their bras for storage purposes. Later, in another added farmhouse scene, she confronts Curley in a ruffled house robe, the slatternly presentation emphasized by an even wider décolletage and an inappropriate combination of jewelry and negligee. For her final departure and death scenes, the outfit is quintessential thirties tart: see-through net blouse, tight skirt, and high heels. A close-up shows penciled eyebrows, polished nails, and lots of cheap jewelry. (See figure 3.) She fits the cultural commonplace of her times that if a woman dressed a certain way, she was "asking for trouble." Hers is clearly the least sympathetic portrayal, but then, in the 1930s, society had more rigid standards by which

Figure 3. Curley's wife, 1939, 1981, 1992: The character's end or death.

women were judged. Mae's dress and make-up mark her. They are not appropriate for a good woman living on a farm.

The 1980s costuming of Cassie Yates is more ambivalent. Little in her costuming or actions communicates the sign of a "floozy." Only in her introductory scene is there some question of décolletage. At the dinner table, Mae is wearing a simple plaid cotton dress, with a few pieces of plastic jewelry. When she reaches into her bodice for the movie flyer, the action is not highlighted. Her costume for her least sympathetic scene, the one where she goes to Crooks's room to dash the men's dreams, is markedly contrary to any depiction of her as a tart or jail bait. Her outfit is almost school-marmish. She is wearing a blouse with a white-eyelet collar and a blue sweater, clothing appropriate for a farm wife. (See figure 2.) In the farmhouse confrontation with Curley, a little-girl hair ribbon offsets her ruffled house-robe. In the death scene, her departure dress is not provocative; it is plain, black, full-skirted, and except for the bare arms, appropriate for a funeral, ironically her own. (See figure 3.) No heavy make-up highlights her close-ups; her face is wistful and tender in the final moments of her presentation. She does, however, wear bright red nail polish. Since the script for the Milestone and Blake versions are almost identical, the marked changes in the way the character is made up and costumed lend credence to the impact of cultural changes in attitudes toward women. Her verbal and visual signs are sometimes incompatible, but in a postmodern age audiences are more comfortable with contradictory and conflicting images. She can look like a sweet farm wife and act like a harpy. It contributes to the complexity of the character.

The costuming in the 1992 production is also sometimes contradictory. After her initial bodice-enhancing dress, there is little that suggests either tart or tramp in the shape or color of the costume or the actions of the character. The dresses are mostly frumpy and formless. In a barn scene, we encounter Curley's wife carrying a book, hardly the emblem of a floozy. This emphasizes the fact that there is more to her than just body. Her postures are often casual, careless. Her hair is long and natural looking; she is not "heavily made up" nor does she have red fingernails. She is a brunette, not a blonde; her voice is not "nasal and brittle," but soft and girlish. Barelegged rather than in black silk stocking, she carries a non-threatening coke bottle for her final encounter with Lennie. The color of her dress in her final scene is white, communicating her innocence. This is in keeping with the earlier added scenes that portray her more as victim than seductress. There is about her a strong evocation of a "little girl lost." (See figure 3.) She is in flat shoes instead of high heels. The flat shoes connote girlishness. The first thing little girls do when they want to play grown up is don high heels. It is significant that the costuming and camera in the earlier versions focus on those high heels. The fact that she has wandered into the barn purposelessly highlights her "lost" quality. In the earlier versions, Mae comes to the barn for a purpose—to get her puppy before she leaves.

Finally, contemporary sensibilities and audience expectations have significantly altered the portrayal of Lennie's killing of Curley's wife. Lennie barely gets to stroke her hair once before Betty Field's character is worrying that he will mess it up, telling him to stop. The camera eye is averted from the actual struggle;

we see only his hand in her hair and then her feet in the air, the dropping of one of her high-heeled black shoes emblematic of her death. When he drops her in the straw, the camera withdraws from the scene, revealing only a partial view of her hip protruding through the hay. This is in marked contrast to the novel, where the narrative focus is on her dead face. Steinbeck's final narrative retrospective on her character presents Curley's wife in a more sympathetic light than elsewhere in the novel. Although he does use the adjective "meanness," the other words he uses to describe her have more to do with her unhappiness and desire for communication. She is also characterized as sweet and simple (90). None of this is conveyed in the 1939 film. The protruding hip maintains the sexualized view of the camera.

Blake's replication of the scene differs little from the Milestone version. The camera does hesitate a little longer on the action. We see Lennie's rough petting of the back of her head as she asks him not to mess it up. Again, we are shifted to her feet, this time in red high-heeled shoes. Television at the time of this filming still showed less graphic violence and overt sexuality than did the movies. In both versions, a hip is all we see of the dead body Lennie drops in the hay. Her sweetness is conveyed only in the close-up of her live face, earlier in the scene, prior to her allowing Lennie to stroke her hair. Our last image is still partial and not inspiring of further thought about her aborted dreams.

Contemporary audiences, on the other hand, have become increasingly desensitized to violence and brutality, especially in the movies. Sex and mayhem, which were only suggested or symbolized in earlier films, are all too graphically depicted on today's big and little screens. Sinise's 1992 version lingers on the death scene, amplifying not only the violence, but also the sexual tension of the interaction. If Curley's wife has been presented in a more sympathetic method earlier in this film, in this scene, the camera eye objectifies her in a near-prurient manner. She and Lennie are presented as much more intimately involved. Rather than beginning side by side as in the earlier films, they are face to face. The scene is played slowly. She responds to his petting, and there is a sensual quality to their interaction as she assures him, "I like it too. It feels nice." This addition implicates her more in what follows. When the scene suddenly turns violent, the camera does not avert its eye. We see her full body struggle, her bare kicking legs, her dress hiked up to her thighs. When Lennie drops her inert body, it is her feet we don't see. Instead the focus is on her backside, dress pulled up, slip showing, the camera moving directly toward her.

In her most recent materialization, Curley's wife is, in Vincent Canby's words, "sort of sweet and none too bright, which is politically correct." She is less blameworthy and more a victim. Jack Garner also registers the change in her characterization, crediting Sinise and Foote with making her "a more complex and sympathetic character, a lonely, warm-hearted woman whose goal is more friendship than seduction." But, if she is a more sympathetic character, in terms of plot, she is made less relevant to the main themes of loneliness and brotherhood, less an actor in the theme of aborted dreams. Since she is not leaving Curley and the farm, carrying a coke bottle to the barn rather than a suitcase, she does not achieve the same tragic status as the men. She is not fleeing to pursue her dream. She is less actor than acted upon. She does not confront Curley as her predecessors did. She is just there, going nowhere, to blame only because she is soft and appealing.

What are we to deduce, then, from the examples of these time-bound presentations of Curley's wife? There is no single answer. The actresses who play the role look progressively younger and their clothing and make-up are less suggestive of the conventional film vamp. Also, as the actresses become younger, the hardness inherent in the earlier portrayals is lost. But even the words "floozy" and "tart" are now culturally anachronistic. The progressively less provocative costuming can also be the result of changing societal mores about dress. In the courts, the rationale that women invite trouble by the way they dress is no longer acceptable. Sherilynn Fenn does not need costuming or make-up to transmit sexual tension. In this post-Lolita era, her very childlike demeanor and voice project their own sexual message. The contradictions and ambiguity in the character are inherent since her conception continue.

Some of these contradictions derive from the conflict between what is still a male-centered and male-driven cinema, what B. Ruby Rich calls "Cinema of the Fathers," and a less homogeneous audience.[7] In 1939 the audience, both male and female, could be expected to share the cultural codes of the time, whereas the audiences for the most recent versions are less likely to view the film from a unified perspective. Today's audiences must wrest meaning out of the struggle and negotiation between competing frames of reference. Nevertheless, the male gaze continues to dominate the camera in the 1990s as it did in the original film and Steinbeck's text.[8] Curley's wife, named or not, is still circumscribed by her position in relation to the men —a wife to Curley, a danger to the men. Though she struggles to define herself as subject, she remains object. If there is anything subversive in the text, as some commentators on her character have argued, it is still struggling to reveal itself. Oddly enough, in the most recent version, the one which should have been most influenced by contemporary cultural critique of woman as object, Curley's wife has even less subjectivity than her earlier manifestations. In the two earliest versions, she is at least shown as challenging Curley's authority, taking a step toward being the subject of her own text. This challenge, plus giving her a name and the added farmhouse scene provide the character some depth and more presence in the story of the earlier versions. Trapped within the patriarchal structure, she asserts herself, struggling to escape. Paradoxically, in the 1990s version, when the women in the audience have enlarged their personal and professional spheres, Curley's wife is more circumscribed than ever. Nameless, unassertive, and purposeless, she is, with a contemporary nod to her victimhood, considerably reduced. Myra Macdonald has noted that in Hollywood movies, woman is usually "put in her due place in the patriarchal order by the end of the film" (27). In the novel, as in the film versions, the threat woman presents is nullified by destroying her. Having done this, the 1990s script allows the camera a final violation as it moves phallically into her backside.

Of Mice and Men has become a classic in our culture and one characteristic of dramatic classics is that they contain characters who invite endless new portrayals, characters who present challenges for each new generation of actors. What else accounts for the numerous film versions of *Hamlet,* just in our generation?

And while I don't mean to suggest any analogy between Curley's wife and Hamlet, they both embody puzzles for their interpreters. Steinbeck understood the sexual objectification of this character, her limitations in a masculine society. He explained to Claire Luce that "No man has ever considered her as anything except a girl to try to make" (*SLL* 154). "It's a devil of a hard part," he concluded, and time has validated his description. In his final view of her, lying dead in a half-covering of yellow hay, the narrator of Steinbeck's novel observes: "the plannings and the discontent and the ache for attention were all gone from her face. She was very pretty and simple, and her face was sweet and young" (90). In death, Steinbeck acknowledges her aborted agency, focusing the narrative eye on her positive characteristics. The camera eye has not been that respectful. In the first two versions, once dead, she is gone, her only function to move the plot to its inexorable conclusion. In the most recent version, while the meanness and the planning are both gone from her character, so is any sense of agency. The problem of Curley's wife, present since her inception, has not been solved. In the medium of film, as on stage and in text, she remains an interpretative puzzle and challenge.

17

Beyond Evil

Cathy and Cal in East of Eden

Carol L. Hansen

When he wrote East of Eden, *Steinbeck recast the story of Cain and Abel, shifting away from the biblical emphasis on clear distinctions between good and evil. Hansen argues that both Cathy and Cal are beyond the conventional oppositions, and that as an amoral monster, a satirical fantasy, and a genetic mutation, Cathy holds a key to the subterranean mystery which lies at the heart of* East of Eden. *She, like Cal, exists beyond evil.*

How can one defend a female character who, at the age of ten, lures boys into sexual experimentation; at age sixteen, drives her Latin teacher to suicide and then incinerates her parents; runs away to become mistress to a brothel owner and, after being brutally beaten by him, marries another man for protection; shoots her husband and deserts her twin sons (one of whom was fathered by her husband's brother on her wedding night); returns to prostitution and murders the madam in order to become madam herself of the most infamous brothel in the west; and commits suicide by drinking poison?

From the beginning, Cathy does not appear to fit into the novel's patriarchal structure postulating free will; rather she eschews a choice between good and evil because she appears driven to defy 19th century conventions which involve binary oppositions between good and evil, specifically the *timshel* theme which, on one level, centers the book. Set outside this framework, Cathy/Kate exists as an amoral monster who brings into question the validity of this theme. She falls into a triploid of familiar associations: an amoral monster, a satirical fantasy, and a genetic mutation, all of which suggest the subterranean mystery at the heart of *East of Eden*.

In his article "The Mirror and the Vamp: Invention, Reflection, and Bad, Bad Cathy Trask in *East of Eden*," Louis Owens raises critical questions about Cathy's character:

> A consideration of *East of Eden* as a self-conscious fiction may also allow us to come to terms with one of the major problems often cited by critics: Cathy Ames Trask. Is Cathy the C. A. T., a genetically misshapen monster who simply is predetermined to be evil because of something she lacks? (Is she, as Benson suggests, a product of Steinbeck's pondering upon the evils of his second wife?) Or is she more psychologically complex than this, as her early and late obsessions with the Wonderland Alice seem to suggest? Why, if *timshel* must apply to all of us, does it seem not to apply to Cathy or Adam, or even Charles, who is incapable of feeling sorry? If this novel is designed to mark the end of an era—naturalism with its emphasis upon pessimistic determinism —as Ditsky has persuasively suggested, why does Steinbeck create absolutists such as Adam and Cathy, who seem, for most of the novel, incapable of free will? (253)

Cathy is beyond evil; she is a monster to those of conventional morals and mores, but, from her perspective, those who judge her are monsters. Steinbeck writes early in the novel:

> to a monster the norm must seem monstrous, since everyone is normal to himself. To the inner monster it must be even more obscure, since he has no visible thing to compare with others. . . . It is my belief that Cathy Ames was born with the tendencies, or lack of them, which drove and forced her all of her life. Some balance wheel was misweighted, some gear out of ratio. She was not like other people, never was from birth. (72)

Here Steinbeck's comments sound more like those of a clinical psychologist than those of an overt moralist, and in his *Journal of a Novel: The East of Eden Letters*, he writes that he, too, in a way, is a monster like Cathy and details fluctuating shifts in her characterization. Moreover, he also describes her enigmatic contradictions in the novel.

> Cathy always had a child's figure even after she was grown, slender, delicate arms and hands—tiny hands. Her breasts never developed very much. Before her puberty the nipples turned inward. Her mother had to manipulate them out when they became painful in Cathy's tenth year. Her body was a boy's body . . . Her feet were small and round and stubby, with fat insteps almost like little hoofs. . . .
>
> Even as a child she had some quality that made people look at her, then look away, then look back at her, troubled at something foreign. Something looked out of her eyes, and was never there when one looked again. (73)

From the beginning, Cathy is seen as the "other," "a girl set apart," and, according to Jackson Benson, is "Steinbeck's non-teleological white whale. Like so many other Steinbeck characters, she is a sport born out of nature who simply does what she does. . . ." (167).[1] In her denial of conventional morality, Cathy questions the binary opposition between good and evil; she exists outside the norm of the biblical symbolism which structures the novel. In her phantasmagoria, she lives as an alien who refuses to fit into the conventional code of the good woman. But in her perversity she remains eerily fascinating, an enigma who cannot be contained. Cathy defies classification in a male-dominated world. From her viewpoint, she is an observer of the true monsters of masculine control as seen in Mr. Ames, her father; Mr. Edwards, her master; and Adam Trask, her husband. Therefore, she is beyond the boundaries of conventional family life as exemplified by the roles of daughter, wife, and mother. Instead she emerges as a force beyond good and evil, a force of perverse freedom. Yet she is more alive than any other character in the novel.[2]

As Mark Schorer notes in his review of the book:

> With Adam Trask we move, too, into the core story, if we accept at all, we accept at the level of folklore, the abstract fiction of the Social Threat, of a Witch beyond women. This account may sug-

gest a kind of eclectic irresolution of view, which is, in fact, not at all the quality of the book. I have hoped to suggest, instead, a wide-ranging imaginative freedom that might save the life of many an American Novelist. (22)

Strangely enough, Cathy is linked not so much to the biblical symbolism of the book's superimposed patriarchal ideologies, but rather to a seemingly innocuous children's fantasy: Lewis Carroll's *Alice in Wonderland.* When Cathy's mother asks, "What's the book you are hiding?" Cathy retorts, "Here! I'm not hiding it." Her mother rejoins, "Oh, *Alice in Wonderland.* You're too big for that." And Cathy replies, "I can get to be *so* little you can't even see me. . . . Nobody can find me" (82). This image of willing herself to become small, this telescoping of self in order to escape the restrictions of control, are repeated near the end of the book when she, like Alice, recalls the literary injunction to "eat me," and "drink me," and she swallows the poisoned tea.

> She thrust her mind back to Alice. In the gray wall opposite there was a nail hole. Alice . . . would put her arm around Cathy's waist, and Cathy would put her arm around Alice's waist, and they would walk away—best friends—and tiny as the head of a pin. (554)

Steinbeck's association of Cathy with Alice is significant in that this fantasy—with its correlation with free imagination and satire —again places Cathy outside the biblical symbolism in the novel. In a sense, the other characters may be seen, from her point of view, as puppets on a string. In an inversion of the norm, she may also be viewed as a bewildered Alice caught in a nightmare world. For, in her mind, she is not culpable but is instead an observer of the true monsters—the mad hatters, the queens and kings of hearts, or as Richard Wallace suggests in a decoding of the word "hearts," *haters* (39).

In a letter to his friend, Carlton Sheffield, written 16 October 1952, Steinbeck says of Cathy's character:

> You won't believe her, many people don't. I don't know whether I believe her either but I know she exists. I don't believe in Na-

poleon, Joan of Arc, Jack the Ripper, the man who stands on one finger in the circus. I don't believe Jesus Christ, Alexander the Great, Leonardo. I don't believe them but they exist. I don't believe them because they aren't like me. You say you only believe her at the end. Ah! but that's when, through fear, she became like us. This was very carefully planned. All the book was very carefully planned. (*SLL* 459)

Indeed, in a sense *East of Eden* may be viewed as an intricately plotted mystery as well as a morality tale. At the heart of the mystery lies the enigmatic Cathy/Kate—a shift in name signifying an ever-shifting characterization—and a split personality. Paradoxically, Cathy appears to develop and change from defiance to fear in the course of the novel. After being brutally beaten by Mr. Edwards, Cathy is next introduced in Chapter 11 as a non-human species:

A dirty bundle of rags and mud was trying to worm its way up the steps. One skinny hand clawed slowly at the stairs. The other dragged helplessly. There was a caked face with cracked lips and eyes peering out of swollen, blackened lids. The forehead was laid open, oozing blood back into the matted hair. (110)

While Charles instinctively gleans the truth about Cathy's character in this scene, Adam benevolently ministers to her every need and sees in Cathy the purpose for his life, a dream built upon the illusion of his own needs. After Adam's proposal to Cathy, we are given a rare glimpse into her motivation for marriage.

She had not only made up her mind to marry Adam but she had so decided before he had asked her. She was afraid. She needed protection and money. . . . And Mr. Edwards had really frightened her. That had been the only time in her life she had lost control of a situation. She determined never to let it happen again. (121)

But it does happen again. Late in the novel Joe Valery convinces Kate that a witness with circumstantial evidence related to the murder of Faye is still alive, and Kate reacts to the news with "almost hopeless fear and weariness."

But Kate is seen not only as powerful or fearful. In a brief reversal from a life of sin, after confronting her twin sons in the brothel, Kate wills her fortune to Aron. After her death, we learn that she has stored her marriage certificate in a safe deposit box, a rather conventional gesture. Earlier, she fantasizes about moving to New York and attending concerts with her fair-haired son Aron. Nearer home, she attends the Episcopal Church in Salinas so that she may view her favorite son Aron. These shades of chiaroscuro in Kate's character, however, mask a sociopathic personality. Alternating between a wish for respectability and a new life with her "angelic" son Aron and a fear of discovery by Cal "the smart one—the dark one—" Kate muses:

> mother of two sons—and she looked like a child. And if anyone had seen her with the blond one—could they have any doubt? She thought how it would be to stand beside him in a crowd and let people find out for themselves. What would—Aron, that was the name—what would he do if he knew? His brother knew. That smart little son of a bitch—wrong word—must not call him that. Might be too true. Some people believed it. And not smart bastard either—born in holy wedlock. Kate laughed aloud. She felt good. She was having a good time.
>
> The smart one—the dark one—bothered her. He was like Charles. (512)

This inner debate is immediately followed by a new dark plan of attack—"a comical murder" of Ethel, the aging prostitute who divines the truth about Kate's murder of Faye. Although changes in her character appear, Kate ultimately runs on parallel tracks that end nowhere. She commits suicide, never achieving a resolution of her self-willed sense of superiority and Cal's unspoken affront. "The glint in his eyes said, 'You missed something. They had something and you missed it'" (554).

In swallowing the final draft of poison, the "drink me" potion, Kate returns to the fantasy world of *Alice in Wonderland*, perceiving herself as a victim surrounded by towering trees of enemies, but never fully confronting her involvement in a life gone awry. She seeks Alice as an innocent feminine icon, but finds herself desolate and isolated from even that fantasy. Steinbeck captures her whirling perceptions: "She thought or said or thought, 'Alice doesn't know. I'm going on past.'" Kate goes on her last adventure alone.

> Her eyes closed and a dizzy nausea shook her. She opened her eyes and stared about in terror. The gray room darkened and the cone of light flowed and rippled like water. And then her eyes closed again and her fingers curled as though they held small breasts. And her heart beat solemnly and her breathing slowed as she grew smaller and smaller and then disappeared—(554)

Steinbeck brilliantly concludes this passage with the dismissal "and she had never been," the total annihilation of her character. The next reference he makes to Kate is clinical:

> Already Kate was on the table at Muller's with the formalin running into her veins, and her stomach was in a jar in the coroner's office. (559)

However, the riddle of Cathy/Kate remains. In willing her fortune to Aron and leaving her marriage certificate behind, she may be subtly reinforcing the *timshel* theme; yet, in Kate's case, the timing suggests a shadow theme: her choice for good may be seen as a kind of epiphany when the reader is dealt a final shock: We remember her not only as the serpentine Eve (or more precisely Lilith) of the beginning, but as a kind of avenging angel at the end.

The mystery of Kate's complex characterization comes full circle. After incinerating her parents and staging a mysterious disappearance, the young "Cathy left a scent of sweetness about her"; the aged Kate leaves a final shock of apparent conversion—until we remember the ugly photographs of her customers—and her determination to blackmail them. Certainly the fearful, tormented Kate at the end is a kaleidoscopic reversal from the defiant and desolate Kate we find in Chapter 25 when she confronts Adam with the fact that perhaps Charles fathered one son. Although Kate prefers Aron, who physically resembles her and, like Adam, represents all she is not, it appears that Cal is the probable son of Charles, the man Kate "could have loved." As Louis Owens notes:

> Caleb and Aron, the twin sons born to Cathy, pick up the Cain and Abel theme introduced in the characters of Charles and Adam and carry it through to the end of the novel. The twins are each "born separate in his own sack" (194), and it is impossible to determine their respective paternity. Again, determinism and psychological realism are confused in the characters of the boys—Is Cal bad because he may be descended from Charles or is he bad because, like Charles, he feels rejected? Is it the "channel in the blood" that makes Cal different from the good Aron, or is it the father's response that determines each son's character? Steinbeck makes it impossible to determine who the boys' respective fathers may be. (*JS's Re-Vision of America* 152)

The multiple ironies of this dilemma both undercut and strengthen the *timshel* theme. If Cal is not Adam's son, his genetic roots lie with Cathy and Charles and hence the question of choosing good over evil becomes more problematic, although, admittedly, he has found his mother out and rejects her. " 'I was afraid I had you in me.' 'You have,' said Kate. 'No, I haven't. I'm my own. I don't have to be you.' " (466). If Cal is not Adam's son, Adam raises himself to a level of spiritual transcendence when he offers Cal the opportunity to choose between good and evil. Like Joe Saul in *Burning Bright,* Adam acknowledges a spiritual paternity which transcends and reconciles the rivalry of three generations of Trasks.

And yet we don't know what choice Cal will make after the final scene; he appears strangely passive and the ending is open-ended, enigmatic, and ambiguous. After all, it is Lee's energy which propels the action at the end of the novel when he delivers his Daedalus-like analogy of a craftsman who had refined his cup with "all impurities burned out," leading to Adam's climactic offering of *timshel.*

Steinbeck notes his exhaustion near the completion of the book in a letter to Covici:

So we go into the last week and I must say I am very much frightened. I guess it would be hard to be otherwise—all of these months and years aimed in one direction and suddenly it is over and it seems that the thunder has produced a mouse. Last week there was complete exhaustion and very near collapse. (*JN* 171)

In a sense, then, the ending of *East of Eden* is as problematic as the characterizations of Cathy and Cal: both bring into question 19th and 20th century attempts to define morality by conventional norms. Indeed, both may be seen as precursors of Generation X's skepticism of conventions, an evolutionary cycle. Almost like *X-Files* detectives, they peer, with x-ray vision, into the raw truth of human behavior and lift the veil of pretense behind hypocrisy. Cal's cry near the end of the novel—"I've got her blood"—questions the predictability of an optimistic, moralistic ending, although Lee and Abra's words offer hope, as does, finally, Adam's labored whisper of *timshel*, which applies to Cal, and today still, to Everyman and Everywoman.

18

Cathy in *East of Eden*

Indispensable to the Thematic Design

Kyoko Ariki

Ariki argues that East of Eden *should be read as a tripartite division of stories—those of the Trasks, of the Hamiltons, and of Cathy Ames/ Trask. In noting the significance of both the theme of love and the Cathy plotline, Ariki refers to Erich Fromm's* The Art of Loving *to help illuminate the significance of love—which Cathy is incapable of giving or receiving—to the human condition.*

I

John Steinbeck's *East of Eden* is composed of three stories—those of the Trasks, of the Hamiltons and of Cathy Ames/Trask. It is so constructed that the novel's central theme emerges at the point where the three stories meet. Unfortunately, however, most Steinbeck critics have considered the novel as simply the saga of the Trasks and the Hamiltons.[1] Joseph Fontenrose and Louis Owens are among the few who refer pointedly to the significance of Cathy. Fontenrose points out that *East of Eden* is made up of three stories and emphasizes the importance of Cathy (118–19). Louis Owens argues that "a way of profitably approaching *East of Eden* is to see the characters of Cathy Trask and Samuel Hamilton as two poles around which the novel revolves and takes form" (74). Indeed, thematic messages come into clear focus only where Cathy works to bridge the Trask story and the Hamilton story. She is, therefore, never a figure to be dismissed as "a monster," "a witch," "a figure of evil," "the most vituperative villainess" and an "enormity of wickedness" (Lisca 267;

French 147; McCarthy 117; Gladstein 98; Heavilin 95). Cathy plays three major roles in *East of Eden:* She connects the two families; she serves as catalyst for change in the Trasks, after which she disappears; and she contributes greatly to the negative presentation of the theme of *timshel,* just as Caleb Trask contributes positively.

II

Love is the thematic foundation of *East of Eden.* At the outset of Part IV, Steinbeck declares that the value of a man depends on how much he is loved:

> In uncertainty I am certain that underneath their topmost layers of frailty men want to be good and want to be loved. Indeed, most of their vices are attempted short cuts to love. When a man comes to die, no matter what his talents and influence and genius, if he dies unloved his life must be a failure to him and his dying a cold horror. (414)

Any person, he claims earlier in the novel, can commit a crime, when love is rejected.

> The greatest terror a child can have is that he is not loved, and rejection is the hell he fears. . . . And with rejection comes anger, and with anger some kind of crime in revenge for the rejection, and with the crime guilt—and there is the story of mankind. (270)

Steinbeck's assertion of love in *East of Eden* is supported by a passage from *The Art of Loving* by the German psychoanalyst Erich Fromm:

> The desire for interpersonal fusion is the most powerful striving in man. It is the most fundamental passion, it is the force which keeps the human race together, the clan, the family, society. The failure to achieve it means insanity or destruction—

self-destruction or destruction of others. Without love, humanity could not exist a day. (15)

Although both Steinbeck and Fromm insist on the instinctive desire for love, there is no denying the possibility that a person can be born without any such desire. Cathy in *East of Eden* is such a person, a mentally crippled figure by nature. She appears as an "animal anomaly" (*JN* 79), because she lacks conscience, kindness, morality and consideration for others, all of which are the products of love toward others. John Timmerman notes appropriately that "Cathy's essential evil is indeed the evil of lovelessness" (219). Steinbeck writes in *Journal of a Novel*, "Yes, I think it is time to wind in the Cathy section. How strange it is and so must be, the animal anomaly" (79). Cathy's story is developed along the lines of her abnormality.

Steinbeck also suggests her important role in his journal, saying, "Cathy is important for two reasons. If she were simply a monster, that would not bring her in" (41–42). Although at the beginning of the novel she is introduced with a malformed soul, "a mental or psychic monster" (72), as the story progresses, Cathy comes to be aware that there is something she lacks. Since she cannot figure out what is missing about her, she fears it, runs away from it and finally attempts to escape from her life forever. In other words she is destined to perish, just like a mutant that cannot adapt itself to the normal environment.

In contrast, the story of the Hamiltons demonstrates affection and warmth, and, as Richard Peterson notes, Samuel is "the God presence" (78). The Trasks, on the other hand, are described as an unhealthy family that cannot foster normal love—Cyrus, his anonymous first wife who committed suicide, the second wife Alice, as well as Charles, and Adam. *East of Eden*, therefore, suggests that the image of the light the Hamiltons shed illuminates the dismal world of the Trasks, eventually helping them toward a healthier direction.

III

The 55 chapters of *East of Eden* are composed of the stories of the Trasks, of the Hamiltons, and of Cathy, each dealing with one particular story or two or even three. As figure 4 shows, the circles represent respectively the stories of the Trasks, of the Hamiltons, and of Cathy, and the numbers in the circles stand for the chapter numbers. Cathy connects the two families. For the first ten chapters each story is told separately until chapter 11, in which Cathy comes to the Trasks in Connecticut, seriously injured, asking for help. While taking care of the wounded Cathy, Adam falls in love with her and soon afterward marries her. Cathy gives Adam the motivation to move west and to build a paradise for her in California, where the Hamiltons live. Indeed there are only three chapters where all the three stories come together (chapters 15, 17, and 31), and the first two of these chapters are very important, for they are the very foundations of the novel from which the Trasks's saga starts. When Samuel visits Adam to dig him a well, he instinctively notices Cathy's abnormalities and warns Adam of this. When he visits the Trasks again to help with her delivery, Cathy bites Samuel's hand like a snake. By thus connecting the Hamiltons and the Trasks, she suggests her strong influence on the relationship of the two families; also, like some catalytic substance, she causes a crucial change in the Trasks.

Cathy also serves as catalyst as Adam eventually learns love from Samuel. The story of the Hamiltons is composed of the episodes concerning his four sons and five daughters. All the episodes, such as Will's practical talent for business, Dessie's broken love and Una's too early death, are so full of love and affection that the reader cannot but feel that Samuel is a leading figure who emits boundless love toward his family. Samuel's love, moreover, is not limited to his family. He loves his useless horse, Doxology, as well as his barren land, saying, "I love it the way a bitch loves her runty pup. I love every flint, the plow-breaking outcropping, the thin and barren topsoil, the waterless heart of her. Somewhere in my dust heap there's a richness" (297). It is quite natural that Samuel, the embodiment of love, can detect almost instinctively the evil of the loveless creature, Cathy.

The Trasks, however, cannot foster love among family members. According to Erich Fromm, a man cannot learn to love others until he is loved by someone; as he says, "the idea of love is

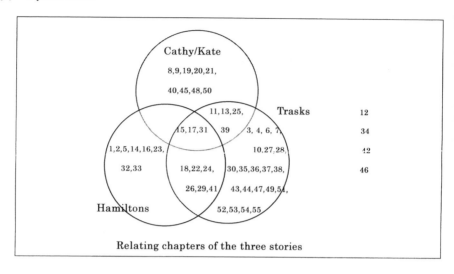

Relating chapters of the three stories

Cathy'/Kate Chapters

(8) From Cathy's childhood to the day when she leaves home.
(9) Cathy becomes a whore. Twisting Edward, the manager of the whorehouse, round her little finger,
   Cathy deceives him. As a   result Edward becomes angry and beats her almost to death.
(19) Cathy comes to Fay's whorehouse with her name changed to Kate and wins her sympathy and trust.
(20) Completely deceived by Kate, Fay makes her will leaving her whole business to Kate(Cathy) after
   her death.
(21) Kate makes a secret plan to murder Fay and carries it out very carefully.
(40) Scared of something she lacks. she hides in her small dark room with no air.
(45)&(48)Kate becomes so frightened at something she can't see that she is driven into a corner.
(50) Finally she makes up her mind to run away from that fear forever,
   and she takes a pill which makes her smaller and smaller and eventually nothing.

Hamilton / Cathy / Trask Chapters

(15) Samuel, who comes to the Trasks to dig a well, warns Adam of Cathy's abnormality.
(17) When he is helping at her delivery.   Cathy bites Samuel's hand.
   After giving birth, Cathy shoots Adam and leaves the house.
(31) Adam visits Cathy to give her the money Charles left after his death.
   He lets her know what she lacks. On his way back he visits Olive and meets Liza and Will.

Cathy & Kate / Trask   Chapters

(11) Cathy comes to the Trasks' house seriously wounded. Adam takes good care of her and marries her.
(13) Adam comes to Salinas with Cathy and plans to make a paradise for his wife.
(25) On his way back home from Samuel's funeral, Adam visits Cathy at her whorehouse   and tells her that
   she hates something in man that she doesn't understand.
(39) Caleb is overjoyed to know that Adam shows him warm affection.   He summons courage to visit Cathy,
   telling her that she is missing something every one of us has.

Figure 4. A brief summary of the Cathy/Kate stories.

transformed from being loved into loving; into creating love" (34). Clearly Steinbeck intends a marked contrast between the Trasks and the Hamiltons. As he writes in *Journal of a Novel*, "This Trask chapter is dark and dour as a damp tunnel. It has to be. And the next chapter is very light and gay. I'll have my contrast all right. It will be all contrasts and balances" (42). Indeed there is no love among the Trask family members. Cyrus's love for his son Adam is nothing more than another expression of his self-love. He wants to make Adam in his own image, as Adam tells Cal later: "My father made a mold and forced me into it" (454). Adam even confesses to Charles, "Maybe it's wrong to feel good when our father's just died, but you know, Charles, I never felt better in my whole life" (64).

But with Cathy as the catalyst, Adam learns what love is from Samuel. This paves the way for Adam to offer love to his troubled son Cal. Samuel's lesson starts (252–72) when he finds Adam totally absent-minded after Cathy has shot him and left the house. When Samuel sees Adam indulging in his sorrow, neglecting the care of his twins, he snarls at him, grasping his throat and crying, "You have no love" (259). Samuel lets him know that there is nothing as dreadful for a child as not being loved and accepted. Knowing that the twins do not have names, he helps Adam name them. The next time Samuel visits him, he gives Adam strong medicine which might kill him if it does not work properly—the truth about Cathy. But the bitter medicine precipitates a change: Adam gains the courage to confirm with his own eyes the ugly business she is doing. After meeting with Cathy/Kate at her whorehouse, he declares, "I'm free, she's gone" (330): and this arouses his interest in his sons. In fact, after he comes back from Salinas, "Cal and Aron were first astonished and then a little embarrassed to find that Adam listened to them and asked questions, looked at them and saw them" (352). It can safely be said that Adam revives from dead indifference, and not only becomes interested in his sons, but comes to love them, as guided by Samuel after he is free of Cathy.

In *East of Eden*, Cal is a Cain figure who commits a terrible crime out of anger of rejected love. To Cal, too, Cathy serves as an important medium. Only after Cal knows the truth about

Cathy can he love his father more. Steinbeck writes, "And in Cal there grew up a passionate love for his father and a wish to protect him and to make it up to him for the things he had suffered" (450). This growing love leads Cal to Cathy's/Kate's whorehouse, because he thinks he needs to know her more in order to protect his suffering father. For the same reason he decides to earn money by going into partnership with Will. Cathy serves as a catalyst, causing chain reactions one after the other among the Trasks. When the fifteen thousand dollars Cal earned for his father is rejected, he feels so hurt and angry that his violent jealousy flashes out against Aron as a murderous weapon. Cal takes his brother to Cathy's/Kate's whorehouse, which drives the latter to enlist in the army and leads eventually to his death. And Aron's death is a factor in causing Adam's stroke. Cathy's role is, throughout, crucial.

IV

Cathy is also a kind of foil to Cal. After causing these crucial reactions in the Trask family, she disappears from the novel. In the thematic frame of the novel the movement of her life toward extinction competes markedly with Cal's new start in life. The clash of these two opposite strong powers generates energy and makes the theme of the necessity of love more impressive and enduring.

As noted earlier, Cathy is an anomaly, lacking the ability to love. Though at first she does not notice what she lacks, she must feel vaguely scared of the people who have what she does not. This is why she destroys her Latin teacher James Grew, her parents, Edward, Adam, and Faye, all of whom offer love to her. Late in the book, Cathy's childhood is revealed:

> She was a very small girl with a face as lovely and fresh as her son's face—a very small girl. Most of the time she knew she was smarter and prettier than anyone else. But now and then a lonely fear would fall upon her so that she seemed surrounded by a tree-tall forest of enemies. Then every thought and word and look was aimed to hurt her, and she had no place to run and no place

to hide. And she would cry in panic because there was no escape and no sanctuary. (551)

The sentences suggest that as a child she was scared of something that she could not understand. As the story progresses, Cathy is increasingly aware that she lacks something that everybody else has. First Adam and then Cal point out what she is missing. When Adam visits her on his way back from Samuel's funeral, he says to Cathy, "I know what you hate. You hate something in them you can't understand. You don't hate their evil. You hate the good in them you can't get at . . . " (323). When Adam visits her again to give her a share of Charles's legacy, he discloses to her something dreadful that she resists. It makes her uneasy and even scares her.

> I seem to know that there's a part of you missing. Some men can't see the color green, but they may never know they can't. I think you are only a part of a human. I can't do anything about that. But I wonder whether you ever feel that something invisible is all around you. It would be horrible if you knew it was there and couldn't see it or feel it. That would be horrible. (385)

Cathy/Kate hears the same thing from Cal, when he visits her in her whorehouse: "Did you ever have the feeling like you were missing something? Like as if the others knew something you didn't—like a secret they wouldn't tell you. Did you ever feel that way?" (465). Furthermore Cal discloses what Cathy/Kate herself is vaguely conscious of: "I don't think the light hurts your eyes. I think you're afraid" (466). All her life, Cathy has run from something, as Steinbeck notes:

> When I said Cathy was a monster it seemed to me that it was so. Now I have bent close with a glass over the small print of her and reread the footnotes, and I wonder if it was true. The trouble is that since we cannot know what she wanted, we will never know whether or not she got it. *If rather than running toward something, she ran away from something, we can't know whether she escaped.* (184, emphasis added)

Eventually she makes up her mind to escape forever from what frightens her and puts the capsule in her mouth. Her death is described with the image of shrinking into nothing like Alice in *Alice in Wonderland*. Indeed, Cathy is the product of a mutation which is destined to become extinct, as Steinbeck writes in *The Log from the Sea of Cortez*, "And our mutation . . . might well correspond to the thickening armor of great reptiles—a tendency that can end only in extinction" (74).

It is evident that the Cain-Abel story is the thematic framework of *East of Eden:* just like Cain's, Cal's malice virtually kills his brother. What is important here, however, is not the structural analogy, but the motivation that drives a man into crazy violence: jealousy gives birth to anger, and this anger becomes a murderous weapon. Cal's jealousy is understandable, for he desperately craves his father's love. In fact it is not Abel but Cain who is the ancestor of all humans. However, Cal is not just a Cain figure. He is also named after Caleb who got out of Egypt and successfully arrived at the Promised Land, while Aaron could not. The narrator of the novel makes Cal declare to Cathy/Kate, "My name is Caleb" and "Caleb got to the Promised Land" (465). While Cal is, in short, presented as a successful or positive figure, clearly Cathy is the negative figure opposed to Cal's positive role. This is demonstrated in the final scene of the novel, when Adam offers his son Cal his blessing, "timshel." This Hebrew word, discussed by Samuel, Adam and Lee, is the key to the novel. When "timshel" is read as "thou mayest," then it promises "the great choice" (303), or man's free will. When Adam whispers "timshel," it suggests that Cal may/can have a chance to be free of his sin. But his father's final blessing contains a further message: "You may/can have a chance to get over your sin, because *I love you*." This message embedded in Adam's final word convinces readers of Cal's future as a man who has learned love. Cathy's life toward extinction for want of love illuminates Cal's life toward a promising future.

V

In *East of Eden* love is clearly shown to be indispensable to humans. Cathy's role is crucial thematically. First, she connects the sagas of both families: the Hamiltons's story which is brightly illuminated with love and the Trasks's story which has the image of a dark, chilly barren land lacking in love. Secondly, she is a catalyst to bring about reactions in Adam and Cal. Through the medium of the malformed figure Cathy, both Adam and Cal undergo change and learn love. And thirdly her life is in marked contrast to Cal's. Because of lack of love she is doomed to extinction, while Cal, because of his earnest craving for love, is offered blessing in spite of his terrible crime. It is not too much to say, therefore, that Cathy is a very influential figure, the one who contributes most to the thematic presentations in *East of Eden*. She is a pivotal figure in the structure of the novel.

IV
Steinbeck's Science and Ethics

19

These Are American People

The Spectre of Eugenics in Their Blood Is Strong *and* The Grapes of Wrath

Kevin Hearle

Noting Steinbeck's disturbing, and otherwise anomalous, reliance upon a racialized, supposedly scientific discourse of "blood" in Their Blood Is Strong, *Hearle offers a few possible reasons for the appearance of this discourse in* Their Blood Is Strong *but not in* The Grapes of Wrath. *He focuses upon the possibility that the influence of science upon Steinbeck's work was not as uniformly positive as literary critics may have believed, and analyzes the racial attitudes of the texts in evolutionary biology whose influence upon Steinbeck has long been acknowledged.*

The notion that an understanding of science, especially of those branches of biology which have an ecological focus, is important to an appreciation of Steinbeck's works has been a critical commonplace since at least Richard Astro's book on Ed Ricketts's influence on the novelist. Brian Railsback's recent study of Steinbeck and Darwin continues this tradition, praising the influence of science in Steinbeck's writing. When it comes to Darwinism and especially to Darwin's bastard offspring the social Darwinists and the eugenicists, there is much reason to examine both the value of some of the so-called "science" which influenced Steinbeck and the role which such pseudo-science played in Steinbeck's works.

Throughout his career, Steinbeck belittled not only notions of racial purity and racial inferiority, but also those who would subscribe to such notions. In *The Pastures of Heaven*, which was only his second published book, the recurrent racism which various characters display is one of the important themes which hold the short story cycle together. In the opening two chapters, Steinbeck presents a little history of Las Pasturas del Cielo. The first white person to view the Pastures was a Spanish corporal who, like his fellow soldiers, commonly raped Indian women at the Carmel Mission. Later, George Battle, one of the first American settlers in the valley, apparently left upstate New York because he was unwilling to fight to free the slaves. He died at 65, stooped from his labors and having never established meaningful emotional contact with anyone. When the novel finally makes it to the twentieth century, race continues to be a problem. For example, in the first two paragraphs of the unpublished manuscript version of what would become Chapter Seven, a paisano denies that he is Indian and proudly lays claim to his Castillian heritage. Steinbeck, however, undercuts the notion of racial superiority by calling the man's Castillian blood "a stain" (Record 37). In Chapter Four, when Tularecito surprises Molly Morgan, she fears both rape and miscegenation at his hands. Similarly, the history of the Whiteside dynasty in the valley is a series of ultimately delusional attempts to maintain a pure lineage.

The case of *Lifeboat*, in the middle of his career, is also illuminating. Steinbeck wrote a script which first MacKinlay Kantor then Jo Swerling and finally Alfred Hitchcock turned into a screenplay. Although the three made so many substantive changes that Roy Simmonds has called *Lifeboat*, "nothing more nor less than a travesty of Steinbeck's intentions and achievement" (216), Steinbeck's outrage focused on the changes made to the character Joe. In a letter to the studio, he wrote,

> While it is certainly true that I wrote a script for *Lifeboat*, it is not true that in that script there were any slurs against organized labor nor was there a stock comedy Negro. On the contrary there was an intelligent and thoughtful seaman who knew realistically what he was about. And instead of the usual colored travesty of the half comic and half pathetic Negro there was a Negro of dignity, purpose and personality. (*SLL* 266)

Steinbeck's depiction of the southern Texas and Louisiana portion of his trip in the non-fiction *Travels with Charley*, during the last decade of his life, is further evidence that his opposition to racism remained steady. The stream of racist jokes at gas stations depresses him, but once he gets to New Orleans his disgust with the pro-segregationist Cheerleaders becomes visceral. Trying to talk his way through his depression as he flees the demonstrations against school integration, he discusses racial tensions with a progressive white Southerner. The man suggests that an America of mixed race people is likely in the future, and the prospect sounds positive to both of them. They are, however, both scared of the violence they expect to erupt, presumably in the names of race purity and retribution, before that mixed race future comes to pass. Later, he picks up a "young Negro student" who is impatient with the pace of social progress (206). Steinbeck conveys his respect for the hitchhiker through his depiction of not only the young man's passion but also his intelligence. It is, however, the redneck Steinbeck kicks out of the truck who most clearly draws the author out on race. When the man calls him a "nigger-lover," Steinbeck replies, "No, I'm not. And I'm not a white-lover either, if it includes those noble Cheerleaders" (205).

Steinbeck's reliance on a conditional phrase at the end of his denial may or may not be significant. If that phrase is merely a rhetorical means of re-introducing his contempt for racists, then perhaps the statement as a whole can correctly be interpreted as a further indication of Steinbeck's long-standing refusal to accept racial hierarchies. Even if Steinbeck is admitting that he doesn't love African-Americans but that he does love white Americans who aren't racists, that doesn't mean Steinbeck was racist or that he thought whites were superior to non-whites. In *Travels with Charley*, Steinbeck at one point comes to regret having made an "old Negro" accept a ride; being alone with a white man—especially one who keeps asking him questions—only serves to make the poor man understandably nervous. From that incident, and from his depiction of Crooks' initial rebuffing of Lennie in *Of Mice and Men*, it is clear that Steinbeck appreciated that one of the fundamental difficulties involved in resolving the nation's racial problems is that racial suspicions—warranted or not—form barriers to honest communication and knowledge. To expect Steinbeck, or anyone else, to love people who will not speak to him, or will speak to him only guardedly, is perhaps to ask too much. Furthermore, his position as a famous author trying to collect material while he travels incognito through a part of the country he knows only as a tourist doesn't allow him anywhere near the same degree of familiarity with African-Americans as his childhood in Salinas or his days working in the fields had once afforded him with paisanos and Mexican-Americans. Throughout his work Steinbeck demonstrates respect for African-Americans and a sympathetic understanding of how racism limits their lives, but, probably because he doesn't know them very well, he doesn't love his African-American characters the way he does his paisanos.

The one notable exception to Steinbeck's generally progressive depictions of race is the series of articles about the Okies which he wrote in 1936 for the *San Francisco News*. That series contains many sections in which racialized discourse drawn from what then often passed for science becomes the grounds for a call to help the downtrodden immigrants from the Dust Bowl. That these articles were part of Steinbeck's preparation for writing *The Grapes of Wrath* makes them especially important. It also suggests the need for a serious reconsideration of the role of race and racialized discourse in that novel.

Because the articles for the *News* were written before *The Grapes of Wrath,* and because the language in those articles is more clearly infused with the pseudo-scientific discourse of race than is the language in the novel, the *News* essays are the logical place to begin an examination of Steinbeck's use of racialized language. As Charles Wollenberg notes, Steinbeck's series of articles prophesizes that because the Okies were white Americans they would, naturally, force reforms upon the Associated Farmers and perhaps end the exploitation of migrant labor upon which so much of California agriculture has long been based (xi). In fact, Steinbeck strikes that note in the first essay:

> It should be understood that with this new race the old methods of repression, of starvation wages, of jailing, beating and intimidation are not going to work: these are American people. (23)

And, lest we have any doubts as to who he means by "this new race," Steinbeck tells us a few paragraphs later that "the names of the new migrants indicate that they are of English, German and Scandinavian descent. There are Munns, Holbrooks, Hansens, Schmidts (23). Still later, he refers to them as "good American stock" (43, 54), and emphasizes that these people, unlike previous waves of migrant farmworkers, will become permanent Californians. There is nothing subtle about this argument. Steinbeck tells his readers that these are white folks; therefore, they are suitable for intermarriage and breeding with established white Californians. Besides, they'll be staying whether we like it or not. Lest his readers somehow miss the implications, Steinbeck states the argument explicitly in the concluding paragraph of the penultimate essay,

> Foreign labor is on the wane in California, and the future farm workers are to be white and American. This fact must be recognized and a rearrangement of the attitude toward and treatment of migrant labor must be achieved. (57)

The question is, though, why does their race seem to matter so much to Steinbeck? And why does Steinbeck privilege whiteness (53–54)? The evidence, after all, indicates that the Okies were far less likely to undertake organized labor actions than were the "foreign migrants" (Steinbeck, *Harvest* 22) who preceded them.

Although definitive answers to these questions are probably no longer possible (and may never have been), there are many avenues of speculation available to us. It is possible that Steinbeck, for all his New Deal liberalism, believed—perhaps only unconsciously—that whites are the superior race. His love of and appreciation of paisanos, Mexicans, Chicanos, and Chinese-Americans would seem to argue against this,[1] as would, for example, his attack on the segregationist "Cheerleaders" in *Travels with Charley,* and also his depiction of the racial isolation and victimization of the stablehand Crooks in *Of Mice and Men.* On the other hand, it is one thing to denounce the oppression of other races and quite another to believe that members of your own socially privileged race could be made to accept similar oppression. The mere fact that we may not want to believe that Steinbeck was racist, however, is not an indication that he wasn't;

it is an indication that we may be unreliable judges of Steinbeck's potential racism.

A second, and not necessarily exclusive, possibility is that Steinbeck's racially tinged discourse is a calculated strategy in which he consciously plays to the prejudices of his audience in order to elicit action from white America to help save the Okies. This theory is supported by the fact that Steinbeck's views on race in his other works appear to be at a variance with his views as stated in the *News* articles, and by the fact that at the same time the *San Francisco News* was printing Steinbeck's series they also ran an editorial making much the same racially based call for labor reform in the fields of California (Wollenberg xi).

It is perhaps even possible to appreciate the irony of Steinbeck's strategic use of discourse steeped in white supremacist ideology. As David Roediger points out, whiteness has been a fluid term in America. For much of the 19th century there was some question as to whether either the Irish or the Germans—who constitute, for example, the majority of Steinbeck's own ancestry—were, in fact, "white." Roediger argues that "whiteness"—which is, after all a social construction rather than a scientific fact—was expanded to include the Irish and Germans in ways which were initially mainly to the advantage of the WASP upper classes (Wheeler A8-A10). Throughout much of the nineteenth and twentieth centuries, recent immigrants and other lower-class Americans of European ancestry have been willing to accept a wage scale equally low or lower than that of native born African-Americans, if they were accorded the social status of being "white" (Roediger 19–31). Steinbeck's use of "white" does, at least, reverse part of this dynamic by calling on the still mostly WASP upper class to take care of their fellow white Americans; however, in its silence about the non-white, Steinbeck's language in *Their Blood Is Strong* also acquiesces to the oppressive force of "whiteness" in the lives of Americans who have non-European ancestry.

A third, and again not necessarily exclusive, possibility is that Steinbeck, in his attempt to maintain some semblance of objectivity, lapsed into a pseudo-scientific and heavily racialized discourse of which he then had insufficient understanding and over which he exercised limited control. His destruction of the

"L'Affaire Lettuceberg" manuscript because it was too one-sided may be evidence for this theory. This possibility suggests once again a less than ideal Steinbeck; however, it does leave open the possibility that Steinbeck was, rather than a mild racist, at least to some extent a less than conscious mouthpiece for a racist pseudo-scientific discourse.

A proper consideration of this last possibility requires an analysis of the discourse of race as it appeared in the "scientific" texts which Steinbeck had read by the late 1930s. In addition to Darwin, Brian Railsback credits each of the following authors as having been influences upon Steinbeck's "scientific" outlook: Jan Christiaan Smuts, John Elof Boodin, W. C. Allee, Mark Graubard, William Emerson Ritter and Ellsworth Huntington. None of these authors claims to be a eugenicist in any of their works which we know that Steinbeck read, and Graubard, in fact, devotes twenty pages to a refutation of eugenics. W. C. Allee, in addition to making no reference to eugenics and taking no readily obvious position in regard to it, uses the term "race" as if it were synonymous with "species." William Emerson Ritter, who also appears to use "race" and "species" interchangeably, is a more complex case. Although Ritter accepts hierarchies of civilization which place European and Euro-American culture at the pinnacle, he belittles eugenicists on the grounds that their project is doomed to at best small success because the differences between people are too slight to allow for much improvement strictly through manipulation of what he calls "the germ plasm" (II: 90).[2]

On the other hand, both Jan Christiaan Smuts and Ellsworth Huntington clearly rely on supposedly scientific notions of white supremacy. General Smuts, who was prime minister of South Africa from 1919 through 1924, deputy prime minister from 1933 through 1939, and then prime minister again from 1939 through 1948, is fairly coy in *Holism and Evolution* about his support for what he calls "the new science of Eugenics" (196). With the possible exception of his capitalization of eugenics, nowhere in his book does Smuts state his support of eugenics; however, his ruminations on the human organism are revealing. For example, discussing the influence of the past on the mind, Smuts claims that

> It [the past] is the contribution of the hereditary structure as
> modified by ancestral experience, which lies behind all indi-
> vidual experience. . . . It gives us our fundamental bias, our points
> of view, our temperament, our instinctive reactions and our par-
> ticular individual ways of looking at persons and things. (255)

A little farther down the same page, Smuts' syntax makes it clear
that "hereditary structure and ancestral past" are separate entities and that both are opposed to "individual experience and development." Without mentioning race, Smuts has nevertheless
managed to invoke the concept of "the volk." We are who we
are, according to this view, not only because of our genes and
our personal experiences but because the cultural heritage of
our ancestors has mysteriously been transmitted to us at birth
(Cashmore 198, 373).

Smuts is deeply concerned that this heritage and everything
else human be transmitted perfectly. For General Smuts the human "Personality" is the highest achievement of creation, and
the "ideal Personality" will be, in his words, "pure" and "homogeneous" (302–303, 314). It is unsurprising then that this man
who seems to have been obsessed with the notion that "there
will be no alien stuff" was also one of the early architects of the
system of racial segregation which would later became codified
as apartheid (314).

Ellsworth Huntington's works are far more obvious than those
of Smuts in both their reliance on pseudo-scientific notions of
white supremacy and in Huntington's support for eugenics. In
Civilization and Climate, for example, Huntington continually
makes claims for the superiority of one race to another. Early
on, he informs his readers that the rise of Greek civilization was
caused by an influx of "blonde Norse invaders" who formed a
crucial class of leaders, and, furthermore, that Greek civilization fell into a precipitous decline when, "the racial elements to
which Greece owed her greatness disappeared, and the country
fell into intellectual insignificance" (23, 27). Later, when he compares "Teutons and negroes," Huntington stereotypically follows the white man's burden school of race relations (31). Having already decided that Africans and African-Americans are
intellectually inferior to whites, he concludes that

Initiative, inventiveness, versatility, and the power of leadership
are the qualities which give flavor to the Teutonic race. Good humor, patience, loyalty, and the power of self-sacrifice give flavor
to the negro. (35)

Huntington's arguments in support of these conclusions are the
social scientific equivalent of the craniometric measurements
which Stephen Jay Gould so wonderfully debunks in *The Mismeasure of Man*. For example, ignoring the accumulated advan-
tages of capital and of established cultural institutions, Huntington claims that the reason for the preponderance of New
Englanders in *Who's Who* is racial. Specifically, he implies a hierarchy of American racial groups: with "people of puritan descent" at the top, followed in descending order by the immigrants
who were middle class in "advanced countries", the recent arrivals who are "scarcely better than the Mexicans", "Mexicans . . .
who possess the greatest proportion of Spanish blood", Mexicans in general, Indians, and blacks (308–310). Huntington follows up his supposedly scientific ranking of the races with a call
to eugenic action. The logic, however preposterous, is chilling,
especially since it was able to validate itself as "science."

As Huntington's hierarchy makes clear, "blood" was definitely not a racially neutral term, so the fact that the pamphlet
which collected Steinbeck's *News* articles bore the title *Their
Blood Is Strong* requires serious consideration in any analysis of
racialized discourse in Steinbeck's works. (Drawing on a phrase
Steinbeck had used in the first essay, the editor of the collection
gave the pamphlet its title.) Although currently the use of "blood"
to designate basic inheritance in general and racial heritage in
particular isn't as common as it was before the discovery of
DNA, when these essays were published in the 1930s "blood"
was an integral part of the construction of race in America (Oxford 930). Although there were no compelling scientific or medical reasons to make racial distinctions on the basis of blood—or
for that matter to make hematological distinctions on the basis
of race—as both a physical entity and a linguistic marker, blood
was nevertheless constructed as a cultural, legal and economic
commodity which defined race ("Racism" 7: 58–59).[3]

The dividing line between white and non-white races in

America was, in fact, explicitly expressed in terms of blood. Shortly after the collapse of Reconstruction, most of the former Confederate states were already using what has been called the "one drop rule" to define racial heritage (Frederickson *White* 130). By that rule a person who had any percentage of blood, in other words ancestry, which was non-white was thereby defined as non-white. As late as 1950, a black World War II veteran was permitted to bleed to death at Duke Hospital because the blood supply was segregated and no "black blood" was available to transfuse him (Love as cited in Tindall). Even now, "blood quantum", which is, in theory, a measurement of the percentage of blood a person carries in them from each of their ancestral races, remains the determining factor for whether or not someone can legally claim membership in an American Indian nation (Cohen 4–5). Therefore, for Steinbeck to use the phrase, "their blood is strong" and to furthermore insist upon the Okies' heritage as Americans with Teutonic sounding names is, at least in part, to base his appeal for the Okies on the now discredited, pseudo-scientific logic of racial superiority.

Of these "scientists", the man whose writing had the most easily traceable influence on Steinbeck's racially inflected "scientific" discourse appears to have been Ellsworth Huntington. In both *Their Blood Is Strong* and *The Grapes of Wrath*, Steinbeck uses the language of eugenics to explicitly accept Huntington's claim that migrations improve the people who undertake them (24). In the first article in his *San Francisco News* series, Steinbeck lists at some length the difficulties which the migrants have faced, and then he concludes, "They have weathered the thing, and they can weather much more for their blood is strong" (22). Shortly after this, he twice calls the Okies, "this new race" (22). The implication is that migration has made a new race of them and it has strengthened their blood.

There are, however, significant differences between Steinbeck's reliance on Huntington in *Their Blood Is Strong* and *The Grapes of Wrath*. Happily, during the two years between his composition of the articles for the *San Francisco News* and his completion of his epic masterpiece, Steinbeck either had a change of heart or finally recognized and repudiated the racism at the core of so much of social Darwinist discourse. In Chapter 14 he still invokes the discourse of biology with his warning to the own-ers, "Here is the anlage of the thing you fear. This is the zygote . . . " (206); however, as Chapter 19 makes clear, in *Grapes* the warning is not about race. Instead, the warning is about how hungry people willing to fight are strengthened in the struggle to survive while the rich grow weak in gorging on their own privileges; the warning is that by testing the strength of the hungry the rich only hasten the day when the hungry will sim-ply take what they need. And this time, to make sure we don't racialize the argument, Steinbeck draws a parallel between the Mexican Californios who were overrun by the invading Yankees and the current land-owning descendants of those Yankees who will in their turn inevitably be overrun by the Okies.

Furthermore, in *The Grapes of Wrath*, Steinbeck doesn't fall back on the discourse of "blood" and doesn't otherwise empha-size the whiteness of the Okies. In fact, in his description of a generic migrant dance in one of the inter-calary chapters (Chap-ter 23), he calls one of the dancers, "the Cherokee girl" and em-phasizes not only her stamina and grace but also implies that she and the "Texas boy" are unstoppably attracted to each other and may well wind up getting married and having mixed race children (449–50). And the tone of the narration is definitely not that of a eugenicist decrying inter-breeding and the supposedly consequent diminishment of the white race. Here, as elsewhere in his work, Steinbeck celebrates sexual attraction as natural and good.

And yet, in the importance Steinbeck places on the difficul-ties imposed by migration it is still possible to trace the influ-ence on *The Grapes of Wrath* of Ellsworth Huntington and his no-tions of improving the race through hardship. Indeed, it is by now a critical commonplace to acknowledge that the central plot of the novel outlines the ways in which hardships strengthen the Okies both by eliminating the weak and by expanding the sense of kinship among those who remain. Grandpa may die in Oklahoma, Noah may head off down the Colorado River, Grandma may die in the desert, and Connie may ditch the fam-ily when things get tough, but as Ma Joad declares in that fa-mous speech, "We ain't gonna die out. People is goin' on— changin' a little, maybe, but goin' right on" (577). And what tends to get ignored in that scene is her answer to Uncle John's doubts, "Ever'thing we do—seems to me is aimed right at goin' on. Seems that way to me. Even gettin' hungry—even bein' sick; some die, but the rest is tougher" (577–78). What has happened here is that Steinbeck has accepted the social Darwinist position that hardship strengthens a people, but he has stripped it of the discourse and of the supposed logic of white supremacy. Race is no longer important. Any people may be tested and strengthened by hardship.

In conclusion, it is important to acknowledge that there is as yet no definitive basis for preferring any one explanation for why Steinbeck used a pseudo-scientific discourse steeped in white supremacist ideology in *Their Blood Is Strong*. It is also important to acknowledge that the language is both disturbing and, in Steinbeck's long career, anomalous. Steinbeck's fans can find solace in that last fact and in the knowledge that when Steinbeck came to write his far better subsequent work on the Okies, he argued for them then on the basis of common humanity rather than on the basis of shared whiteness.

20

The Global Appeal of Steinbeck's Science

The Animal-Human Connections

James C. Kelley

Since the late 1930s, Steinbeck has been severely criticized for reducing humans to the level of animals and for endowing animals with human emotions and sensitivities. Noting the tenor of this criticism, Kelley untangles this human/animal connection in Steinbeck's work, analyzes Steinbeck and Ricketts's non-teleological viewpoint, and surveys relevant scientific criticism on human/animal connections.

John Steinbeck was most successful when writing of the Salinas Valley in California; in 1933 he writes: "I would like to write the story of this whole valley. . . . I would like to do it so that it would be the valley of the world" (*SLL* 73). One way he succeeds in creating this global appeal is through the use of the methods of scientific observation which he learned from Ed Ricketts. In the pre-war period during which he and Ed Ricketts were in closest collaboration (1930–1941), he often employs what the two called "non-teleological thinking," by which they meant careful and objective observation, without assigning a causal agent. The ideas of superorganism, the phalanx and "group-man" and the tide pool metaphor—all ideas discussed with Ed Ricketts—form the fundamental themes of Steinbeck's greatest novels and short stories of the 1930s. His recurring theme is the relationship of humans to animals. From Thomas Wayne's attachment to animals in *To a God Unknown* and the Pirate's love for his dogs in *Tortilla Flat*, through Jody's boyhood with *The Red Pony*, Steinbeck explores the subject. Some critics deplored his "animalizing tendency" as Edmund Wilson phrased his attack (qtd. in

McElrath 186). They complained that he was obsessed with animals and reduced humans to the level of animals, stripping them of all the noble qualities of humanity as we know it.

If Steinbeck was criticized for comparing humans to animals, many also decried his tendency to blur the lines between "respectable people" and lowlives of various forms: Mack and the boys, Danny and the paisanos and the Okies. He also writes of mentally challenged people, Johnny Bear in *The Long Valley*, Tularecito in *The Pastures of Heaven*, Lennie in *Of Mice and Men*, Noah in *The Grapes of Wrath*, the Pirate in *Tortilla Flat*, and Frankie and Hazel in *Cannery Row* and treats them with respect. But the most serious of his sins, in the minds of some of his critics, was in the way he portrayed animals and humans as part of a continuum of life forms, sharing both nobility and biology. Steinbeck seems aware of the hazards as well as the value of this approach when he writes in *Sea of Cortez:* "It is difficult, when watching the little beasts, not to trace human parallels. The greatest danger to a speculative biologist is analogy. It is a pitfall to be avoided—the industry of the bee, the economics of the ant, the villainy of the snake, all in human terms have given us profound misconceptions of the animals. But parallels are amusing if they are not taken too seriously as regards the animal in question, and are downright valuable as regards humans" (79).

Today, however, human-animal associations, analogies and comparisons have become the subject of large and popular fields of study (evolutionary psychology, ethology, sociobiology and the philosophy of consciousness) and of popular political movements (animal rights and ecological activism). To some degree the continuing popularity of Steinbeck's writing may result from the fact that he and Ed Ricketts were far ahead of their time in understanding the evolutionary thread that binds together all living things. The growing global concern over humans' role in the degradation of our environment and the exploitation of our natural resources has brought into question the notion that mankind can live separate from and superior to the natural world. We are encouraged to emulate the natural world, to learn from it how to sustain the global ecosystem. The "animalizing tendencies" of John Steinbeck are becoming rather fashionable, and this contributes to his continued popularity around the world.

To recognize the enormity of that shift a reader need only survey contemporary criticism of Steinbeck's two most incisive treatments of ecological holism—*Sea of Cortez* and *Cannery Row.* The former, published in 1941, was a book that thoroughly confused many reviewers. The interweaving of Steinbeck's rich descriptive narrative with Ricketts's philosophical essays was not universally acclaimed. In his review of *Sea of Cortez*, Edmund Wilson writes, in a rather positive piece: " . . . even those who, like this reviewer, have occasionally deplored Steinbeck's inclination to sentimentalize and even glorify the subhuman, will agree that when he has his sense of humor along he can make a kind of hilarious Valhalla out of this subhuman world" (*Baltimore Sun* 54). Writing for *Harper's*, John Chamberlain weighs in more critically: "[Steinbeck's] mind is here revealed as a 'cold' mind, interested more in 'what is' than in what might be or 'ought' to be. However, the 'coldness' is in reality, part of a great tenderness that does not blame unfortunate human beings (or animals) for predicaments into which they have been shoved by the competition of life." And a more amusing critique came from Harry Hansen, of the Norfolk, Va. *Pilot:* "It stands to reason that if you have a lot to do with fish and you begin to think about men, the similarities offer comparisons, not always flattering to the human race. But with an author as interested in subjective reactions as Steinbeck you can't keep to the subject of fish without getting the human race and the universe involved in it" (6).

The harshest criticism, however, was directed toward *Cannery Row* (1945). Margaret Marshall, writing in *The Nation* takes him to task:

> The great defect grows out of Steinbeck's attitude toward the people he has chosen to portray. He professes to love them; he probably thinks he does. But his real attitude, except in the case of Doc, is nine parts condescension and one part sentimentality. In *Cannery Row* Mr. Steinbeck handles human beings as if they are species of small animal life. They exist and have their being on the same level as the frogs and dogs, the cats and octopuses

> he is so fond of watching. Their 'happiness' is that of insects, and his 'love' for them is that of a collector. Conversely, and significantly, he humanizes frogs and dogs, cats and octopuses in a way that becomes at times repellant as well as embarrassing. (qtd. in McElrath 281)

Such comments were all too typical. David Appel of the *Chicago Daily News* observes: "The portraits all have the virtue of simplicity and a certain reality, but they never come alive. Under Steinbeck's ever present microscope they are tiny squirming social specimens just like their marine counterparts" (13). And Orville Prescott of the *New York Times* states that "The general atmosphere is one of biological benevolence, or a sort of beaming approbation for human activities conducted on an unthinking level far below the demarcation line of pride, honesty, self-respect and accomplishment" (qtd. in McElrath 277).

Why did these contemporary reviewers object to Steinbeck's treatment of humans and animals? Some of the answers are found in religion and philosophy.

Ethicist James Rachels, in his book *Created by Animals: The Moral Implications of Darwinism*, argues that Darwinian evolutionary theory effectively undermines what he calls the "Human Dignity Thesis." This thesis argues in favor of a separate and, of course, superior role of humans in the cosmos. The thesis is based upon two fundamental pillars: 1) the claim of Western religion that humans are created in the image of God, and 2) the secular claim that humans are special because of their unique rationality. Philosopher Daniel Dennet writes that the thesis can be traced to John Locke and his "Essay Concerning Human Understanding" which argues for the primacy of the human mind. This is an idea which is perpetuated today in the creationist literature (*Darwin's Dangerous Idea* 26). To creationist writers the idea that the human mind might have evolved, and that it therefore shares some aspects of its brain physiology and behavioral responses with other animals is a very uncomfortable notion. They much prefer a human mind-brain separately created in the image of the Creator.

It is interesting to note that John Locke did discuss the possibility of rational thought in animals, arguing that the Creator surely had the power to cause animals to think and even speak, as in the case of Balaam's donkey (Locke 467).[1] While Locke argued that "reason stands for a faculty in man; that faculty whereby man *is supposed to be distinguished* from beasts, and wherein it is evident that he much surpasses them" (567 emphasis added), he recognized that humans are animals and used the following syllogism to express his ideas on the matter:

Omnis homo est animal
Omnis animal est vivens
Ergo omnis homo est vivens.

And even Charles Darwin, in the *Descent of Man,* notes, "I fully subscribe to the judgment of those writers who maintain that of all the differences between man and the lower animals, the moral sense of conscience is by far the most important . . . It is the most noble of all the attributes of man" (97).

The Human Dignity thesis was certainly alive and well in the 19th century and was supported through the 20th by both religion and philosophy. Perhaps the finest articulation of the matter occurs in the film *African Queen* when Humphrey Bogart wakes up with a serious hangover to see Katherine Hepburn pouring the last of his gin supply into the river. He says, "Have a heart, ma'am. It's only human nature." And she replies, "Nature, Mr. Alnut, is what we are put on earth to rise above."

In the years immediately after World War II, as the details of the wartime atrocities of Nazi Germany and Imperial Japan were made public, the notion of the "dignity" of humankind lost some of its luster. While "respectable people" may have been able to rationalize the injustices visited upon migrant farmworkers in California, no one could justify genocide. Out of the sympathy for the victims began the development of social concern for oppressed people around the world, and today this concern is manifested in various activities designed to protect the "rights" of groups perceived to be less able to speak for themselves: marginalized people, women, ethnic minorities, the disabled. Some of the most militant activities have centered on protecting the "rights" of those with the least ability to plead their own case, unborn babies and, of course, animals.

In the case of animals it is helpful to examine our perceptions about the relationship between humans and animals and how those perceptions have changed in the last 50 years. Two positions are common. One is that humans and animals are very different, as described in the previous section. The second is that they represent points on a continuum, sometimes called "The Great Chain of Being," which links humans not only to animals which are warm and fuzzy (e.g. Bambi, Thumper and Flipper) but also to the simplest invertebrates, to bacteria and even to plants. The former argument seems to have been favored by some of Steinbeck's critics. Of the latter, the most significant argument in favor of the continuum comes, at least for the vertebrates, from Charles Darwin. In the *Descent of Man* he writes: "Thus we understand how it has come to pass that man and all other vertebrate animals have been constructed on the same general model, why they pass through the same early stages of development, and why they retain certain rudiments in common. Consequently we ought frankly to admit their community of descent: to take any other view, is to admit that our own structure, and that of all the animals around us, is a mere snare laid to entrap our judgement" (97).

Beyond the physical traits shared by humans and animals, the mental differences and similarities have received a great deal of attention both in the past and today. In the *Descent of Man*, Darwin argues "Nevertheless the difference in mind between man and the higher animals, great as it is, certainly is one of degree and not of kind. We have seen that the senses and intuitions, the various emotions and faculties, such as love, memory, attention, curiosity, imitation, reason &c., of which man boasts, may be found in an incipient, or sometimes even well-developed condition, in the lower animals" (126). In the same work Darwin argues for the evolution, through natural selection, of morality, often presented (as above) as the singular distinguishing characteristic of humans. He writes, "Selfish and contentious people will not cohere, and without coherence nothing can be effected. A tribe rich in the . . . qualities [of sympathy, fidelity and courage] would spread and be victorious over other tribes: but in the course of time it would, judging from all past history, be in its turn overcome by some tribe still more highly endowed. Thus the social and moral qualities would tend slowly to advance and be diffused throughout the world" (130).

In his speculations on the evolution of human behavior and morality Darwin anticipated the rapidly growing field of evolutionary psychology whose proponents argue for the evolution, through natural selection, of much of human behavior. The field is based on analyses of human behaviors which are common to people in many places and many cultures and the argument that these widespread behaviors must have biological rather than social explanations. An excellent overview is provided by Robert Wright in *The Moral Animal,* whose title reflects the issue well. In this book, Wright explores the Darwinian evolution of the moral sense and the moral codes which govern human behavior. Evolutionary psychology has itself evolved from earlier biological work, notably that of the sociobiologist Edward O. Wilson. Since the proposed mechanism for the evolution of behavior is (as is true of physical evolution) genetic, much of the literature addresses human sexual behavior and argues that much of the rest of human behavior is based upon sexual selection. In *The Evolution of Desire,* David M. Buss outlines this behavior and discusses the evolutionary reasoning behind it. Certainly John Steinbeck and Ed Ricketts would be receptive to these interpretations—in fact, they anticipated many of them in the 1930s.

One of the sticky points for the critics of evolutionary psychology is over the apparent inevitability of human conflict. Evolutionary psychologists have attributed human conflict to battles over women and some studies have shown that this is a prime motivator even among relatively peaceful groups. A classic work is that of Napoleon A. Chagnon on the Yanomamo, who kill one another to assure better breeding rights (*Science* 985). The report shocked those who wanted to believe in a more harmonious existence. As Buss says: "According to one of these views, 'natural' humans are at one with nature, peacefully coexisting with plants, animals, and each other. War, aggression, and competition are seen as corruptions of this essentially peaceful human nature by current conditions, such as patriarchy or capitalism" (17). Buss points out that this denial response is not new. He says "Evolutionary theory has appalled and upset people since Darwin first proposed it in 1859 to explain the creation and organization of life. Lady Ashley, his contemporary, remarked upon hearing his theory of our descent from nonhuman primates: "Let's hope that it's not true: and if it is true, let's hope that it does not become widely known" (16).

A passage from the *Sea of Cortez* looks at man's aggressions in precisely the same manner as Buss:

> We have looked into the tide pools and seen the little animals feeding and reproducing and killing for food. We name them and describe them and, out of long watching, arrive at some conclusion about their habits so that we say, "This species typically does thus and so," but we do not objectively observe our own species as a species, although we know the individuals fairly well. When it seems that men may be kinder to men, that wars may not come again, we completely ignore the record of our species. If we used the same smug observation on ourselves that we do on hermit crabs we would be forced to say, with the information at hand, "it is one diagnostic trait of *Homo sapiens* that groups of individuals are periodically infected with a feverish nervousness which causes the individual to turn on and destroy, not only his own kind, but the works of his own kind. It is not known whether this be caused by a virus, some airborne spore, or whether it be a species reaction to some meteorological stimulus as yet undetermined." (15)

Another line of scholarly inquiry which relates to the issue of human/animal relationships is best exemplified by the work of Daniel C. Dennett on the nature of consciousness and how it might differ between humans and animals. In his latest work, *Kinds of Minds: Toward an Understanding of Consciousness*, Dennet directly addresses the issue of the continuum and finally decides that humans are distinctly different from animals because animals are without language. He writes:

> It would be reassuring if we had come to the end of our story and could say something along the lines of "And so we see that it follows from our discoveries that insects and fish and reptiles aren't sentient after all—they are mere automata—but amphibi-

ans, birds and mammals are sentient or conscious just like us!
And for the record, a human fetus becomes sentient between fifteen and sixteen weeks." Such a neat plausible solution to some
of our human problems of moral decision making would be a
great relief, but no such story can be told yet, and there is no reason to believe that such a story will unfold later. It is unlikely
that we have overlooked a feature of mentality that would make
all the difference to morality, and the features we have examined
seem to make their appearance not just gradually but in an un-
sychronized, inconsistent, and patchy fashion, both in evolutionary history and in the development of individual organisms . . .
In our survey of minds (and protominds) there does not seem to
be any clear threshold or critical mass—until we arrive at the sort
of consciousness that we language-using humans enjoy. That sort
of mind is unique, and orders of magnitude more powerful than
any other variety of mind, but we probably don't want to rest too
much moral weight on it. (161–62)

Though humans may sometimes be distinguished from animals by our desire to understand the thoughts of others, our
sense of morality, our facility with language or even our understanding of death, a good deal of scholarly activity seems to be
converging on the idea of a continuum. But sympathetic academic discourse alone cannot account for the continuing appeal
of Steinbeck's work even if the appeal were solely based on the
human-animal relationship. We must ask what is going on in
society at large, globally, which continues to make us so receptive to his work.

In addition to the trend in academic discourse toward recognizing human/animal connections, and perhaps quite independent of it, there are important changes in public thinking regarding the "rights" of groups perceived as less able to control
their own destinies. One of the effects of this rising popular
concern has been the evolution of a set of ideas regarding the
relative importance of members of politically and socially marginalized groups in society or in the world. The increasingly
prevalent sentiment seems to be that these populations and individuals are every bit as important and worthy of respect and
equitable treatment as is everyone else. And this increased sen-

sitivity to the marginalized may be in part responsible for the continuing popularity of John Steinbeck's work.

If we view Steinbeck's "less noble" fictional characters (the bums, the hookers, the paisanos, the Okies, the mentally challenged, and the animals) through the eyes of a generation or two which have come to accept the idea of the nobility of all living things, the objections of Steinbeck's contemporary critics seem a bit quaint. When he is a champion of the underclass—of the Okies and the paisanos, of the bums and the hookers—he sounds a voice sympathetic with the United Farm Workers, with civil rights organizations, with homeless advocates and with C.O.Y.O.T.E.[2] When he ennobles Rose of Sharon's stillborn baby by sending him, like Moses, down the river to free the people, he is an advocate of respect for fetal life. When he describes the talents of Tularecito and Johnny Bear and understands the struggles of Hazel and Noah and Frankie and Lennie, he fosters respect for the mentally challenged. Today we are not so shocked by this frankness and compassion and when he unflatteringly compares these lives with those of "better" people, the Blues and the Greens of the Great Roque War (*ST*), the Growers and the Cannery Owners (*IDB* and *TGOW*) and all the other faceless wealthy and respectable characters in his works, we share both his amusement and his disdain.

It is with his animals, however, that we see both his own love and Ed Ricketts's fascination. Steinbeck wrote to Robert Ballou after the death of his beloved Airedale, Tillie Eulenspiegel, commenting, "It was much more important to us that she be alive than that people like Hearst and Cornelius Vanderbilt foul up the planet. *She* was house broken" (*SLL* 66). Here we see the same contrast as between his "less noble" characters and the "better" people. But when he explicitly compares the stories of the people of Cannery Row with the animals of the tide pool he is engaging in a wonderful example of Ricketts's non-teleological thinking. At the beginning of *Cannery Row* he writes:

> How can the poem and the stink and the grating noise—the quality of light, the tone, the habit and the dream—be set down alive? When you collect marine animals there are certain flat worms so delicate that they are almost impossible to capture

whole, for they break and tatter under the touch. You must let them ooze and crawl of their own will onto a knife blade and then lift them gently into your bottle of sea water. And perhaps that might be the way to write this book—to open the page and to let the stories crawl in by themselves. (6–7)

It is this "is thinking" that so bothered Steinbeck's critics. But for those who have never subscribed to the thesis of the great nobility of mankind and the centrality of humans in the cosmos it provides a very comfortable perspective. John Steinbeck, as usual, says it best in *Sea of Cortez:* "We are no better than the animals. In a lot of ways we aren't as good" (58).

21

The Philosophical Mind of John Steinbeck

Virtue Ethics and His Later Fiction

Stephen K. George

With an emphasis on virtue ethics—focusing on the actor rather than the action, on issues of individual moral character rather than on ethical principles and duties—George examines two of Steinbeck's later works, East of Eden, *and* The Winter of Our Discontent. *He shows that Steinbeck shifts his emphasis from broad social issues to individual moral concerns that have their basis in virtue ethics.*

> We have only one story. All novels, all poetry, are built on the never-ending contest in ourselves of good and evil. And it occurs to me that evil must constantly respawn, while good, while virtue, is immortal. Vice has always a new fresh young face, while virtue is venerable as nothing else in the world is.
>
> *East of Eden* 415

> [T]he work of the moral imagination is in some manner like the work of the creative imagination, especially that of the novelist. . . . [A]ccording to this conception, the novel is itself a moral achievement, and the well-lived life is a work of art.
>
> Martha Nussbaum, *Love's Knowledge* 148

John Steinbeck was never a writer who fit neatly into any one category. His interests were varied, reaching from tidepool specimens to King Arthur's legends, from the environment and ecology to social criticism and politics. His writing endeavors have also been endlessly, yet paradoxically, categorized; Steinbeck was both a realist and a romantic, an unapologetic naturalist who also believed in the perfectability of man. Yet one thing is clear: Steinbeck the writer was also a serious philosopher, as his early insistence with Edward Ricketts on a non-teleological approach to life attests. Though sharply attacked for his "tenth-rate philosophizing" by certain of his contemporaries (Mizener 45), Steinbeck, to the end, was a student of human behavior, "a philosopher who listened to ditch-diggers" and "a ditch-digger who thought philosophically" (Timmerman 270).

Most of the scholarship concerning the philosophical nature of Steinbeck's fiction has focused on the early ecological and holistic views he shared with Ed Ricketts, especially their perception of the world from a biological standpoint (biological naturalism) and their concern with "what is" (non-teleological thinking) and not the question of "why it is." Little has been done, however, with Steinbeck's later novels, which mark a philosophical shift from social criticism, group dynamics, and a non-teleological perspective to an emphasis on individual moral character and the specific causes of good and evil within us and within our societies. In the past Steinbeck's later work has been regarded as inferior; according to Richard Astro, when Steinbeck "plunge[s] into the confines of traditional morality (with its heavy emphasis on the role of the individual in the search for salvation)," his "efforts . . . lack range and power" (224). More bluntly, Peter Lisca pronounced some years ago that Steinbeck "cannot seem to say anything significant" when he "attempts [in his later works] to project an image of man based on . . . Christian morality and ethical integrity" (10).

However, more recent critics, such as Louis Owens, now see a "psychological complexity" in *East of Eden*, which "may be the most misunderstood of all of Steinbeck's creations" (84–5). Likewise, as Michael Meyer argues, "*The Winter of Our Discontent*, though greeted with heavy criticism at its publication, appears to have weathered the years well," with critics now finding in this "interweaving of biblical, historical, and literary texts" a moral insight and "complexity" which was initially overlooked (268).

These later novels require a philosophical approach that will comprehend Steinbeck's focus on good and evil, the individual in conflict with these forces, and his or her subsequent moral development. Within the discipline of philosophy, that critical approach is known as virtue ethics, a branch of ethical inquiry, as old as Aristotle and Aquinas, which focuses on the actor rather than the action, on issues of individual moral character rather than on ethical principles and duties. The central ethical question of virtue ethics is not "What is the right thing to do?," but rather "What traits of character make one a good person?" (Rachels 160). In addition to character traits such as courage, generosity, and jealousy, virtue ethics also examines concepts that provide a "necessary background for any psychology of the moral life," including such subjects as emotions, intention, willpower, and pleasure (Kruschwitz 2).

John Steinbeck has long been accused of sentimentality by his severest critics. But this charge, with a few exceptions, is both unfair and unjustified. Steinbeck himself explained that since our emotions are part of our human experience, a writer would be either blind or dishonest to not include them in his portrayal of that experience. Hence, an author like Steinbeck is perfect for a virtue ethics analysis because he took seriously the emotions, virtues, and vices of his characters and was extremely careful, as Jackson Benson notes, to give those characters "psychological validity" (151, 173).

Two of Steinbeck's later major works—*East of Eden* and *The Winter of Our Discontent*—make particularly good resources for a virtue ethics analysis. The intense focus of these works on human beings struggling with the forces of good and evil gives these novels their particular status as Steinbeck's "moral fiction." Although earlier novels, such as *The Grapes of Wrath* and *Of Mice and Men*, deal with powerful moral issues, they lack the focused attention to character development and the question of evil that exists in these later works. In *East of Eden* and *Winter* Steinbeck purposefully follows the Trask, Hamilton, and Hawley families over three generations in order to trace the effect of environment and heredity on moral character development. For an early Steinbeck confirmed in non-teleological thinking, the origins of depravity meant little, for the aim was to comprehend the whole—such as the Okies' disaster in California—without imposing a design or demanding a cause. A more mature and experienced Steinbeck now openly questions why people are as they are, for (as he admits in *East of Eden* concerning Cathy

Ames) knowing someone is evil means very little unless one knows why (184).

In *East of Eden*, the author gives a paradigm for the development of irrational and destructive emotions, or what we would describe in psychological terms as the states of emotionally disturbed people. As the Chinese servant Lee (a frequent mouthpiece for the author) explains to Samuel Hamilton:

> The greatest terror a child can have is that he is not loved, and rejection is the hell he fears. I think everyone in the world to a large or small extent has felt rejection. And with rejection comes anger, and with anger some kind of crime in revenge for the rejection, and with the crime guilt—and there is the story of mankind. I think that if rejection could be amputated, the human would not be what he is. Maybe there would be fewer crazy people. I am sure in myself there would not be many jails. It is all there—the start, the beginning. One child, refused the love he craves, kicks the cat and hides his secret guilt; and another steals so that money will make him loved; and a third conquers the world—and always the guilt and revenge and more guilt.... [T]his old and terrible story [of Cain and Abel] is important because it is a chart of the soul—the secret, rejected, guilty soul. (270–71)

Steinbeck's *East of Eden* specifically focuses on such ethical topics as emotional development and the connections between emotions such as fear, anger, and hatred and more lasting character traits such as cruelty and dishonesty. Such concerns are of particular interest to philosophers in the field of virtue ethics. Justin Oakley, in *Morality and the Emotions*, argues that the emotions are complex entities comprised of affective, cognitive, and motivational elements. Or, in other words, our emotions are not merely subjective feelings over which we have no control, and hence amoral entities; rather, emotions are also based on certain beliefs and actually move us to do certain things. As such complex entities, it is no surprise that healthy emotions play a crucial role in our achieving clear perception and understanding, in motivating us to act in accordance with our values, and in forming "such morally significant relationships as love and friendship" (35, 57). Emotions, Oakley argues, are central to the development of stable and virtuous people.

As *East of Eden* and *The Winter of Our Discontent* affirm, however, emotions are also a factor in the development of unstable and even evil people, for irrational emotions seem to be sequential in nature: people who feel a misplaced and extreme fear often progress to states of irrational anger, hatred, and guilt. For example, in *East of Eden* Cal Trask's deepest fear is that he cannot be loved, that in comparison to his blond and blue-eyed brother, Aron, he will never be loved (379, 422). This fear (irrational in that Cal is worthy of love) leads Cal to anger and hatred, and finally to the cruel act of showing Aron his real mother, Cathy Ames, the sadistic brothel owner. Cal later feels immense guilt for this, almost so much that he wants to take his life, as did the guilt-driven son of Samuel Hamilton, Tom. The destructive effects of these emotions clearly follow the sequential pattern described by Lee to Samuel, showing with poignant clarity the blindness and irrational acts that such emotions encourage; as Donald Capps observes, to be angry is often to lash "out against the other in blind fury" without the "judicious self-restraint" that is needed "to assess carefully our own desires and interests" (83).

Steinbeck's "teleological" fiction also offers explanations for such extreme emotions. Part of the answer (within the age-old dialectic between "nature" and "nurture") seems to be as a consequence of one's natural tendencies; for instance, Cathy Ames is evil, at least partly, because she was born that way, with her bizarre physical traits (cat-like features, "nipples turned inward") mirroring her inherent moral or spiritual abnormalities (72–73). But Cathy is not simply a monster (as Steinbeck himself later suggests), for "some of . . . [her] cruelty," according to Mimi Gladstein, could be "a result of her mother's influence," given Mrs. Ames's own sadistic tendencies (35). As Steinbeck, the participating author, rethinks this character, the question of "why" Cathy is evil becomes all important; simple determinism seems too easy, especially since it would remove Cathy entirely from the moral realm, as well as run counter to *East of Eden*'s dominant theme of "Timshel," or "Thou mayest" (303).

Concerning the moral and psychological development of

Aron, Adam, and Charles Trask, it is clear that parental neglect and/or abuse play a primary role in their emotional instability, as when Adam grows up essentially motherless and as a young child longs for a mother's "holding" and "rocking" and "breast and nipple." Because of this parental neglect, Adam comes to look at life as if from the end of a long tunnel and thus is unable to really see people for who they are or to bond effectively with others (20–22). His blindness leads to his shattering break with Cathy, and to the neglect of his own sons, Cal and Aron, who grow up starved for love and acceptance and susceptible to their own irrational emotions. As Steinbeck forcefully shows with the Trask family, emotional instability often passes from one generation to the next in a terrible cycle of family dysfunction.

Moreover, a virtue ethics analysis of these novels reveals the connections of these emotions to more permanent character dispositions. As John Timmerman notes, Cathy Ames, "who uses people as things and destroys them for her own malevolent end," "never acts positively or creatively out of love, but only negatively and out of fear" (220). Throughout the novel we see how Cathy's extreme fears of men and of vulnerability provide the motivation behind her unthinkable acts of cruelty, which include murdering her parents, shooting Adam and leaving him to die, abandoning her infant sons, and torturing the male clientele of her whorehouse. Cathy gets a sick satisfaction out of fixing "the gray slugs that come" to her brothel to "dump their nasty little loads—for a dollar" (236). Her irrational fears and gender hatred, which psychologist Gerald Schoenewolf describes as "the most primal of hates" (107), blind her to the humanity and potential goodness of the other sex, and thus enable and motivate her horrible cruelty; the vice of cruelty often includes the emotions of fear and hatred at its core.

But the power that comes with cruelty, with "the maiming of" another person's "dignity" (Hallie 11) and taking pleasure in his suffering (Taylor, Richard 43), only temporarily relieves the fear that drives the obsession of someone like Cathy because the underlying terrors of the cruel person remain unresolved. At the end of *East of Eden*, Cathy becomes an example of this insufficiency within the power dynamics of cruelty. Having lost her beauty, and hence much of her sexual power, she can no longer personally tempt men into her web of depravity. She has also begun to lose control over her employees (as evidenced by Joe Valery's secret mutiny) and thus resorts more and more often to hiding in her little gray room. Pained with arthritis and with no one to turn to, Cathy finds herself "cold and desolate," "a sick ghost, crooked and in some way horrible" (553). Upon finally admitting to herself that she may not be inherently superior to others, that they may indeed have had "something she lacked," she can no longer avoid her inner psychological horrors; her only escape becomes suicide or swallowing the little "capsule" around her neck which beckons, "'Eat me'" (553–54). But even this brings no relief, for suicide, in many ways, is the ultimate act of surrender and loss of control. As Steinbeck writes, the once powerful and cruel madam leaves this world shaking with "nausea" and staring "about in terror" (554), unable to escape the fears that have driven her whole life.

Ethan Hawley's dishonesty and lack of moral integrity in *The Winter of Our Discontent* also seem, at least partially, to be motivated by irrational emotions. Ethan is a man filled with fear, shame, and anger—even the novel's opening pages resound with his humiliation at being nothing more than "a goddam grocery clerk in a goddam wop store in a town . . . [his family] used to own" (4). Ethan's identity as a provider, businessman, and Hawley is at stake, for he feels himself a failure—a man working in a store that used to be his own and near the "half block of real estate [he had to sell] to stock it" (14). Yet his fears—which later move him to betray his closest friend and his own moral principles—are largely irrational, given their basis in New Baytown's corrupt moral standards, a town where "the meanings of . . . good and evil" are "reversed" (Hayashi 111) and where "selling one's soul has become the norm" (Meyer 255). Ethan is in the process of accepting the tenet that a "gentleman without money is [only] a bum" (34), that money, given enough time, inevitably conveys respectability. This mistaken belief, encouraged by and consisting within his irrational fears, makes him unable to assess his personal worth on more enduring aspects of his life, such as his adherence to moral principles and fidelity to his wife. Vices such as dishonesty and lack of integrity may often have irrational emotions such as these at their core.

Furthermore, as *The Winter of Our Discontent* shows, these forces internal and external—his fears, a "false shame" that has inflicted a very real "injury to [his] self-respect" (Taylor, Gabriele 140), his family's desires for status, his peers' opinions—bring about a shocking change in Ethan Hawley's moral character. Before, Ethan had believed that certain attitudes and actions were not a part of his nature, but no longer (88). The new Ethan Hawley hungrily eyes Margie Young-Hunt's assets, holds out for more money from Mr. Biggers (the drummer from B.B.D. and D.), goes along with others' follies for his own use, and then scrubs the day's business off his hands with a little soap. Hawley, Steinbeck's "Everyman," has begun a rebirth during this Easter season that "is the reverse of Christ's," for while "Christ dies to sin, . . . Ethan's sinless life dies" (Meyer 253). This reborn man is now willing to sacrifice almost anything, be it people or principles, in order to be successful.

Which is what Ethan does. Three elements, or what could be loosely called thought processes, mark his loss of integrity: his rationalizations concerning his behavior, his belief in extreme moral relativity, and his turning morality into a sort of game or recreation. Ethan's primary rationalization for temporarily laying aside his principles and commitments comes from his analogy (shaky at best) between business and war, both of which, as he maintains, are worlds based on survival of the fittest. For Ethan, "there is no doubt that business is a kind of war" (92) and money a necessary evil, an objective to be won in order to provide peace and security for himself and his family (104). This reduction of all business affairs to a sort of jungle warfare is encouraged by the transition of Ethan's moral foundation from a belief in certain absolute standards of right and wrong to an acceptance of a code of extreme ethical relativity. Such relativity not only encourages Hawley to see his world in a purely naturalistic or Darwinian light—a world of "the eaters and the eaten"—it also enables him to question if "the eaters [are any] more immoral than the eaten," for "in the end all are eaten—all—gobbled up by the earth, even the fiercest and the most crafty" (46).

Finally, out of Ethan Hawley's rationalizations and belief in ethical relativity comes his new willingness to test the moral limits by mentally playing with ideas and conduct that before would have been unthinkable—a sort of recreation with morality (or immorality) that eventually bridges the gap between his inner change and outer behavior. This recreation, encouraged by the relativistic view that morals are but playthings anyway, takes many forms with Ethan. It surfaces as a game with Mr. Biggers to see if Hawley can get six percent instead of five, as a toying with his boss Marullo to find out his immigration status, and as a flirtation with Margie lined with undertones of infidelity. The fallen Ethan, who sees his world with playful "new eyes" (133), can now flirt with crime and immorality, or (as he calls it) engage in "a game of imagining" (134), because there is really no such thing as morality anymore. Ultimately, this recreation serves to move Ethan from playing with crime to participating in it. As Ethan reveals concerning his plan to rob Mr. Baker's bank:

> If my plan had leaped up full-grown and deadly I would have rejected it as nonsense. People don't do such things, but people play secret games. Mine began with Joey's rules for robbing a bank. Against the boredom of my job I played with it and everything along the way fell into it. . . . As a game I timed the process, enacted it, tested it. But the gunmen shooting it out with cops—aren't they the little boys who practiced quick draws with cap pistols until they got so good they had to use the skill? I don't know when my game stopped being a game. (213–14)

This brief summary of ideas concerning irrational emotions, cruelty, and loss of moral integrity clearly illustrates the philosophical richness of Steinbeck's later works. What these novels have to say about the importance of the emotions within the moral realm adds depth and breadth to the work of such philosophers as Justin Oakley, Donald Capps, Philip Hallie, and Gabriele Taylor. Steinbeck, who suffered himself from an emotionally withdrawn father, gives in *East of Eden* "a shockingly believable tale of family pathology" (Parini 362). In both of these novels we see irrational emotions in action: Charles Trask's rage at his father's rejection and his attempt to murder Adam in revenge; Cathy Ames's gender hatred toward the men in her brothel of horrors; Ethan Hawley's psychological disintegration as he allows his shame and fear to destroy Danny, Marullo, and others. Moreover, we see the causes of such emotions, particularly the neglect and rejection of children by their own parents. Sociologists and psychologists such as David Blankenhorn and Gerald Schoenewolf concur in these findings on the importance of parental love and discipline to the moral development of children. The answers concerning moral development found within Steinbeck's later fiction have never been more relevant.

Furthermore, these novels exemplify the crucial role literature in general can play in philosophical endeavors. Martha Nussbaum of Brown University has observed that "what we now call philosophical inquiry in ethics" was never neatly divided anciently into "aesthetic questions and moral-philosophical questions, to be studied and written about by mutually detached colleagues in different departments." Instead, there was one question pursued by both poets and philosophers alike: "namely, how human beings should live" (15). It is literature, with its rich levels of observation, explication, and psychology, that finally does justice to the human experience, not the "abstract, hygienically pallid" prose of traditional philosophy, whose "style" often seems to serve as an "all-purpose solvent" for neatly disentangling any moral quandary (19). As Nussbaum persuasively argues, any ethical inquiry that excludes the richness of literary sources is ultimately incomplete (23–4).

The use of literature to provide answers to such moral questions as how we should live and what kind of person we should be—while derided by some as meaningless in a postmodern age of deconstruction and relativity—is actually a long-held tradition within philosophical studies and a primary reason for Steinbeck's appeal to so many people around the world. His interdisciplinary approach to life and to observing and capturing human experience in print touches fundamental chords within all of us. Clearly this appeal did not end, as some critics maintain, with *The Grapes of Wrath* or *Cannery Row*; it continued with vibrancy in *East of Eden* and *The Winter of Our Discontent* for those with an ear to hear it. The candor of Reloy Garcia in his re-evaluation of Steinbeck's last novel is instructive. He confides:

In preparation for this brief introduction I reread that book [*The Winter of Our Discontent*], in the process immodestly reviewing my own theme. Reality is a harsh mistress, and I would write that essay differently today. . . . The book I then so impetuously criticized as somewhat thin, now strikes me as a deeply penetrating study of the American condition. I did not realize, at the time, that we had a condition. His [Steinbeck's] work thus rewards a returning reader, is seemingly amplified by our own enriched experience. (4)

Steinbeck's later fiction indeed speaks with a clear moral voice, a voice concerned not only with our moral development as individuals, but with the ability of those same individuals to provide a light by which others may see the way. This later fiction has in the past been ignored or misunderstood, at least from a philosophical perspective. But its worth for us as carriers of the light is still there if we will only look and listen. Perhaps, in the final analysis, it is not we who will judge the worth of Steinbeck's later works, but the literature which will judge us.

22

Dreams of an Elegant Universe on Cannery Row

Brian Railsback

With Ed Ricketts, Steinbeck read texts on physics, and his conception of non-teleological thinking, accepting what is—as well as his acute awareness of the frivolity of perception—owes much to his reading of physics. In Cannery Row *"he nearly touches upon what is now known as the Ultimate Theory—the unified field theory that connects all, micro and macro universes."*

> "Oh! Blessed rage for order, pale Ramon,
> The maker's rage to order words of the sea,
> Words of the fragrant portals, dimly-starred"
> Wallace Stevens, "The Idea of Order at Key West," 1934

By the time we arrive at Wallace Stevens's famous passage, we feel the thump of a refrain, a culminating song, that describes a *leitmotif* in great American literature: the need to find some comprehensible meaning in the nature of things. Anne Bradstreet's speaker is torn apart by the question of where the soul sits with God in "The Flesh and the Spirit"; Ben Franklin's autobiography clicks with the assurance of a deistic universe in time with Newtonian physics; Melville's Ahab dies trying to penetrate the universal question begged by the white whale; Robert Frost's speaker looks with wonder into the same impenetrable whiteness in a spider; F. Scott Fitzgerald's characters meet the threat of disorder in a Jazz Age crack-up of broken dreams; Hemingway tackles the universe head-on with an internal, face-saving code; and Faulkner looks into the frightening chaos of the human soul at war with itself (curiously returning us to Bradstreet's poem). In this quest for order our acclaimed authors give us, ultimately, a sense of great fear. Our authors make us feel that without some understanding of the universe, of Why, we would be confused, broken, lost.

For his time, John Steinbeck is the great exception.

Because of the unusual way that Steinbeck approaches the universe, he walks out of step with his contemporaries and ahead of the science that informed him. With his fellow investigator, the marine biologist Edward F. Ricketts, Steinbeck embraced the paradoxes and disorder of the world around him and said it is enough to see what is there. In a famous discussion of his and Ricketts's non-teleological philosophy from *The Log from the Sea of Cortez*, this approach is succinctly defined: "Non-teleological thinking concerns itself primarily not with what should be, or could be, or might be, but rather with what actually 'is'— attempting at most to answer the already sufficiently difficult questions *what* or *how*, instead of *why*" (112). Their path to "is" depends on inductive thinking, free of preconceptions, that will lead one to ever-widening circles expanding outward from the original question: "the whole necessarily includes all that it impinges on as object and subject, in ripples fading with distance or depending upon the original intensity of the vortex" (*LSC* 123). As we seek to understand the whole, we can only hope to recognize what "is" in an infinitely expanding horizon. Why becomes impossible, and the amazing thing about John Steinbeck's work is that not knowing why is perfectly acceptable, even expected. He stands before the frightening, infinite, paradoxical—indeed chaotic—universe and informs us that seeing these things is quite enough. For Steinbeck, the quest is not to understand the whole but rather to see, to embrace, as much of it as possible. Steinbeck asks us to constantly widen our apertures to view something that can never be big enough.

What informs his view? A glance at Robert DeMott's *Steinbeck's Reading: A Catalogue of Books Owned and Borrowed* shows us that the novelist's holistic philosophy derives not surprisingly from many disciplines: anthropology, Eastern mysticism, history, philosophy, psychology, and sociology. However, Steinbeck's reading of science (and no doubt his discussion of such matters with Ricketts in Monterey during the 1930s) most strongly supports his consideration of the whole. The influence of biological science and methodology has been thoroughly studied by Richard Astro, Jackson Benson, and myself in *Parallel Expeditions: Charles Darwin and the Art of John Steinbeck*. Another, most intriguing area of science for Steinbeck and the study of the author's cosmology is physics; specifically relativity, quantum theory, and the attempt to reconcile the two in an overarching theory, the Holy Grail of physics, in the unified field or what has been called the Ultimate Theory. We find Steinbeck's view of the whole well-informed by the physics of his day, as described in his greatest nonfiction work, *Sea of Cortez*, and playfully dramatized in one of his greatest novels, *Cannery Row*. Through the power of his imagination, the author widened the aperture and saw beyond what he knew of physics into theory that has only been recently described for the general public in Brian Greene's 1999 masterpiece, *The Elegant Universe*.

John Steinbeck owned or read two books that would have given him the macro (universal) and micro (subatomic) views in physics for the layman of his day: Albert Einstein's *Relativity* and Arthur Eddington's *The Nature of the Physical World* (DeMott *Reading* 36, 37). In *Sea of Cortez*, Steinbeck makes direct reference to Einstein and Eddington (*LSC* 178, 125). Throughout *Sea of Cortez* he makes use of ideas found in both books, and some possibly derived from another book he owned, *Quantum Mechanics*, by Edward Condon and Phillip Morse (DeMott *Reading* 28). Steinbeck and Ricketts (who had a copy of Eddington's text in his library), had read enough between them to understand and quite possibly be attracted to several aspects of physics in the early twentieth century: that Einstein's theory of relativity radically altered Newtonian or Classical physics (much in the same way Darwin's theory of evolution shook up nineteenth century natural science); that measurement of space and time are relative to our position—there are no absolutes; that physics at the quantum level admits only to describe accurately *what* but not *why*; that at the quantum level there are probabilities but no absolutes—a hint of chaos in the nature of things; that a great paradox exists as quantum theory and relativity do not agree—concepts that explain the subatomic universe do not work for the cosmic universe; that therefore to contain all, a unified field theory is needed that does not yet exist. In short, physics as Steinbeck might have understood it would have been very exciting to him, and his exuberance for the questions raised shows itself in *Sea of Cortez* and *Cannery Row*.

Steinbeck's universe lacks absolutes, as he makes clear from the beginning of *Sea of Cortez*. In March and April of 1940, Steinbeck, Ricketts, and the crew of the *Western Flyer* (a purse-seiner out of Monterey) traveled into the Gulf of California (Sea of Cortez) to collect a variety of littoral marine specimens. In the subsequent journal of the trip, originally published in 1941, Steinbeck notes the limitation of their observations in curiously Einsteinian language. The trip forms itself from the "boundaries [of] a boat at sea" with "its duration a six weeks' charter time": neatly defined in space and time (*LSC* 1). Further, their observations must be "warped, as all knowledge patterns are warped," and knowing this allows them to "maintain some balance between our warp and the separate thing, the external reality" (2). In reference to the ways of observing a fish, the Mexican sierra, Steinbeck notes we can take measurements of it or experience the feel of it, the excitement of it, on the line and therefore "a whole new relational externality has come into being—an entity which is more than the sum of the fish plus the fisherman" (2). As they go into the Gulf, Steinbeck and the crew will not be "betrayed by this myth of permanent objective reality" but will instead be a small part of the ecology: "And if we seem a small factor in a huge pattern, nevertheless it is of relative importance" (3). The ground rules laid out in these first pages demonstrate Steinbeck's view that the trip, though measured in time and space, is entirely a matter of perspective: all things are relative, dependent on one's particular warp, so the reality is very fluid.

The idea that the "myth" of objective reality is shattered by one's position in time and space and relative perspective might have been underscored for Steinbeck in Einstein's *Relativity*. All physical laws come under Einstein's principle of relativity: when determining speed and direction of motion, "we must specify precisely who or what is doing the measuring" (Greene 28). Motion is relative. In *The Elegant Universe*, Greene imagines a case of two spacewalkers coming toward each other: who is moving depends on the perspective of the other. One astronaut would say he is stationary while the other is moving by, and the other would say the same thing—by Einstein's principle of relativity, though both appear to disagree, they are both correct. Eddington's *The Nature of the Physical World* makes a similar point with the more complicated situation of Earth's travel through space (9–11).

The notion of reality dependent on one's perception in place and time must have been intriguing to Steinbeck and Ricketts. The novelist has some fun with this concept in regard to Tony Berry, skipper of the *Western Flyer,* who, according to Steinbeck, is an absolutist and a man who believes in an objective rightness and wrongness about things. To Berry's dismay, the *Coast Pilot,* a navigational guide, is not always accurate because points in the Gulf have changed over time. "Tony is uneasy in the face of variables," Steinbeck writes. "The whole relational thinking of modern physics was an obscenity to him" (*LSC* 18). Steinbeck has more fun with Tony when the skipper sees a shoreline of mirages: "here right and wrong fought before his very eyes, and how could one tell which was error" (68). The reality Tony and the rest of us face in an Einsteinian universe of relativity is a realization that the "limitation of the seeing point in time, as well as in space, is a warping lens" (218).

While the planets, stars, and cosmos spin around us in a mind-boggling blur dependent on one's perception of speed, time, and place, the micro view afforded by quantum mechanics adds its own little chaotic universe to our understanding. In his reading of quantum theory, Steinbeck might well have appreciated the fact that this science must accept what is, but cannot account for why. Surveying the development of quantum theory, Greene writes, "those who use quantum mechanics find themselves following rules and formulas laid down by the 'founding fathers' of the theory—calculational procedures that are straightforward to carry out—without really understanding *why* the procedures work or *what* they really mean" (87). Steinbeck would have encountered what Greene calls "microscopic weirdness" at the quantum level in Eddington's book (85). For example, Werner Heisenberg's uncertainty principle (or principle of indeterminacy, as Eddington refers to it), shows "a particle may have position or it may have velocity but it cannot in any exact sense have both": we can measure one or the other at any given time but not both at once with absolute accuracy (Eddington 220). To make things even more baffling to the layman, "Such uncertain aspects of the microscopic world become even more severe as the distance and time scales on which they are considered become ever smaller" (Greene 424). Further, Greene observes, this "implies that the microscopic realm is a roiling frenzy, awash in a violent sea of *quantum fluctuations*" (424). We can be fairly certain that Steinbeck read the passage about the uncertainty principle, as he makes direct reference in *Sea of Cortez* to Eddington's discussion of a "q number," a mere ten pages away from Eddington's section on the principle (125). As a science of variables and probabilities, absent in comforting absolutes, quantum mechanics invites speculation and even mysticism. Eddington moves his discussion of the natural world from the realm of physics into the mystic and even supernatural in the last four chapters of his book. He begins this discussion in a chapter entitiled "Science and Mysticism" with a comparison of a study of the "Generation of Waves by Wind" from a mathematical perspective and a poetic one (316–17). The discussion is strikingly similar to Steinbeck's comments on the different ways of seeing the Mexican sierra. The poetic, emotional view Eddington labels an "illusion," but he adds that the mathematical perspective is also a "fancy projected by the mind into the external world" (318). The baffling and at times inexplicable world at the quantum level invites a fluid, ever-changing perception of the universe and comes down to our perspective or, as Steinbeck might put it, our "warp" or our "peephole" (*LSC* 2; *CR* 5).

Steinbeck's reading of physics was no doubt without an understanding of the underlying math (as is my own!), but even a rudimentary understanding of this ever-expanding field of science and the sort of mystifying consideration of the universe it invites should have underscored the novelist's notion of "is" thinking. For an author who enjoyed portraying paradoxes in his nonfiction and fiction, the great paradox between relativity and quantum theory would have been fascinating. As Greene summarizes at the opening of his book, physics has been confronted with the problem that general relativity provides a frame-work for understanding the macro universe (planet, stars, etc.) and quantum theory does the same for the micro universe. However, as "they are currently formulated, general relativity and quantum mechanics *cannot both be right*" (3). "The two theories underlying the tremendous progress of physics during the last hundred years," Greene adds, "are mutually incompatible" (3). Steinbeck would not have easily gleaned this paradox from his reading of Einstein or Eddington, but *Sea of Cortez* demonstrates that he was aware of the dilemma. For the answer to the problem, a theory which bridges the gap, is often referred to as the unified field theory. In Steinbeck's time, a workable theory, one that would bridge the whole, did not exist. Yet Steinbeck clearly was familiar with the term and at some level aware of the incompatibility of the micro and macro worlds. In his discussion of teleological and non-teleological thinking, Steinbeck writes that a "parallel to these two types of thinking is afforded by the microcosm with its freedom or indeterminancy, as contrasted with the morphologically inviolable pattern of the macrocosm" (*LSC* 112). "Statistically, the electron is free to go where it will," he adds. "But the destiny pattern of any aggregate, comprising uncountable billions of these same units, is fixed and certain" (112). Later in the same discussion, as he focuses on "the universality of quanta" Steinbeck writes that if an "investigation is carried deep enough, the factor in question, instead of being graphable as a continuous process, will be seen to function by discrete quanta with gaps or synapses between, as do quanta of energy, undulations of light" (118). He notes that such an investigation will lead to connections so that what appear to be "closed systems" are actually representative of "kingdoms of a great continuity bounded by the sudden discontinuity of great synapses which eventually must be bridged in any unified-field hypothesis" (118). Perhaps from the very model of the physics of his day, Steinbeck realized that as we pursue the whole there will be paradoxes and "gaps" to contain in a unified field theory that might account for all.

I would not argue that John Steinbeck had a full understanding of physics but rather that he was inspired by a science that reveals the universe's disorder and order, its grand paradoxes, and above all—more than any other branch of science—considers things in the widest scope, from the infinitesimal to the infinite. "I have been having a good bit of fun with the quantum theory," Steinbeck writes in a 1929 letter, "not that I understand it at all even in its primer for the man in the street stage" (DeMott *Reading* 28). Robert DeMott writes that Steinbeck had been familiar with at least quantum theory before engaging in conversation about such things with Ed Ricketts (Steinbeck and Ricketts met in 1930); by 1933 Steinbeck could refer to the names of several physicists, including Heisenberg (140). The most significant source for Steinbeck in this area of science was likely Eddington's book, to which Steinbeck refers in *Sea of Cortez*, and which does a splendid job of covering the full range of physics for Steinbeck's "man in the street." Indeed, Eddington's work, ranging from theories of the micro world to the galaxies and even beyond the scientific borders into the mystical had the widest kind of aperture—more than enough to inspire an author determined to go after the whole.

While *The Log from the Sea of Cortez* provides a great source for Steinbeck's consideration of physics in a nonfiction work, *Cannery Row* proves the richest dramatization of the author's interpretation of physics in a novel. This 1945 work is in fact illuminated in interesting ways by Steinbeck's ideas about the physical universe from the quantum to the cosmic. *Cannery Row* embraces the whole—in style, form, and content—attempting to contain the peculiar problems of "warp," micro and macro worlds, and grand paradoxes. Ultimately, the novel suggests we may find sanity in an apparently chaotic universe by attaining some sense of the unified field. Steinbeck had only music to articulate a theory that did not begin to exist until the year the novelist died in 1968. His philosophical extrapolations of physics, played out in *Cannery Row,* were so prescient no theory could support them fully until just recently—where most artists reflect existing science if they choose to do so at all, Steinbeck's *Cannery Row* considers a theory ahead of his time, one that physics has only just caught up to: superstring theory, the so-called Ultimate Theory. Hence, Greene's *The Elegant Universe*, a book as significant to the close of the 20th Century as Eddington's was in 1929, helps us to more fully comprehend *Cannery Row.*

A major stylistic device in *Cannery Row* is the list. In one of Steinbeck's most famous passages, the novel begins with a listing of perceptions of the Row, and touches on major lists of actions and things in at least ten places in the novel, including the last two lines (5, 10, 27, 72, 74, 121, 148, 173, 182, 185). The lists remind us of the collecting expedition Steinbeck took in the Gulf of California; they exist as a stylistic symptom of an author who had spent six weeks collecting marine specimens for cataloging, and in fact the author refers to the collection of marine animals as he describes the way *Cannery Row* is put together (6–7). The lists are also evidence of Steinbeck's desire to contain the whole in his novel; as things, events, and people become swept up in lists—sometimes in a rather random order—we see in action Steinbeck's assertion that "The Word is a symbol and a delight which sucks up men and scenes, trees, plants, factories, and Pekinese" (*CR* 17). The novel's impulse to capture the whole of Cannery Row, as a sort of parallel to *The Log from the Sea of Cortez*, has long been recognized by critics, from Richard Astro to Susan Shillinglaw. Yet an attempt to go after the whole, the impossible attempt to contain it all, bears some resemblance to the probably impossible goal of physics to do the same thing.

Cannery Row opens with its consideration of the problems of perception, "warp," and relative positions, subjects covered in *Sea of Cortez*. As in Einsteinian physics, much of our sense of reality depends upon where we are when we observe it. Steinbeck neatly sums up the problem in *Sea of Cortez* in a discussion of sea waves and how they are perceived as breaking at Point Sur: "And so on and on to the shore, and to the point where the last wave, if you think from the sea, and the first if you think from the shore, touches and breaks. And it is important where you are thinking from" (31). Of course, "where you are thinking from" is of great importance in *Cannery Row,* and readers are instructed to consider this as we look at the Row: "Its inhabitants are, as the man once said, 'whores, pimps, gamblers, and sons of bitches,' by which he meant Everybody. Had the man looked through another peephole he might have said, 'Saints and angels and martyrs and holy men,' and he would have meant the same thing" (5). So much of Steinbeck's fiction reminds us that truth is relative to the position from which one stands: in *The Pastures of Heaven* the collection of stories concludes with a group of tourists admiring the valley below from an idealistic perspective that counters the stories from inside the pastures. *In Dubious Battle* studies a strike from the differing perspectives of strike organizers and the laborers they are supposed to serve, just as a strike is seen from the inside and the outside in *The Grapes of Wrath*. Often, as in the case of physics outlined in Eddington's text, the perspectives—what we see through the peepholes—differ widely from the micro and macro view.

Throughout *Sea of Cortez*, Steinbeck considers the wide sweep, from the micro to macro perspectives, as a part of his larger desire to see relations within the whole. In a discussion of steering a boat and maintaining a course, he notices the smaller "internal factors" of the boat against the larger "external factors" of the sea (*LSC* 32). "The working out of the ideal into the real is here—the relationship between inward and outward, microcosm to macrocosm," he writes, considering the problem of reconciling the two factors in steering a boat: "There is probably a unified-field hypothesis available in navigation as in all things" (32). Later on the trip, as the *Western Flyer* makes its way back into the Pacific, Steinbeck observes "We could not yet relate the microcosm of the Gulf with the macrocosm of the sea" (223). But as he thinks further on this "little expedition" to the Gulf, he realizes that "it was a thing whose boundaries seeped through itself and beyond into some time and space that was more than all the Gulf and more than all our lives" (223). So often with Steinbeck there is this balancing of the two peepholes, the small and personal to the great and infinite; parallel to it is the strong desire to relate the views to all or, in his fiction, the truth. His greatest dramatization of this desire is *The Grapes of Wrath*, structured so we see the micro view of the Joads against the macro panorama of migrants, California history, and dispossession portrayed in the intercalary chapters.

Cannery Row, in a less rigid structure, does the same thing as we follow the story of Mack and the boys' attempt to pull off a party for Doc, against the larger picture of Monterey and its surroundings. The novel careens from a view as small as a gopher's attempt to make a home for itself (Chapter 31) to Doc's journey of several hundred miles to collect marine specimens in La Jolla (Chapters 17 and 18). A most interesting presentation of the micro and macro view occurs when a little boy, Andy, taunts a mysterious old Chinaman. The man turns, and his eyes spread out until the boy is engulfed by one single eye; the boy sees a vast world reminiscent of the Gulf mirages that so annoyed the skipper of the *Western Flyer:* a fantastic world of "mountains shaped like cows' and dogs' heads and tents and mushrooms" (CR 25). This is a dizzying moment for the boy—as it might have been for Tony Berry as he looked upon a headland with a "mushroom" shape and islands appearing to float in the air (68). The moment is as disorienting for the reader of *Cannery Row;* has the boy been swept into the mind's eye of the Chinaman, into a tiny micro universe? Or has the Chinaman's giant eye grown outward, so the boy perceives a vision of a colossal universe in which he is but a tiny, lonely part? The old man has provided a glimpse of the chaotic universe—quantum, cosmic, or both— and for a little boy not ready to look through that peephole it is a terrifying experience.

What readies us for that particular view, for a consideration of the whole? *Cannery Row* suggests, more so than any of Steinbeck's other works, that the key is embracing the disorder and especially the paradoxes that life and the universe present to us. Because of its wide scope, physics must do exactly this: comprehend the bewildering reality of quantum theory and relativity and the fact that the two views—at least in Steinbeck's time— seem impossible to reconcile. The grand paradox is the fact that working explanations for the quantum universe do not work for the cosmic universe, and vice versa. Hence the need for the unified-field theory Steinbeck refers to, which will contain this gigantic contradiction. Steinbeck not only embraces paradoxes, he delights in presenting them. If a chief stylistic device in *Cannery Row* is the list, the driving force of the novel's plot, humor, and theme is paradox.

Paradox as a device runs throughout Steinbeck's work, from his first novel, *Cup of Gold* (in which the pirate Henry Morgan achieves his quest for La Santa Roja only to find she destroys him) to his last book, *America and Americans* (in which he lists American peculiarities in a chapter, "Paradox and Dream"). His emphasis on paradox reaches its zenith in *Cannery Row*. The central plot of the novel is itself a paradox: when Mack and the boys plan a party it is a disaster, when they don't plan it the party succeeds. All predictions of how the second, successful party will be are also wrong: "it is also generally understood that a party hardly ever goes the way it is planned or intended" (*CR* 172). In other words, in order to have a fun party, don't try to plan or understand it—let it come. Of course the same can be said for the structure of the novel, for Steinbeck tells us that the best way to capture *Cannery Row* "alive" is "to open the page and to let the stories crawl in by themselves" (7). The quickest way to lose control of a party or novel is to start by planning and controlling. In *Cannery Row,* the disastrous first party for Doc proves this thesis.

The novel's humor, its satire, and even its tragedy derive from paradox, and most of the characters are defined by paradox. Mack and the boys are content because they do not work for contentment, and those who do are miserable: "What can it profit a man to gain the whole world and to come to his property with a gastric ulcer, a blown prostate, and bifocals?" (18). Dora Flood, a madam who runs a "stately whore house," lives in a paradox: "Being against the law, at least in its letter, she must be twice as law abiding as anyone else" (19, 20). Hazel asks questions of Doc but never listens to nor cares about the answers. Henri builds boats but is afraid to finish them because that would mean he would have to set them on the water, and Henri hates the water. Frankie is a boy with no one to love until he finds Doc, and falling in love with Doc is his undoing when he breaks into a store to get his father figure a birthday present. Chapter 25 opens with the observation that people on the Row do not believe in superstitions although they certainly act on them, including Doc, who "was a pure scientist and incapable of superstition and yet when he came in late one night and found a line of white flowers across the doorsill he had a bad time of it" (147). The paradoxical focuses on something as small as a gopher who builds a perfect home that he cannot live in for lack of a mate, to sweeping statements about the world, such as Doc's observation that "The things we admire in men, kindness and generosity, openness, honesty, understanding and feeling are the concomitants of failure in our system" and "those traits we detest, sharpness, greed, acquisitiveness, meanness, egotism and self-interest are the traits of success" (135).

In such a confounding world and universe, a dizzying whirl-wind of paradox, *Cannery Row* suggests an added, perhaps fright-ening, dimension: most if not all of it *cannot be explained.* "Why" is a dangerous word on Cannery Row, where the inexplicable abounds. No one likes William, the watchman at Dora's Bear Flag Restaurant, and he kills himself; the next watchman, Alfred, is liked by everyone—in both cases, no one could really say why. Eddie the bartender cannot predict what will be in the jug of half-finished drinks he collects for Mack and the boys—one night ten men might order Manhattans and then that particular drink might not be ordered but twice in the next month. "Oh, the infinity of possibility!" Steinbeck opens a section in which Gay goes for a part to fix a truck and winds up in jail through a series of "unrelated, irrelevant details and yet all running in one direction" (66). After the disastrous party for Doc, a collec-tion of bad events descend on the Row. "There is no explaining a series of misfortunes like that," Steinbeck writes, adding that perhaps there is evil or "One man may put it down to sun spots while another invoking the law of probabilities doesn't believe it" (137). A mere ten pages later the collective mood on Cannery Row lifts, gladness spreads out from the boys' Palace Flophouse and good things happen across town and even out into the sea, where "The sea lions felt it and their barking took on a tone and a cadence that would have gladdened the heart of St. Francis" (148). Everyone and everything feels it, now all is moving in one direction that is positive, but the general good feeling over such a wide area is about as explicable as the general bad feeling that hung over the place earlier. Perhaps it is the paradox of the next party, unplanned, not centrally organized, in which "no one was invited" but to which "Everyone was going" (156).

How does Steinbeck suggest we survive such a paradoxical universe? We must widen the aperture to contain as much of it as possible, to contain the chaos by not explaining it. "The pro-cess of gathering knowledge does not lead to knowing," Stein-beck writes in *Sea of Cortez.* "A child's world spreads only a little beyond his understanding while that of a great scientist thrusts outward immeasurably" (*LSC* 137). All is infinitely large, "And in a unified-field hypothesis, or in life, which is a unified field of reality, everything is an index of everything else" (213). The greatest expression of this widening of fields, of perspectives, in *Sea of Cortez* occurs when the apparent waste of fish in Japanese dredge boat operations is considered. For Tiny, a fisherman on the *Western Flyer*, the waste of marine life cast aside as excess in the great dredging process is horrifying but then "We discussed the widening and narrowing picture" (217). In the micro view—Tiny's view—there is waste, but as the view widens what appears to be waste goes into the sea and feeds a variety of species from sea birds to bacteria: "in the macrocosm nothing is wasted" (217). Chaos to Tiny is reconciled as the view widens and widens—the illusive gap between the micro and macro view closes and one comes closer to the whole. This infinite widening is suggested by the expanding eye of the old Chinaman on Cannery Row; he seems to have contained the whole and all its weirdness and paradox.

Doc, as the unconventional hero of *Cannery Row*, is himself a paradox who has learned to take in larger paradoxes and indeed more of the whole than anyone else in the book (with the possible exception of the Chinaman). He is described as a man whose "face is half Christ and half satyr," a man with a "cool warm mind" who "can kill anything for need but he could not even hurt a feeling for pleasure" (29). Doc is a scientist with superstitions, a center of Row society but "a lonely and set-apart man," a man who loves true things but knows that sometimes it is easier to lie—give the expected explanation—for those who cannot understand, a man who makes his livelihood in tide pools but is deathly afraid of even a single drop of water on his head (96). Doc also has the ability to take in the widest possible view: "His mind had no horizon—and his sympathy had no warp" (30). His ability to widen the aperture is put to the test when Mack visits the lab after the first party has left it in ruins; after initial rage, Doc takes in the wider view. Going forward in time, he sees that though Mack plans to repay Doc for the damage, it will never happen: holding Mack and the boys to the debt would only make them "uneasy" and they "wouldn't pay for it anyway" (125). Very quickly, Doc takes in and adapts to the chaos that the party has made of his lab and home. Doc in *Cannery Row* embodies the paradoxical and the sweep of the unified field. He possesses the ever-expanding mind of a scientist, transcends the micro and macro, the sensual and intellectual. More than any other character in the novel, he comes closest to comprehending all—the convergence of things. Beyond Doc, this convergence of everything, the unified field, manifests itself in *Cannery Row* as sunrise and sunset, and as music. The Chinaman walks in and out of the between time, the small "quiet gray period" at dawn and sunset (24). These times of convergence, of peace between the daylight and nighttime boundaries, are the only times the mysterious Chinaman appears. They are periods of "magic" on the Row, when the place "seems to hang suspended out of time in a silvery light" (81). As we see in Chapter 14, in which two soldiers and two women take an early morning stroll to Hopkins Marine Station and blithely ignore the admonitions of the watchman there, this is a time of peace when the rules do not seem to apply; this is "the hour of the pearl" (82). For Doc, such moments can be savored at other times, for he literally tunes into the whole, the unified field, through music. Throughout the novel, we know Doc appreciates music of all kinds, including Gregorian chants, fugues, concertos. Angry at Mack after the destruction of the lab, he turns to the phonograph for comfort only to find it is destroyed; it doesn't matter, as Monteverdi's music fills his head anyhow.

In one of the novel's most striking chapters, 18, Doc keys into the whole through music that is inside his head and around him as well. Beginning work at dawn, Doc spends the morning collecting specimens at the tide pools of La Jolla when at the outer barrier before the deep he discovers a drowned girl wedged in the rock. She presents an immediate paradox for Doc: there is the fearful tragedy of a drowned girl, and at the same time the scene is strikingly beautiful: "on [her] face was only comfort and rest" (105). Doc's reaction is a mixture of emotion; he shivers, his heart pounds, his eyes grow moist but are "wet the way they get in the focus of great beauty" (105). Sitting on the beach, he seems to go outside himself—in place and time—for the picture of the girl's face is "set for all time" (105). As he extends into the whole, he hears music: piercing flutes in his mind from "a melody he could never remember" against "a pounding surf-like wood-wind section" (105). The microcosm of his mind tunes into the macrocosm of the sea; the tragedy of death for a moment greatly enhances Doc's life. He taps out the rhythm of the sea with his hand, while the "terrifying flute" plays in his head (106). The next line is disembodied: "The eyes were gray and the mouth smiled a little or seemed to catch its breath in ecstasy"; this is the girl or Doc or both. He is knocked out of this reverie by the intrusion of a man who becomes interested in reporting the girl for the bounty offered; Doc is torn from the much greater place where he has been residing—he walks to his car with tiny reverberations of flute music still in his head.

In this crucial scene, Doc, a man after the whole, connects to it—in Steinbeck's language this is a moment when Doc keys into the unified field. This is a time when, as Steinbeck describes it in *Sea of Cortez*, "one has a feeling of fullness, of warm wholeness, wherein every sight and object and odor and experience seems to key into a gigantic whole" (101). Such a time, when one can see "that man is related to the whole thing" is what makes "a Jesus, a St. Augustine, a St. Francis, a Roger Bacon, a Charles Darwin, and an Einstein" (*LSC* 178). It also makes a Doc. His impulse, his quest to connect it all together, embodies the ultimate goal of physics through the unified field. Steinbeck dramatizes a theory that did not exist yet, and curiously in *Cannery Row* he uses music as a metaphorical device to suggest the infinite interrelations. With his rudimentary understanding of the physics of his day, Steinbeck manages to forecast in metaphor the great unifier that has only recently been expressed—superstring theory; the author proves ahead of his time. In the part of *The Elegant Universe* entitled "The Cosmic Symphony," Brian Greene observes that from the Pythagorean "music of the spheres" onward "we have collectively sought the song of nature in the gentle wanderings of celestial bodies and the riotous fulminations of subatomic particles" (135). "With the discovery of superstring theory, musical metaphors take on a startling reality, for the theory suggests that the microscopic landscape is suffused with tiny strings whose vibrational patterns orchestrate the evolution of the cosmos" (135). He adds that the "winds of change, according to superstring theory, gust through an aeolian universe" (135). In the simplest terms, superstring theory suggests that all, from the micro to the macro, is bound by interlocking loops of vibrating string, rather than the scattered assortment of subatomic *particles* that we have been accustomed to visualizing. Steinbeck himself came close to expressing the same view, as he refers back to Einstein, Darwin, and others: "Each of them in his own tempo and his own voice discovered and reaffirmed with astonishment the knowledge that all things are one thing . . . plankton, a shimmering phosphorescence on the sea and the spinning planets and an expanding universe, all bound together by the elastic string of time" (*LSC* 179).

Alone among the writers of his time and stature, John Steinbeck wanted to teach us that the disorder and paradox we perceive in our world is relative—a figment of our own peculiar warp. If we move beyond our own boundaries, we might sense an unseen order in things and therefore we may allow ourselves to stand before the universe without raging for order, without trembling in fear, when we cannot discern an order to our liking. Through his unique perspective, enlightened by the science of his day, Steinbeck made it clear that an order exists *outside of us*—exists even if the greatest scientific or philosophical minds cannot explain it. Going as far out as an author might, he nearly touches upon the Ultimate Theory—the unified field that at last connects all—in superstring theory. To go there, we must embrace the micro and macro universes, and we are gently asked to do so at the ends of *Cannery Row* and *Sea of Cortez*. The final image of the novel is of white rats scampering in cages, while in their glass tanks "the rattlesnakes lay still and stared into space" (185). "It is advisable to look from the tide pool to the stars and then back to the tide pool again," Steinbeck writes toward the end of *Sea of Cortez*. "The shape of the trip was an integrated nucleus from which weak strings of thought stretched into every reachable reality," Steinbeck concludes. "There was some quality of music here, perhaps not to be communicated, but sounding clear and huge in our minds" (224). Like the aeolian harp Greene makes reference to when introducing superstring theory, the final image in *Sea of Cortez* is the guy wire of the *Western Flyer*, pointing from the bow of the little boat into the infinite sky, and making "its vibration like the low pipe on a tremendous organ" (224). Like a physicist who may demon-strate what but not always why, or a character who can tune into the whole when confronted with the chaos of a smashed lab or a drowned girl, John Steinbeck exhibits a deep faith that can weather our bewildering, elegant universe.

23

The Place We Have Arrived

On Writing/Reading toward Cannery Row

Robert DeMott

DeMott approaches Steinbeck's 1945 novel, Cannery Row, *by first unpacking two neglected terms in Steinbeck's aesthetic vocabulary—"participation" and "the new." The former was his term for creating a dimension of audience involvement in his fictional texts (an early example of reader-response dynamic). The latter was his code word for developments in contemporary physics (quantum mechanics, particle physics) that had changed the way the world was perceived. The two concepts merge in that the effect of quantum physics is to break down the barriers between observer and observed, and make the world a "participatory universe," to use physicist John Wheeler's phrase. Understanding the implications of "participation" and the "new" helps contextualize Steinbeck's attempt to write a radically indeterminate and interdisciplinary novel.[1]*

> The luck of the book is that we then may go back, to the top of
> the page, and begin to arrive again.
>
> Muriel Rukeyser, *The Life of Poetry*

On 13 November 1939, seven months after the publication of *The Grapes of Wrath*, which had become a run-away best seller, an exhausted and dismayed John Steinbeck confessed to Carlton Sheffield that he had worked the "clumsy vehicle" of the novel as far as he could. He also announced his plan to explore uncharted creative horizons informed by contemporary developments in theoretical physics, among other disciplines (including marine biology, mathematics, anthropology, and psychology), which he dubbed "the form of the new" (*SLL* 194). The immediate result of Steinbeck's recuperative self-fashioning was a collaborative volume written with marine biologist Edward F. Ricketts, *Sea of Cortez: A Leisurely Journal of Travel and Research*, published in December, 1941 (a decade later, the volume's narrative portion appeared as *The Log from the Sea of Cortez*, with Steinbeck listed as sole author). But the long-range result of his broad inter-disciplinary exploration appeared six years later in *Cannery Row*. In the following essay, I offer some avenues of approach for understanding the place Steinbeck has brought us to/to us in his quest for the "form of the new." As with so many Steinbeckian locales it is not the simple nostalgic regional place we once imagined it to be, but a rich, inflected, interstitial site, a contested space where a number of disciplinary "borders and boundaries" (Tatum 318) have been crossed, joined, and redrawn. In order to offer some speculations and approximations about the layered complexities of Steinbeck's novel, I must detour into a couple of underlying, neglected Steinbeckian tropes —"participation" and "the new"—both of which converge in *Cannery Row* and emphasize the novelist's prescient ecological belief that "[e]verything impinges on everything else, often into radically different systems . . . " (*LSC* 118). Examining these overlapping concepts might rectify the belief that "no key" exists with which to unlock "the secret structural design at the center" of *Cannery Row* (Benson "Reconsideration" 13). If, after all is said and done, the novel still remains a "puzzle" to us, it will probably be for other reasons.

I. Participation: A Short (Hi)story of a Word

[T]he law of participation. . . . At the moment it would be difficult to formulate this law in abstract terms.
                              Lucien Levy-Bruhl, *How Natives Think*

A few years ago, a Monterey tabloid, the *Coast Weekly*, ran a front cover headline, "Who Owns Steinbeck?" Inside, the investigative story centers on the unresolvable "tug of war between commemoration and commercialization," and highlights the necessarily inconclusive "battle" between "the Monterey Peninsula and the Salinas Valley asserting their ties to the essential Steinbeck" (Duman 10). But perhaps it isn't a question of who owns Steinbeck, but how it is that he own us, compels us to respond? To put it another way, books are metaphors as well as material products, which is to say—not to put an excessively commodificational twist to it—they can be made "use" of in any number of both routine and unexpected ways. Steinbeck understood that multiplicity better than many writers when he claimed in 1936 that reading "certain books" was "realer than experience" (DeMott *Reading* xx)—in other words, the result of virtual textual seduction becomes the equivalent of an event actually happening to us. That a Steinbeck novel happens to us is not an accident, because positing the presence of a participatory "reader" was always part of his basic story-telling project.[2] As recent commentators have realized, Steinbeck has not been adequately or widely enough credited for having an abiding, generative, ideational aesthetic (Benson *True Adventures* 231; Timmerman 3–15; Ditsky 5), though in fact he wrote from a consistent (though unpretentious) set of operative principles, and a healthy dose of pragmatic optimism that his words would communicate on a variety of levels to his audience. He told George Albee in 1934 that "The Chrysanthemums" story "is designed to strike without the reader's knowledge. I mean he reads it casually and after it is finished feels that something profound has happened to him although he does not know what nor how" (*SLL* 91). In the individual space opened up by the reading experience, in the aftermath of contemplating the "what" and the "how," Steinbeck expected we would talk back, breach boundaries, and become, in short, not merely consumers of culture, but its participants.

From the start of his mature career, then, Steinbeck imagined a dynamic, interactive equation configured around a cooperative triad of Writer-Text-Reader. In the 1930s and 1940s—generally well ahead of its time—Steinbeck worked out a homemade reader-response theory, which he dubbed "participation." For instance, in *The Forgotten Village* Steinbeck and director Herbert Kline attempted to "draw" a portrait of the indigenous Mexican culture with "something like participation." In the Preface Steinbeck elaborated: "Birth and death, joy and sorrow, are constants, experiences common to the whole species. If one participates first in the constants, one is able to go from them to the variables of customs, practices, mores, taboos, and foreign social patterns. That at any rate was our theory and the pattern in which we worked" (5). No single Steinbeck text embodies all these elements in the same proportion, but they appear in sufficient regularity and concert to look like a definable pattern, embedded particularly in *The Grapes of Wrath, Cannery Row, The Pearl,* and *East of Eden.* In much of his major writing, then, Steinbeck consciously sought to achieve a strong participatory effect by reaching a "common ground" between text and audience, a liminal site, a contact zone, where a reader can take from his book "as much" as he or she can "bring to it" (*JN* 11, 17).

It is impossible to know where Steinbeck first encountered "participation." It is reasonable to surmise that Ed Ricketts, Joseph Campbell, and Evelyn Ott aided and abetted Steinbeck's study of Carl Jung and other influential psychologists, mythologists, and anthropologists (DeMott *Reading* lxxii, 62–63, 156–57). The fortieth definition of "Psychological Types," which appears in chapter X, paragraph 781, of Jung's *Psychological Types,* reads in part: "Participation mystique is a term derived from Levy-Bruhl [in *How Natives Think*]. It denotes a peculiar kind of psychological connection with objects, and consists in the fact that the subject cannot clearly distinguish himself from the object but is bound to it by a direct relationship which amounts to partial *identity. . . . Participation mystique* is a vestige of this primitive condition" (456). Whether Steinbeck, guided by Jung's attribution, bothered to go next to Lucien Levy-Bruhl's chapter, "The Law of Participation," in his sociological study of primitive collectivism, *How Natives Think* (originally published in French in 1923, then in English in 1926), is unknown, but is highly likely.[3] In speaking without condescension of primitive subject/object perceptions, Levy-Bruhl claimed that "in various forms and degrees they all involve a 'participation' between persons or objects which form part of a collective representation. . . . " This interaction he termed *"the law of participation"* (76).

Steinbeck appropriated the Levy-Bruhl/Jung idea (and adopted both writers' tone of acceptance and understanding) for his own enabling ends, as he often did with inspiring sources. In this instance, seeking a new way to mediate experience, Steinbeck metaphorized the metaphor itself. Steinbeck discovered in Levy-Bruhl's "multipresence" (96) and his "ensemble which depends upon the group, as the group depends upon it" (99), and in Jung's "transference relationship" (457) not an isolated primitive or mystical condition or an aberrant, fetishistic psychological quirk, but a kind of immanent palimpsest of interaction, a cognitive bridge with which to link author, text, and reader in an evolving, non-hierarchical, ecological phalanx of interpretation and perpetual (re)construction of meaning. Levy-Bruhl's investigations highlighted issues of "collective representation" (76) and affective social "communion" (90), and Jung's dealt with multiple and reciprocal attachments (456–57). Both are analogous to Steinbeck's preoccupation with phalanxes of natural and human social organization, a developing pattern of aggregate stimulus, action, and perception he had been working out since the early 1930s (Steinbeck "Argument of Phalanx").

A great deal has been written about this "group man" theory and Ricketts's important role in it, especially regarding how, when humans operate in aggregate they function in ways different than those of the individual (Astro 43–60; Benson, *True Adventures* 264–70). Nothing has been said, however, about Steinbeck's writerly role in regard to the social phalanx, so it is worthwhile to focus briefly on that aspect. Steinbeck keyed into a particular kind of scriptive role as a recorder of group activity. For Steinbeck, the recording figure—the artist with small "a"—is the egoless "spokesman" of the phalanx, "the one in whom the phalanx comes closest to the conscious." He continued to George Albee in 1933: "When a man hears great music, sees great pictures, reads great poetry, he loses his identity in that of the phalanx. I do not need to describe the emotion caused by these things, but it is invariably a feeling of oneness with one's phalanx" (Letter to George Albee [1]).[4] The spokesperson, who is capable of writing the "tremendous and terrible poetry" of the moment ([3]), appears when he is needed to express a group's most important or pressing needs. Thus, paradoxically, although the artist is *constructed* by social desire/political necessity and the conjunctive pressures of history, economics, and geography, he *expresses* himself not only according to the degree of felt life he brings to his work, but also according to his inventive and suasive capacities regarding theme, style, and form. "Man's art always reflects the nature and emotion of his phalanx. If it does not, it is not art, it is simply technique" (Letter to George Albee [2]). The central point in this paradoxical dance of unconscious desire and conscious craft is to break through the old monolithic, totalizing conventions—the "obstacles" (Steinbeck "Suggestion" 541)—of ignorance and oppression by building approximate living structures in language that in turn will invite audience empathy, imaginative participation, and even social action. These ends are achieved not by mystical means, but through emotional identification and psychological investment with the mediating textual object. "Art is the phalanx knowledge of the nature of matter and life," which is to say, it is a way of expressing experience through apt form: "Art form is nature form," he concludes emphatically (Letter to George Albee [2]).

For example, *The Grapes of Wrath* demonstrates this breakthrough toward participation in a variety of ways (Owens *The Grapes of Wrath* 28), but in addition to its radical political thrust it also enacts an aesthetic gambit, especially in Chapter 23, which is devoted to the migrants' pleasures. Their pleasures include a storytelling round where "people gathered in the low firelight to hear the gifted ones. And they listened while the tales were told, and their participation made the stories great" (444). The whole passage (at 549 words, too long to quote here) also presents an eponymous speaker's haunting account of his reluctant but complicitous involvement in the United States Army's murderous campaign against Apache leader Geronimo in 1885–1886, and offers a parable of a slaughtered brave and a dead cock pheasant. This section functions as an elaborate trope for the key social themes of *The Grapes of Wrath,* including tyranny of surveillance, arrogance of power, and willful destruction of peoples and resources—all those unconscionable acts that cause us to "spoil" something better than ourselves, to destroy something in ourselves that can never be "fixed up" (445). The oral performance, including the nameless recruit's confession, is at once realistically (re)presented and textually (re)flexive, because it mirrors in miniature Steinbeck's methodology regarding his writerly situation: note that the storyteller is positioned not above his auditors but at their level so that they can key into his narrational experience and thereby lend it additional power and meaning. "Their participation," Steinbeck writes, "made the stories great" and allows the man's confession to become not self-indulgent posturing, or empty technique, but a redemptive gesture applicable to the entire community of listeners both inside and outside the book. In this transactional configuration, at its most basic level, lies part of the secret of Steinbeck's appeal and success. Hearing, reading, participating, we readers willingly transgress fixed boundaries to help create and re-create the text in front of us. Being a "gifted one" in this narratological context, then, refers to Steinbeck's mediating attention toward vocal presence and his embedded—and often unavoidably self-conflicted—role in the complex, shifting, indeterminate relationship among groups of people, events, things, words, and audience.

Steinbeck's life changed drastically in the years following the success and notoriety of *The Grapes of Wrath*. In an abstract sense *The Grapes of Wrath* no longer belonged to Steinbeck at all but to an army of anonymous readers who reinvented it according to their own predilections, experiences, and desires. If this satisfied the social usefulness of proletarian literature, the theoretical destiny of phalanx art, and the power of Steinbeck's own participatory aesthetics, it did little to explain the personalism of the moment. In fact, Steinbeck resented the reductive implications of an exchange that, instead of expunging him from the public gaze, could produce a monstrous, distorted "straw man," a "fictitious so-and-so . . . out there in the public eye," as he told interviewer Tom Cameron of the *Los Angeles Times* in July of 1939 (*Conversations* 18). Instead, he tried to leave behind the part of him that made *The Grapes of Wrath*, but it always proved difficult, primarily because his critics and reviewers expected him to write the same thing over again. But he was a relatively resilient if not always utterly centered person, and one of his responses to his own cynicism and cautionary backlash was to embark on several different kinds of writing, to reinvent himself, and to become, in effect, a man of letters. "I have to go to new sources and find new roots," he confessed on 16 October

1939 (*WD* 106). Between 1940 and 1945, he brought forth a film-script (*The Forgotten Village*, produced and directed by Herbert Kline), two works of non-fiction (*Sea of Cortez* and *Bombs Away*), a play novella (*The Moon Is Down*), a series of war dispatches for the *New York Herald Tribune* (later published as *Once There Was a War*), and, finally, a novel (*Cannery Row*). In addition, he had a hand in the first Viking Portable anthology which appeared in 1943, edited and selected by Pascal Covici, Steinbeck's editor at the Viking Press.

The clearest theoretical statement of the writer's participatory method appears in one of the oddest documents in the Stein-beckian archive. "Introduction by Pascal Covici" was handwritten in late September 1942 by Steinbeck himself and perhaps intended to be used or drawn upon by his Viking Press editor Covici as he arranged the publication of the *Viking Portable Stein-beck*.[5] Though it has never been published in its entirety, this is an especially valuable document because Steinbeck attempts to codify the affective and intuitive dimension of reading as a way of experiencing reality:

> There are some books, some stories, some poems which one reads over and over again without knowing why one is drawn to them. And such stories need not have been critically appreciated—in fact many of them have not been. The critic's approach is and perhaps should be one of appraisal and evaluation. The reader if he likes a story feels largely a participation. The stories we go back to are those in which we have taken part. A man need not have a likeness of exact experience to love a story but he must have in him an emotional or intellectual tone which has keyed into the story and made him part of it. No one has ever read *Treasure Island* or *Robinson Crusoe* objectively. The chief characters in both cases are merely the skin and bones of the reader. The poetical satires of Gulliver have long been forgotten but the stories go on. The message or the teaching of a story almost invariably dies first while the participation persists. Perhaps the best balance of message and participation in all literature is the story of Jesus—for there step by step the mind is opened by association with the man and his suffering to the things he said. ("Introduction" [1]; DeMott *Typewriter* 195–96)

Steinbeck's testimony—it had by this juncture of his career become a signature rationale, even a personal manifesto, which is to say, both hopeful and resistant—is a summation of a decade's preoccupation with trying to accomplish a fundamental yet mysterious affective task: to create a "true" theory of writing which linked non-telological observation with an affective dimension of "religion and emotion and poetry" (Letter to George Albee [2]; DeMott *Typewriter* 195) in order to make us "see a little play" in our heads, as he had once claimed in a brief essay in *Stage* magazine (50). This is not to be confused with pejorative notions of "escape writing and reading" for as far as Steinbeck is concerned, "all art is escape" into a fuller dimension of reality:

> One escapes into the painter's eye, and brain in a Rembrandt, one escapes into the rich reality of Tolstoy out of the muddy and troubled reality of oneself. One escapes into the clear thinking of a physicist[,] into the glowing emotion of a poem. It is all escape—Next to the eating and reproducing urges it is probably that man's greatest quality is his instinct for rebellion and escape. His religion, and all his arts and all his sciences are simply the results of his beating against the bars of his world. It is natural enough that the dull coarse mind should escape into the super reality of the success-love story of the magazine. The hungrier and sharper mind may chose [*sic*] the paths of astrophysics, of poetry, or ethics. But the escape effort is everywhere. ("Introduction" [2])

Steinbeck's 1942 rationale not only summed up his major work to date, but also forecast writing yet to be done in *Cannery Row, The Pearl,* and *East of Eden.* This desired end required a new way of writing that avoided "the usual narrative method"—a storytelling strategy "so natural and unobtrusive that an audience would not even be conscious of it" (*FV* [6]). It is debatable how unobtrusive Steinbeck's method was, especially in his post-1950 works; nevertheless, composing with a response theory in mind allowed Steinbeck to create a silent "wall of background" and a "picture-making state," which would allow the "unexpected" to emerge, as he claimed in his *Long Valley* notebook (qtd. in Benson *True Adventures* 331), or to create a broadly "relational" effort that requires "living into" for its optimum effect (*LSC* 117).

Two years almost to the day after Steinbeck had written his ghosted "Introduction" he told Carlton Sheffield, "I finished the book called Cannery Row. . . . I don't know whether it is effective or not. It's written on four levels and people can take what they can receive out of it. One thing—it never mentions the war—not once. . . . " (*SLL* 273). Steinbeck did not consider those levels a "preconceived structural pattern," as Roy Simmonds rightly notes (226), but rather as fluid, interpenetrative layers which attempt to replicate life's complex holism. Steinbeck's text, then, is relational—so that classifying distinct, sharply etched referential categories is less important than seeing the interrelated pattern they create (Shillinglaw xxiv–xxv). Indeed, *Cannery Row* is almost anti-literary, because it avoids "elaborate, formal, literary structures" (Benson "Reconsideration" 23), and builds on Steinbeck's strategy of democratically inviting us in at the outset to share the perplexing task of telling a story for which there is no preferred, favored vantage point with which to approach it, and there are no clear lines between historical reality, thinly disguised fictional creations, and utterly imagined and made up events. Steinbeck's conundrum becomes our shared interpretative puzzle and requires our active involvement to concretize it:

> How can the poem and the stink and the grating noise—the quality of light, the tone, the habit and the dream—be set down alive? When you collect marine animals there are certain flat worms so delicate that they are almost impossible to capture whole, for they break and tatter under the touch. You must let them ooze and crawl of their own will onto a knife blade and then lift them gently into your bottle of sea water. And perhaps that might be the way to write this book—to open the page and to let the stories crawl in by themselves. (7)

Cannery Row explicitly foregrounds both the basis of Steinbeck's real-life experience (his association with Ed Ricketts and memories of Cannery Row as an historical place) *and* the materiality of his writing (his aesthetic difficulties in achieving written representation of, or objectivity toward, oral/folk experience). The narrator's problematic position frames, or focalizes, the text. Because ideally his stance purports to be non-judgemental, it also undercuts traditional authorial privilege, in that the narrator, like the teller in Chapter 23 of *The Grapes of Wrath,* is situated at the same level as his audience and provides one perspective among many possible perspectives on the action and characters (5). He asks how the Row's intangible, evanescent qualities can "be set down alive?" His response is not transcendent or imperial, but rather tentative, qualified, conditional—"perhaps that might be the way," he admits. The image of coaxing marine worms into bottles, Jackson Benson claims, "suggests to us that this will be a rather daring experiment—a non-teleological novel, a fiction as unordered as possible by previous conceptions and structures, dealing not even with a hero (the anthropocentric view of life) or with plot (concern with cause and effect), but with life as an ongoing 'is' process" ("Reconsideration" 23). If Steinbeck relied on raw emotional power to implicate us in *Of Mice and Men* and *The Grapes of Wrath,* in this fiction he has more figuratively and subtly made us accomplices, co-conspirators in his eco-textual and language project, and has allowed us to enter the frame with him to witness the inherent difficulty of representing "the flow and vitality" (13) of Cannery Row. Contemplating these elements brings to mind Steinbeck's closing words in his "Introduction by Pascal Covici": "When reader and writer go together into a story . . . pleasure is the result" ([3]).[6]

Toward that end, *Cannery Row* utilizes a few subtle, almost transparent strategies to encourage our participation: lyrical place descriptions help readers locate geographically and spatially; relatively sketchy physical descriptions of characters encourage readers to envision them in their mind's eye; emphatic dialogue creates the illusion of eavesdropping on private conversations. In addition, Steinbeck employs structural and stylistic innovations to effect our involvement. Digressive interchapters establish a rhythmic or thematic counterpoint to the main narrative, while other evocative chapters withhold disclosures and direct the reader's eye or ear toward the unsaid, perhaps even the momentously unsayable (Andy's inscrutable experience with the elderly Chinese man in Chapter 4, the drowned woman Doc discovers in Chapter 18), or the egregiously unthinkable (William's suicide in Chapter 3, Gay's beating of his wife in Chapter 6). In order to arrive at a fuller-than-usual understanding of the novel, these episodes require completion by an audience keyed into Steinbeck's text, readers receptive to powers of suggestion, randomness, and spatial form (*SLL* 91).

In fact, because a kind of unique heterodoxy and diversity results when barriers are broken down, and boundaries crossed, *Cannery Row* is purposely full of inviting, seductive gaps, shadows, discontinuities, and margins. As most scientists, naturalists, and ecologists know, life at these transitional sites, these eco-tonal margins, is often thickest, most vital, diverse, and interesting. Steinbeck's references to hybrid micro-cosmic locations (Lee Chong's grocery, Palace Flophouse), physical edges and contact zones (land/sea, vacant lot/busy street, whorehouse/marine lab), and to temporal boundaries between day and night, such as dusk, and especially dawn, which he names the "Hour of Pearl" (82, 121), all open up primary, originary spaces where readers can go beyond mere "skin and bones" and imagine the whole fabric of experience, the place where paradox rules: Lee Chong is a "hard man with a can of beans—a soft man with the bones of his grandfather (17); Doc's face is "half Christ and half satyr" (29). Overseeing this aesthetics of the edge, this "edgesthetics" (to coin a term), Steinbeck invokes "Our Father who art in nature" (18) as a validating spirit of the paradox, hybridity, bricolage, simultaneity, and randomness necessary for survival at "the margins of society" (Shillinglaw ix). "Monterey is lousy with this kind of paradox," Steinbeck noted in the margins of *Cannery Row*'s galley proof (*Complete Archive* [5]).

If Steinbeck's desire for his audience to share his perplexity frames one end of *Cannery Row*, then Doc's second party, a hymn to quantum unpredictability, frames the other. In order to appreciate Steinbeck's statement that "the nature of parties has been imperfectly studied" (172), we need to attend one. This party is full of festivity, rowdy shenanigans, and unexpected changes; indeed, far from being innocuous, escapist fare, it reveals Steinbeck's sense of performativity and cultural spectacle.

Moreover, Doc's party calls attention to its own "spontaneity," its sense of "play" (Meeker 10, 18)—induced by music, poetry, and lots of booze, the revelers dance, eat, and even fight with abandon. This carnivalesque scene, to borrow loosely Mikhail Bakhtin's term from *Rabelais and His World*, undoes the quotidian world, unsettles the social order, undercuts authority, destroys the boundaries between hierarchies, and invites us to go beyond reading subjectively to momentarily transgressing:

> And then the party really got going. The cops came back, looked in, clicked their tongues and joined it. . . . You could hear the roar of the party from end to end of Cannery Row. The party had all the best qualities of a riot and a night on the barricades. The crew from the San Pedro tuna boat crept humbly back and joined the party. They were embraced and admired. A woman five blocks away called the police to complain about the noise and couldn't get anyone. The cops reported their own car stolen and found it later on the beach. Doc sitting cross-legged on the table smiled and tapped his fingers gently on his knee. Mack and Phyllis Mae were doing Indian wrestling on the floor. And the cool bay wind blew in through the broken windows. It was then that someone lighted the twenty-five foot string of firecrackers. (178)

This scene indicates the degree to which Steinbeck, a writer given to exploding "closed systems" (*LSC* 118) of all kinds, was continually revising the traditional novelistic contract, the philosophical either/or proposition. Furthermore, if we remember that Steinbeck told Carlton Sheffield *Cannery Row* does "not once" mention World War II, then the novel can be seen not only as personal therapy for (and a kind of exorcism of) nausea brought on by his recent tour abroad writing "crap" military journalism (*SLL* 273), but also as a return to the familiar ground of localized (hi)story (Shillinglaw xviii–xix) and the empowering, anarchic potential of the "little" narrative (Lyotard 60). *Cannery Row* anticipates what Jean Lyotard has called the "postmodern condition" by resisting grand, totalizing narratives of universal truth, institutional certainty, and consensual normalcy; rather, in its satiric thrust, it functions as a critique of bourgeois pomposity, pretentiousness, entitlement, arrogance, and hypocritical respectability. In Steinbeck's turn toward subverting officially sanctioned grand narratives and exalted literary techniques (his own included) he was making room for the reader, who, in the new non-teleological dispensation, becomes part of the text's conspiratorial hermeneutic process. And yet there is more to Steinbeck's participatory theory than I have thus far assayed. In the closing segment of this essay I will focus on another dimension of Steinbeck's new futuristic method in *Cannery Row*, his "escape" into the "clear thinking" of physics.

II. "A new world is growing under the old"

A Challenge/A Question

> What we observe is not nature itself, but nature exposed to our method of questioning.
>
> Werner Heisenberg, *Physics and Philosophy*

On 13 November 1939, besides lamenting that the novel was a worked-out genre, Steinbeck also told Sheffield, "[T]he real origin of the future" lies with physicists, who, "puzzled with order and disorder in quantum and neutron, build gradually" a new picture of order. "I have too a conviction that a new world is growing under the old, the way a new finger nail grows under a bruised one. . . . " Steinbeck didn't know what the form of the new would be, but he knew it would be "shaped by the new thinking" (*SLL* 194). Multi-layered *Cannery Row* benefitted from Steinbeck's excursions into scientific realms, and would exemplify Steinbeck's new form.[7] Indeed, the "new" was Steinbeck's code word for relativity theories, particle physics, and quantum mechanics, whose dizzyingly complex development in the previous forty years or so had disturbed the universe mightily and caused a severe break with classical, deterministic, Newtonian physics. Startling breakthroughs in the structure of micro-reality by the great visionary physicists Albert Einstein, Max Planck, Erwin Schrödinger, Niels Bohr, Werner Heisenberg and other pioneers in that era (not all of whom were in agreement) had not just scientific, but philosophical and cultural ramifications far beyond the rarefied world of the laboratory (Kragh 441, 449). Steinbeck's concept of participation and fictional form as a "field" of related energy units was aided and abetted by his explorations into the literature of new physics. Stephen Katz, who has studied the relationship of the new physics and reader-response criticism, has found both to be revisionist "expressions of a movement away from the formalistic, rationalistic epistemology embodied in Newtonian" world view, and proof of the possibility of bridging "humanistic and scientific disciplines . . . " (4–5). Steinbeck's formulation in "Argument of Phalanx"—"Art form is nature form"—has particular resonance here, for as Katz avers: "in New Physics and Reader Response Criticism the subjective process of reading nature and reading text seems to be similar . . . " (42).

That Steinbeck was aware of this conceptual linkage is evident in his correspondence. Steinbeck praised the technical achievements of "Schondringer [*sic*], Planck, Bohr, Einstein, Heisenberg," who were "all headed in the same direction," and he indicated that he was not only becoming familiar with their scientific projects, but considered them part of a combined effort (his own included) to ensure "the logical conclusion of my thesis" which is "exactly that destruction of boundaries."[8] Besides revolutionizing views of the material world and scientific paradigms in their own right, these discoveries had immediate philosophical and metaphorical charge (Jones). Concepts such as Bohr's so-called Theory of Complementarity (opposing, logically exclusive, seemingly incompatible entities, such as particles and waves, may be separately true at different times in a micro system) and Heisenberg's Uncertainty Principle (also known as Principle of Indeterminacy), formulated in 1927 (the velocity and location of an electron can't be measured at the same time) became part of the new matrix of thought for many American writers who reveled in their metaphoric potential (Scholnick 14), Steinbeck among them. In the "new epistemology," so termed by British astronomer Arthur S. Eddington in his 1927 Gifford Lectures, *The Nature of the Physical World* (a touchstone text quoted on several occasions in *The Log from the Sea of Cortez*), subjectivity, plurality, uncertainty, interrelatedness, participation of the measurer in the measuring process (in which the act of observation affects the object observed)—all became defining markers of the radical new world view. "The principle of indeterminacy is epistemological," Eddington states emphatically, and continues: "It reminds us once again that the world of physics is a world contemplated from within surveyed by appliances which are part of it and subject to its laws" (225).

In his marvelous book, *The Tao of Physics*, Fritjof Capra notes, for instance, that human consciousness becomes part of the process of observation in the new physics, and that observations are best understood in a context, a defining field of interrelated forces (140). The placement of *Cannery Row*'s narrator (and his readers) inside the "frame" of the narrative takes on a new significance when one considers Steinbeck's technique in light of physicist John Wheeler's statement: "Nothing is more important about the quantum principle than . . . that it destroys the concept of the world as 'sitting out there,' with the observer safely separated from it by a 20 centimeter slab of plate glass." To describe the conceptual change accurately, he continues, "one has to cross out that old word 'observer' and put in its place the new word 'participator.' In some strange sense the universe is a participatory universe" (qtd. in *Tao of Physics* 141).

The implications of quantum physics on *Cannery Row* are significant, and except for David Farrah's brief article, entirely unremarked upon. The Great Tide Pool Steinbeck takes us to in Chapter 6 is a major metaphor in *Cannery Row*, a window into a remarkable ecological world of biodiversity and marine difference, but the microcosmic site can also be seen as a contextual matrix/system of sub-human forces impinged upon by the narrative observer who cannot retain his "objectivity" (the octopus is described in freighted terms as a "creeping murderer"). Principles of indeterminacy can be seen in the many random, seemingly unplotted events that take place in the novel (Farrah 28). Characters enter and veer off in all directions, such as this moment in Chapter 11, when Steinbeck writes:

> Oh, the infinity of possibility! How could it happen that the car that picked up Gay broke down before it got into Monterey? If Gay had not been a mechanic, he would not have fixed the car. If he had not fixed it the owner wouldn't have taken him to Jimmy Brucia's for a drink. And why was it Jimmy's birthday? Out of

all the possibilities in the world—the millions of them—only events occurred that lead to the Salinas jail.... (66)

In a strictly naturalistic, deterministic world, or in a strictly realistic novel (if such a thing exists), these "unrelated, irrelevant details" would have no place; but in Steinbeck's quantum fictional landscape, coincidence and accident add their part to the overall "web of related discourses" (Strehle 19). In fact, it is possible to see, metaphorically anyway, complementarity operating in *Cannery Row*, not only in real life human beings (Red Williams) interacting with fictional (Hazel, Henri) or quasi-fictional ones (Doc, Mack), but also the larger design of chapter organization, in which the causality of Doc's birthday party plot is disrupted with the equally important, though digressive and non-sequential episodes. While these elements are superficially or apparently oppositional, and perhaps even seemingly incompatible, the fact is in Steinbeck's expanding quantum universe they complement each other in a dimensional literary structure where space (digressive chapters) and time (plot chapters) not only create a simultaneous command on our attention as readers, but for full integrative effect require our "imaginative engagement" with the text to complete the experience: "There is no such thing as an objective observer or reader in an interconnected universe, even in the fictive one of *Cannery Row*" (Farrah 23, 25).[9]

In *The Cosmic Web* N. Katherine Hayles remarks that "[t]he twentieth century has seen a profound transformation in the ground of its thought, a change catalyzed and validated by relativity theory, quantum mechanics, and particle physics." But the shift in perspective, she continues, "was by no means confined to physics; analogous developments have occurred in a number of disciplines, among them philosophy, linguistics, mathematics, and literature" (15). In *Cannery Row*, Steinbeck drew deeply from this historical moment of radical change. Steinbeck was one of the few major novelists of his era to participate in the discourse of the new sciences, to assimilate their spirit, and to employ congruent philosophical attitudes, beliefs, procedures from allied areas. Whether they came from anthropology, psychology, philosophy, marine science, or physics, in their metaphoric immediacy such concepts as participation, carnivalization, indeterminacy, and complimentarity all allowed Steinbeck to exceed imposed limits, to transgress and reconfigure boundaries, to bring the margins toward the center.

In the long run, that achievement may have been precisely what allowed Steinbeck to "outlast" so many other modern writers (Owens "Where Things Can Happen" 154). Steinbeck's achievement can be understood to have been partly predicated on his ability to interrelate literature and science—two traditionally oppositional cognitive and intellectual disciplines— and to traverse the otherwise contested "permeable boundaries" between the two discourses, so as to mutually inform "their interaction" within our culture (Scholnick 3; Barthes 4). Steinbeck's intertextual gambit, his discovery of "a great poetry in scientific thinking" (Fensch Steinbeck and Covici 31; SLL 232), points up a paradox, because if Steinbeck's adoption of scientific elements in his writings put him at risk with many established literary critics and influential cultural taste-makers such as Edmund Wilson and Clifton Fadiman (McElrath, Crisler, Shillinglaw 183–87; 204–05; Benson "Novelist as Scientist" 15), his "interdisciplinary habit of mind" may have been the very move, the definable "difference," that allowed Steinbeck to be "unique" by allowing him to appeal to a much wider reading public than many other fictionists of his time (Beegel, Shillinglaw, Tiffney 20; Railsback 7).

Steinbeck's admission, a kind of New Deal–inspired belief, that his "whole work drive has been aimed at making people understand each other" (WD xl) has relevance here, as do the affective dimensions of his preference for "symbol people," and "psychological sign language" (JN 27), as well as the far-reaching theoretical implications of considering his fiction as being essentially fabular (French and Kidd 199; Jones 10–11), which is to say, considering his texts as participatory parables that aim "to involve the reader in the story and to make the story live in the reader" (Timmerman 7). "The Word" does indeed "suck up" everything on Cannery Row/Cannery Row (17), including its readers, so that the place we have arrived at is not an absolute destination, but a way station in the indeterminate border country between culture and nature, writing and speech, fiction and science. Reading *Cannery Row,* then, is nothing less than an entrance into a "radically different system" (*LSC* 118). Even those of us who have participated in the discourse on/of Steinbeck, those of us who have been complicit in constructing an evolving narrative of cultural/literary identity, can still be challenged by the places Steinbeck traveled in his effort to uncover a nonhierarchical related field, a place where "everything is an index of everything else" (*LSC* 213). But the real challenge now and in years to come is to revise our portrait of Steinbeck the humanist, Steinbeck the social chronicler, Steinbeck the popular icon, by adding these new colors: Steinbeck the quantum mechanic, Steinbeck the conceptual thinker, Steinbeck the ecologist, Steinbeck the metaphorist. Who would have thought it?

Notes

Chapter 2. *The Ghost of Tom Joad*

1. In 1988, two years before *Human Touch,* Springsteen acknowledged his debt to Guthrie by contributing to *Folkways: A Vision Shared,* a tribute album to Guthrie and his sometime musical partner, Leadbelly.

2. Cullen points out that "Streets of Philadelphia" is a telling landmark in that it was commissioned. Springsteen, suggests Cullen, "may well have regarded tailoring a piece of music for someone else's purposes beneath him at an earlier point in his career" (192).

3. Dale Maharidge, cited by Cullen, is quoted in Tom Schoenberg. Nicholas Dawidoff's cover story is also cited by Cullen.

4. See John Dos Passos "Joe Hill" in *USA.* The same paradox existed for the movie, of course. As Bluestone notes, on one hand you had a reporter "poking fun at the grandiose premiere," attended not only "by glamorous stars adorned in jewels and furs" but "by the representatives of the very banks and land companies that had tractored the Joads off their farms." On the other hand, you had "the industry's discomfort" because the adaptation of Steinbeck's book "came as close as any film in Hollywood's prolific turnout to exposing the contradictions and inequities at the heart of American life" (Bluestone 168).

5. See Sandford 378–79. Springsteen has never been averse to interspersing his songs with exposition. But while this tended to be personal and anecdotal in earlier years, more recently it has reflected his evident sense of himself as an artist in the Steinbeck mold. Sandford records *Los Angeles Times* reporter Mark Arax witnessing Springsteen making "a pitch for the plight of migrant farm-hands" at a Fresno concert. Such exposition did not go down too well in Fresno. "Despite

several pleas from the stage, not a single cent was collected for their cause among the audience. A handful of fans even asked for—and were given—their ticket money back. Later, Springsteen wrote the local workers' union a personal cheque."

Chapter 3. Changing Perceptions of Homelessness

1. Labor Secretary Frances Perkins also visited the homeless migrants and, even though she had not read Steinbeck's novel, she quoted it during her comments praising the migrants. Many other groups and individuals toured the valley on fact-finding missions and returned to fulfill people's curiosity about migrant living conditions.

2. Estimates of the numbers of homeless migrants in the state were as high as 500,000. Although it was not possible to accurately count the homeless population, Works Progress Administration statistics revealed that California contained a disproportionately high number of homeless persons compared to other states. In 1935 California contained 13.8 percent of all the needy transients in the nation, yet in 1930 California comprised only 4.7 percent of the country's entire population (California State Chamber of Commerce).

3. The public discussion of homeless migrants occurred in a variety of forums, including the mass media, government reports and hearings, and community meetings.

4. Other reformers and artists, of course, also had an important impact on perceptions of the migrants. Shindo provides skillful explanation and analysis of the contributions of Paul Taylor (an economist and reformer), Dorothea Lange, John Ford, Woody Guthrie, Robert Sonkin (a folklorist), Charles Todd (a folklorist), and the Farm Security Administration photographic project.

5. The British were certainly not alone in their tendency to fear and disdain the transient outsider. Indeed, this custom permeates Western society. The treatment of gypsies throughout Europe testifies to this fact. Yet, the British had the most direct impact on the United States, providing the framework for American thought and legal and institutional systems dealing with homeless transients. For comprehensive discussions of homelessness in England and the United States, see Crouse, Miller, and Simon.

6. In a 1936 report, the California State Relief Administration acknowledged that in California in the mid-1800s "when public assistance became necessary all new comers were excluded according to the pattern of the English Poor Law at the time of Elizabeth" (5).

7. Politicians capitalized on fears of the homeless and squatters to

appeal to voters. In a 1934 media-based campaign to defeat the socialist Democratic gubernatorial candidate, Upton Sinclair, Republicans accused Sinclair of attracting transients and squatters into the state with his social welfare proposals. For a thorough account of the campaign, see Mitchell.

8. See also Hendricks (461) and Darton.

9. Tom Collins disputed the choice of the term "gypsies" in the title of Steinbeck's collection, saying that he was "stunned by the title" and abhorred "labels of any kind attached to humans, especially the under privileged" (Collins, "Report . . . October 24, 1936"). Collins absolved Steinbeck of guilt for the choice of the title, but he cut the word "gypsy" out of the copies of the book that he distributed to Arvin camp residents. The Arvin Camp Committee and Collins wrote a letter to Steinbeck thanking him for the articles and recognizing the importance of eloquent advocates on their behalf: "We think you did a fine job for us and we thank you. This is a big battle which cannot be won by ourselfs. We kneed friends like you to help us get decent camp places" (Collins, "Report . . . October 24, 1936").

10. For further discussion of Jeffersonian small farmers and the agrarian myth in *The Grapes of Wrath*, see Eisinger (46–57).

11. McWilliams later explained that the consecutive publication of the books was not planned. McWilliams never met Steinbeck, but they shared the broader public fascination with the migrants (McWilliams, *Factories* ix–x).

12. Of course many other people, aside from McWilliams, came to the defense of Steinbeck's novel, including Eleanor Roosevelt who said she had seen and held in her hand the fliers urging migrants to come to California ("State Lucky").

13. Representing a sizable group of farmers who challenged the accuracy of McWilliams' book, Roy Pike charged that a list of all the factual inaccuracies would be too long and tiresome to detail.

Chapter 5. Propaganda and Persuasion in John Steinbeck's *The Moon Is Down*

1. See especially Donald Coers, Jackson Benson, and Roy Simmons for valuable information concerning the production and reception of the book in the United States and Europe.

2. Peter Lisca, Richard Astro, Lester Marks, Warren French, Howard Levant, John Timmerman, and others like Robert Morsberger have provided useful contextual insight into the book's form and genesis.

3. Peter Lisca, for example, claims the book fails as art because

"it carries stylization beyond the limits where it concerns us" (196). Richard Astro calls *The Moon Is Down* a "quasi-fictional philosophical debate" that unsuccessfully relates "abstract philosophical vision to concrete reality" (150). For Howard Levant, the novel contains a three-part theatrical structure that presents characters as flat generalizations or types (146–48). In addition, John Timmerman observes that the "repetitively short sentences" in the work reveal a "failure of language and stylistic technique" (184–85). And even Donald Coers, whose *John Steinbeck as Propagandist* gives the most thoroughly researched account of the novel's impact on Nazi-occupied Europe, says little about Steinbeck's actual propaganda technique.

4. Philosophically, the mayor-as-idea also affords a convenient rhetorical vehicle for Steinbeck to articulate his theory of groups, particularly his belief that everything, man included, is ultimately part of a single organism (*SLL* 79; Ross 173). In *The Moon Is Down*, for instance, the notion gets expressed using "free men" like Orden to embody what Steinbeck elsewhere describes as "non-teleological" or integrative impulses (see *LSC* 115, 136).

Chapter 8. "Consonant Symphonies"

1. *Cup of Gold*, according to Fontenrose (10), is a story that skillfully uses three legends—the Grail, the Trojan and Faust—to emphasize heroic quest, shattered dreams and unattainable ambitions. *In Dubious Battle* is a blend of the Grail legend and the battle waged by Satan against God. The Exodus, the Gospel story and St. Paul's story of the New Testament, along with the Monistic concept of the *Vedas* have been syncretically combined in *The Grapes of Wrath*. See also Pratt 13–14.

2. As for the green rock discovered by Joseph in a pine grove, Western critics have generally perceived it as a symbol of great significance. Leiber regards it as a protective symbol (266–67); Le Master sees the rock as a Grail symbol (10).

3. Joseph tells Juanito, "Elizabeth once told me of a man who ran away from the old Fates. He clung to an altar where he was safe" (168). Orestes in a Greek myth was pursued by the Furies, but he never "clung to an altar." In the context of Steinbeck's interest in ancient Hindu texts, it is probable that he alludes to the Indian legend of *Markandeya*. Destined to die at the age of sixteen, Markandeya clung to the main deity in a Shiva temple when pursued by the corps of the god of death with the noose. At the critical moment, Lord Shiva appeared on the scene and not only saved the youth from death, but granted him

the boon of everlasting youth. Thus, the name Markandeya has come to mean 'evergreen' in all Indian languages.

4. *Rama*, the Hindu God-incarnation, the hero of the epic *The Ramayana*, is a male and a model for many virtues. Steinbeck, however, in a syncretic exercise, names the wife of Thomas so. A similarity might be noted. Cf. "The laws of Rama never changed, bad was bad and bad was punished, and good was eternally, delightfully good. It was delicious to be good in Rama's house" (20).

5. The main form of Lord Shiva is the *Lingam*, a pear-shaped smooth rock, cylindrical, and rounded off at the top, rising from a circular bed. The divine vehicle of this God is a hornless bull, called the *Nandi*. Huge carvings of the *Lingam* and the *Nandi* in black granite can be found in some ancient temples of South India.

Chapter 9. Living In(tension)ally

1. Lisca's original insights into the *Tao*'s relationship to *Cannery Row* can also be found in a special 1975 issue of *San Jose Studies* edited by Arlene Okerlund, in an article entitled "*Cannery Row* and *Tao Teh Ching*."

2. Other scholars who have suggested the influence of Eastern philosophy on Steinbeck include Tsuneko Iwase, Soiku Shigematsu, M. R. Satayanarayana, Mashkoor Ali Syed and Malithat Promathatavedi. Several of these authors' speculations are included in *John Steinbeck: Asian Perspectives*.

3. Similar readings of *The Tao* can be found on pages 59 and 66 of the Mitchell translation and include Chapters 57 and 64 of the manuscript. Line numbers of *The Tao* have not been cited since they vary, based on the translator's interpretation of the original Chinese. Readers of older translations will also note a difference in the numbering of the chapters of *The Tao*. This dual numbering system is based on the fact that earlier translations cannot take into account the finding of the Ma-Wang-tui manuscripts in 1973 in which the two major sections of *The Tao* were found in reverse order. Hence translations relying on the newer archeological find will encounter a different numbering system than those translations that were composed previous to its discovery. The citations here are based on the Mitchell translation and the 1973 manuscript.

4. See also Steinbeck's comments about collaboration in *Journal of a Novel* (76).

5. See Kevin Hearle, "The Boat Shaped Mind," for more detail on Steinbeck's use of language.

Chapter 15. Beyond the Boundaries of Sexism

1. See Erich Neumann, *The Great Mother*, for a thorough discussion of the archetype. See also Lorelei Cederstrom, "The 'Great Mother' in *The Grapes of Wrath*" which describes Steinbeck's extensive use of this archetype in another context.

2. This discussion of the archetypal Green Man is based on Anderson and Hicks' *Green Man: The Archetype of Our Oneness with the Earth*, and Frazer's *The Golden Bough*. Jay Parini in *John Steinbeck: A Biography* notes Steinbeck's reading of several mythological sources, including Frazer. He writes: "[Steinbeck] had been reading James Frazer's *The Golden Bough* . . . and he was familiar with the primitive vegetation myths and tales of the dying and reviving god" (181).

3. I share with Joseph Fontenrose a confusion over the distinction that Steinbeck makes between the teleological process of discovering an answer to What? or Why? and the answer to the non-teleological How? (91).

4. Jungian psychologists Anne and Barry Ulanov have detailed many of the complexities of anima projection, including those in which Adam Trask is enmeshed. They write: "If a man tends to project all the power of his anima onto a woman, resisting the task of examining it in himself, he may find he has endowed the female with witchlike powers and fall completely under her spell. He has identified her with his projected anima image" (91). However, since Adam Trask is forced into the recognition of his projection and withdraws that projection consciously, Cathy still retains her unconscious hold over him and his anima remains unassimilated.

Chapter 16. *Of Mice and Men*

1. Judith Crist was a guest for a film festival at the University of Texas at El Paso in the early eighties. We were discussing Boorman's *Excalibur* when she made this observation to me. Since that time, whenever I am watching a period piece, I am struck by the perspicacity of her remark. It seems particularly apt in terms of this text.

2. My thanks to Albert Wong for making the illustrative drawings, taken from relevant scenes in the videos of these three productions. Though I would have liked to reproduce stills from the films, permission costs are prohibitive.

3. One marked difference is the addition of the character of Aunt Clara who is only spoken about in the Milestone original and in Stein-

beck's text. In the Blake version, a scene where George and Lennie visit with Aunt Clara comes early in the script. The scene illustrates the close bond between the dissimilar men. George tries to leave Lennie with Aunt Clara, but cannot. E. Nick Alexander is given credit for the teleplay.

4. Marilyn Monroe was the prototype for a new kind of sex-goddess. Unlike her femme fatale predecessors, Marilyn projected a wraithlike image. She looked seductive and voluptuous, even hard, but the minute she opened her mouth, she communicated helplessness and vulnerability. One of her signature songs was her sensuous rendition of "My Heart Belongs to Daddy." Gloria Steinem comments on the critical praise Monroe elicited for acting "babyishly seductive" (119).

5. In her chapter on seductive imagery, Ruth Rubinstein notes that in the 1800s and 1900s sexual liaisons between older men and young females were satirized and discouraged, but that in the 1950s "the vulnerable look" as an alluring image initiated by men was legitimized (118–19). Audrey Hepburn, whose body was adolescent and boyish, was seen as a seductive ideal. The baby doll look was the accompanying fashion. Rubinstein also notes that since the 1950s our society has "sexualized the 'childlike' look" (121). The globalization of this infantilization of sexuality is further evidenced by a 1997 *New York Times* story from Japan: "A Plain School Uniform is the Latest Aphrodisiac." This story reports that schoolgirl uniforms are the latest turn-on for Japanese businessmen who frequent the brothels in Tokyo.

6. Rubinstein defines clothing semiotics as a "language" of clothing derived from "the storehouse of images," in our Western history and "significant only when used in a specific social context" (7).

7. Christine Gledhill also argues that films present us with a version of woman that we, as female spectators, must reject because of the "ideology privileged as the film's 'message'" (115).

8. Laura Mulvey's influential article established the priority that classic American film gives to the male perspective, both narratively and visually. She shifted the questions of gender in film from the representations on the screen to the psychodynamic between spectator and screen.

Chapter 17. Beyond Evil

1. According to Richard Lee Hayman, of the National Steinbeck Center in Salinas, California, the character of Cathy/Kate is modeled after a combination of someone Steinbeck knew in Salinas at one time,

and his second wife, Gwendolyn Conger Steinbeck. Robert DeMott writes, "Through another imaginative, linguistic investiture that compensated for his real-life experience, Steinbeck reprised his tumultuous marriage to Gwyn in the pathetic *Burning Bright* and went a long way toward exorcising his memory of her in the devastating portrait of the evil, conscienceless Cathy Ames in *East of Eden*" (Hayashi, *JS: The Years of Greatness* 44–45).

2. In an article entitled "The Neglected Rib: Women in *East of Eden*," Beth Everest and Judy Wedeles conclude that Kate's bitterness comes from her dealing with men like Mr. Edwards, who somehow manages to manipulate her. She punishes men simply for their maleness and finds them most vulnerable when sexually aroused. She is able to manipulate men because she sees their weaknesses (20).

Chapter 18. Cathy in *East of Eden*

1. Peter Lisca, a pioneer Steinbeck researcher, for instance, reads the novel as the story of the two families, and he finds it a failure: "the Trasks and the Hamiltons pursue separate courses, and nothing results from their juxtaposition" (265). Warren French also regards the novel as centered on two families, claiming that "rather than counterpointing each other, however, the two stories clash" (151–52). For Richard Astro, *East of Eden* is nothing more than "an epic study of three generations of the two families" (207). Though Lester Jay Marks and Paul McCarthy consider it a successful novel, neither acknowledges the importance of Cathy's story (Marks 116; McCarthy 118–24). Barbara A. Heavilin studies the novel's basis of good and evil, emphasizing "the balance between the enormity of Cathy's wickedness, . . . and the goodness of the Hamilton women" (95).

Chapter 19. These Are American People

1. His admiration for Mexicans and Mexican Americans is clear in *To a God Unknown, The Long Valley, The Forgotten Village, The Log from the Sea of Cortez, The Pearl, The Wayward Bus* and *Viva Zapata!* Similarly, his affection for the mixed race paisanos is evident throughout *Tortilla Flat*, and his respect for the Chinese-American Lee in *East of Eden* is no less obvious. Although these depictions probably no longer qualify as ideals of racial sensitivity, Steinbeck's racial attitudes were progressive for their time.

2. Ritter Volume I, 89, 333–36, 353–57. Strangely enough, Ritter de-

votes many pages to blaming German social Darwinists for World War I in language which manages to condemn eugenic leanings while at the same time seeming to make it part of the German racial heritage. That this ignores the early 20th century dominance of eugenics by Americans (Degler 41–46) is intriguing. It is also interesting that neither "biology" nor "philosophy" on page 356 is capitalized; however, "Eugenics" on page 89 is.

3. Of the "scientist" authors who influenced Steinbeck, William Emerson Ritter and John Elof Boodin are the two who seem to take the notion of blood as a racial entity most seriously, but their statements on the matter either display a fair degree of ambivalence or are ambiguous. Ritter notes the then recent discovery that blood from one animal is incompatible with blood from another animal (Volume I, 100–101), but his rather loose use of the term "race" makes it difficult to know if he is referring to eugenics or, if he is, to measure his tone toward eugenics, when he states, "Its [the incompatibility of blood from different species] bearings on problems of affinity and racial descent, for example, have elicited their due of interest" (I, 100). If Ritter means "racial descent" to designate separate races of humanity here—and it is by no means certain that is his intention—does "their due of interest" indicate that eugenics is owed serious attention or that eugenics has already received as much attention, if not more, than it deserves? There is little, if any, basis for preferring one interpretation of that sentence over another.

With John Elof Boodin, there is still another difficulty. For Boodin, blood appears to be an agent of inheritance and may even be racialized; however, Boodin doesn't privilege "white blood." Instead, Boodin accepts the distinction between so-called "primitive peoples" and "civilization" and then proposes the possibility (He emphasizes the conditionality of his proposition by using "if" twice in the statement of the idea) that civilized life, because it tends to offer "abstract" stimuli rather than the more "immediate" stimuli of primitive life, is the least healthy condition of the two (167).

Chapter 20. The Global Appeal of Steinbeck's Science

1. After Balaam beat his donkey three times "The Lord opened the donkey's mouth, and she said to Balaam 'What have I done to you to make you beat me these three times?' Balaam answered the donkey, 'you have made a fool of me! If I had a sword in my hand, I would kill

you right now.' The donkey said to Balaam, 'Am I not your own donkey, which you have always ridden, to this day? Have I been in the habit of doing this to you?' 'No,' said Balaam" (Numbers 22).

2. C.O.Y.O.T.E. (Call Off your Old Tired Ethics) is a support organization for prostitutes founded in Seattle and San Francisco in 1973 by Margo St. James.

Chapter 23. The Place We Have Arrived

1. My work on Steinbeck has long been encouraged by Warren French, who has challenged me year after year to "arrive again." I thank him for many years of stalwart friendship, lively conversation, and critical insight. This essay is one of three related critical narratives in progress on aspects of Steinbeck's writing imagery. The others are on *The Grapes of Wrath* as ecological text, and the poetics of presence in Steinbeck's journals.

2. "Reader" is a term I use here loosely as a hybrid amalgam of actual, hypothetical, implied readers and "narratees" to whom I have attributed a cheerful, rather than hyper-critical or hyper-skeptical attitude. I am not concerned with the ideological particularities or hairsplitting distinctions of and among different methods of audience-oriented interpretative strategies, but rather I am interested in *reading back* on Steinbeck the general, symbolic implications of reader-centered criticism's cumulative effect: "all reader-response criticism has shared in shifting attention from the inherent, objective characteristics of the text to the engagement of the reader with the text, and the production of textual meaning by the reader" (Childers and Hentzi 253).

3. Passages on cause-and-effect reasoning and naive acceptance of the *post hoc, ergo propter hoc* fallacy in the exploration of non-teleology which appear in the "Easter Sunday" chapter of *The Log from the Sea of Cortez* (116–17) bear a striking resemblance with Levy-Bruhl's prominent statements on that same reasoning fallacy and on related naive causal relations. Especially pertinent is Levy-Bruhl's tone throughout *How Natives Think*—he is never condescending toward primitive world views, but posits the need to understand difference and otherness as a primary effect; certainly this dimension is apparent throughout Steinbeck's works.

4. Steinbeck's 1933 letter to George Albee, which is 3¼ typed pages long, appears in edited form in *Steinbeck: A Life in Letters* (79–82). The published version excludes a number of Steinbeck's statements on,

among other things, the phalanx artist's role, and for that reason I refer to the original text of the letter from here on.

5. Written in Steinbeck's hand, "Introduction by Pascal Covici" is 2½ pages long and is accompanied by a 26-line handwritten letter from Steinbeck, composed in September 1942 from Sherman Oaks, California, where Steinbeck and his soon-to-be second wife, Gwyn, were living. "I have a little time today," Steinbeck wrote Covici, "and will take a crack at this introduction you asked me to do. Don't know how it will be but I'll give it a try. . . . There I finished it and I hope it is what you want." Both documents are in the Covici collection at the Harry Ransom Humanities Research Center, University of Texas, Austin.

6. Although it has not been my angle here, an alternate and less overtly pleasurable analysis of *Cannery Row* is possible for the resisting reader who approaches Steinbeck's text from perspectives of ethnicity, race, and/or gender.

7. The letters, sources, and texts scholars such as Richard Astro and Brian Railsback have employed to demonstrate Steinbeck's immersion in evolutionary biology indicate that, in constructing his phalanx thesis, Steinbeck also boned up on other branches of scientific discourse, including mathematics, especially the work of Paul Dirac, and that he was dipping into literature about contemporary physics as early as 1929 when, after reading Edward U. Condon and Philip M. Morse's theoretically detailed and equation-heavy *Quantum Mechanics*, Steinbeck told Robert Cathcart, "I have been having a good bit of fun," though he admitted to not understanding the theories even in their "primer for the man in the street stage" (qtd. in DeMott, *Steinbeck's Reading* 28). Steinbeck's claim that "the only true poets are found among the physicists, mathematicians and biochemists," which was quoted by Stanley Brodwin as an epigram to his excellent essay on *Sea of Cortez* (142), again reveals a wider interest on Steinbeck's part in branches of science than has been acknowledged. In the decade following his admission to Cathcart, Steinbeck seems to have remedied his deficiencies not so much in the realm of hard, practical science, but in the philosophical and metaphoric implications of the new physics. Nuclear chemist Peter Englert argues that in *Sea of Cortez* Steinbeck and Ricketts's "use of terms borrowed from quantum mechanics, relativity theory, and field theory is doubtful in many respects" (186), but he also finds value in the authors' approach: "one can cross boundaries of traditionally separate subject areas with an ease that facilitates in-

novative discussion. Such openness can lead to speculation as well as to simplified statement, but the risk is worthwhile" (192). In *The Epistemic Music of Rhetoric*, Katz considers crossing boundaries between literature and science as a kind of "imperative," which "underlie[s] the nature and pursuit of knowledge across disciplines and constitute[s] cultural ways of knowing" (20).

8. Steinbeck wrote this letter to Carlton Sheffield on 30 June 1933, but unfortunately the section I quote was excised in the published version *(Steinbeck: A Life in Letters* 78). The original is in Stanford University's Department of Special Collections (Riggs 80).

9. The fullest explanation of Steinbeck's ordering of plot and digressive chapters in the manuscript, typescript, and published text of *Cannery Row* (they differ) occurs in Simmonds (321–22). Given the novel's elastic form, in which all chapters (each their own quanta of energy) are supposed to fit equally into the overall (though ultimately incomplete) design of the novel, one puzzle remains, and that is why Steinbeck took out a chapter called "The Day the Wolves Ate the Vice Principal" (Simmonds calls it a "self-contained short story"), which was later published independently in *'47 Magazine of the Year.* Editor Susan Shillinglaw states that thematically the interchapter fits the novel "seamlessly" *(Fiftieth Anniversary* 10). She proposes several reasons why Steinbeck might have omitted the chapter, but they remain conjectural.

Bibliography

Principal Collections

Bancroft Library, University of California, Berkeley, California.
Bracken Library, Ball State University, Muncie, Indiana.
Center for Steinbeck Studies, San José State University, California.
Columbia University, New York, New York.
Humanities Research Center, University of Texas, Austin, Texas.
National Steinbeck Center, Salinas, California.
Pierpont Morgan Library, New York, New York.
Stanford University Library, Stanford, California.
University of Virginia Library, Charlottesville, Virginia.

Published Works by John Steinbeck

Editors' Note: Whenever possible, the works of John Steinbeck are
cited from the Twentieth Century Classics editions of Steinbeck
texts.
The Acts of King Arthur and His Noble Knights. Ed. Chase Horton. New
York: Farrar, Straus, and Giroux, 1976.
America and Americans. New York: Viking, 1966.
Burning Bright: A Play in Story Form. 1950. New York: Penguin, 1994.
Burning Bright: Play in Three Acts, Acting Edition. New York: Dramatists
Play Service, 1951.
Cannery Row. 1945. New York: Penguin, 1994.
Conversations with John Steinbeck. Ed. Thomas Fensch. Jackson: UP of
Mississippi, 1986.
"Critics, Critics, Burning Bright." *Saturday Review* 33 (11 Nov. 1950):

20–21. Rpt. in *Steinbeck and His Critics: A Record of Twenty-Five Years.* Eds. E. W. Tedlock, Jr., and C. V. Wicker. Albuquerque: U of New Mexico P, 1957. 43–47.

Cup of Gold. 1929. New York: Penguin, 1995.

East of Eden. 1952. New York: Penguin, 1992.

The Forgotten Village. New York: Viking, 1941.

The Grapes of Wrath. 1939. New York: Penguin, 1992.

The Harvest Gypsies. 1936. Berkeley: Heyday, 1988.

In Dubious Battle. 1936. New York: Penguin, 1992.

Journal of a Novel: The East of Eden *Letters.* 1969. New York: Penguin, 1990.

The Log from the Sea of Cortez. 1951. New York: Penguin, 1995.

The Long Valley. 1938. New York: Penguin, 1995.

The Moon Is Down. 1942. New York: Penguin, 1995.

The Moon Is Down: A Play. New York: Dramatists Play Service, 1942.

Of Mice and Men. 1937. New York: Penguin, 1994.

Of Mice and Men: A Play in Three Acts. New York: Covici-Friede, 1937; rpt. Kyoto: Rinsen, 1985.

"My Short Novels." Tedlock and Wicker 38–40.

"The Novel Might Benefit by the Discipline, the Terseness of the Drama." *Stage* 15 (1938): 50–51.

Once There Was a War. 1958. New York: Penguin, 1994.

The Pastures of Heaven. 1932. New York: Penguin, 1995.

The Pearl. 1945. New York: Penguin, 1994.

A Russian Journal. 1948. New York: Penguin, 1999.

Sea of Cortez: A Leisurely Journal of Travel and Research. Edward F. Ricketts. New York: Viking, 1941.

The Short Reign of Pippin IV. 1957. New York: Penguin, 1994.

"The Soul and Guts of France." *Collier's* 30 Aug. 1952: 26–30.

Speech Accepting the Nobel Prize for Literature. New York: Viking, 1962.

Steinbeck: A Life in Letters. 1975. Eds. Elaine Steinbeck and Robert Wallsten. New York: Viking, 1989.

"Suggestion for an Interview with Joseph Henry Jackson." *The Grapes of Wrath: Text and Criticism.* Ed. Peter Lisca with Kevin Hearle. Viking Critical Library. Updated edition. New York: Penguin, 1997. 640–43.

Sweet Thursday. 1954. New York: Penguin, 1998.

"The Time the Wolves Ate the Vice-Principal." *'47 Magazine of the Year* Mar. 1947: 26–27. Rpt. in *The Steinbeck Newsletter* 9.1 (1995): 10.

To a God Unknown. 1933. New York: Penguin, 1995.

Tortilla Flat. 1935. New York: Penguin, 1997.

Travels with Charley in Search of America. 1962. New York: Penguin, 1997.
Un Américan à New York et à Paris. Trans. Jean-François Rozan. Paris: René Julliard, 1956.
The Wayward Bus. 1947. New York: Penguin 1995.
The Winter of Our Discontent. 1961. New York: Penguin 1996.
Working Days: The Journals of The Grapes of Wrath, *1938–1941.* Ed. Robert DeMott. New York: Viking, 1989.
Viva Zapata! Ed. Robert Morsberger. New York: Viking, 1975.

Published Works about John Steinbeck

Astro, Richard. *John Steinbeck and Edward F. Ricketts: The Shaping of a Novelist.* Minneapolis: U of Minnesota P, 1973.
"Auto Trek to Check 'Grapes of Wrath.'" *San Francisco Chronicle* 5 Nov. 1939: n. pag.
Bakersfield Californian 21 Sept. 1936: n. pag.
Beegel, Susan F., Susan Shillinglaw, and Wesley N. Tiffney, Jr., eds. *Steinbeck and the Environment: Interdisciplinary Approaches.* Tuscaloosa: U of Alabama P, 1997.
Benson, Jackson. "John Steinbeck's *Cannery Row:* A Reconsideration." *Western American Literature* 12 (1977): 11–40. Rpt. as "*Cannery Row* and Steinbeck as Spokesman for the Folk Tradition," Benson, *Short Novels,* 132–42.
——, ed. *The Short Novels of John Steinbeck: Critical Essays with a Checklist of Steinbeck Criticism.* Durham, NC: Duke UP, 1990. 132–42.
——. "The Novelist as Scientist." *Novel: A Forum on Fiction* 10 (1977): 248–64.
——. *The True Adventures of John Steinbeck, Writer.* New York: Viking, 1984.
Bloom, Harold, ed. Introduction. *John Steinbeck: Modern Critical Views.* New York: Chelsea House, 1987.
Brodwin, Stanley. "'The Poetry of Scientific Thinking': Steinbeck's *Log from the Sea of Cortez* and Scientific Travel Narrative." Beegel, Shillinglaw, and Tiffney 142–60.
Cassuto, David. "Turning Wine into Water: Water as Privileged Signifier in *The Grapes of Wrath.*" Beegel, Shillinglaw, and Tiffney 55–75.
Cederstrom, Lorelei. "The 'Great Mother' in *The Grapes of Wrath.*" *Steinbeck and the Environment.* Beegel, Shillinglaw, and Tiffney 76–91.
Chamberlain, John. "The New Books." *Harper's* Dec. 1941: n. pag.
Choi, Jin Young. "Steinbeck Studies in Korea." Nakayama, *Asian Perspectives,* 19–25.

Coers, Donald V. *John Steinbeck as Propagandist:* The Moon is Down *Goes to War.* Tuscaloosa: U of Alabama P, 1991.

"Congress May Help the Joads If Hue and Cry Continues." *San Francisco News* 8 Apr. 1940: n. pag.

Covici, Pascal, ed. *The Portable Steinbeck.* Enlarged Edition. New York: Viking, 1946.

Cox, Martha H. "Steinbeck's *Burning Bright.*" Ed. Tetsumaro Hayashi. *A Study Guide to Steinbeck (Part II).* Metuchen, N.J.: Scarecrow, 1979. 46–62.

DeMott, Robert. *Steinbeck's Reading: A Catalogue of Books Owned and Borrowed.* New York: Garland, 1984.

———. *Steinbeck's Typewriter: Essays on His Art.* Troy, NY: Whitston, 1996.

———, ed. *Working Days: The Journals of* The Grapes of Wrath. New York: Viking, 1989.

Ditsky, John. *John Steinbeck and the Critics.* Rochester, NY: Camden House, 2000.

Duman, Jill. "Searching for Steinbeck." *Coast Weekly* 4 Aug. 1994: 10, 12–13, 15.

Eden no Higashi [East of Eden]. Produced by Takarazuka Revue Company. Takarazuka. 1995.

Eisinger, Chester E. "Jeffersonian Agrarianism in *The Grapes of Wrath.*" *University of Kansas City Review* XIV (Winter 1947): 149–54.

Englert, Peter A. J. "Education of Environmental Scientists: Should We Listen to Steinbeck and Ricketts's Comments?" Beegel, Shillinglaw, and Tiffney 176–93.

Everest, Beth, and Judy Wedels. "The Neglected Rib: Women in *East of Eden.*" *Steinbeck Quarterly* 21.1–2 (1988): 13–23.

Farrah, David. "'The Form of the New' in Steinbeck's *Cannery Row.*" *Shoin Literary Review* 25 (1992): 21–30.

Fensch, Thomas, ed. *Steinbeck and Covici: The Story of a Friendship.* Middlebury, Vermont: Paul S. Eriksson, 1979.

Fiedler, Leslie. "Looking Back After 50 Years," *San Jose Studies* 16.1 (1990): 54–64.

Fontenrose, Joseph. *John Steinbeck: An Introduction and Interpretation.* New York: Barnes and Noble, 1963.

French, Warren. *John Steinbeck.* New York: Twayne, 1961.

———. *John Steinbeck's Fiction Revisited.* New York: Twayne, 1994.

———. Introduction. *In Dubious Battle.* John Steinbeck. New York: Penguin, 1992.

Garcia, Reloy. Introduction. Hayashi, *Study Guide,* 4–5.

Garner, Jack. "'Of Mice and Men' Touches the Heart." *Gannett News Service* 15 Oct. 1992.

George, Stephen K. "Of Vice and Men: A Virtue Ethics Study of Steinbeck's *The Pearl, East of Eden*, and *The Winter of Our Discontent*." Diss. Ball State U, 1995. UMI, 1995. 9538187.

Gladstein, Mimi Reisel. "Abra: The Indestructible Woman in *East of Eden*." Bloom, *John Steinbeck*: 151–53.

———. *The Indestructible Woman in Faulkner, Hemingway, and Steinbeck*. Ann Arbor, Michigan: UMI Research P, 1986.

———. "The Strong Female Principle of Good—or Evil: The Women of *East of Eden*." *Steinbeck Quarterly* 24 (1991): 30–40.

"'The Grapes of Wrath' Yield Golden Wine." *San Francisco News* 7 Jul. 1939: n. pag.

Hashimoto, Izo. *Eden no Higashi [East of Eden]*. Final Script. Tokyo: TBS, 1997.

Hatsukanezumi to Ningen [Of Mice and Men]. Produced by Independent Group. Tokyo, 1939.

———. Produced by Tokyo Pikaderi Jikken Gekijo. Tokyo, 1950.

———. Produced at Chiyoda Kokaido. Tokyo, 1957.

———. Produced by Haiyuza Theater. Tokyo, 1994; Osaka, 1995.

Hawkins, William. "Heir's the Thing in 'Burning Bright.'" *New York World-Telegram & The Sun*. 19 Oct. 1950. Rpt. in *New York Theatre Critics' Reviews 1950*. XI-29. Ed. Rachel W. Coffin. 31 Dec. 1950. 238–40.

Hansen, Harry. "The First Reader." *Norfolk (Va.) Pilot* 9 Dec. 1941: 6.

Hayashi, Tetsumaro, ed. *John Steinbeck: The Years of Greatness, 1936–1939*. Tuscaloosa: U of Alabama P, 1993.

———, ed. *A New Study Guide to Steinbeck's Major Works, With Critical Explications*. Metuchen, NJ: Scarecrow, 1993.

———, ed. *John Steinbeck on Writing, Steinbeck Essay Series*. Indiana: Steinbeck Research Institute, 1988.

———. "Steinbeck's *Winter* as Shakespearean Fiction." *Steinbeck Quarterly* 12 (1979): 107–15.

Hearle, Kevin. "'The Boat Shaped Mind': Steinbeck's Sense of Language as Discourse in *Cannery Row* and *Sea of Cortez*." *After The Grapes of Wrath: Essays on John Steinbeck in honor of Tetsumaro Hayashi*. Eds. Don Coers, Paul D. Ruffin, and Robert J. DeMott, Athens, Ohio: Ohio UP, 1995: 101–12.

———. *Regions of Discourse: Steinbeck, Cather, Jewett and the Pastoral Tradition of American Regionalism*. unpublished Ph.D. dissertation, U of California at Santa Cruz, 1991.

Heavilin, Barbara A. "Steinbeck's Exploration of Good and Evil: Structural and Thematic Unity in *East of Eden.*" *Steinbeck Quarterly* 26 (1993): 90–100.

Ikari no Budo [The Grapes of Wrath]. Produced by Mingei Theater. Tokyo, 1994.

——. Produced by Subaru Company. Tokyo, 2001.

Jones, Lawrence William. *John Steinbeck as Fabulist.* Ed. Marston La-France. *Steinbeck Monograph Series*, No. 3. Muncie, IN: Ball State University/John Steinbeck Society of America, 1973. Rpt. *The Betrayal of Brotherhood in the Work of John Steinbeck: Cain Sign.* Ed. Michael J. Meyer. Lewiston, NY: Edwin Mellen, 2000. 53–97.

Le Master, J. R. "Mythological Constructs in Steinbeck's *To a God Unknown.*" *Forum* 9 (1971): 8–11.

Levant, Howard. *The Novels of John Steinbeck: A Critical Study.* Columbia: U of Missouri P, 1974.

Lewin, Frank. *Burning Bright: Opera in Three Acts.* Princeton, NJ: Parga Music, 1989.

——. *Burning Bright: The Genesis of an Opera—An Interview with Composer Frank Lewin.* Guilford, CT: Lyrica Society, 1985.

Lieber, Todd M. "Talismanic Patterns in the Novels of John Steinbeck." *American Literature* 44 (1972): 262–75.

Lisca, Peter. "*Cannery Row* and *Tao Teh Ching.*" *San Jose Studies* 1 (Nov. 1975): 21–27. Rpt. Benson, *Short Novels*, 111–19.

——. *Nature and Myth.* New York: Crowell, 1978.

——. "Steinbeck's Image of Man and His Decline as a Writer." *Modern Fiction Studies* 11 (1965): 3–10.

——. *The Wide World of John Steinbeck.* New Brunswick, NJ: Rutgers UP, 1958.

Marks, Lester. *Thematic Design in the Novels of John Steinbeck.* The Hague: Mouton, 1969.

McCarthy, Paul. *John Steinbeck.* New York: Frederick Unger, 1980.

McElrath, Joseph, Jr., Jesse S. Chrisler, Susan Shillinglaw, eds. *John Steinbeck: The Contemporary Reviews.* Cambridge: Cambridge UP: 1996.

"McWilliams, Bancroft Debate 'Grapes' at Commonwealth Club." *San Francisco News* 30 Mar. 1940: n. pag.

McWilliams, Carey. "What's Being Done About the Joads?" *New Republic* 20 (Sept. 1939): n. pag.

Metzger, Charles R. "Steinbeck's *Cannery Row.*" *A Study Guide to Steinbeck: A Handbook to his Major Works.* Ed. Tetsumaro Hayashi. Metuchen, N.J.: Scarecrow, 1974. 19–28.

Meyer, Michael. "Steinbeck's *The Winter of Our Discontent* (1961)." Hayashi, *New Study Guide*, 240–73.

Millichap, Joseph R. *Steinbeck and Film*. New York: Frederick Unger, 1983.

Mizener, Arthur. "Does a Moral Vision of the Thirties Deserve a Nobel Prize?" *New York Times Book Review* 9 Dec. 1962: 45.

Moore, Harry T. *The Novels of John Steinbeck: A First Critical Study*. Chicago: Normandie House, 1939: 2nd ed., with a contemporary epilogue. Port Washington, New York: Kennikat, 1968.

Morsberger, Robert E. "Steinbeck's War." *The Steinbeck Question: New Essays in Criticism*. Ed. Donald Noble. Troy, NY: Whitston, 1993. 183–212.

———. "Steinbeck's Happy Hookers." *Steinbeck's Women: Essays in Criticism*. Ed. Tetsumaro Hayashi. Steinbeck Monograph Series (9) 1979. 36–48.

Nakayama, Kiyoshi, Scott Pugh, and Shigeharu Yano, eds. *John Steinbeck: Asian Perspectives*. Osaka: Osaka Kyoiku Tosho, 1992.

Ogoshi Kazuso Sensei Taishoku Kinen Ronshu [A Festschrift of Professor Kazuso Ogoshi]. Kyoto: Aporonsha, 1990.

Ohtani Joshidagaku Eigo Eibunngaku Kenkyu [English Studies of Ohtani Women's University]. Osaka: Ohtani Women's University, 1995.

Owens, Louis. *John Steinbeck's Re-Vision of America*. Athens: U of Georgia P, 1985.

———. "The Mirror and the Vamp: Invention, Reflection and Bad, Bad Cathy Trask in *East of Eden*." *Writing the American Classics*. Eds. James Barbour and Tom Quirk. Chapel Hill: U of North Carolina P, 1990. 235–57.

———. "Steinbeck's *East of Eden* (1952)." Hayashi, *New Study Guide*, 66–89.

———. *The Grapes of Wrath: Trouble in the Promised Land*. Boston: Twayne, 1989.

———. "Where Things Can Happen: California and Writing." *Western American Literature* 3 and 4 (1999): 150–55.

Parini, Jay. *John Steinbeck: A Biography*. New York: Henry Holt, 1995.

Peterson, Richard F. "*East of Eden*." Hayashi, *Study Guide*, 63–86.

Pratt, J. C. *John Steinbeck: A Critical Essay*. Writers in Christian Perspective Series. Grand Rapids: Eerdmans, 1970.

Railsback, Brian. *Parallel Expeditions: Charles Darwin and the Art of John Steinbeck*. Moscow: U of Idaho P, 1995.

Riggs, Susan F. *A Catalogue of the John Steinbeck Collection at Stanford University*. Stanford: Stanford U Libraries, 1980.

Ross, Woodburn O. "John Steinbeck: Earth and Stars." Tedlock and Wicker 167–82.

Rucklin, Christine. "Steinbeck as a Reader of Frazer in *The Grapes of Wrath.*" *Mythes, Croyances et Religions dans le Monde Anglo-Saxon* 13. (1995).

———. "Steinbeck and the Philosophical Joads," *The Steinbeck Newsletter* 10.1 (1997): 11–13.

Sathyanarayana, M. R. "The Unknown God of John Steinbeck." *Indian Journal of American Studies* 3.1 (1973): 97–103.

Schorer, Mark. "*A Dark and Violent Steinbeck Novel.*" *The New York Times Book Review* 21 Sept. 1952: 22.

Shillinglaw, Susan. Introduction. *Cannery Row.* By John Steinbeck. New York: Penguin, 1994. vii–xxvii.

———, ed. *Cannery Row Fiftieth Anniversary Edition. The Steinbeck Newsletter* 9.1 (1995).

Simmonds, Roy S. *John Steinbeck: The War Years, 1939–1945.* Lewisburg: Bucknell UP, 1996.

Steinbeck, Elaine. "A Message from Elaine Steinbeck." *Eden no Higashi [East of Eden].* Takarazuka, Takarazuka Kagekidan, 1995.

Takamura, Hiromasa. *Sutainbekku to Engeki [Steinbeck and Drama].* Kyoto: Aporonsha, 1989.

Tani, Masazumi. Myujikaru *Eden no Higashi, Sutainbekku Gensaku [Musical, East of Eden: Based upon the novel "East of Eden" by John Steinbeck].* Takarazuka: Takarazuka Revue Company, 1995.

Taylor, Frank. "California's *Grapes of Wrath.*" *Forum* CII (Nov. 1939): 232–38.

Taylor, Ralph. "Farmers' Corner: Fictionists' Tale Gives Misleading Picture of State's Agricultural Situation." *Merced Express* 23 Nov. 1939: n. pag.

Thomas, David. Steinbeck Documentary. *The Late Show.* London Weekend Television Productions, 1994.

Timmerman, John H. *John Steinbeck's Fiction: The Aesthetics of the Road Taken.* Norman and London: U of Oklahoma P, 1986.

Valjean, Nelson. *John Steinbeck, The Errant Knight: An Intimate Biography of His California Years.* San Francisco: Chronicle, 1975.

Wallace, Richard. "Malice in Wonderland." *Harper's Magazine* Nov. 1996: 37–39.

Whitebrook, Peter. *Staging Steinbeck: Dramatising* The Grapes of Wrath. London: Cassell, 1988.

Wilson, Edmund. *Baltimore Sun* 21 Jun. 1942: 54

Wollenberg, Charles. Introduction. *The Harvest Gypsies.* Berkeley: Heyday, 1988.

Other References

Alexie, Sherman. *The Summer of Black Widows.* Brooklyn, NY: Hanging Loose, 1996.

Allee, W. C. *Animal Aggregations.* Chicago: U of Chicago P, 1931.

Anderson, William and Clive Hicks. *Green Man: The Archetype of Our Oneness with the Earth.* London: HarperCollins, 1990.

Appel, David. "Turning a New Leaf." *Chicago Daily News* 3 Jan. 1945: 13.

Bakersfield Conference on Agricultural Labor. "Report of the Bakersfield Conference on Agricultural Labor—Health, Housing, and Relief." 29 Oct. 1938. Simon J. Lubin Society Collection. U of California, Berkeley. Carton 11.

Bakhtin, Mikhail. *Rabelais and His World.* Trans. Helene Iswolsky. Cambridge, MA: MIT P, 1968.

Baldwin, James. "Everybody's Protest Novel." *Within the Circle: An Anthology of African American Literary Criticism from the Harlem Renaissance to the Present.* Ed. Angelyn Mitchell. Durham, NC: Duke UP, 1994. 149–55.

Bardo, Susan. "True Obsessions: Being Unfaithful to 'Lolita.'" *Chronicle of Higher Education* 24 Jul. 1998: B7–8.

Barnes, Julian. *Flaubert's Parrot.* London: Picador, 1984.

Barthes, Roland. *The Rustle of Language.* Trans. Richard Howard. Berkeley: U of California P, 1989.

Baxter, Leone. "Uncensored." *Crescent City American* 15 Mar. 1940: n. pag.

Bay Area Committee to Aid Agricultural Workers. "Report to State Relief Administration Re: Migratory Workers." San Francisco, 1939.

Bentman, Raymond, ed. *The Poetical Works of Burns.* Boston: Houghton Mifflin, 1974.

Blankenhorn, David. *Fatherless America: Confronting Our Most Urgent Social Problem.* New York: Basic Books, 1995.

Bluestone, George. *Novels into Film.* 1957. Berkeley: U of California P, 1966.

Boodin, John Elof. *Cosmic Evolution: Outlines of Cosmic Idealism.* New York: MacMillan, 1925.

———. *God and Creation: Three Interpretations of the Universe.* New York: MacMillan, 1934.

Boren, Lyle. *Cong. Rec.* 1940. 76th cong., 3d sess., 86, pt. 13: 139–40.

Bradstreet, Anne. "The Flesh and the Spirit." 1678. *Anthology of American Literature.* Eds. George McMichael, et al. 7th ed. Vol. 1. Upper Saddle River, New Jersey: Prentice Hall, 2000. 137–39.

Burke, Kenneth. *The Philosophy of Literary Form: Studies in Symbolic Action.* 3rd ed. Berkeley: U of California P, 1973.

Buss, David M. *The Evolution of Desire.* New York: Basic Books, 1994.

California State Chamber of Commerce. Migrant Committee. *Migrants: A National Problem and Its Impact on California.* San Francisco: California State Chamber of Commerce, 1940.

California State Relief Admin. *Transients in California.* San Francisco: CSRA, 1936.

Canby, Vincent. "New Facets Highlighted in a Classic." *New York Times* 2 Oct. 1992: Weekend C5.

Candland, Douglas K. *Feral Children and Clever Animals: Reflections on Human Nature.* New York: Oxford UP: 1993.

Capps, Donald. *Deadly Sins and Saving Virtues.* Philadelphia: Fortress, 1987.

Capra, Fritjof. *The Tao of Physics: An Exploration of the Parallels Between Modern Physics and Eastern Mysticism.* Berkeley: Shambala, 1975.

Carson, Diane, Linda Dittmar, Janice R. Welsch, eds. *Multiple Voices in Feminist Film Criticism.* Minneapolis: U of Minneapolis P, 1994. 109–23.

Cashmore, Ellis, et al., eds. *Dictionary of Race and Ethnic Relations.* 4th ed. New York: Routledge, 1996.

Chagnon, Napoleon A. "Life Histories, Blood Revenge, and Warfare in a Tribal Population." *Science,* 239 (1988): 985–992.

Chandruang, Chonprakan. *The New Heritage.* Bangkok: n. pag., n.d.

Chaplin, Charles. *My Autobiography.* Boston: Plume, 1992.

Childers, Joseph, and Gary Hentzi, eds. *The Columbia Dictionary of Modern Literary and Cultural Criticism.* New York: Columbia UP, 1995.

Cohen, Felix S. *Handbook of Federal Indian Law.* 1942. Rpt. as *Felix S. Cohen's Handbook of Federal Indian Law.* Albuquerque: U of New Mexico P, 1971.

Collins, Thomas. "Report for Week Ending April 4, 1936: Kern Migratory Labor Camp." Paul Taylor Papers. U of California, Berkeley. Carton 10.

——. "Report for Week Ending February 22, 1936: Kern Migratory Labor Camp." Paul Taylor Papers. U of California, Berkeley. Carton 10.

——. "Report for Week Ending October 24, 1936: Kern Migratory Labor Camp." Simon J. Lubin Society Papers. U of California, Berkeley. Carton 12.

Coltelli, Laura. *Winged Words: American Indian Writers Speak.* Lincoln: U of Nebraska P, 1990.

Condon, Edward, and Phillip Morse. *Quantum Mechanics.* New York: McGraw-Hill, 1929.

Coyle, David Cushman. "Depression Pioneers." Washington, DC: GPO, 1939.

Crouse, Joan. *The Homeless Transient in the Great Depression: New York State, 1929–1941.* Albany: State U of New York P, 1986.

Cullen, Jim. *Born in the USA: Bruce Springsteen and the American Tradition.* 1997. London: Helter Skelter, 1998.

Darton, Byron. "Migrants' Dream of Owning Land Makes Them Conservative Lot." *New York Times* 6 Mar. 1940: n. pag.

Darwin, Charles. *Descent of Man and Selection in Relation to Sex.* New York: Appleton, 1895.

Dawidoff, Nicholas. "Steinbeck in Leather." *New York Times Magazine.* 26 Jan. 1997: n. pag.

Degler, Carl N. *In Search of Human Nature: The Decline and Revival of Darwinism in America.* New York: Oxford UP, 1991.

Dennett, Daniel. *Darwin's Dangerous Idea.* New York: Simon and Schuster, 1995.

———. *Kinds of Minds: Toward an Understanding of Consciousness.* New York: Basic Books, 1996.

Doob, Leonard W. *Propaganda: Its Psychology and Technique.* New York: Henry Holt, 1935.

Dos Passos, John. *USA.* London: Constable, 1938.

Eddington, A. S. 1929. *The Nature of the Physical World.* Ann Arbor: U of Michigan P, 1963.

Eggleston, Arthur. "The Labor Scene: A Small Revolution is Taking Place in California; Migrant Problem is Respectable." *San Francisco Chronicle* 30 Oct. 1939: n. pag.

Einstein, Albert. *Relativity.* 1920. Trans. Robert W. Lawson. New York: Crown, 1961.

Eliade, Mircea. *Cosmos and History: The Myth of the Eternal Return.* Princeton: Princeton UP, 1954.

Emerson, Ralph Waldo. "The Poet." *The Selected Writings of Ralph Waldo Emerson.* Ed. Brooks Atkinson. New York: Modern Library, 1950. 319–341.

Fiedler, Leslie. *Love and Death in the American Novel.* New York: Dell, 1996.

"Film Stars May Attend Migrant Camp Opening." *Sacramento Union* 28 Jan. 1940: n. pag.

"First Lady and Film Stars to Visit the Migrant Camps." *San Francisco Chronicle* 3 Apr. 1940: n. pag.

"First Lady is New Ally of State in Migrant Stand." *Fresno Bee* 5 Apr. 1940: n. pag.

Fisher, H. A. L. *A History of Europe.* London: Eyre and Spottiswoode, 1936.

Fisher, Philip. *Hard Facts: Setting and Form in the American Novel.* New York: Oxford UP, 1987.

Foulkes, A. P. *Literature and Propaganda.* London: Methuen and Co., 1983.

Franklin, Benjamin. *The Autobiography.* 1791. Anthology of American Literature. Eds. George McMichael, et al. 323–440.

Fredrickson, George M. *The Black Image in the White Mind: The Debate of Afro-American Character and Destiny, 1817–1914.* New York: Harper & Row, 1971.

———. *White Supremacy: A Comparative Study in American and South African History.* New York and Oxford: Oxford UP, 1981.

French, Warren, and Walter E. Kidd, eds. *American Winners of the Nobel Literary Prize.* Norman: U of Oklahoma P, 1968.

Fromm, Erich. *The Art of Loving.* New York: Harper & Row, 1974.

Frost, Robert. "Design." *The Poetry of Robert Frost.* Ed. Edward Connery Lathem. New York: Holt, Rinehart, Winston, 1969. 302.

Garner, Jack. " 'Of Mice and Men' Touches the Heart." *Gannett News Service* 15 Oct. 1992.

Gilmore, Mikal. "*The Ghost of Tom Joad:* Year-End Album Review." *Bruce Springsteen: The Rolling Stone Files.* Parke Puterbaugh. London: Pan, 1997. 434–36.

Gledhill, Christine. "Image and Voice: Approaches to Marxist-Feminist Film Criticism." Carson, Dittmar, and Welsh 109–23.

Gould, Stephen Jay. *The Mismeasure of Man.* New York: W. W. Norton, 1981.

Graubard, Mark. *Man the Slave and Master.* New York: Covici-Friede, 1938.

Greene, Brian. *The Elegant Universe.* 1999. New York: Vintage, 2000.

Gregory, James. *American Exodus: The Dust Bowl Migration and Okie Culture in California.* New York: Oxford UP, 1989.

Guizot, Francois. *L'Histoire de France racontée a mes petits-enfants depuis les temps les plus reculés jusqu'en 1789.* (Paris: Hachette, 1872) Robert Black, trans. NY: J. B. Allen, 1884.

Hallie, Philip. "From Cruelty to Goodness." *Virtue & Vice in Everyday Life.* 2nd ed. Eds. Christina Sommers and Fred Sommers. San Diego: Harcourt, 1989. 9–24.

Hayles, N. Katherine. *The Cosmic Web: Scientific Field Models and Literary Strategies in the 20th Century.* Ithaca, NY: Cornell UP, 1984.

Hefferan, Harold. "Filming May Solve the Problem." *San Francisco Chronicle* 14 Oct. 1939: n. pag.

Heisenberg, Werner. *Physics and Philosophy: The Revolution in Modern Science.* New York: Harper, 1958.

Henderson, John C. "Your Government At Your Service." National Broadcasting Company. 21 Oct. 1938.

Hendricks, Hazel. "Farmers Without Farms." *Atlantic Monthly* Oct. 1940: 461–68.

Hepworth, David. Interview with Bruce Springsteen. *The Late Show,* London Weekend Television Productions, 15 June 1992.

Hibbs, Ben. "Footloose Army." *Country Gentleman* Feb. 1940.

Hinz, Evelyn. "Hierogamy versus Wedlock: Types of Marriage Plots and Their Relationship to Genres of Prose Fiction." *PMLA* 91 (1976): 900–13.

"Housing for Migratory Agricultural Workers." *Public Welfare News* Jul. 1939: n. pag.

Huntington, Ellsworth. *Civilization and Climate.* New Haven: Yale UP, 1924.

Jaffe, Eli. "The Farms Blew Away." *NM* 14 May 1940: 15–16.

Jones, Roger S. *Physics as a Metaphor.* Minneapolis: U of Minnesota P, 1982.

Jowett, Garth S. and Victoria O'Donnell. *Propaganda and Persuasion.* Newbury Park, CA: Sage Publications, 1986.

Jung, Carl. *Psychological Types: The Psychology of Individuation.* Trans. H. G. Baynes. New York: Harcourt, Brace, 1923; Psychological Types. A Revision by R. F. C. Hull of the Translation by H. G. Baynes. Bollingen Series XX. Princeton: Princeton UP, 1971.

Jung, Emma. *Animus and Anima.* Dallas: Spring Publications, 1985.

Katz, Stephen B. *The Epistemic Music of Rhetoric: Toward the Temporal Dimension of Affect in Reader Response and Writing.* Carbondale: Southern Illinois UP, 1996.

Kern County Health Dept., Sanitary Division. *Survey of Kern County Migratory Labor Program, Supplementary Report as of July 1, 1938.* 1938.

King, Thomas. *Medicine River.* Toronto: Penguin, 1991.

Koffka, K. *Principles of Gestalt Psychology.* New York: Harcourt, 1935.

Kragh, Helge. *Quantum Generations: A History of Physics in the Twentieth Century.* Princeton: Princeton UP, 1999.

Kruschwitz, Robert B., and Robert C. Roberts. Introduction. *The Vir-*

tues: Contemporary Essays on Moral Character. Belmont: Wadsworth, 1987.

Kuhn, Thomas S. The Structure of Scientific Revolutions. Chicago: U of Chicago P, 1970.

"L.A. Police Chief Uses Freight to Move Out Bums." Nevada State Journal 11 Feb. 1936: n. pag.

Lao Tze. Tao Teh Ching: A New English Version. Translated by Stephen Mitchell. New York: Perennial Classics, 1991.

Levy-Bruhl, Lucien. How Natives Think. Trans. Lillian A. Clare. London: Allen and Unwin, 1926.

"Lilith." The Concise Columbia Electronic Encyclopedia. 3rd ed. 1994.

Locke, John. An Essay Concerning Human Understanding. Amherst, New York: Prometheus, 1995.

Love, Spencie. One Blood: The Death and Resurrection of Charles R. Drew. Chapel Hill: U of North Carolina P, 1996.

Lukàcs, Georg. Writer and Critic, and Other Essays. 1970. Trans. Arthur Kahn. London: Merlin, 1978.

——. The Meaning of Contemporary Realism. 1963. Trans. John and Necke Mander. London: Merlin, 1978.

——. The Historical Novel. 1962. Trans. Hannah and Stanley Mitchell. Harmondsworth: Penguin, 1986.

Lyotard, Jean-François. The Postmodern Condition: A Report on Knowledge. Trans. Geoff Bennington and Brian Masumi. Minneapolis: U of Minnesota P, 1984.

MacDonald, Chris. Ed. 1996. <www.ethics.ubc.ca/~charismac/phd/biblio.html>

Macdonald, Myra. Representing Women: Myths of Femininity in the Popular Media, London: Edward Arnold, 1995.

Maxwell, T. S. The Gods of Asia: Image, Text, and Meaning. Delhi, India: Oxford UP, 1997.

McWilliams, Carey. "California Pastoral." Antioch Review II (Mar. 1942): 103–21.

——. Factories in the Field. 1939. Santa Barbara: Peregrine Smith, 1971.

Meeker, Joseph. The Comedy of Survival: Literary Ecology and a Play Ethic. 3rd ed. Tuscon: U of Arizona P, 1997.

Melville, Herman. Moby Dick. 1851. New York: Vintage, 2000.

"Migrant Camp Expansion Opposed by Californians." Brawley News 17 Feb. 1940: n. pag.

"Migrant Camp is Red Hot Bed." Yuba City Herald 9 Jul. 1936: n. pag.

"Migrant 'Smear' Novels Denounced By Speakers at Pro-America Meet." *San Francisco Chronicle* 22 Aug. 1939: n. pag.

"Migratory Workers Subject of Review." *San Francisco Chronicle* 27 Jan. 1939: n. pag.

Miller, Henry. *On the Fringe: The Dispossessed in America.* Lexington: Lexington Books, 1991.

Mills, C. Wright. *The Power Elite.* Oxford: Oxford UP, 1956.

"Missionary Work Among Migrants Told to Baptists." *Brawley News* 22 Mar. 1940: n. pag.

Mitchell, Greg. *The Campaign of the Century: Upton Sinclair's Race for Governor of California and the Birth of Media Politics.* New York: Random House, 1992.

"Mrs. FDR Talks Here, Plans Yosemite Trip." *San Francisco Chronicle* 5 Apr. 1940: n. pag.

Mulvey, Laura. "Visual Pleasure and Narrative Cinema," *Screen* 16 (Autumn 1975): 6–18.

Neumann, Erich. *The Great Mother.* New York: Pantheon, 1955.

"New Attitude Noted Toward Migrants." *San Francisco News* 1 Nov. 1939: n. pag.

Nussbaum, Martha C. *Love's Knowledge: Essays on Philosophy and Literature.* New York: Oxford UP, 1990.

Oakland Tribune 20 Jul. 1937: n. pag.

Oakley, Justin. *Morality and the Emotions.* London: Routledge, 1992.

"Opinion Shifts to Help Dust Bowlers Living in California." *Dinuba Sentinel* 9 Apr. 1940: n. pag.

Owens, Louis. *Other Destinies: Understanding the American Indian Novel.* Norman: U of Oklahoma P, 1992.

———. *Wolfsong.* Albuquerque: West End, 1991.

Pike, Roy. "Facts From the Field: Being a Review of Carey McWilliams Book Entitled 'Factories in the Field.'" San Francisco: Dettners Printing House, 1939.

"A Plain School Uniform is the Latest Aphrodisiac." *New York Times* 2 Apr. 1997: A4.

"A Plea for the Unhappy Émigré." *San Francisco Chronicle* 16 Jun. 1939: n. pag.

Pomeroy, Harold. "Agricultural Migratory Laborers in San Joaquin Valley, July and August 1937." Sacramento: California State Relief Administration, 1937.

"Pro-America Group Gives 'Other Side' of Migrant Case." *San Francisco News* 22 Aug. 1939: n. pag.

Punyanubhab, Sujib. *Some Prominent Characteristics of Buddhism.* Bangkok: Buddhist UP, 1965.

Qualter, Terence H. *Propaganda and Psychological Warfare.* New York: Random House, 1962.

Rachels, James. *Created From Animals: The Moral Implications of Darwinism.* Oxford: Oxford UP, 1990.

———. *The Elements of Moral Philosophy.* 2nd ed. New York: McGraw, 1993.

Rich, B. Ruby. "In the Name of Feminist Film Criticism." *Multiple Voices in Feminist Film Criticism.* Carson, Dittmar, and Welsch 27–47.

Ritter, William Emerson. *The Unity of the Organism, or The Organismal Conception of Life.* Boston: Richard G. Badger/ The Gorham, 1919.

Roediger, David R. *The Wages of Whiteness: Race and the Making of the American Working Class.* London: Verso, 1991.

Rock, Irvin. *The Logic of Perception.* Cambridge, MA: MIT P, 1983.

Rubinstein, Ruth P. *Dress Codes.* Boulder: Westview, 1995.

Rukeyser, Muriel. *The Life of Poetry.* 1949. Ashfield, MA: Paris, 1996.

San Francisco Examiner. 24 Nov. 1931: n. pag.

Sandford, Christopher. *Springsteen: Point Blank.* London: Little, Brown, 1999.

Schoenberg, Tom. "Professor's Research Inspires Rock Star." *Chronicle of Higher Education.* 19 Jan. 1996: A7.

Schoenewolf, Gerald. *The Art of Hating.* Northvale: Jason Aronson, 1991.

Scholnick, Robert J., ed. *American Literature and Science.* Lexington: UP of Kentucky, 1992.

"'See For Yourself' Caravan to Visit Cotton Country." *Labor Herald* 8 Nov. 1939: n. pag.

Sharma, Arvind. *The Philosophy of Religion and Advaita Vedanta: A Comparative Study in Religion and Reason.* Delhi, India: Sri Satguru, 1997.

Shindo, Charles. *Dust Bowl Migrants in the American Imagination.* Lawrence: UP of Kansas, 1997.

Showalter, Elaine, ed. *The New Feminist Criticism: Essays on Women, Literature, and Theory.* New York: Pantheon, 1985.

Simon, Harry. "Towns Without Pity: A Constitutional and Historical Analysis of Official Efforts to Drive Homeless Persons From American Cities." *Tulane Law Review* 66 (1992): 632–76.

Smith, Huston. *The Religions of Man.* New York: Harper, 1958.

———. *The World's Religions.* San Francisco: Harper, 1991.

Smith, Stephen F. "Is Darwinism a Religion?" *The Catholic World Report.* Dec. 1996: 50–55.

Smuts, Jan Christian. *Holism and Evolution*. New York: MacMillan, 1926.

Snow, C. P. *The Two Cultures and the Scientific Revolution*. New York: Cambridge UP, 1959.

"Speakers Agree Federal Government Should Handle Migratory Labor Problems." *Sacramento Bee* 8 Mar. 1940: n. pag.

"Stage Star Makes Plea for Migrants." *P.A. Free Press* 8 Sept. 1939: n. pag.

"State Lucky to Get Dust Bowl Refugees." *San Francisco Chronicle* 5 Apr. 1940: n. pag.

Steinem, Gloria. *Marilyn*. New York: Henry Holt, 1986.

Stevens, Wallace. "The Idea of Order at Key West." *The Palm at the End of the Mind*. Ed. Holly Stevens. New York: Vintage, 1972. 97–99.

Strehle, Susan. *Fiction in the Quantum Universe*. Chapel Hill: U of North Carolina P, 1992.

Tapasyanada, Swamy. *Swamy Vivekananda: His Life and Legacy*. Madras, India: Sri Ramakrishna Math Publications, n. d.

Tatum, Stephen. "Topographies of Transition in Western American Literature." *Western American Literature* 32 (1998): 310–52.

Taylor, Gabriele. *Pride, Shame, and Guilt: Emotions of Self-assessment*. Oxford: Clarendon, 1985.

Taylor, Paul. "Migratory Farm Labor in the United States." *Monthly Labor Review* (Mar. 1937): 537–49.

Taylor, Richard. "Compassion." *Virtue & Vice in Everyday Life*. Ed. Christina Hoff Sommers. San Diego: Harcourt, 1985. 40–52.

Thomas, P. *Epics, Myths and Legends of India*. Bombay, India: D. B. Taraporevala Sons, 1980.

Tompkins, Jane. *Sensational Designs: The Cultural Work of American Fiction, 1790–1860*. New York: Oxford UP, 1985.

"Truth Finally Dawns." *San Francisco News* 3 Apr. 1940: n. pag.

Ulanov, Ann and Barry. *Transforming Sexuality: The Archetypal World of Anima and Animus*. Boston: Shambhala, 1994.

Walker, Barbara G. *The Crone: Woman of Age, Wisdom, and Power*. New York: HarperCollins, 1998.

Watts, Michael. "Lone Star." *Classic Rock Interviews*. Ed. Allan Jones. London: Mandarin, 1994. 42–56.

Welch, James. *The Death of Jim Loney*. New York: Penguin, 1987.

Weybright, Victor. "Rolling Stones Gather No Sympathy." *Migrant and Farm Labor* 1 (Jan. 1937).

Wheeler, David L. "A Growing Number of Scientists Reject the Concept of Race." *Chronicle of Higher Education*. 17 Feb. 1995: A8.

Whitman, Walt. "A Backward Glance O'er Travel'd Roads." *Leaves of Grass.* Ed. Sculley Bradley and Harold W. Blodgett. New York: Norton, 1973. 561–74.

Wilson, Edmund. *Classics and Commercials: A Literary Chronicle of the Forties.* New York: Farrar, Straus and Co., 1950.

Wright, Robert. *The Moral Animal.* New York: Vintage, 1994.

Manuscripts

Steinbeck, John. "Argument of Phalanx." Unpublished essay. Typed ms. Ca. 1935. Bancroft Library. U of California, Berkeley.

——. "Burning Bright." ts. First copy. 1950. The Rare Book and Manuscript Library, Butler Library, Columbia U, New York.

——. The Complete Archive of *Cannery Row* by John Steinbeck. Stanford: Stanford U Libraries, 1975.

——. "Introduction by Pascal Covici." Unpublished essay. Autograph ms. [September 1942]. Harry Ransom Humanities Research Center. U of Texas, Austin.

——. Letter to George Albee. Thursday [1933]. George Albee Papers. Bancroft Library. U of California, Berkeley.

——. *The Record Book, mss.* Department of Special Collections—Stanford University, 1929–1932.

——. Unrevised galley-proof of "In the Forests of the Night." The Rare Book and Manuscript Library, Butler Library, Columbia U, New York.

Tindall, Bruce. "drew love." Death/Charles Drew. Hp. 31 Jan. 1996. Article 264284 of alt.folklore.urban. Jason R. Heimbaugh, ed., n.p. Online. *The AFU and Urban Legend Archive.* Available: <http://www.urbanlegends.com/death/charles.drew/drew_love.html.> 10 Mar. 1997.

Williams, Annie Laurie. Letter to John Steinbeck. 16 May 1950. The Rare Book and Manuscript Library, Butler Library, Columbia U, New York.

Contributors

Kyoko Ariki is a Professor of English at Okayama College and earned her Ph.D. from Okayama University in 2000. She has published articles on Steinbeck and Willa Cather, is a co-translator of *East of Eden* (1999), and is co-editor of *Re-Reading John Steinbeck* (2001). Professor Ariki is a member of the American Literature Society and one of the directors of the Steinbeck Society of Japan.

P. Balaswamy is Professor of English at Pondicherry University. A teacher at the collegiate level for over 30 years, he has worked in one of the oldest colleges of India, Presidency College, Madras. He conducted his research at the University of Madras on the American novelist, John Steinbeck, under the title, *Allegory in the Early Novels of John Steinbeck*. Out of his love for the contemporary literature in Tamil, his first language, Dr. Balaswamy has translated *Sembaruthi*, a six-hundred-page modern Tamil classic, which is slated for publication. His articles on American and Comparative Literature topics have appeared in anthologies and journals such as *Indian Response to John Steinbeck, American Studies in India, and The Indo-American Review.* In addition to attending the Fourth International Steinbeck Congress at San Jose, California, in 1997, he has been a Visiting Professor at the University of Re Union, Re Union Island, off Mauritius, for a brief period, and has given a series of talks on Indian Fiction in English.

Lorelei Cederstrom is a professor of English and Women's Studies Co-Ordinator at Brandon University in Manitoba, Canada.

In addition to Steinbeck, Dr. Cederstrom's research and publication interests include Whitman, Shakespeare, Jungian literary theory, and 20th Century fiction by women. She is the author of two books, the first, *Fine-Tuning the Feminine Psyche: Jungian Patterns in the Novels of Doris Lessing*, was published in 1990, and the second, *The Unknown Face: Jungian Archetypes in 20th Century Women's Literature*, should be published this year. The latter includes discussions of Atwood, Beresford-Howe, Byatt, Chopin, Dick, Drabble, Engel, French, Jong, Laurence, Lessing, Morrison, Piercey, Siddons, Tan, and Wharton. When she is not teaching, Dr. Cederstrom resides on an island on The Lake of the Woods where she works on her creative writing projects, which include an illustrated collection of poems, *Lopez Lazuli*, a nonfiction work about German-American culture in Milwaukee and a novel, tentatively titled *Free Women*.

Gavin Cologne-Brookes is senior Lecturer in English and Creative Studies at Bath Spa University College, England. He is the author of *The Novels of William Styron: From Harmony to History* and *Dark Eyes on America: The Novels of Joyce Carol Oates;* and he is co-editor (with Neil Sammells and David Timms) of *Writing and America*.

Robert DeMott is Edwin and Ruth Kennedy Distinguished Professor at Ohio University. A recipient of numerous teaching awards, he has published widely on Steinbeck and American literature. Recent books include *Steinbeck's Typewriter* (1996), essays, *Dave Smith: A Literary Archive* (2000), a bio-bibliography and memoir, *The Weather in Athens* (2001), poems, and *Conversations with Jim Harrison* (2002), interviews. He is editor, with Elaine Steinbeck as Special Consultant, of Library of America's three volume Steinbeck project (1994, 1996, 2002).

John Ditsky has had over 1400 of his poems accepted by the major and "little" magazines of half a dozen countries. His poem collections include *The Katherine Poems, Scar Tissue, Friend and Lover,* and *The Naked Man On the Road.* Teacher of American literature, modern drama, and creative writing at the University of Windsor, Ontario, he has also published five critical volumes

(Essays on *East of Eden; The Onstage Christ; John Steinbeck: Life, Works and Criticism; Critical Essays on Steinbeck's* The Grapes of Wrath, and *John Steinbeck and the Critics*) and well over 100 critical articles, notes, and chapters on a variety of subjects.

Warren G. French is Professor Emeritus of English at Indiana University—Purdue University at Indianapolis, and Honorary Professor of American Studies, University of Wales, Swansea. He holds a Ph.D. in English from the University of Texas, Austin and a D.H.L. from Ohio University. He was the founding President of the International John Steinbeck Society. He has published and edited a number of books, including the Twayne United States Authors Series titles on contemporary American literature and Twayne's Filmmakers' Series. He has also contributed numerous articles to professional journals, especially on John Steinbeck, J. D. Salinger and the Beat Generation.

Stephen K. George is a professor of English at Brigham Young University—Idaho. Dr. George has published some 30 articles, reviews, and introductions in such venues as *The Steinbeck Newsletter,* the *Steinbeck Yearbook,* and *The Steinbeck Encyclopedia,* as well as editing a forthcoming anthology entitled *John Steinbeck: A Centennial Tribute.* His research interests include Steinbeck's role as a moralist/philosopher and the critical worth of *The Winter of Our Discontent,* the author's last novel. George currently resides in the quiet town of Rexburg, Idaho, with his wife and five children.

Mimi Reisel Gladstein is a Professor of English, Theatre Arts, and Women's Studies at the University of Texas at El Paso. She has chaired the English and the Philosophy departments, was the first director of the Women's Studies Program, Director of the Western Cultural Heritage Program and Associate Dean of Liberal Arts for the Humanities. Recognition for her work on Steinbeck includes the John J. and Angeline Pruis Award for Teaching and the Burkhardt Award for Outstanding Steinbeck Scholar. She is the author of *The Indestructible Woman in Faulkner, Hemingway, and Steinbeck* and has contributed numerous articles to scholarly anthologies and journals. John Ditsky credits Gladstein with a "brand of feminist thinking [that] finally pulled criticism of Steinbeck's work regarding female characterizations into the late twentieth century."

Christina Sheehan Gold is a Visiting Assistant Professor at Loyola Marymount University in Los Angeles, California. Her dissertation, *Hoovervilles: Homelessness and Squatting in California During the Great Depression,* asserts that traditional ideas about private property, hard work, gender, and family guided how the poor built and lived in Hoovervilles and that public policy dealing with homelessness was based on centuries old punitive policies. Her current research explores the historical roots of contemporary homelessness policy.

Charlotte Hadella (Ph.D. American Literature, University of New Mexico, 1989) is a Professor in the Department of English and Writing at Southern Oregon University in Ashland, Oregon. She teaches courses in American Literature and English Education, and directs the Oregon Writing Project. In addition to articles on American short story writers, she has published two books: *Of Mice and Men: A Kinship of Powerlessness* (New York: Twayne Publishers, 1995), and *Warm Springs Millennium: Voices from the Reservation,* co-authored with Michael Baughman (Austin: University of Texas Press, 2000).

Paul Hadella (Ph.D. American Literature, University of New Mexico, 1990) has published a number of articles and book reviews. He owns and operates a music and book store in Ashland, Oregon.

Carol L. Hansen received a BA in English from San Jose State University, an MA in English from U.C. Berkeley and a Ph.D. in English from Arizona State University. She is the author of *Woman as Individual in English Renaissance Drama: A Defiance of the Masculine Code* (New York: Peter Lang, 1993, 1995, 2000) and *The Life and Death of Asham: Leonard and Virginia Woolf's Haunted House* (London: Cecil Woolf, 2000). For the past fifteen years she has taught English at City College of San Francisco and College of San Mateo, as well as one semester in London and at

California State University, Monterey Bay and the University of San Francisco. Having lived on the Monterey Peninsula for ten years, she is a devotee of John Steinbeck's life and writing.

Kevin Hearle has been a member of the editorial board of *The Steinbeck Newsletter* and with Peter Lisca edited the 2nd Viking Critical Edition of *"The Grapes of Wrath": Text and Criticism*. His essays, interviews, poems, and reviews have been published widely, and he has taught at Coe College, the University of California at Santa Cruz, San José State University, California State University at Los Angeles, Santa Clara University, and Notre Dame de Namur University.

Hiroshi Kaname is a Professor of English at Osaka Prefecture University in Osaka, Japan. He has published other articles on Steinbeck in various scholarly publications.

James C. Kelley is an oceanographer and geologist who received his academic training at Pomona College and the University of Wyoming. For nine years he was a member of the Oceanography faculty at the University of Washington and has been dean of science and engineering at San Francisco State University. He has taught, together with colleagues from the English department, a course titled "John Steinbeck and Ed Ricketts: Literature and the Sea," as part of San Francisco State University's NEXA Program. He has been chief scientist and expedition leader on more than fifty scientific and natural history expeditions in the oceans of the world and has published widely on the productivity of the nearshore environment.

Michael J. Meyer is the new Steinbeck bibliographer (Scarecrow 1998) and his essays on Steinbeck have appeared in numerous books and journals. His most recent Steinbeck scholarship is *Cain Sign: the Betrayal of Brotherhood in the Work of John Steinbeck* (Mellen 2000). He also serves as co-editor of the new *Steinbeck Encyclopedia* (Greenwood, forthcoming), and is working on a book which will trace the scholarly reactions to Steinbeck's *Of Mice and Men*.

Kiyoshi Nakayama is a professor of English at Kansai University in Suita, Osaka, Japan. He is the co-editor of *Selected Essays of John Steinbeck* (1981), the co-translator of *Sweet Thursday* (1984), the editor of *Uncollected Stories of John Steinbeck* (1986), and the compiler of *Steinbeck in Japan: A Bibliography* (1992), among other notable works. Currently he is the director of the John Steinbeck Society of Japan, and one of the executive directors of the American Literature Society of Japan (1997–2002).

Malithat Promathatavedi received her B.A. (cum laude) from Miami University as a grantee of the Thai government scholarship, where she was a member of Phi Beta Kappa; her M.A. in English is from the University of Wisconsin, Madison. She began her teaching career at Chiang Mai University in the north of Thailand, and is presently an Associate Professor in the Department of English and Linguistics, Faculty of Humanities, Ramkhamhaeng University, where she has taught since 1973. She also served as Department Head and Associate Dean for Academic Affairs, and her current position is Deputy Department Head. Her field of specialty is literature and translation. A member of PEN International Thailand-Center and Writers Association of Thailand, she is the author of several textbooks and translations.

Brian Railsback teaches creative writing and American literature at Western Carolina University, where he has served as the department head of English and the founding dean of The Honors College. He has published numerous articles and book chapters on John Steinbeck and published *Parallel Expeditions: Charles Darwin and the Art of John Steinbeck* (Idaho UP, 1995). Presently he is co-editor, with Michael Meyer, of *A John Steinbeck Encyclopedia* for Greenwood Press.

Rodney P. Rice is an Associate Professor of English at the South Dakota School of Mines and Technology. He received his Ph.D. in English in 1987 from the University of Nebraska-Lincoln. His publications have appeared in *Great Plains Quarterly; Mid America; Texas Books in Review; Texas Review; War, Literature, and the Arts; Western American Literature; The Journal of Business and*

Technical Communication; and *IEEE Transactions on Professional Communication.* Two recent essays, "The Construction of Social Reality in John Steinbeck's *Tortilla Flat,*" and "Group Man Goes to War: Elements of Propaganda in John Steinbeck's *Bombs Away,*" are forthcoming respectively in *The Steinbeck Centennial Anthology* (Creative Press), and in *War, Literature, and the Arts: An International Journal of the Humanities.*

Christine Rucklin, an independent scholar living in France, has contributed many articles about Steinbeck to *The Steinbeck Newsletter* as well as numerous other scholarly publications.

John Seelye is a Graduate Research Professor of American Literature at the University of Florida in Gainesville and is the general editor of the Penguin American Classics editions. He has authored numerous books and articles on American Literature.

Susan Shillinglaw is a Professor of English and Director of the Center for Steinbeck Studies at San José State University. She edits the award-winning *Steinbeck Studies* (previously *The Steinbeck Newsletter*) published twice yearly by the Center. She has published several articles on Steinbeck and co-edited four books, most recently *America and Americans and Selected Nonfiction* with Jackson Benson (Viking P) and *John Steinbeck: Centennial Reflections* (Center for Steinbeck Studies).

Hiromasa Takamura is currently a Professor of English at Ohtani Women's University in Osaka, Japan. He received his M.A. from Kansai University and his Ph.D. from Okayama University. He also studied at the University of Hawaii and Adelphi University, and did research at the Steinbeck Research Institute as a Visiting Fellow at Ball State University. In addition to his essays and books on Steinbeck, he has written frequently on such American playwrights as Arthur Miller, Tennessee Williams, and William Inge. He has also edited and translated a children's book, *Canadian Folklore,* among his ten published books.

Index

References to endnotes include the relevant chapter number in parentheses when the page includes more than one note with the same number.